ISBN 978-0-243-54071-6
PIBN 10803495

1 MONTH OF
FREE
READING

at

www.ForgottenBooks.com

By purchasing this book you are eligible for one month membership to ForgottenBooks.com, giving you unlimited access to our entire collection of over 1,000,000 titles via our web site and mobile apps.

To claim your free month visit:

www.forgottenbooks.com/free803495

English
Français
Deutsche
Italiano
Español
Português

www.forgottenbooks.com

Mythology Photography **Fiction**
Fishing Christianity **Art** Cooking
Essays Buddhism Freemasonry
Medicine **Biology** Music **Ancient
Egypt** Evolution Carpentry Physics
Dance Geology **Mathematics** Fitness
Shakespeare **Folklore** Yoga Marketing
Confidence Immortality Biographies
Poetry **Psychology** Witchcraft
Electronics Chemistry History **Law**
Accounting **Philosophy** Anthropology
Alchemy Drama Quantum Mechanics
Atheism Sexual Health **Ancient History**
Entrepreneurship Languages Sport
Paleontology Needlework Islam
Metaphysics Investment Archaeology
Parenting Statistics Criminology
Motivational

THE

$3\frac{6^L}{4\,7}.2$

QUARTERLY JOURNAL

OF THE

AMERICAN UNITARIAN ASSOCIATION.

VOLUME II.

BOSTON:
AMERICAN UNITARIAN ASSOCIATION,
21 BROMFIELD STREET.
1855.

CAMBRIDGE:
METCALF AND COMPANY, PRINTERS TO THE UNIVERSITY.

CONTENTS.

No. I.

No. II.

No. III.

No. IV.

THE

QUARTERLY JOURNAL.

VOL. II.   BOSTON, OCTOBER 1, 1854.   No. 1.

SOCINUS.

THE traveller who passes by railway from Milan to Venice will get a glimpse of the beautiful town of Vicenza, thirty-five miles this side of the latter city. The cars glide along the skirts of the town, just near enough to enable the eye to survey its position, to mark the broad and fertile plain on which it stands, and to observe the white wall of the Alps some twenty or thirty miles to the north. As the train stops but a few moments, one carries away a confused picture of open squares, triumphal arches, churches, bridges, palaces, monasteries, and long rows of Lombardy poplars; and were it not for the superior attraction of the wonderful city of Venice, he feels that he would like to stop at the quaint old town, which numbers about thirty thousand inhabitants, and contains, as the list reads, " a castle, twenty-two churches, thirty-three oratories, seven colleges, twenty-seven hospitals," beside many handsome buildings of the celebrated architect Palladio, who was born here.

Vicenza has a peculiar interest to us as Unitarians. It

was here, in the very earliest dawn of the Reformation, that
a little band of Unitarians had communion together, encouraging one another in earnest inquiries after the truth as it
is in Christ, and sharing the dangers incurred by their departure, in that age of persecution, from the creeds of the
Church. It was not long before the Inquisition disturbed
them. Some of their number were put to death, and others
fled to distant countries.

Among this last class was Lælius Socinus. The son of
a lawyer of great eminence, he was himself educated for
the legal profession. A diligent perusal of the Scriptures,
undertaken in order that he might go back to the origin of
all laws, disclosed to him the truth, so often obtained by
impartial inquiry, that many of the doctrines of the Church
were as contradictory to revelation as they are repugnant
to reason. The discovery gave a new direction to his life,
and he sought religious sympathy in Vicenza. In his subsequent exile, he travelled in Germany, France, England,
Poland, and Switzerland, and finally made a home in Zu-
rich, where he applied himself to the study of theology.
His investigations were pursued under the advantage of
familiarity with many Oriental languages, while his learning, judgment, prudence, good temper, and pleasing manners, won for him a large circle of friends among persons
of eminence and rank. He maintained a correspondence
with Melancthon, Calvin, and other leaders of the Reformation. He died in 1562, in the thirty-seventh year of his
age. His papers, containing the results of his critical inquiries, and a full statement of his opinions, passed into the
hands of his nephew, Faustus Socinus, who became in
time the more eminent man, and the leader in the movement of thought which is historically marked by his name.

At the time of his uncle's death, Faustus was twenty-three years of age, having been born at Siena, in Tuscany, December 6, 1539. His father had been a Professor of Law in Padua; but both father and mother died when the son was yet young. In consequence of this loss his uncle felt a peculiar interest in the young man, whose rare endowments he discerned, and whose future eminence he predicted. Theology, however, did not at first engage his attention. He passed twelve years at the Court of Francis de Medici, the reigning Duke of Tuscany, where he was intrusted with many honorable employments.

In 1574, at the age of thirty-five, Faustus Socinus went to Germany and Switzerland. He selected Basle as his residence. This city had long been renowned for its freedom, and the peaceful shelter it gave to scholars of all names. Here Erasmus had not long before closed his career, after having published an edition of his voluminous works, and bequeathed an example of profound and extensive learning, and of free and bold inquiry. Aided by the papers of his uncle, and the library and instructors of the University, Socinus for three years devoted himself to the study of Theology.

Among the many objects of interest which the traveller finds in Basle, two will especially engage his attention. One is the cathedral of red sandstone, grotesquely covered with tiles of various colors, beneath which repose the remains of Erasmus; the other is the Council-Room of the University, where assembled, in 1431, the famous Council which declared that a General Council was superior to the Pope, and consistently followed up the position by dethroning the reigning Pontiff, Eugene the Fourth. In these halls Erasmus and Socinus had mused and studied. But, though probably agreeing in many fundamental points of theology, in character they were widely different. A quiet life of study was all that the former desired, and he was willing to purchase it by means which exposed him to the charge of insincerity and timeserving. Socinus, on the other hand, with less learning but more courage, preferred to enter the world of action, both in controversy with error and earnest labors for the diffusion of the truth. In 1577 he had reduced the science of theology to a system, which he felt it to be his duty to teach. Public disputations constituted one mode of disseminating the truth which was in fashion in that age. Every one remembers the story of Luther's nailing up his theses on the great door of the church in Wittenberg. This took place only sixty years before the time to which we now refer. In like manner Socinus held public discussions, maintaining the cardinal doctrine of his system, — that the Father alone is God. Meanwhile, a distant field was in preparation, to become in time the scene of his labors.

It was one consequence of the Reformation to stir up inquiry and thought in all directions. Freed from the weights of prescription and authority, thousands began to question many of the doctrines which Luther and Calvin received. They saw no reason for making Popes of these men in place of the more generally acknowledged Pontiffs at Rome. It was doubtless a time of much peril and fanaticism, and it was natural that the leaders of the movement should become alarmed, and finally resolved to fix the limits beyond which, in the matter of creeds, the Reformation should not go. For this reason, they employed the weapons of persecution from which they had themselves but recently made their escape. Especially were they determined to suppress any opposition to the doctrine of the Trinity. Calvin's treatment of Servetus was only an expression of the general spirit of the times. But everywhere there were those who had been led, like Socinus, to see the fact that this doctrine has no foundation in the Scriptures. In Poland they found a country which permitted unlimited toleration of opinions, and here accordingly they gathered in great numbers. Churches of anti-Trinitarians were formed in all the principal cities. Their influence became so great, that nearly all the Reformed clergy ranked themselves on their side, and a formal separation from the Lutheran and Calvinistic churches took place in 1565.

But while they were united in a disbelief of the Trinity, on other points of doctrine there was not much harmony among them. They differed especially in regard to the degree of honor which should be bestowed upon Christ. That he was not God, they were clear; but precisely what he was, and what he claimed for himself, and what homage it was - proper for believers to render him, were unsettled points, to which the temper of that age attached great importance, and which led to endless controversy and strife.

To this people Faustus Socinus came to be in effect their common head and leader. Those who do not sympathize with any of his opinions must yet confess that he rendered great and important services to the churches afterwards called by his name. To a large and flourishing sect he was the Luther and Calvin in one, organizing their religious institutions, and giving form and consistency to their faith. He established a college, set up a large printing-house, encouraged Biblical literature, raised up a generation of scholars, and gave an impress and mould of his own belief and character which survive to this day. We will name some of the events of his career.

In 1579, George Blandrata, physician to the king, and a man of much influence, invited Socinus to Poland, in the hope that he would be an instrument to compose their re-

ligious differences. At the head of the prevailing party
was Francis David, who maintained that to God alone can
all our prayers be properly addressed, and that to direct
them to Christ is to take the glory of God and give it to
another. This was not the opinion of Socinus. He held
that, as Christ is the Mediator between God and man, our
supplications should be addressed to him, asking for that
guidance and blessing which, under the Father's appointment, it is in the province of the Son to bestow. To the
combatants it appeared like a question between a true worship and idolatry. Logically the party of David could be
most easily defended. But in a question like this something more than logic always enters. There was the habit,
confirmed by ages, of addressing Christ in prayer, and there
were liturgies and hymns for this worship without number.
Reverential and holy feelings towards the Saviour pleaded
for a direct address to him, which seemed also to be encouraged by the Saviour's own words, that prayer was to be
offered " through him," and " in his name." If, among
Unitarians, general practice has conformed to the rule of
praying only to the Father, it is but fair to acknowledge
that both the party of David and the party of Socinus have
their representatives among us to this day; and some, un-
edified by prayers in which the name of Jesus rarely if ever
occurs, would rejoice in a direct address, by hymn and
apostrophe, to that Saviour who, under God, is our Master
and the Captain of our Salvation.

We have not very ample materials relating to the controversy that followed. All accounts agree, however, in
describing it as earnest and excited, and not unstained by
party excesses and violence. It was in vain that Blandrata brought the two disputants together, and, that they
might confer with each other, boarded them for many

THE

QUARTERLY JOURNAL

OF THE

-AMERICAN UNITARIAN ASSOCIATION.

VOLUME II.

BOSTON:

AMERICAN UNITARIAN ASSOCIATION,

21 BROMFIELD STREET.

1855.

debted to quotations from his works, and to the celebrated Racovian Catechism, — a work begun by Socinus himself, though it was not completed and published until after his death.

He believed that the Divine Essence is numerically one, containing one person only, God the Father, to whom unlimited Power, Wisdom, Goodness, Rectitude, and Equity belong.

He believed that Christ was a man, conceived without human intervention by the power of the Divine Spirit, and in consequence of this Divine Sonship he is the king over God's people, whom all men are to honor even as they honor the Father, for he is the medium through whom God governs his Church and all things that have any connection with its members, and therefore ought to be continually adored by them, and with confidence invoked in their necessities.

He rejected the doctrine of " original sin," as it is called, which teaches that there are certain innate desires, or evil concupiscence and proneness to sin in man, which opinion, he says, cannot, on three accounts, be true : —

" First, because it is not clear that this concupiscence, or proneness to sin, is in all men. And then, although this should be evident, it does not follow that the cause of it is that Adam, from whom we all sprung, transgressed the Divine command. Lastly, because this evil desire or proneness to sin, since it has not guilt joined with it, cannot properly be called *his* sin in whom it exists. Moreover, these evil desires which it is asserted are born with most men do not flow from the sin of the first man, but from this, that man, by frequent acts of sin, hath contracted the habit of sinning, and hath corrupted himself, which corruption descends by propagation. For this one sin by itself could not have the power of corrupting even Adam himself, much less all his posterity. And we nowhere read this corruption was the effect of the counsel of God as a punishment of that sin. And indeed it is highly incredible, nay, impious, to suppose that God, the author of all righteousness, could in any way be the cause of this pravity; which pravity, so far as it is derived to men, as it was said, by propagation, cannot properly be said to be sin."

Of the method of our salvation, Socinus says : —

" Three things are signified by God's being propitious to us in Christ Jesus : — First, that God hath by Jesus Christ announced, testified, and confirmed his own free and voluntary propitiousness to us and our sins. Secondly, that it is necessary, if we would be partakers of this great blessing, to be in Christ, and be members of him by faith, and by the same spirit of obedience which he possessed. Thirdly, that God causeth us to experience all the effects of this his own propitiousness by Christ, and by him alone carrieth it on to its last and most perfect issue and end.

" That God was not in the least made propitious or appeased by Christ, but was of his own free will propitious to us in him is clear from this : first, that Christ is never in the Sacred Scriptures said to appease God. Besides, we there read that God, because he loved us, sent Christ into the world (1 John iv. 10) ; and that Christ visited us according to the tender mercies of our God (Luke i. 78) ; and from many other passages it is plainly concluded that God was propitious and benevolently disposed towards mankind before Christ began to enter upon his office. To this add, that the forerunner of Christ preached the baptism of repentance for the remission of sins, from whence it appears there was no necessity that Christ should appease God, or that on that account a decree to forgive sins, and the publication of that decree, should take place."

In another place, commenting on the text, " the Lamb of God, that taketh away the sins of the world," Socinus says : —

" Without doubt he alluded to the expiatory sacrifices ; yet I do not apprehend that by this language he refers only to the sacrificing of a lamb, or to Christ as so sacrificed, but to Christ in his whole character, who in many ways takes away the sin of the world. It may be alleged as a proof of this, that in the expiatory sacrifices of the Law, which were expressly offered for sin, no lamb was sacrificed ; from which it appears that, when the Baptist called Christ a lamb, he had a reference to something else beside those sacrifices, and had respect to the purity, innocence, and meekness of Christ, and designed in some measure to represent the office of Christ in general by that metaphor. For Christ took away sin, that is, wrought out our exemption from the punishment of sin, as he was the first since the beginning of the world who in the name of God offered the pardon of all sins, even the most heinous, to all who should repent according to his directions, and confirmed these overtures by an everlasting covenant. Christ takes away sin, because he allures, and has power to engage men, by heavenly and most sublime promises, to practise that repentance by which their sins will be blotted out. Christ takes away sin, because he hath not only taught the method of their being blotted out, but hath also proved the infallible truth of his doctrines by many, and those very amazing, evidences. Christ takes away sin, because he hath the power of remitting the sins of whomsoever he pleaseth, either on earth, as he could when he was mortal, or even in heaven, which he was authorized to do after he was made immortal. Christ takes away sin, because, separately from the offering of himself, he prevails with us, by the efficacy of his doctrine and the wonderful confirmation it received, to forsake our sins. And, to omit other considerations, Christ takes away sin, because he excites all who are not past recovery, by the example of his own most pure life, to leave their sins, and cordially to pursue sanctity and righteousness."

The commonly received doctrine, that Christ procured our salvation by rendering a satisfaction to God, is thus treated : —

" No man of judgment and piety ought to entertain the idea of a satisfaction for sin, since it plainly does very much derogate from the power and authority or goodness and mercy of God.

Nay, it neither ever has or ever can be the case that any one should be delivered from the punishment of his sins by the efficacy of a satisfaction ; for the Divine justice can by no other means be satisfied, than by the sinner's suffering the punishment of his sins : but every one will perceive that to suffer the punishment of our sins, and to be exempted from the punishment of them, are totally irreconcilable to each other. Neither can one person suffer punishment for another, as one may pay the money another owes ; for punishment cannot, like money, be transferred from one to another. Forasmuch as money, to use the style of lawyers, is somewhat real, and can therefore be transferred ; but punishment, which we here speak of, and which, according to the law, is due to the sins of men, is something personal, and therefore of such a nature as always to adhere to the person who suffers it, and does not admit of being transferred to another. To this let it be subjoined, that God himself hath expressly forbidden that one should be put to death for another, though nearly related (Deut. xxiv. 16 ; 2 Kings xiv. 6), and hath most plainly declared that he will by no means do this (Ezek. xviii. 20)."

In regard to the ordinances of religion, Socinus held that the Lord's Supper is no grant or ministration of some divine blessing for a particular class of persons, but is a Eucharist, an act of thanksgiving for the remembrance of Christ, in which all may unite who wish joyfully and gratefully to call him to mind. The baptism of water he did not regard as a perpetual ordinance in the Church. It failed to carry with it its proper meaning, he thought, if applied to those who from their earliest years have been instructed in the Christian discipline, for they are already in the Christian fold, and are consecrated to God. He maintained that, if water-baptism be retained in the Church, it should be confined to converts from other religions. Hence he objected to the practice of infant baptism, — a point in which he agreed with the Unitarian churches in Poland. On one other matter in regard to this ordinance he was totally at

variance with them, as they practised immersion on an
adult profession of belief, without which none were admitted to their communion.

The general view of Christianity as held by Socinus will
sufficiently appear from the above extracts. It is substantially the same view as that taken by Unitarians at the
present day, though in some points, it will be seen, they do
not follow him.   All the works of this author show his profound belief in the Divine authority of the Christian religion, his high conception of the attributes of God, his devout
love for the Saviour, his reverence for the Scriptures, his
clear discrimination and good sense.   Historical notices of
him bear witness not only to the great influence exerted on
his age by his learning and ability, but to the integrity of
his character and the purity of his private life.   The fact
is not without its interest, as a mere illustration of mental
strength, that he so completely emancipated himself from
the past, avoiding alike the accumulated errors of the Pa-
pists and the metaphysical subtilties of the Calvinists, evolving a system of religion so plain and intelligible, and, as we
think, so agreeable to the simplicity that is in Christ, and so
prophetic of the future progress of the broad current of
Protestant thought.

The paragraph in Mosheim's Ecclesiastical History
which sums up the results of the life of Socinus may here
be recalled.

"The affairs of the Unitarians assumed a new aspect under the
dexterity and industry of Faustus Socinus, a man of superior
genius, of moderate learning, of firm and resolute spirit, less eru-
dite than his uncle Lælius, but more bold and courageous. When,
after various wanderings, he went among the Polish Unitarians, in
1579, he at first experienced much trouble and opposition from
very many, who accounted some of his opinions wide of the truth.

And in reality the religious system of Faustus (which he is said to have derived from the papers left by Lælius) had much less simplicity than that of the Unitarians. But the man by his wealth, his eloquence, his abilities as a writer, the patronage of the great, the elegance of his manners, and other advantages which he possessed, overcame at length all difficulties; and by reasonably yielding at one time, and contesting at another, he brought the whole Unitarian people to surrender to those opinions of his which they had before contemned, and to coalesce and become one community. Through his influence, therefore, the ill-digested, dubious, and unpolished religion of the old Unitarians became greatly altered, was more ingeniously stated, and more artfully and dexterously defended. Under the guidance of so spirited and respectable a leader, the body also, which before was a little feeble flock, rose in a short time to distinction and honor, by the accession to it of great numbers of all orders and classes, among whom were many persons of illustrious birth, of opulence, influence, eloquence, and learning." — *Cent.* 16, Sec. 3, Part 2, chap. 4.

From Toulmin's Life of Socinus we learn that in person he was tall and slender, having a high forehead, a penetrating eye, pleasing manners, and altogether of such rare gifts that Ashwell, a writer against Socinianism, says : " He so excelled in fine parts and lofty genius, such were the strength of his reasonings and the power of his eloquence, he displayed in the sight of all men so many distinguished virtues, that what Augustine said of Faustus Manichæus may not improperly be applied to Faustus Socinus, that he was *Magnum Diaboli Laqueum*, the Devil's chief decoy."

Writing of the deep religious spirit which distinguished Socinus, Toulmin says he was especially remarkable for " a calm and steadfast faith in a future life as a continuation and perfection of the present existence ; and to one far advanced in years, who showed him a tomb he had built for himself, adding, as a token of piety, that his mind was

continually engaged upon death, Socinus replied, ' He
would have been much better employed if he had contemplated the evidences and nature of the resurrection of the
dead.' "

The strong praise bestowed by Archbishop Tillotson upon
the Socinian writers was intended as much for Socinus as
any of his compeers, though the good Archbishop's careful
discrimination between the merits of the advocate and the
merits of his cause was yet not enough to save himself
from suspicion of a decided leaning towards the condemned
theology. " To do right," says he, " to the writers on that
side, I must own that generally they are a pattern of the
fair way of disputing and debating matters of religion, without heat, and unseemly reflections upon their adversaries.
They generally argue matters with that temper and gravity,
and with that freedom from passion and transport, which
become a serious and weighty argument, and for the most
part they reason closely and clearly, with extraordinary
guard and caution ; with great dexterity and decency, and
yet with smartness and subtlety enough ; with a very gentle
heat and few hard words ; virtues to be praised wherever
they are found, yea, even in an enemy, and very worthy
of our imitation. In a word, they are the strongest mana-
gers of a weak cause, and which is ill-founded at the bottom,
that perhaps ever yet meddled with controversy ; insomuch
that some of the Protestant, and most of the Popish writers,
and even of the Jesuits themselves, who pretend to all the
reason and ability in the world, are, in comparison of them,
but mere bunglers. Upon the whole matter, they have this
one great defect, that they want a good cause and truth on
their side, which, if they had, they have reason and wit
and temper enough to defend it."

As these pages are passing through the press, we observe

that another prelate of the English Church has lately referred to Socinus in terms of high respect. The Bishop of
Exeter, in his Pastoral Letter to the Clergy of his Diocese,
at the triennial Visitation, in the spring of this present year,
having occasion to support some critical observations he
made, says: "A not less distinguished and trustworthy
guide than Socinus himself has put forth the same statement."

These references to the great heresiarch of the sixteenth
century are in a different temper from those which have been
so common, for several generations, upon any allusion to
Socinus or Socinianism. These have been, as everybody
knows, objects of unmitigated scorn and loathing. To be
a Socinian was, in the estimation of many, to be an infidel,
a blasphemer, the most detestable and atrocious heretic,
and an outcast from all hope of mercy. "Its hissing sound
has great sneering capabilities," said an English friend,
"and if you had lived in England you would have acquired
some greater idea of the degree of scorn and contempt
which it can express." Very likely ; though we have some
suspicion that religious scorn and contempt are not peculiar
to England. We have even thought that we have seen
something pretty strong in this way nearer home. But
though these feelings have been so common, and have been
often shared, too, by men otherwise of many excellences
of character, we have not ceased to wonder how any fol-
lower of Jesus Christ can feel at liberty to indulge them, or
how the teachers of religion and guides of public opinion
can justify themselves in urging the multitude to bark and
gnash their teeth at the name and memory of a man of
such pure life and such sincere faith. We say this without
any sectarian bias. We have no particular interest in rescuing the name of Socinus from contempt. We do not

hold some of·his opinions. We refuse to be called after him. Content with the name of Christ, we do not want to add to that the name of Socinus or of Calvin; though, if we were compelled to choose between them, on the score of greater likeness to the character and temper of Him after whom the whole family in heaven and on earth are named, we should not for a moment hesitate which to take.

Socinus died in 1604, in the sixty-fifth year of his age. On his tombstone was placed the following epitaph : —

"Tota licet Babylon destruxit tecta Lutherus,
  Muros Calvinus, sed fundamenta Socinus "; —

which has been translated in these words : " Luther took off the roof of Babylon ; Calvin threw down the walls ; but Socinus dug up the foundations."

We will add a few facts relating to the subsequent history of Socinianism in Poland. The Racovian Catechism, begun, as we have before stated, by Socinus, but not completed by him, was published in 1609. Its title was as follows : "The Catechism of the Churches who in the Kingdom of Poland, and in the great Dukedom of Lithuania, and in other Provinces belonging to that Kingdom, affirm that no other Being beside the Father of our Lord Jesus Christ is the One God of Israel ; but acknowledge and confess that the Man of Nazareth who was born of a Virgin, and no other besides or before him, is the only-begotten Son of God." This Catechism was dedicated to James the First, who, shortly before its publication, had begun his reign in England, and was then the chief hope of the Protestant world. Not many years after this, in 1638, the Unitarians drew upon themselves the odium of the Roman Catholics, by their opposition to Popish superstitions and abuses ; and the act of some students in the Unitarian College at Racow, who threw stones at a crucifix outside of the town, was the signal for attempts to break up the churches of the Unitarian faith. In the political changes which followed, the Roman Catholic party had the ascendency, and a decree was passed, closing the University, banishing the Professors, and shutting up the churches. In 1658 the Unitarians were driven out of the kingdom, and the profession of their faith was made a capital offence. Many found a refuge in Transylvania, and some repaired to Holland and England. The churches in the first-named country have remained to this day. We know little of their present condition. Not many years ago, George Sylvester, a Unitarian Professor of Theology at Clausenburg, sent a letter to the Unitarians in England, in which he says that the Unitarians in Transylvania have 123 churches, a college at Clausenburg, and two academies. We infer, however, from his statements, that as a sect they are poor, and that they possess but the shadow of their former strength and prosperity.

" BODILY EFFECTS OF RELIGIOUS EXCITE-MENT."

In a volume of " Theological Essays reprinted from the Princeton Review," there is a remarkable paper with the above title. A note appended to it informs the reader that the article " was originally in the form of a letter from one who was well acquainted with the facts detailed." It adds, that these facts " are highly instructive, and ought to be recorded and remembered for the benefit of the coming

generation."   Viewing the subject in this light ourselves,
we propose to give a brief account of the article, with quotations of its most important paragraphs.   It will at least
show that those who lived before the days of table-moving,
spiritual rapping, clairvoyance, and mesmeric influences,
were not so unfortunate as we may imagine. They had
other things to excite their wonder and try their credulity.
It may suggest, also, that, in the present state of information concerning a most interesting department of the physi-
ology of the human system, some caution may be justified
in regard to the claims of hastily formed theories.

The preliminary statements of this article we shall con-
dense.   An account is given of a revival of religion in the
southern and western sections of Kentucky in 1800 and the
three following years.   Before this, that region had been in
a state of great coldness and declension.   The country was
new, and a heterogeneous population had pressed into it.
The religious services were of a formal and tedious character, and were to a great degree neglected by the young.
Signs of a reviving interest, in 1799, encouraged ministerial
labor, which was occasionally concentrated in places of
most promise ; and as no churches were large enough to
accommodate all whom curiosity or anxiety brought together, there arose the plan — afterwards widely adopted
in other parts of the country — of " protracted meetings "
and " camp-meetings."

The first bodily exercise that followed from long-continued preaching, praying, singing, and shouting was what
was called " the falling exercise," in which a person was
said to be " struck down."   The subject was at first seized
with a kind of convulsive trembling, till, overcome by his
feelings, he would fall prostrate on his face, and lay for a
length of time in a swoon.   On recovering, crowds would

press around him to learn the result of the exercise, and visions were reported, and prophecies uttered, in the assured belief that these had been supernaturally communicated. We need not dwell on these events, as exercises of a similar kind are to this day, we believe, among the phenomena of a Methodist camp-meeting.

We pass on to more remarkable bodily exercises, an account of which is given by " a contemporary brother minister, on his own personal knowledge, during a revival in 1800 – 1, near the borders of the State of Tennessee." We shall here quote the article in the Princeton Review.

" We proceed to relate a case or two respecting the exercise called the ' jerks.' This succeeded some time after the falling exercise, and, I believe, had its origin in East Tennessee ; at least it was, to use a commercial phrase, first imported into Kentucky from that quarter. It affected the good and the bad, the aged and the young. It was entirely involuntary, dreaded, and hated, and even cursed by some ; while it was desired and coveted and highly prized by others. It came on something like the hiccough, without any premonitory symptoms, and left the subject equally without any sensible effect. During its prevalence we made several experiments ; being inexperienced in the ministry, we knew not what to do with it. While preaching, we have, after a smooth and gentle course of expression, suddenly changed our voice and language, expressing something awful and alarming, and instantly some dozen or twenty persons, or more, would simultaneously be jerked forward, where they were sitting, with a suppressed noise, once or twice, somewhat like the barking of a dog. And so it would either continue or abate, according to the tenor or strain of my discourse. The strong sympathy and intimate correspondence between the mind and the body was fully manifested by this experiment producing the exhibition which immediately followed. The first subject of this exercise that attracted our attention was the pious wife of one of our elders. She was affected by this operation very gently ; she felt no pain whatever, but rather the

reverse, a pleasing sensation ; could give no satisfactory account
of its operation. She went to the country village on a public day
to do a little shopping ; we accompanied her on our way home.
She was entirely free from any operation of the jerks. We therefore determined to try an experiment, conversed freely and somewhat jocularly with her on secular matters, to divert her mind as
far off in that direction as we thought necessary, and then immediately changed the subject to that of a very serious and solemn
character. We are certain not two minutes had elapsed before
she was considerably affected with this exercise. Her body, from
the saddle and upwards, appeared to pitch forward half-way to
the horse's neck, six or eight times in a minute. We were fully
satisfied she could not prevent it. Our mind became, some time
after, greatly perplexed about this exercise. We could not encourage it, and yet, being a young minister, we were afraid to say
anything against it publicly, as it had many advocates and friends.
At length it was found to be detrimental in various ways; besides
interrupting public worship, it deterred many from attending altogether, being impressed with the belief that it was 'catching.'
But it was not confined to the public assembly ; it invaded the
private and domestic circle, while engaged in domestic business
or travelling on the road. The same individual was frequently
the subject of it ; young and old, male and female, refined and un-
refined, the pious and the wicked, were alike under its operation.

" Take another singular case, stated to us by Mr. M'Gready.
A young man, son of an elder, to avoid attending a camp-meeting
in the neighborhood with the family, feigned himself sick. On
the morning of the Sabbath he continued in bed until the family
had all started for the meeting ; he being left alone, except a few
small blacks. When thus alone, he congratulated himself on his
success by the deception he had practised on his parents. He
raised up his head, and, looking all round the room, smiled at
the adventure ; but lest it might not be complete, lest some one
might have occasion to linger or return, and so he be detected, he
resumed his clinical position, covering over his head, and in a
short time directed his thoughts towards the camp-ground. He
fancied the multitude assembled, the services commenced, the

bodily exercises, as he had seen them, now in operation. He
fancied a certain female now in full exercise : ' Now she 's at it!
now she 's at it!' In a moment he was taken with the same exercise (the jerks), was hurled out of his bed, and jerked hither
and thither all around the room, up against the wall, and in every
fashion. He had never been affected by bodily exercise before,
but now found himself perfectly unmanageable. He had heard it
said, and indeed witnessed the fact, that praying would cause the
jerks to cease. He tried it ; the desired effect followed immediately. He felt no more the effects of the exercise, than a person
does after the hiccough. He supposed it all a dream, a mere conceit, illusion, or something of the kind, resumed his bed, commenced his pranks again, and again was the scene acted over, only
a little worse. The same remedy was resorted to, and he again
became *in statu quo*. He arose, dressed himself, sauntered about
awhile, wanted some employment to pass the time away, be-
thought himself of a dog-skin in the vat that needed unhairing,
drew it out, laid it on the beam, rolled up his sleeves, grasped the
graining-knife, lifted it up to make the first scrape, when lo ! it
was instantaneously flirted out of his grasp, and he was jerked
back, over logs, against the fence, up and down, until he resorted
to his old remedy again, and obtained relief. Feeling, as before,
perfectly free from any sensible or evil effects, as strong and resolute and determined and reckless as ever, he ventured again.
He assumed his instrument, and resumed his posture over the subject of his intended operation, when immediately, before he could
make one stroke, the whole scene, only, if possible, tenfold worse,
was acted over again ; it was much more severe, and greatly protracted. The usual remedy at first failed ; he became alarmed ;
thought the Lord was now about to kill him ; became deeply convicted of his great folly and wickedness ; became composed again
in body, but now greatly agitated and concerned in mind ; called
a little black, pointed him to the dog-skin, which he was afraid
now to approach, directed where to lay it away, returned to his
room weeping and crying to God for mercy, and in this condition
was found on the return of the family. He shortly afterwards
obtained a good hope through grace, applied for the privileges of

the Church, gave this relation of facts to the Session, was received, and, in the judgment of Christian charity, gave satisfactory evidence, by a Scriptural experience and godly living, that he was a renewed man and redeemed sinner saved by grace.

" We shall add only one case more. One evening we rode six miles up Green River, and preached at a Mr. M'Whorter's, in a Baptist settlement. The house was crowded. The people were attentive until we had finished the discourse and had prayed, and were about to sing the last hymn, but were forestalled by an enthusiastic kind of man who started a song with a lively tune. Several young women began to jerk backwards and forwards. The seats were immediately removed, to afford room and prevent them from being hurt. One young woman had what we would call the whirling exercise. She went round like a top, we think at least fifty times a minute, and continued without intermission at least an hour. It exceeded by far anything of the kind we had ever witnessed. We were told that she had had the jerks nearly three years. She did not appear exhausted; complained of pain or distress if the by-standers did not continue singing. We became perfectly tired. Our preaching seemed to be all gone, and to have been rather in the way, from what took place afterwards. We remonstrated with some of them, and cautioned them. Thus, you see, this exercise continued more or less in one or another place for a long time. It however, in the general, gradually disappeared, especially from the Presbyterian Church; and thus afforded us a very happy relief. We were heartily glad when it was entirely gone. After all these novelties left us, the Church, like one enfeebled and exhausted, sunk down into formality and apathy."

The writer of the article in the Princeton Review, commenting upon the above, subjoins some further particulars relating to the " jerks."

" The only appearance known to us which bears a resemblance to it is the jumping exercise in Wales, of which Dr. Haygarth has given an account in his treatise ' On the Effect of the Imagination in the Cure of Bodily Diseases.' The same facts are referred to in Sidney's Life of Rowland Hill. This extraordinary nervous agitation commenced, as above stated by our correspondent, in East Tennessee, at a Sacramental meeting ; and we have been informed that on that day several hundreds of persons, of all ages and sexes, were seized with this involuntary motion. It was at first almost uniformly confined to the arms, and the motion proceeded downwards from the elbow, causing the arm to move with a sudden jerk or quick convulsive motion, and these jerks succeeded each other after short intervals. For some time no religious meeting was held in which this novel involuntary exercise was not exhibited by more or less of the audience in that part of the country where they originated. And generally all those who had once been the subjects of it continued to be frequently affected, and not only at meeting, but at home, and sometimes when entirely alone. After the commencement of the jerks, they spread rapidly in all directions. Persons drawn by curiosity to visit the congregations where they existed were often seized, and when they returned home they would communicate them to the people there. But in some instances they occurred in remote valleys of the mountains, where the people had no opportunity of communication with the infected. In East Tennessee and the southwestern part of Virginia, their prevalence was the greatest; and in this region persons of all description were seized, from the aged, gray-headed preacher down to children of eight or ten years of age. Soon, however, the ' exercise ' began to assume a variety of appearances. While the jerks in the arms continued to be the most common form, in many cases the joint of the neck was the seat of the convulsive motion, and was thrown back and forward to an extent, and with a celerity, which no one could imitate, and which to the spectator was most alarming. Another common exercise was dancing, which was performed by a gentle and not ungraceful motion, but with little variety in the steps. During the administration of the Lord's Supper, in the presence of the Synod of Virginia, we witnessed a young woman performing this exercise for the space of twenty minutes or half an hour. The pew in which she was sitting was cleared, and she danced from one end to the other; her eyes were shut, and her countenance calm.

When the dancing terminated, she fell, and seemed to be agitated with more violent motions. We saw another who had what was termed the 'jumping exercise,' which resembled that of the jumpers in Wales. It was truly wonderful to observe the violence of the impetus with which she was borne upwards from the ground : it required the united strength of three or four of her companions to confine her down. None of these varieties, however, were half so terrible to the spectator, as that which affected the joint of the neck. In this, it appeared as if the neck must be broken; and while the bosom heaved in an extraordinary manner, the countenance was distorted in a disgusting way.

" Besides the ' exercises ' already mentioned, there were some of the most curious and ludicrous kind. In one, the affected barked like a dog ; in another, they boxed with fists clenched, striking at every body or thing near them. The running exercise was also one of the varieties, in which the person was impelled to run with amazing swiftness. There were many other singular motions in imitation of persons playing on the violin, or sewing with a needle, &c., &c."

We have now quoted the most important facts in the article named in the beginning. Further acquaintance with . the effect of mental excitement upon the nervous system will yield an explanation of the above events, and of many reported marvels of our day. It will be remembered, that the scenes here narrated were first witnessed in the Presbyterian churches of the West. It is a cause of gratitude that increasing intelligence soon banished from these churches the "exercises," which were fruitful, first of intense curiosity and wonder, then of suspicion and ridicule, and finally of disgust and infidelity. In like manner we trust the day for the more recent extravagances of Burchard, Knapp, and others has gone by. It is among the encouraging signs of the times, that all denominations are coming to see that the religious life is to be begun and built up by a process of calm, but earnest, religious instruction. What resources had the Son of God to work up the human mind to a state of frenzy! Through his knowledge of what was in man, and his power of performing miracles, how easily he might have touched the springs of passion, and tossed all into a tempest of excitement! How did he veil his godlike powers, that his words of holy wisdom and tranquil instruction might descend like dew on the tender grass! Who can doubt that they imitate their Master best whose reliance is the most firm and abiding on the moulding power of *instruction*. Slow and laborious this process may be, and every now and then there will be those who will cry, " See here! " or, " See there! " but after all, this, through God's grace, is the only true refiner of character and reformer of the world; and hence the noble words of Paul, " I had rather speak five words with my understanding, that by my voice I might *teach* others, than ten thousand words in an unknown tongue," merely to *startle* and *astonish*.

A PERSONAL DEVIL.

A FRIEND once meeting Rev. Robert Robinson, the well-known English preacher, asked, " Do you believe in a Devil, Mr. Robinson? " To this the reply was, " No, I believe in God: don't you? " If my faith is indicated by this answer, if I hold that the Christian idea of God and the Pagan notion of a Devil are inconsistent with each other, I am still bound to explain to myself how the belief in a personal Devil originated, and why the phraseology concerning his supposed agency took the form which it still preserves. The inquiry cannot be without interest, to every reader of the Bible. Our children there see the word Devil; they find it in our literature; they hear it in sermons; and sometimes, though I hope not often, it occurs in the conversation of those who think it a strong word, if it be not exactly fit for ears polite. As long as it thus presents itself to the public eye and ear, and forces itself upon the attention of the young and inquisitive, so long we need to be ready to give an answer to the inquiry, What does it mean?

In undertaking to state the answer which best satisfies my mind, I shall speak for no one but myself. I do not suppose that I shall touch a point which is regarded as essential by any one. No creed I ever heard of requires a belief in the Devil. The Apostles' Creed, the Athanasian Creed, the Thirty-nine Articles of the Church of England, and the unnumbered articles of our modern creed-making churches, not one of them, so far as I know, has the clause, " I believe in the Devil." But a traditional recognition of this point survives more or less distinctly in nearly all denominations, and perhaps in some cases it appears among us. It is not my purpose to dogmatize. I mean to state my impressions frankly, and they will pass for what they are worth.

All that need be said by way of historical comment may be compressed within the compass of half a dozen sentences like the following; — that it has been quite common with heathen nations to divide the empire of the universe between two beings, a good being and an evil being; that the Jews received all their ideas of a Devil from the Babylonians, during the time of the captivity; that opinions thus imported into the Jewish mind from a heathen source, and forming no part of any revelation from heaven, soon suggested and stereotyped those modes of speech which referred all evil to the agency of a malignant being; that Jesus when he appeared in the world found these modes of speech though covering up varying and undefined opinions, a part of the popular language of his day, which language he adopted as his own, avoiding any side controversies and leaving it to the gradual effect of the doctrines he taught to root out these heathenish ideas; that there has been, with a progressive light and civilization, less and less faith both in diabolical agencies and in the existence of a diabolical being; though, finally, with some denominations of Christians, as we have before intimated, there is still a vague and fearful belief in a personal Devil, a belief which they think a right interpretation of Scripture demands, and which therefore they must not give up.

In relation to this latter point, how much they who accept " the doctrine of devils " really believe on this subject, it is difficult to tell. Probably they could not tell themselves. It has never been with them a matter of critical investigation; it is solely an hereditary superstition. It seems protected and countenanced by the literal words of the Bible, and it makes strong appeals to their imagination and fears. I suppose that no one now holds opinions on this point such as were maintained generations ago. No one believes, I presume, that Satan, in a visible form, with horns on his head, and with his cloven foot, has his haunts in lonely places, or in scenes where great crimes have been committed, and is trying to lure the unsuspecting traveller or visitor to ruin ; nor that he sometimes shows himself to human sight in circles of profane and boisterous revelry, or as dogging the steps of the man who is meditating a deed of blood, or as mounting a gale of wind, which he makes his chariot to bear him to distant scenes of mischief and crime. These superstitions, firmly believed ages ago, have now, as I take it, all passed away. It is indeed but lately that they have left us.   Only one hundred and fifty years ago it was believed that the Author of evil had power to send his imps into the minds of human beings, whereby they became possessed, bewitched, themselves the agents of Satan, and fit only for the gallows or the fagot.   How strange to reflect that, four generations ago, the inhabitants of the whole region around us were carried away with this delusion, which terminated amid awful scenes of blood !   What a cause for thankfulness, that, if men must yet longer have a Devil, they have now a so much better one than our fathers had in those days of witchcraft !

After all, I fear there is no reason to think that his nature is changed.   Burns, as all readers remember, prayed for the conversion of the Devil; but there is no evidence that the prayer was answered.   If Satan adopts new modes of operation from age to age, he is accounted just as malignant as ever, perpetually busy at his old work, the inspirer of wars, treasons, robberies, thefts, murders, the grand author of all rebellion against the sovereignty of God ; and if now grown too cunning to assume human shape and show himself to human eyes, it is because he finds himself more successful in usurping dominion in the empire of the thoughts and will.   No doubt, the very mystery in which this subject is enveloped may make it seem more awful to the imagination. Perhaps the little that is said about it in any of the methods of public instruction may invest it with an air more terribly sacred and wonderful.   Whence come our evil thoughts, if *he* does not dart them into our mind ?   Whence come these determinations to do wrong, which at times so unaccountably take strange possession of our souls, and draw us captive after them, if he, the Tempter of all souls, does not breathe them within us ?   And then the common experience of our hearts, our wilfulness, our hankering for what we know to be wrong, our love for what is low and unworthy, our irresolution, our delay, our doubts, our weakness when great things are at stake ; and then, too, far worse things than these, the envy, the enmities, the pride, the selfishness, which I find lurking like a serpent in the bottom of my heart the deeper down I probe there, — all these things how am I to explain, except by admitting that there is a being disturbing the dominion of my soul and warring with it? You may call it by what name you will, — Devil, Satan, the old Serpent, the God of this world, the Prince of the power of the air, — but must there not be some being trying to draw me under his power, and whom I am to resist?

I do not doubt that there are hundreds and thousands, who, looking at the subject in this point of view, still hold to the doctrine of a personal Devil with as much firmness as that doctrine was ever held ages ago. It is a part of their religion. They believe in a Devil just as much as they believe in a God, perhaps even more. The conception is vague, undefined, mysterious, and on men of blunt and coarse minds will have no more than the average influence of other religious ideas. But what tremendous power it must have over sensitive and imaginative persons, if to them it once becomes a reality! A Devil sitting on the throne over which waves the banner of opposition to the throne of God, mustering the hosts of hell against the hosts of heaven, this world the scene of the warfare, human souls the prizes for which they contend, and we ourselves at one moment led by an angel-spirit and at another borne along by a goblin damned, — this is awful imagery and machinery, somewhat worn, it is true, by too frequent use in poetry and sermons, but still of sufficient power, if one can really be-

3 *

lieve it to be true, to upset the balance of the mind, as here and there it does, and to leave it a crazed and ruined wreck.

We have all seen maps of the world colored to represent the different shades of civilization, in which, for example, England is represented by a white color, as of the highest civilization, and other countries are shaded off with progressive darkness according to their rank as semi-civilized, barbarian, or savage. Were I to construct on a similar plan a map of theological doctrines, I should place in a white color those truths which are a manifest revelation from heaven, such as the paternal character of God, his universal and unresisted agency, the doctrine of a future life, the mission of an inspired Teacher from heaven; while I should put down the doctrine of the Trinity in the color in which China and Japan are placed in the other map; the doctrine of total depravity would be black as Africa; and this doctrine of a personal Devil would be my Otaheite. These shaded spaces would represent territories of opinions not yet Christianized, still sitting in part or entirely in the old pagan darkness. The doctrine of a personal Devil is a remnant of the mythologies of heathenism, received by the Jews, as I have said, during their captivity in Babylon, coloring through the influence of language the current of thought in all Christian times,— a doctrine softened down from age to age, but not yet rooted out; so that here is a territory of thought not yet brought into full Christian light. How strange that this shadow of paganism should survive to this day! Other gods of the old mythologies have long since been dethroned, the god that presided over storms, the god that presided over darkness, the god of the hill, the god of the valley; but this false god, the Devil, that presided over evil, we have still retained. We do not yet see that evil is an instrument not in the hands of the Devil, but in the hands of the one true God, who uses it only as a means of greater good.

" I have not a Devil," said Jesus, intending to rebut the charge that he was possessed by an evil spirit. But do I misrepresent the mind of the Saviour if I understand his words in a wider sense ? as if he meant, " I do not acknowledge the doctrine of a Devil, it forms no part of my religion; there is but One who has sway in the empire of the universe, and that is the Father. Of him, and through him, and by him are all things; and if I use the language which speaks of a ' Devil,' I use it as a part of the common and established idiom of the day, in its popular and figurative sense, with no intention of sanctioning what this language may literally imply."

And taking these words of Jesus in this broad signification, and applying them to that system of religious doctrines which I profess and believe, I may say, " I have no Devil." I do not want a Devil. I do not need a Devil. That is, I can explain the phenomena of the world better without a Devil than I can with one, beside getting rid of the Devil himself, — the hardest thing to be explained after all. These evil thoughts that come into our minds, these wicked desires that take possession of our hearts, why not look upon them just as we look upon the pains that sometimes seize our limbs, or the aches that sometimes afflict our head, which we need no Devil to explain, for either they are hints from a good God of a danger which we are to avoid, or they are trials appointed by a good Father to strengthen our patience and faith.

Nevertheless, though I speak so disrespectfully of this false god, whom I would dethrone, drive out, and never permit to set his cloven foot again on the territory of

Christian belief, yet, mindful of that proverb which tells us
to give even him his due, I must acknowledge that he has
not been without some use in the world. We are to consider how much mankind in all ages have been governed by
sheer bugbears, and it has undoubtedly been far better for
them to have been governed by these than not to have been
governed at all. The conception of a personal Devil has
given point, force, a lively and dramatic power, to precepts
and principles essentially true ; nor can any one estimate
the extent to which, as a mere figure of speech, it has filled
the imagination, and affected the sensibilities, and influenced
the will. I think there are always some tokens of a Divine
Providence even in the errors which are permitted to keep
a footing in the world, and it must gratify every benevolent
heart to find something good even in the Devil.

Nor is it at all likely that this doctrine of a personal Devil
will soon altogether die out, even from the most enlightened
Christian lands. It finds a lodging-place in some of the
weak corners of man's heart, and there it will yet abide.
How soothing to ascribe all our errors and failings, our
weaknesses and sins, to somebody beside ourselves ! What
a humiliating thing it would be if men were to refer to their
own folly and neglect the infirmity and wickedness which
they now charge upon the Devil, and what more convenient
arrangement can there be than to have this one grand head
to whom all our short-comings may be imputed ! About a
century ago, in England, in an age of extreme scepticism,
a writer undertook to set forth " the disadvantages of abol-
ishing Christianity " ; and among them he names this, that
the abolition of the Christian priesthood would take away
from the public one of their most convenient and innocent
occasions to find fault ; for, considering man as naturally a

fault-finding animal, and remembering that he might find fault with more important things if some innocent substitute be not provided, the writer thought it would be unwise to put away the ministers of religion, with whom all were at liberty to find fault as much as they pleased. Some consideration like this will long uphold among men the reign of the Devil, who, bearing so much the load of their sins, will be the most convenient relief they can have.

But if our faith does not present to us a fabulous demigod on whom we may lay the burden of our sins, we may the more truly feel that these sins are *ours*, and that there is no one to share the blame of them with ourselves. No malignant being divides the empire of the universe with the all-good Father in Heaven. Evils there are in the world, but the evils only of imperfection, appointed to try us and strengthen us, and subordinate, therefore, to our good. Come, thou, who didst of old cast out the evil spirits, cast all thoughts of them out from our minds, all superstitious fears of their power, all flattering excuses of their agency, — cast them all out, and teach us that there is no power above us but that of God, and no one whom we need fear but ourselves.

UNSCRIPTURAL WORDS AND PHRASES.

It may not be so generally known, perhaps, as it ought to be, that there are many terms and expressions current in popular theology which are not to be found in the Bible, but which have acquired an authority and sanction as if they were derived from an inspired source. Among these are

the following : " Original sin " ; " Experiencing religion " ;
" New birth " ; " Change of heart " ; " Holy Trinity " ;
" Triune God " ; " God-man " ; " God the Son " ; " Three
persons in the Godhead " ; " Human nature of Christ " ;
" Divinity of Christ " ; " Atoning Lamb " ; " Eternal
Son " ; " Imputed righteousness " ; " Self-righteousness " ;
" Absolute election " ; " Decrees of God " ; " Being under
concern " ; " Ark of safety " ; " Obtained a hope " ; " In-
terest in Christ " ; " Seed of grace " ; " Unpardonable
sin " ; " Merits of Christ " ; " Christ died in our stead " ;
" His death was expiatory," &c.

The above form a kind of technical language, by which it
is readily known to what creed those who use it are attached.
It exercises a greater influence than is usually supposed in
shaping the religious opinions of the mass of Christian believers and worshippers, and causes " their minds to be corrupted from the simplicity that is in Christ." This phraseology, which gives an unvarying tone to almost every
sermon, prayer, and religious conversation of a certain
class, crept into Christianity very probably by degrees, as
the fruit of human invention, and only by degrees can it be
extirpated, as the language of the New Testament more and
more becomes the medium by which the doctrines and precepts of religion are expressed. The language which Christ
and his Apostles used to define the doctrines and duties of
religion can require no improvement from fallible hands;
and it is not a little surprising that mankind should fabricate
terms to define their position in the Christian fold, which in
many instances convey a meaning quite different from anything contained in God's revelation to man. This course
has had the direct tendency to erect partition-walls, and sow
the seeds of discord among brethren.

During the early period of Christianity, when disciples taught and received their views of faith and duty in the uncorrupted language of Scripture, there were no very serious controversies in the Church ; but when they began to invent new terms to be used as a key to unlock, as it was mistakenly thought, the divine mysteries, and to talk of " hypostatical union," " trinity," " original sin," " transubstantiation," &c., then discord entered the family of Christ, and has ever since disturbed its peace. It is only by laying aside language of human authority, and adopting that which the Holy Spirit has dictated and sanctioned, — and let this be our aim and work as Liberal Christians, — that the followers of the same Master can best express their doctrinal views and understand each other, at the same time allowing to every one the liberty to put his own interpretation upon it. Those who are willing, in all meekness, to take this course, will be more likely to attain to a correct faith and to a plainer course of duty, and they will do much to diffuse brotherly love and universal charity. *This*, and only this, can restore a divided household to " the unity of the spirit in the bonds of peace."

P. S.

FIFTH AND LAST LETTER TO PARISHES.

FRIENDS, in speaking of the " Sphere of the Pulpit," I have shown, I think, that it is nothing new, but a practice as ancient as preaching itself, for the preacher, prophet, or reformer to speak of the nature and the measures of government, the conduct of rulers, and the wickedness of oppression, as well as every other kind of wickedness, in high or low life, religious, civil, or mercantile relations. All that is new about it is the extreme sensitiveness of the American people in regard to anything national and political, when rebuked or censured from the pulpit. For the first time almost in the history of nations, the pulpit is forbidden to speak upon anything but the "Gospel"; and then every man defines the Gospel for himself, and expects the preacher to keep within his definition. In this assumption there lie many evils, active causes of disaffection and separation. A reference to some of these will meet the other points named in my last letter, and close this short series of familiar communications.

I doubt if many parishes are aware how rapidly and hugely the habit of which I speak has grown of late, — the habit of extreme sensitiveness, and suspiciousness also, in regard to the preacher's topics of discourse. The suspiciousness is really laughable, leading, as it does, to so many blunders. We have known ministers to be suspected and charged with preaching on subjects which had not entered their minds. The minds of the hearers are filled with these subjects; and a particular word, as "bondage," "law," "compromise," "traffic," or any other that chanced to be common at the time, falls on some sensitive, perhaps sleepy ear, and sets in motion a whole host of suspicions and complaints. The innocent preacher, who thought he was preaching on a very religious, Scriptural theme, hears the next day that one or more of his parishioners will stop their tax, or withdraw their patronizing presence at church, if he ever preaches again on the higher law or temperance legislation, — matters that he may not have touched or thought of at that time. This is no exaggeration. We could name instances in which sermons, written and preached without any thought of the delicate or offensive topic supposed, have been considered as designed specially for that, and designed also to be personal. We have heard of hearers who " suspected what was coming " from the text or the introduction, and so shut their ears against all the rest, and boasted of having done it, when a very little continued attention would have shown them that the preacher was speaking of something else, and something which they needed as sinners. The use of the word " platform,"² at a time when political parties were identified with the Baltimore or Buffalo platform, of which the minister knew little and cared less, has given such offence as to cause threats of withdrawal, and very nearly the dissolution of the pastoral relation. And nothing is more common than for discourses written many years before, and preached again just as they first stood, to be taken as new issues, aimed at a special party, at this critical juncture. " Our minister must be careful what he says, or he will make trouble for us and himself too."

All this is childish and pernicious. Even if it were true that the sermon did allude to the matter in question, it may have contained much more on other points, and offered counsel or reproof which every serious mind or penitent heart should welcome. It is seldom that the really humble and devout are offended with that which is well meant, or fail to find some needed instruction. When any of your parishes, or any members of your parish, become restive, complaining, and threatening, observe them well, and see how much they are concerned for that cause for which ministers are ordained, the cause of " righteousness, temperance, and judgment to come," or how much they really

young men will not enter it, older men worth retaining will not remain in it, unless they can have perfect freedom in interpreting the Gospel, and applying it to all the relations and pursuits of life, to all the evils that obstruct its progress, to all the sins of the heart, temper, tongue, and conduct.

But will not this freedom be abused ? Of course it will. All freedom is abused ; and ministers are as likely to abuse it as any others. When they do abuse it, tell them so, kindly but faithfully. You will not find ministers so unwilling to be told their faults or errors as you may think; not so unwilling, perhaps, as some of their parishioners are. There are not many. ministers who will not thank their parishioners·for any frank, friendly counsel. The difficulty is, that parishioners are not frank or communicative to the minister. To others they may be. They may talk a great deal *about* the minister, but say very little to his face with a view to a full understanding of the questions between them. If there were more freedom of intercourse and interchange of thought, there would be less danger of misconstruction and evil every way. The common course is to keep the minister in the dark ; and the more he is criticized and blamed, the more reserve is there and silence, perhaps an intentional civility and show of kindness, the better to hide the dislike that is fomenting and the storm that is preparing to burst upon his head. And all for what ? Because, in the case we are supposing, he uses the liberty which every one uses, of forming and expressing his own opinion on the great moral movements of the age.

But enough. More than enough may have been written of late upon pastors and parishes, — such a torrent of this one kind of literature, that I will omit all else that I had thought of saying, and refer you to some of the books in question. Not all of them should any one be doomed to read, and of those I have read I would recommend the " Voice from the Parsonage," as containing many good hints and true experiences, though not offered in the best style. The tendency with us always is to overdo these things, when we begin to talk and write about them. We make too many books, and too partial statements, or exaggerated in some way. Few are content to be moderate. The favorers of reform and its opposers tend alike to some extreme. One minister never touches any of the contested matters, another never enters the pulpit without handling them ; and of the two, if we *must* choose between these ultraists, we could bear the former more patiently than the latter, — the extreme right rather than the extreme left. If a man conscientiously abstains from all discussion of matters considered by him foreign to the sphere of the pulpit and preacher, we can respectfully submit, even if we regret. But when a man singles out one precept or duty, and makes it the theme of every sermon and every prayer, we should doubt our patience and *long*-suffering, or the virtue of exercising it.

Let the whole question be viewed religiously. Let the pulpit assert its rights, but forget not its great object, — the saving of men's souls. Let the people be regarded as having rights also, and especially the right of being addressed chiefly as sinners, with a care, earnestness, and solemnity which shall show that their minister desires nothing so much as to convert the sinner from the error of his way, and save a soul from death. And whatever is said, and whatever heard, let it be in a calm, gentle, Christian temper. No good can be effected by any other temper. No cause was ever aided by violence and intolerance, unless through a

4*

reaction. The very best thing had better remain unsaid or undone, than be said or done in a bad way. Bad temper, violent abuse, indiscriminate denunciation, wrath, malice, falsehood, are as flagrant evils, and may prove as great sins, as war, intemperance, or slavery. And this is to be remembered both by pastor and parish. They are not accountable for any evils which they cannot remove lawfully and in the temper of the Gospel. They *are* accountable for the indulgence of any other temper, for every unlawful, unchristian word or deed.

Let me close these letters as I began them, by entreating that the quality most sought and prized in a minister may be Piety, and the result or effect most coveted by the people be also Piety. It may seem useless to urge this in any given case, but it is no less a duty, and cannot be wholly in vain, to keep it before the minds of pastor and people. They will own that there is nothing else of half the importance that this is, or rather, that nothing else is worth striving for in comparison with this, and as the result of such outlay and effects as are needful for the very support of the ministry. An immense amount of money, time, toil, and feeling is expended upon this institution; and if it fail of its object, if it be fruitful only of uneasiness, complaint, and variance, or in any way come short of the one great end, — piety, religion, salvation, — it is an enormous waste and a frightful perversion. If the end be kept in view and attained, no matter how much it costs. But sad, if this be overlooked and lost, though all else were gained. What if a man shall gain the whole world and lose his own soul! Cannot pastors and parishes apply the principle to their own connection, and its object ? *Do* they apply it ? In these days of discord especially, amid this ceaseless controversy

about rights, liberty, independence, and encroachment, is
not that for which alone parishes exist, and the ministry is
sustained, in danger of being wholly lost sight of? How
many parishes, in settling a minister or dismissing him,
think chiefly of religious character and religious issues?
How many judge of a preacher's fitness or success by his
Christian character, his power of making a religious impression, and leading men to repentance and holiness? Nay,
how many ministers themselves set this before them as the
one paramount object, and think more of winning one soul
to Christ than of filling a church, selling pews, and keeping
the people quiet?

It is not to be doubted that there is great fault on both
sides in all these things, and it is not worth while to attempt
to decide where is the greatest blame. Let each party look
to its own dangers and defects, leaving the other until these
are considered. There must be higher and more serious
views of such relations and their consequences, or evils will
multiply, and the whole cause of religion suffer. Men of
principle and piety must evince more anxiety to give a religious direction and decision, than to assert the rights of
either party, or complain of any political bearing. Ministers must show that they desire nothing so much as to do
good to the mind, the heart, the soul, good to society, and
particularly to their own people, in a religious way and for
an endless existence. And if ministers do show this disposition, leaving no doubt as to its sincerity and prevailing
power, we believe they will be allowed to express any opinion they may honestly hold on any subject, moral or social.
Let them express it in a Christian temper, as decidedly and
independently as they will, showing at the same time that
they care more to advance the moral improvement and

spiritual growth of their people, than to win a victory or vindicate a right; and then if the people complain, and would hamper or dismiss their minister, the fault is all on one side; such a people will not be likely to get or retain any minister worth having, nor likely to be profited by any dispensation of the Gospel of Christ. An earthly, selfish, quarrelsome, restless parish is a pitiable object, *needing* the Gospel as much as the heathen, and more hopeless.

The Christian Ministry is the hope of the world. Not necessarily in its present form, and not as standing in men's wisdom, but in some form, as a Divine institution calling for human co-operation, as the embodiment and instrument of the highest trust and power given to man, this ministry is essential to the welfare of society, the regeneration and perfection of humanity. Let no petty jealousies, no personal prejudice or pique, no temporal policy or passing interest, stand in the way of such an institution, or fritter its energy and delay its work. Let all parishes which really desire to find and retain a humble, faithful, independent, pious, and Christ-like pastor remember the end for which Christ lived and preached, endured and died, and think *him* alone who looks to this end, and labors to accomplish it with singleness and devoutness, a successful minister.

Your friend and servant in the Gospel ministry,

E. B. H.

SPIRITUALISM.

SUCH is the name given, as is well known, to the belief that departed spirits send messages to the inhabitants of earth, by means of table-tipping, or an overpowering influence guiding the hand of an amanuensis. Leaving the alleged phenomena to be explained by the physiologist, there are some religious aspects of this subject which seem worthy of notice.

A strange opinion on this subject by here and there one — the idiosyncrasy of an eccentric mind — would afford no matter of surprise. But " Spiritualism," started only a half-dozen years ago, has run through the whole land. It numbers its receivers by hundreds of thousands. It has its books and papers and expounders. In New York, Ohio, and other Western States, it prevails, as we are told, more extensively than in New England. It has entered churches, startling their ancient slumbers, and creating divisions which neither creeds nor discipline can heal. Simple-minded men in whom the religious element may be strong, and incredulous men who have for the most part stood aloof from the subject of religion, here meet in company. Already a church of the Spiritualists is talked of, and a sect is prophesied, powerful in numbers and zeal.

Of course there must be some widely diffused cause to make such facts as these possible. Some find it in the shallow education which, notwithstanding our continual and empty boasts, and perhaps in consequence of them, our common schools impart. Others name the materialistic tendencies of our times, seeking to find a solution of problems, hitherto invested with doubt and awe, by some positive and palpable evidence. No doubt these and other causes have co-operated. But perhaps the main cause may be found in another direction, — *in the character of the prevalent religion.* There are two features of that religion which, as we think, have prepared the way for this state of things, and are to a great degree responsible for this state of things. One is the awful distance and sepulchral gloom in which the spiritual world is regarded by the prevalent religion, and the other is the utter incapacity which it has begotten in the popular mind of discriminating between what is reasonable and unreasonable in religious belief.

" Spiritualism " is a reaction against the terrible background of the generally received theology. The human heart does not love to feel that all messages from the Good Father of Spirits ceased when the New Testament was finished, near two thousand years ago. It craves some tokens now that he feels for his children and loves them. It wants to draw nigh to him, and to feel assured that he has a benignant interest in their daily lot. The theology that is most preached does not give a God whom the heart can approach, nor one whom the heart can love. And then, all its representations of the spiritual world are revolting. Departed souls are borne off to some far-distant region, to await the resurrection of their bodies, after which the immense majority are to undergo inconceivable and unending retributions. Thus shut out from all communion with a Father, and from all consciousness of any near relation to the millions who have gone before, we, miserable inhabitants of the earth, must feel that we ourselves are in a dungeon, a tomb. The cold and everlasting walls are around us. Everlasting blackness, or, worse still, hopeless despair, rests upon the future ; and hearts are crushed beneath this awful burden. All the joyful currents of life are frozen up, and thousands leap at a chance of relief offered any way.

"Spiritualism" is a protest against the whole of this. Seizing hold of some as yet unexplained laws of our mental constitution, it rushes to the hope that all these representations of the great family of Spirits, and of the great Father of Spirits, are false ; it believes that it gets a hint that God has a paternal interest in each of his children now ; that death is not that boundless separation ; that the future is not that black despair ; that the departed are happy ; that they sustain conscious and benignant relations to us, and only thin partitions separate us. What fresh interest these thoughts give to life! what new and cheering views of death! what awakening and inspiring hopes! The past, with all its grim theologies, and nightmare dreams, and awful forebodings, rolls away, and a new universe opens at once, with a living and loving God, while the present life and the future life are brought near and are made one. "Spiritualism," we repeat, owes its growth to a dark and false theology. It is a protest against it. It is a satire upon it. Sceptics will sooner receive it than receive the old hereditary dogmas. For ourselves, we do not wonder at it. Most of the table-messages we have heard of seem more heaven-inspired than a large part of the creeds of some churches. We cannot regret that thousands are leaving the latter for the former. If we have reason to fear the first effects of these storms of fanaticism and superstition, we remember that the old, gnarled oaks must first be uprooted before the beautiful and fruit-bearing trees can be planted in their place. Few, understanding and receiving our liberal theology, have believed in "Spiritualism" as a supernatural manifestation. Give the whole country our

conception of God as a Father, and our belief of the spiritual world as closely allied to this, and " Spiritualism " would
find no food on which to live.

But some may think that we are attaching altogether too
much importance to " Spiritualism " by the supposition that
it has any intelligent and rational connection with religion.
What is it? they may ask.   A vile imposition with some,
a love of novelty and talk in others, a most unthinking and
stupid willingness to be deluded on the part of the most.
Can any man, in the exercise of his common sense, believe
that Spirits in heaven would choose reeling tables for their
instruments of communication, or would break the awful
silence of eternity with such messages as have been reported ?

" In the exercise of his common sense ? " it is asked.
We take up these terms of the question ; and we reply by
asking, What has the prevalent religion done to educate
man's common sense on this subject of religion ?   Has it
not here denied to him the use of his common sense ? . Has
it not poured forth all terms of reprobation and scorn against
the use of it ?   Has it not told him again and again, that in
religion mere faith, blind, unquestioning faith, is everything ?
Worse than this, has it not demanded assent to propositions
which do the utmost violence to his rational nature, — propositions which require him to say that two and one do not
make three, and which go farther than contravening the
laws of his rational nature by contradicting his clearest
convictions of what is morally right and just ?   And now,
having broken down man's perceptions of what is reasonable and unreasonable in the subject of religion, having
destroyed in the public mind generally the capacity of discriminating between what is likely to be true and untrue in

this matter, they have no reason to be surprised that men will receive what is so revolting to common sense. Common sense they have frightened away from this field, and it will not return at *their* call. Chained, starved, and poisoned by them, how can they expect it will now exert a strong and healthy action?

The truth is, we never know how far the human mind will wander after it has once renounced its allegiance to what seems reasonable. It is like sailing on an ocean without sun, star, compass, or rudder; and though a man is almost sure to be shipwrecked somewhere, he cannot tell in what strange sea it may be. We sometimes wonder at the pitch of absurdity to which superstition in Roman Catholic countries often mounts, — thousands prostrating themselves before a holy coat, or, as recent papers tell us, immense processions of bishops, priests, and monks, in that most detestable of all Italian cities, Civita Vecchia, visiting the portrait of a Madonna, the eyes of which a little girl saw move. But why be surprised at this, or at any thing? Judgment, reason, common sense, have there long been driven away from the whole subject of religion. They are intruders; they are carnal. Yea, the merit of faith is greater, the more irrational it is; and the saying of the old Churchman, " I believe because it is impossible," indicates the perfection of submission. And so in our country, at the present time, in regard to believers in Spiritualism; as the most of them have never been trained to use their reason, but have been taught to distrust it and to do violence to it, how can we expect them to stop at the line which separates the probable from the improbable, or to stop anywhere, if under the impulse of long-suppressed, but now freed and glowing, yearnings of their hearts?

For this second reason, then, we may justly hold the

prevalent religion responsible for Spiritualism. The numerous so-called Evangelical sects are active and proselyting; they tell us of the vast enterprises of their zeal, and enumerate the ever-increasing census of their converts; but what does all their labor amount to? It is as clear as noonday that, everywhere, in the midst of their own churches, there is an appalling amount of secret scepticism, and that, under the discipline of all their meetings and mutual oversight, the faith and allegiance of thousands can be shaken by table-turnings. We said that this was " appalling," but we take that back. It is hopeful. It shows that all the arts of proselytism, and the surveillance of party drill, cannot, after all, bind the mind; and regarding "Spiritualism" as a symptom of a desire to throw off the bondage of old dogmas, and to receive a faith more in accordance with some of the deep longings of the heart, we feel encouraged to increased activity in the dissemination of the truth. In the discussion of the questions that are agitated, men will read other books than those prescribed by sectarian leaders; and the fresh and cheerful light in which religion is presented in our literature makes it welcome to a continually increasing circle of readers. Hence the need and promise of the movement in which, as Unitarians, we are now engaged; and we are gratified by assurances that our friends will help us send forth to thousands, here in our own land, as much benighted and deluded as are others in the pagan islands of the sea, the true interpretations of that Gospel which gives a spirit of love and of a sound mind. Some of the aspects of the present age seem to devolve the strongest obligations upon enlightened Christians to increased activity in giving a pure and saving truth to the world, that men may thus be rescued from the delusions of ignorance, and the superstitions of unbelief.

LOVE FOR THE SAVIOUR.

As we obtain a deeper sense of the blessedness of the Christian faith, we shall naturally have a stronger love for him who, under God, gave us this " unspeakable gift." A growing sympathy with his work and spirit must awaken a growing interest in him personally, and give a more quickening sense of the reality of his life, and set him distinctly before us as one on whom the tenderest and holiest affection will rest. It is a confirmation of this, that those experiences of life which bring the soul into harmony with the mind of Jesus tend also to call forth a more earnest love for him. What expressions of a vital and fervent affection for the Saviour have come from a sick and dying bed l There the delusions of the world are dispelled, the soul deals with reality, it has a juster perception of the character and work of Christ, and " Jesus," " blessed Jesus," " my Lord and Saviour Jesus," are the words uttered with the deepest and tenderest emotions. We were told the other day of a young person who died after a gentle decline, during which all the mental powers were bright, and the spiritual nature shone with unearthly beauty. Every preparation was made by the departing one, even to the naming of the headstone to be placed at the green mound in the cemetery. " And on that have the word ' Jesus,' — nothing else, — ' Jesus.' " So much had the soul been with Jesus that that name was above every name on earth, nor did it need other words to express the boundless affections associated with it. Look, too, to the old martyrs. In our day of peace and ease they are somewhat apocryphal characters. Still, none doubt, we suppose, that there were men who triumphantly gave up life in the midst of flames of fire. As little can we doubt

what image it was that filled their souls, and kept up their
courage, and made them conquerors.   It was the image of
Jesus ; and the cry of the first martyr, " Lord Jesus, receive
my spirit ! " has been repeated by thousands of sufferers
since, who have felt the presence and power of Jesus giving
them the victory.

We would turn now into our own hearts ; and, in order
that we may prove and know them, we would ask ourselves,
do *we* love the Lord Jesus Christ ?   Do we set him before
our minds as a real person ?   Have we a conscious sympathy with the object for which he lived, and the work in which
he died ?   Do some of the tenderest and warmest affections
of the soul go forth to embrace him, and to rest on him ?
And if, in that truthfulness with which in solemn moments
of self-examination we would deal with ourselves, we cannot answer these questions as we would, let us be assured
there is something wrong in the life that we lead.   We are
estranged from Jesus.   We must come into his sphere, and
must seek to fill our souls with love for him by a deeper and
holier comprehension of the mind that was in him.   We are
to love the Saviour as the *Son* of God.   Much of that affection which Christians of other denominations express for
Christ, belongs, according to our convictions, to the Father
alone.   In their theology, the Son has every tender, confiding, and lovely attribute ; while God the Father represents
only majesty, justice, and power.   Not so with us.   We
see one higher than Jesus, " his Father and our Father, his
God and our God " ; around Him would we gather every
endeared, filial association, so that Him and Him only we
may love with all the heart, soul, and strength.   Jesus we
would love with an affection which, though it may seem cold
compared with that of others who see none higher than he,
should yet be one of the vital powers of the soul.   And we

would love him, too, not by mere words and high-sounding phrases. We remember his own striking saying, "Lovest thou me? Feed my sheep. Feed my lambs." "If ye love me, keep my commandments." He sought not an affection dissipated in mere emotion and high-wrought fervors; but one conducting to a steady, consistent, and holy life.

We have heard it said that Unitarians do not love the Saviour. Too true, we fear, is this charge. Compared with the degree in which we ought to love him and obey him, our hearts plead guilty. Whose hearts do not? Instead of sitting in judgment on one another, and magnifying our warmth by contrasting it with others' coldness, let us all give a better proof than this of our sympathy with the mind of Jesus. And if we carry the spirit of our Master into our daily life, filling it with pure affections and kind deeds, seeking to bring others to the knowledge of the truth, testifying against the wrongs and oppressions of the world, and doing all this from a truthful love of Christ, we need not fear what others may say. Enough for us what Jesus has said: "He that hath my commandments and keepeth them, he it is that loveth me, and he that loveth me shall be loved of my Father."

EXTRACTS FROM THE JOURNAL OF OUR MISSIONARY.

(Continued from the April Number.)

North Cambridge. A few days in February were spent in calling upon the members of the Unitarian Society in North Cambridge. A sufficient sum was subscribed to make their pastor, Rev. James Thurston, a life-member of the Association, and several sets of the Works and Life of Dr. Channing were sold.

.   .   .   .   .   .

New North Society, Boston. Part of the same month was spent in calling on the members of the New North Society in Boston. One hundred and thirty-two volumes were sold, consisting mostly of the Works and Life of Dr. Channing, Sears's Regeneration, and Eliot's Lectures. About twenty subscribers were also obtained to the Quarterly Journal. At the time these calls were made, this Society had already given indications of increased activity and growth, and there has since been no abatement in these respects. I had the pleasure and privilege of attending one of its conference-meetings, on one of the evenings of my service there, and of offering some remarks on the new field of enterprise upon which the Association has entered, in the publication and distribution of religious books, and the duty of Unitarians to co-operate in the work.

.   .   .   .

Providence, R. I. A good part of the month of March was spent in Providence. There are here many warm friends of the American Unitarian Association, and the cause to which its energies are devoted, — earnest believers in our form of Christian faith, and liberal in their contributions for its promulgation. My chief service here was the solicitation of contributions to the Book and Mission Fund of the Association from the members of both societies. In this labor I had the kind co-operation and assistance of Rev. Dr. Hall, and of two or three of the members of each society. A part of the time Dr. Hedge was not at home. The whole amount contributed was three thousand dollars, about two thirds of the amount coming from the older and larger Society, Rev. Dr. Hall's, and the other third from the Society of Rev. Dr. Hedge. More than seventy subscribers to the Quarterly Journal were obtained, and books were sold to the amount of nearly fifty dollars, mostly the Works and Life of Dr. Channing.

* * * * *

Sterling. During the month of April I spent a week among the people of Sterling, selling Unitarian books. As a contribution for the general purposes of the Association had been previously taken up by the Secretary at the time of his annual visit, no subscriptions to our funds were obtained. It was a very rainy week, but a young friend drove me through the parish with a horse and carriage, and I sold about fifty dollars' worth of books, mostly Osgood's Hearthstone, and Martineau's Endeavors after the Christian Life. But few of Channing's Works and Life were sold here, as they are in the parish library, and have been generally read. I feel under many obligations to the Rev. Mr. Allen, who is successfully engaged in teaching a private school for boys in this place, having retired from the pastorship of the Sterling parish, and to Dr. Peck, at whose house I stopped during my stay.

* * * * *

Salem. A few days in March, and parts of the month of May and June, were spent in canvassing the four Unitarian Societies in Salem, for subscriptions to the Book Fund and to the Quarterly Journal of the Association, and in selling Unitarian books. The results of my labors here were eight hundred and forty dollars for the Book Fund, over three hundred dollars for the general purposes of the Association (including four life-memberships and one fifty-dollar subscription), and over sixty dollars for books, — in all about twelve hundred dollars. To the ministers for their kindness in giving notice of my labors, and to those who responded to my calls, either in kind words or in material aid, I return my heartfelt thanks. Among the pleasant reminiscences I shall have of Salem will be the fact of having sold a large number of Channing's Works and Life among the working-men of that city, some of whom were not of our own denomination of Christians.

    .   .   .   .   .

Cambridgeport. During the month of July I spent a fortnight in Cambridgeport selling Unitarian books in the parish of Rev. Mr. Ware, and among a few of the Lee Street Society. I met everywhere a cordial and friendly reception. Almost every family improved the opportunity of procuring some of our choicest books. In a circle of one hundred families I sold three hundred and fifty volumes, amounting to one hundred and seventy-five dollars, and there are other households to call upon when they have returned from the watering-places. Mr. Ware was particular to give notice of my work to his people ; and to his hearty explanation and commendation do I chiefly attribute my success.

Such are the principal incidents attending my labors up to the end of July. My experience has been somewhat varied. Home cares, and occasional sickness of some member of my household, have discouraged and hindered me. Yet I have gone on thus far with a good degree of success, and have laid out an important and useful work. Whether my circumstances will permit me to occupy this field any great length of time I cannot tell ; but should I feel called to relinquish it, and to enter upon the quiet labors of the preacher and pastor again, I trust it will not be left vacant, and that some persevering, earnest, and capable man will carry forward so important and useful a work.

MEETINGS OF THE EXECUTIVE COMMITTEE.

THE first meeting of the Executive Committee for the year 1854 – 5 was held June 5, and all the members were present. It having been customary to appoint at this meeting the Standing Committees for the year, the following were appointed : —

On Missions. — Messrs. Hall, Fearing, and Briggs.

On Publications. — Messrs. Lothrop, Lincoln, and Alger.

On General Business. — Messrs. Fairbanks, Clarke, and Callender.

The Secretary is *ex officio* a member and Secretary of each.

The Rev. Mr. Windsor, of Rockford, Illinois, appeared before the Committee, and favored them with some account of the condition, growth, and prospects of the Unitarian Society in that place. This is a post in which much interest has been felt by many Unitarians in this vicinity, and a considerable sum has here been raised to aid in building a church. It gave us pleasure to hear of the prosperity of the Society, and we may reasonably hope that it will erelong become one of our strongest and most active Western churches.

At this meeting a consultation was held in regard to procuring suitable books for distribution. The character of our publications was felt to be a subject of the first importance, and the conviction was generally expressed, that they should not be altogether of a controversial or dogmatic character, but should be designed also to appeal to the religious feelings, and to awaken the spiritual life. Popular and able works on the basis of a true theology, presenting religion in earnest and quickening lights, — these are the books which it will be our study to procure. Some measures were discussed towards supplying this demand, and inquiries instituted which may lead to results to be hereafter named.

A vote was unanimously passed, continuing Rev. Charles Briggs in the relation which he sustained last year to the Association.

July 10, 1854. The Committee held a meeting this day; — absent, Messrs. Briggs, Fearing, Callender, Clarke, and Alger.

A letter was read from the Society in Milwaukee, asking aid in sustaining preaching in that place; and upon consideration of its revived prosperity, and the success attending the ministry of Rev. Mr. Tenney, an appropriation was made in its behalf.

A proposal to publish a volume of select articles from the series of the Christian Examiner came up for consideration, and various suggestions were offered in relation to it. The subject was finally referred to the Committee on Publications.

The accounts of Rev. J. G. Forman, and Rev. C. G. Ward, missionaries and book distributers of the Association, were presented, and were referred to the Committee on Business. Mr. Ward has travelled extensively through the Western States, carrying our publications with him, and selling them wherever he met with purchasers. He has also procured subscribers to the Quarterly Journal, and has lectured and preached as opportunity presented. He leaves the service of the Association to prepare himself to enter in the autumn upon the duties of a Minister at Large in St. Louis, to which office he has recently been invited.

August 14, 1854. All the members of the Committee were present at the meeting this day.

Reports from the Business and Publication Committees

were submitted. Proposals from Mr. John Owen, of Cambridge, to sell to the Association the balance of the edition of the late Professor Norton's work on the Genuineness of the Gospels, were considered, and were finally referred to the President and Secretary, with full power.

The Secretary stated that he had received a visit from the President of " William Jewel College " in Missouri, who asked for a copy of all our publications for the library of that institution.; and that he had made up and forwarded a package of books as a donation to the college. It was voted to approve of the action of the Secretary.

The Committee heard with pleasure of the formation of a Liberal Society in Cleveland, Ohio, under hopeful auspices, and the Secretary read a letter he had received from the committee asking for the sympathy and encouragement of the Association. It was voted to appropriate three hundred dollars in aid of the Society in Cleveland, to which it is understood Rev. Mr. Mayo, now of Gloucester, is to minister, in the hope that this may be the beginning of a tie of sympathy and interest which shall be strengthened and long continued, — a source of satisfaction to each of us, and fruitful of good influences to many others.

EXTRACTS FROM LETTERS.

DURING the last summer there has been occasional Unitarian preaching in Carrolton and Bloomington, Illinois. Rev. Mr. Haley of Alton has officiated there, and feels much confidence in the establishment of good Societies in both of those places.

We understand that the new church which our friends in Alton, Ill. are erecting, is advancing towards completion as rapidly as could be expected considering the great heat of the summer, and the sickness in that city. The Society meanwhile continues to prosper, and through the labors of their earnest and faithful pastor their prospects are most promising.

From Rev. Mr. Bradley of Belvidere, Ill., we have received an interesting letter, relating to the growth of that place, and the hope of a Unitarian Society. We give the following extract : —

" The village of Belvidere is on the north side of a pleasant river. It contains about two thousand five hundred inhabitants, and has a Presbyterian, a Baptist, a Methodist, and a Universalist church. In addition to these, the Congregationalist Society is building a house of worship, and the Episcopalians are making arrangements to build. All these churches are on the north side of the river. But the growth of the village will be on the south side, from the fact that the Chicago and Galena Railroad has within two or three years been opened there, and there the business must go. Recently streets have been laid out, and many acres divided into building lots, not a few of which have been bought, and already stores and dwellings are being erected. On this side we propose to build our church. We feel assured of a field of great Christian usefulness. Indeed, I think any Society established on the south side must grow up to be large. With the power we derive from a reasonable and Scriptural theology, connected with an earnest and spiritual religion which we hope to preach and live, we have hopes of great prosperity. Our plan is to build a small, neat house, in such a form as will admit of enlargement as the wants of our congregation may demand."

Mr. Bradley proceeds to name the resources of the Society, and to express a wish that aid to the amount at least of a few hundred dollars may be extended to it. The Ex-

ecutive Committee of the Association have felt an interest
in the cause of our friends in Belvidere, and they hope
they may find assistance, at least to the humble extent indicated.

We have had an interesting communication from Rev.
Leonard Whitney of Keokuk, Iowa, who is the pastor of a
new Society in that place. Mr. Whitney has been a
preacher of our faith only a few years, and was formerly
connected with the Baptist denomination. In the growing
town above named he has gathered a Society of much
promise, — the first and the only Unitarian Society in Iowa.
Mr. Whitney informs us of the interest with which our
views of Christianity are received, and of his hopes, not
only of establishing a strong society, but of circulating extensively our religious literature. We are glad to welcome
among us this new and earnest laborer.

In the Quarterly Journal for January of this year we
gave notice that the Rev. Charles T. Brooks of Newport,
R. I., had been requested, by a vote of the Executive Committee, to improve the opportunity which his proposed voyage to India would afford for obtaining some information in
regard to the state of Unitarian Christianity in that land,
and to favor the Association with some communication on
that subject.

Mr. Brooks sailed for India on the 20th of October,
1853, and returned to Boston on the 26th of last August.
In compliance with the request of the Association, he has
placed in the hands of the Secretary a communication,
which we are happy in now presenting to our readers. It
is as follows: —

" To the Executive Committee of the American Unitarian
Association.

" Brethren, — When I left home last October, on a voyage

to India for the sake of my health, you requested me, through
your Secretary, to find out, so far as I might be able, the situation and prospects of our Unitarian faith in that part of the world.

" At that time I confidently hoped that a voyage round the
Cape would so far restore me, that, even if I were not able to
preach in any foreign place, I might at least go about freely and
talk with the scattered professors or friends of our religious
views, and thus get considerable knowledge of the condition, if
not do something for the help, of our simple and precious doctrines among missionaries and heathen.

" But our passage, from various causes, was, unexpectedly, so
long and trying, especially to an invalid, that when, after a hundred and forty-three days, we landed at Madras, my hoarseness
of throat and depression of spirits compelled me to make the nurs-
ing of health my main business, and to forego very greatly both
the gratification of curiosity and the satisfaction of being useful to
the religious cause we all have at heart.

" Nevertheless, I did what I could (and could have done more
than I did had not the heat made it too oppressive to go about
much while the sun was up) ; and I will now proceed to give you
the result of my interviews and inquiries, first in Madras.

" You had requested me to inquire into the state of the Society
in charge of the Rev. William Roberts.   The officers of our
Association, as well as many of the members, have undoubtedly
been informed, for several years, through the medium of the
British Unitarian Association, that a Mr. Roberts has been for
some years ministering to a Unitarian congregation in Madras,
and many of us have heard something of the history of his late
father, a contemporary and fellow-laborer (at some distance) of
Rammohun Roy.   But I confess, for one, to have been so ignorant, as to have supposed, until my arrival and inquiries at Madras,
that this Mr. Roberts was an Englishman, settled over an English
Society, instead of a native, preaching in the native Tamil to a
congregation entirely composed of native Unitarian Christians.

" Two or three days after my arrival, I drove out, with such
very vague and general directions as I could get, in quest of Mr.

Roberts. The vast city of Madras, originally consisting of the
fort and the houses within and huts around it, gradually, like
London, devoured as it grew the crowded villages for miles
round, and they are now, under their own names, incorporated as
wards (so to speak) of the swarming metropolis. I was told that
Mr. Roberts lived in ' Vepery '; but, after driving and stopping
and inquiring the whole of a hot forenoon, (sent about from one
padre to another,) at last, in ' Pursewankum,' I drew up before
a veranda on which a school of children were chanting their lesson from palm-leaves; and this, I was told, was one of the schools
connected with Mr. Roberts's chapel (which I saw in the yard
behind), but that he himself lived in Royapettah. I left my
name, as a Unitarian minister from Boston, and returned home.

" The next day, Mr. Roberts called on me; a young man, of about
thirty-three, with a remarkably animated, radiant, and intellectual
countenance. The tears glistened in his eyes when he expressed
his disappointment at learning that I had not come out as a missionary; he said that, when they got my card, they were sure
that now at length their prayers for a missionary were answered,
and the disappointment was bitter indeed. He gave an affecting
account of the poverty and perplexity of his little flock. He said
that the other denominations held out strong temptations, by gratuitous boarding-schools, for instance, to the natives to become
' rice-Christians ' (loaf-and-fish disciples), and that the poor Unitarian was sorely, and sometimes successfully, tempted to aposta-
tize for the sake of a living. Even his own elder brother, who
had been taken to England by his father and there educated and
sent back expressly to be his successor had lost his interest in
the cause, and had accepted a tutorship in an Orthodox family; and
thus it was that he (the youngest), out of *pride in his father's
memory*, as well as devotion to truth and justice, was compelled to
buckle on the armor and train himself for the service.

" The Sunday following I went to his chapel, where I found an
audience of about fifty (men, women, and children), following the
preacher very attentively with their Bibles before them, as he read
at a table in front of the pulpit. The book of service was a trans-

lation of our English Expurgated Prayer-Book into the native Tamil, the hymns at the end being the composition of Mr. Roberts's father. The text of the sermon (suggested, as I afterwards learned, by my arrival) was Acts xxviii. 22, 'Concerning this sect, we know that everywhere it is spoken against.' There was one custom which enlivened the delivery of the discourse; whenever there was a text to be quoted, the preacher would just name the place in the Bible, and then any one of the hearers who found it first would read (or chant) it out, and then the sermon would proceed. After service a circle was formed close up round me, — children in front and old men behind, (several of them peering over with their bald heads like snowy mountain-peaks, as a writer expresses it, out of the vale of past years,) and through Mr. Roberts, as interpreter, I had some conversation with the little group, which made their eyes glisten and caused my heart to feel for them sincerely. Three old men were pointed out to me as three of the four founders of the Society in 1800. I shall not soon forget the look of those aged, eager, imploring eyes, as of Simeon yearning to see the Church of the one God on a sure foundation among them, and a missionary from their English or American brethren in the field, that they might look up thankfully and depart in peace. They seemed to be waiting for the consolation of their little Israel. Mr. Roberts told me that most of his congregation were servants, and that they were very poor. ·The interview closed with their unitedly beseeching me to represent their situation to their brethren in America. Some days after they wrote me a letter, signed by the leading members of the church both in English and in Tamil, which accompanies this.

"A few days after, I called to see Mr. Roberts at his house (which, however, might as properly be called a cavern, and made me think of the rock stable in which our Saviour is said to have been born). There I found the brave young defender of the faith at his desk, with piles of his own and· his father's manuscripts around him (among the latter an entire Commentary on the New Testament), near him the *Book and Tract Department*, contained in a couple of chests, and several scribes, catechists, and other disciples, engaged in their several offices. He then entered into the particulars of his situation. He said his father had left a house, adjoining a chapel, as a parsonage, but that his brother had mortgaged it for $ 350. If he could redeem that, he would be in a much more favorable position for making Unitarianism known and promoting its interests. But at present he scarcely received from England the small amount he had been led to expect from there, about $ 150 annually. With this and a small sum obtained from instructing the child of a Mahometan, .he has to support his family, pay one of his schoolmasters $ 3.50 a month, another $ 2.50, a catechist and chorister $ 1.75, and a tract distributer the same. He seemed to feel as if the defection of his elder brother had occasioned a little coolness of zeal on the part of the English committee. They had recently voted a small sum of money to the veteran Abraham Chiniah, at Secunderabad, towards the building of a chapel (to which the American Association had voted to add $ 100); but without disparaging the claims of the cause in that place (and also at Salem, where there was a strong cry for a shepherd), he still felt that the Madras post had the first claim, and that just now it was especially pressing.

" The next day Mr. Roberts called on me and introduced a very agreeable and ingenious Mussulman, brother-in-law of the Nawab, who argued with remarkable ability against the claims of our Bible to be the last and great revelation of religion for the world, but ended with expressing his warm sympathy with us in the doctrine of the Divine Unity, and handing me a letter to our Association, which I herewith deliver. I should add, that in Madras the only European Unitarians I found were a gentleman who used to hear Mr. Fox in London, and a young officer (Captain Mercer) who was about going to England, and promised to urge Mr. Roberts's case there. There is also an editor of a paper in the city who freely admits articles of a liberal religious character.

" Painfully regretting my inability to help them as my heart would have prompted, I left Mr. Roberts and his little band, with some strong impressions, which I take the liberty of submitting to you.

6 *

"I felt that there was something of the moral sublime in this little handful of poor people thus continuing to hold forth, year after year, the light of the simple Gospel, between the native idolatry, on one hand, and the Trinitarian idolatry and Calvinistic superstition (which, while nominally warring with it, are also working with it), on the other. I look upon them as a little band of martyrs, for poverty and obloquy are their only earthly reward.

"I was moved solemnly to promise them and myself that I would plead for them with my brethren in America,—which I now do. They seem to me to need, immediately, and deserve, our pecuniary assistance. If the Association would vote them a sum, say of $500, and afterward an annual appropriation, it would be money well spent; it would plant roses in the wilderness and kindle the star of hope in a dreary sky. It would trim a light for the Gentiles and for them that sit in the shadow of death.

"And, then, I would submit whether, by and by, our Association might not combine with the British in sending out a missionary, who, assuming the general oversight of the stations, Calcutta, Madras, and the interior, might perhaps make his head-quarters at the first of these places, and there organize a Society.

"And this brings me to the part of my report which relates to Calcutta. It was here that I had expected to make my chief stay while abroad. But the lateness of my arrival, the heat of the season, and other unexpected events, left me only three weeks in that place, weeks shortened by languor and the necessary preparations for the return voyage, so as to prevent my doing more than a very little, even in the way of inquiry, respecting our Unitarian cause. Could I have given a lecture or two, I might have discovered considerable interest in our views. As it was, I could only ascertain that there were two or three English and Americans who felt a practical zeal for Unitarianism; one particularly, an English gentleman of great activity and influence, Hodgson Pratt, Esq., under-secretary of the Bengal government, whom I interested in behalf of the Madras Society, and who has promised to write me a letter overland, containing his views on the feasibility of organizing Unitarianism in India, the contents of which, when received, I will forward to you. As regards Rammohun Roy, I was sorry to find such an unfavorable testimony everywhere, among both English and natives, as to the claim of his Unitarianism to be called Christianity. I was assured that he was simply a Deist. As to the purity and loftiness of his character, of course there was but one voice. Whatever may have been his precise ideas of the Christian Scriptures, he was certainly a Unitarian in his faith and a Christian in his spirit. The only followers of his existing are a Society of so-called Vedantists, philosophers who maintain that the Hindoo scriptures (the Veds), in their primitive purity, teach the unity of God. But I doubt not that they and many other Hindoo sceptics and seekers might without great difficulty be won to the Gospel as presented by a Unitarian.

"Regretting that the state of my health, want of time, and other causes, prevented my gathering more than this meagre report, deeply feeling how much the light of our simple faith is wanted on those shores so darkened and deadened with sin and superstition, and hoping that your zeal and wisdom may devise some mode of relief, I remain, in the faith and fellowship of the Gospel,

"Your brother,

"C. T. Brooks."

We would express our sincere thanks to Mr. Brooks for the above interesting communication. While we regret that his limited time, and the state of his health, forbade his obtaining exact knowledge as to the probable number of professed Unitarians in India, we are glad that he accomplished the main object of his voyage, the improvement of his health, and has opened for us a communication with fellow-believers in that distant land. Certainly there are many motives that plead for efforts to extend the lights of learning and a pure faith at a point so open to the labors of a Christian missionary from our body. We well remember the great interest awakened in this subject among the Unitarians of New England twenty-five years ago, and have always regretted that our Christian enterprise and courage as a denomination were not equal to our opportunities. We hope to obtain further information upon this subject, and, if successful, shall present it to our readers.

Mr. Brooks refers to a letter from some Mussulmans. This also has come to hand, and we give it below. It is one sign among a great many presented on all sides, of a willingness on the part of the more intelligent followers of Mahomet to regard the Christian faith with a friendly eye. This state of things in India is another door opened for usefulness to a missionary, who would doubtless find that the corruptions of Christianity, and especially the doctrine of the Trinity, are the great obstacles to the reception of the Gospel.

" To the President and Members of the American Unitarian Association, etc.

" Gentlemen, — Most respectfully we beg to bring to your kind consideration that we were much interested to understand that among Christians there is a party who are called Unitarians, and that they labor hard to prove the self-existence and unity of God. Being very desirous of meeting an individual of this profession, we were long in search of one. A few years ago we came to know that one Mr. William Roberts, in Royapettah, at Madras, is a preacher of Unitarian Christianity. We sent for him, and conversed on religious subjects. Both his answers and queries concerning the unity of God were so interesting to us, that we always find it to be a pleasure to converse with him. We here beg to inform you, gentlemen, though we have been long acquainted with several of the European missionaries at Madras, yet we have not found one of them so pleasing to us as Mr. Roberts. At the kind recommendation of Mr. Roberts we have attentively perused several of the Unitarian books, such as ' The Improved Version,' Yates's ' Vindication of Unitarianism,' ' Porter's Four Days' Discussion with Begott,' Wright's ' Essay on the Miraculous Conception of Jesus Christ,' Wright's ' Essay on the Doctrine of the Trinity,' &c. The perusal of all these works has given us great pleasure."

" Being much delighted both by the conversations of Mr. Roberts and by the books he kindly provided us with, we were induced to purchase some books for our own use, and to lend to others also who may have a delight to know what Unitarianism is. Several of these books are now in circulation among our community.

" Some time in the last year we addressed a letter to the British and Foreign Unitarian Association, informing them of our views and motives; but to our surprise we are sorry that our letter has not been yet replied to, but lately we have been given to understand by Mr. Roberts that the Committee in England intend to do so.

" Having met the Rev. C. T. Brooks on the 31st ultimo, we were much pleased with his conversation, and we invited him to our place on the 3d instant, when we think he was kindly interested by several of our men. On his recommendation we now address this to your respectable Association, to inform you of our desire to be acquainted with Unitarian Christians both at home and abroad.

" We here beg leave to be permitted to inform you that Mr. Roberts, in propagating Unitarian Christianity, takes the greatest possible pains; but we are sorry to see that no notice is taken of him and his poor family by the Unitarian Association, either in England or in America. Now, as his duty and his respectable birth require a decent living for himself and family, we trust that you will be pleased to set him at ease of mind by relieving him from the pitiful hardships that he endures. I think that he is worthy of your notice in all respects, both by the Association in England and America.

" Should a European or American Unitarian missionary be sent to Madras, we have no doubt that it would be of great advantage to the cause of Unitarian Christianity in India. Many persons who are ignorant of the Divine Unity will embrace Unitarian Christianity. We have informed the Rev. C. T. Brooks of this subject, as also of Mr. Roberts, whose services we trust will be of great assistance to the missionary that may be sent out to Madras. We beg to commend this to your mature and benevolent consideration.

"As we consider Unitarians to be the true worshippers among Christians, and it is our opinion that the knowledge of the unity of God is the source of wisdom, we shall be much delighted to hold correspondence with you, with every hope that it would be of improvement of mind both to us and you.

"We further beg to inform you, that we, being firm believers in the Mahometan religion, are as much persecuted among nominal Mussulmans-as you Unitarians are among your fellow-Christians, and both for the same cause, that is, for endeavoring to put down Polytheism and Idolatry and establish the Unity of God. With this view we beg to offer to you our friendship, and solicit yours in return, which we trust will not be refused. When we say friendship, we wish you to bear in mind that we do not wish any pecuniary aid or assistance, but your correspondence and well-wishes. With every hope of receiving a reply, we beg to conclude with prayers to the Almighty for the spread of the doctrine of the Divine Unity, both at home and abroad.

"We beg to remain, gentlemen, yours faithfully,

"RHANAY ALUM KHAN,
JANAY JAHAN·KHAN.

"*Royapettah, Madras, 10th April, 1854.*"

Mr. Brooks has placed in our hand the letter he received from the members of Mr. Roberts's Society in Madras, and we are happy in being able to present this to our readers, who will obtain from it still further information relating to the condition and wants of the Unitarian Christians in that place. It is as follows : —

"To THE REV. C. T. BROOKS, UNITARIAN MINISTER, ETC.

"Reverend Sir, — It is with due respect and attention that we the undersigned, natives of the Madras Unitarian Congregation of Pursewankum, beg leave most respectfully in a concise manner to convey to your kind notice our grievances, on which intrusion we entreat your kind pardon.

"For the present permit us very submissively herewith to state to you, that ever since the demise of the late Rev. Mr. William Roberts, deceased, we have aspired to obtain a person competently qualified for conducting the missionary avocations here; and as, upon several probationary tests, we found his son, Mr. William Roberts, was worthy of the important office vacated by the demise of his father; and as we likewise cherished an ample and satisfactory hope, that one of his offspring might succeed to labor in the vineyard of the Lord, — Mr. William Roberts began to perform, and is performing, with great zeal, the arduous duties of the mission ; and up to this very date we can find no reason to reprove him, but, on the contrary, we are compelled to vouch in the superlative degree that his conduct towards us, and his indefatigable labors for the spread of the truth, are indeed very satisfactory to us all, and we feel equally confident in affirming that the same opinion is prevalent among all those who have a regard to the cause of Christ.

" With regard to his conduct, both public and private, we can with full reliance testify, that he is in all respects sober, diligent, and assiduous, sharing the benevolent disposition of his late father, and worthy of the ministry he now holds.

" Still, reverend sir, our unfeigned wish is, that either an European or American missionary may be sent to us. The united labor of Mr. W. Roberts and of the European missionary will, without doubt, afford a great satisfaction to our benefactors. To have an European or American missionary in India will be an honor to us, as all other Christians here with the exception of us have Europeans, and in consequence of which we are very much disregarded by others. We therefore have no other alternative but to pray, trusting that you will be kindly pleased to take this our wish into your mature consideration, and condescend to communicate the purpose of this our case to the British and Foreign Unitarian Association, as well as to the American Unitarian Association. We further crave you will always remember us in your prayers.

" May the Lord Almighty, the God and Father of our Lord Jesus Christ, guide you safe to your native land, to the caressing

arms of your worthy family and relatives; and that you and they
may enjoy longevity, success, and happiness is our cordial wish
on your arrival.   We trust you will not fail personally to bring
our wants and wishes to the benevolent notice of the American
Unitarian Association.   This is the fervent prayer of, reverend
sir, your most obedient and very humble servants,

" T. DAVID,	MOSES M. MICHAEL,
C. AMOORTHAPEN,	SAMUEL DAVID,
M. MICHAEL,	DAVID CAVARYMOOTOO,
ISAIAH LAZARUS,	PAUL DAVID,
DAVID NANAMOOTTOO,	JOSEPH DAVID.
A. AROKEEM,	

" *Madras*, 1854."

We need not add, that the above communications awakened great interest in the minds of the Executive Committee of the Association, who passed the following resolutions : —

" *Resolved*, That we have heard with great satisfaction the report of Rev. Charles T. Brooks relating to his visit to India, and
hereby express to him our earnest thanks for the kindness which
has procured for us a statement so full and interesting respecting
the condition of Unitarian believers in that land.

" *Resolved*, That we learn with deep emotions of sympathy of
the wants of our Unitarian brethren in Madras; and of the wishes
of some believers in the Mahometan faith for the distribution of
our Christian publications in India ; and that the sum of two hundred dollars be appropriated to aid Rev. Mr. Roberts in missionary
labor in Madras, and the further sum of fifty dollars be given to
him for the distribution of Christian books in such places where
he may judge they will be of most use."

OBITUARY.

Hon. Daniel Wells, who deceased at Cambridge, June 23, 1854, deserves honorable mention in our Journal.

Whitefield said, he could not pronounce a man good until he had seen him at his own fireside. It was our privilege to see Judge Wells there, loving and beloved, consistent and unpretending in piety, generous yet unostentatious in benevolence, more patient with others' faults than his own, encouraging inquiry even when its results were what he could not accept, ready to sacrifice for others' happiness what he would ask no one else to sacrifice for his.

In the early days of the Unitarian Church at Greenfield, he went beyond his means in its support. It was a precious cause to him, and his sincerity did not evaporate in words. He had " searched " out its truths in the Scriptures; and when they were most unpopular he professed them before the world at no little cost. As he advanced in life his mind underwent the same change as that of Dr. Channing, and he devoted the leisure of his profession to philanthropy. No one of the modern enterprises of humanity failed to find a deep lodgement in his earnest heart, and his friends remember how indignant he was at the Court-House being bound with chains when the fugitive slave was upon trial, and he himself obliged to creep through these emblems of tyranny to his seat upon the bench. But criminal reform naturally engaged the most of his attention. He could not dismiss the poor prisoner when he had finished the trial, but anxiously sought how the punishment of the guilty might minister reformation, and save the community from the increase of crime. He was one of the first to see the importance of the Temperance enterprise, had a living faith in the cause of Peace, and permitted no claim of humanity to pass unregarded, whether it tasked his crowded hours, emptied his slender purse, or required his invaluable counsel.

Greenfield owes to him not a little of its prosperity ; not only by an example of worth in the highest station, the District Attorney gathering the lambs of the flock together for Sunday instruction, leading the devotions of the household, allowing no pressure of care to keep him from the village church, making his religion no more a matter of question than his professional diligence ; but by his encouragment of every improvement, especially of that new road through the mountain which has suffered a severe blow by his death, as it was prompted and sustained very much by his energy and hope.

His death seemed to us beautiful as his life had been. Though suddenly called away, his family, with one exception, were around him. He was tried by no prolonged suffering, but passed away before his physician could come to give him relief. He would no doubt have rejoiced to make better provision for his family, had he known his departure was at hand ; but he could rejoice that he had done everything which education and example could do to fit them for the warfare of life, and had bequeathed the richest treasure, a character without stain and above reproach.

His age was sixty-three years, ten of which he had passed as Chief Justice of the Court of Common Pleas of Massachusetts.

NOTICES OF BOOKS.

Sunny Memories of Foreign Lands. By Mrs. HARRIET BEECHER STOWE. Boston : Phillips, Sampson, & Co. 2 vols.

ALMOST everybody will have read this book before this notice of it is published, and any praise here will be only an echo of the general commendation with which it has been received. Not that it has escaped criticism, especially in English papers and reviews, which speak of it as egotistical, personal, gossiping, at times indelicate and irreverent, and in its criticisms of art ridiculous. Like objections we have occasionally seen in American notices of this book; though, on the whole, the tone of criticism on this side of the Atlantic has been much more complimentary. The explanation of these facts we take to be this, — that the English people, in the *furor* of their demonstration, saw the celebrated authoress only in a haze of admiration, and attributed to her all imaginable gifts and graces of genius, and now feel disappointed in finding by further acquaintance that she is not so well informed and high-bred as they had fancied ; while the American people, on the other hand, sore on the subject of slavery, and shrinking from the thought of having its enormities shown up to the world, were disposed to underrate the ability of their countrywoman, and to attribute her success to the accident of her subject, rather than to the extraordinary powers which these volumes of travel demonstrate that she possesses. It is an illustration of the proverb, that time holds the balance, and in the end weighs and stamps all according to their true worth. It is evident what *her* standing is to be with all excepting those just emerging from the excitement of an excessive and bewildering adulation. These volumes give proof of a rare combination of powers, strong good sense, close observation, knowledge of human nature, command of a forcible and picturesque style, cheerfulness, wit, freedom from all cant, and, above all, a heart sympathizing with the deep wants of humanity, and tenderly and faithfully loyal to the cause of Christian righteousness and truth. There are other fields of service in which these powers, we believe, will win still nobler laurels ; and the trust of a talent to interest and influence the world — as solemn as it is rare — will be neither misemployed nor misdirected. Should there be any who have not read these volumes, we can assure them that the "Memories" will be "Sunny" in the mind of the reader. As for the criticisms on art, we like the independence of which they give proof. Mrs. Stowe did not speak as an artist, nor pretend to. Let it be that she gave the impression that was made on an unpractised eye, and, in this department, an uninformed mind ; still it was a frank and honest statement, and as such has its worth. There is a prodigious deal of cant and bondage to opinion and authority in these questions about art. We are glad our authoress meant to see with her own eyes, and advocate, not only civil freedom at home, but some mental freedom abroad. We respect her for it. It would have been quite as easy to echo the opinions of the circles in which she visited. One fresh and independent observation is worth all the echoes.

———

Sermons, by Rev. Joseph Harrington *of San Francisco, California, with a Memoir by* William Whiting. Boston : Crosby, Nichols, & Co.

The general facts pertaining to the life of this gifted and devoted brother are known to most of our Unitarian friends ; but so full a knowledge of his fine genius, and pure spirit, and enterprising faith and courage, is presented in this Memoir, that it seems as if a new friend had been introduced to our heart. It is not often that we read a biography so simple, modest, yet tender and touching, as this ; while the seventeen sermons that follow indicate a far higher power than we had attributed to him, though we knew him to be one of our most effective preachers. Delivered with that finished elocution for which he was remarkable, they show a rare combination of qualities for the highest pulpit eloquence, and gave promise of great eminence had his life been prolonged. We are deeply thankful that his many friends in California, Chicago, and New England have this endeared memorial of him. We heartily commend it, as a valuable addition to all our parish libraries, and as furnishing an attractive and inspiring example to young men. We understand that the proceeds of sales will enure to the benefit of his widow, who we hope will receive some substantial evidence of the high regard in which Mr. Harrington was held.

———

History of Cuba; or Notes of a Traveller in the Tropics. By MATURIN M. BALLOU. Illustrated. Boston : Phillips, Sampson, & Co.

THIS is not what the French call a mere *livre d'occasion.* It is a work of permanent interest and value. Following a brief account of the colonization of the island, and of the successive revolutions it has witnessed, it gives careful statements of its climate, productions, the character of its people, their employments, amusements, exports, imports, &c. The book is written in an easy, pleasing style, and great pains evidently has been taken to make its statements correct. For this purpose its author consulted various Spanish books and pamphlets, some of which were kindly placed at his disposal by Hon. Edward Everett. It is published in the beautiful style in which Phillips, Sampson, & Co. are getting out many books, and it will be sought by all who wish for information on the interesting subject of which it treats.

———

Book of Worship for the Congregation and the Home, taken principally from the Old and New Testament. Second Edition. Boston : Crosby, Nichols, & Co.

THIS is a new edition of Mr. Clarke's liturgical forms for the use of the Church of the Disciples. It is the basis of the Service-Book noticed in our last number, and prepared by Dr. Gilman and Mr. Tagart for the Society in Charleston, S. C. Its adoption substantially by those gentlemen is not the only evidence of its great merit ; and were we to introduce a Service-Book in aid of public worship, the simplicity of its arrangement, the good taste of its selections, its devout spirit, and Scriptural phraseology, would give it high claim to be preferred.

7 *

The Stars and the Earth: or Thoughts upon Space, Time, and Eternity. Third American from the Third English Edition. Boston : Crosby, Nichols, & Co. 1854.

It is a good sign when successive editions of a work like this are called for. We know not the other example where so many thoughts of a fresh, sublime, and profoundly religious interest are crowded into so few pages. Science is here presented in her true light as handmaid to Faith, and we see how the fact of a future retribution may be as certain as the physical laws of the universe. We know of cases where the oldest classes in our Sunday schools have made this little work a text-book, and found it fruitful in deep interest and solid instruction.

Sin and its Consequences. Boston : American Unitarian Association, 21 Bromfield Street.

This is a reprint of the remarkable sermon of Dr. Channing on the " Evil of Sin," and the equally striking discourse of Dr. Dewey on the " Law of Retribution." They are here reproduced in the form of a neat little book, designed as a present to the young. The importance of giving to them thoughtful and solemn views on the subjects of future punishment, no one can deny. Such views are here stated positively, with no extravagance of assertion on the one side and no laxity of doctrine on the other, with no language of cant and no appeal to mere fear. We look to parents and teachers to give this book a wide circulation. Of course it is not a work which those who most need to read it will naturally buy. It must be given to such, and we trust it will be purchased by many with a view of making presents to such as need — and what young man does not need — the guiding and restraining influence of the great doctrine of revelation " of a day when God shall judge the world by that man whom he hath appointed."

We have received also, — *The Spirit of Devotion and of Trade. Mr. Osgood's Sermon before the Western Conference of Churches, at Louisville, May* 14, 1854, — characteristic of its author's tact in gracefully grouping subjects together, and in finding illustrations in a wide acquaintance with books and men : *The Two Stand-Points and the Contrast, a Discourse delivered by Rev. Charles M. Tagart, on the Thirty-third Anniversary of the Charleston Unitarian Book and Tract Society,* — a clear statement of the characteristic differences and contrast between the liberal and austere theology, with an appropriate reference to the annual meeting of a society which is four years older than the American Unitarian Association: *The Spirit of Truth, a Sermon by Dr. Hall of Providence, delivered June 28, 1854, at the Dedication of the new Divinity Hall in Meadville, Pa.,* — a sermon which one who heard it said flowed on in the delivery like a majestic river, and which in its clear arrangement, its just thought, its Christian freedom and earnestness, cannot but leave a salutary impression upon the reader. It discusses timely topics with the wisdom characteristic of the author, and is one of the best occasional sermons which his pen has furnished.

RECORD OF EVENTS AND INTELLIGENCE.

JUNE 15, 1854.—The beautiful and costly stone church, erected by the Unitarian Society in Jamaica Plain, Roxbury, was dedicated to the service of one God the Father, through Jesus Christ. The sermon was preached by the pastor, Rev. Grindall Reynolds.

JUNE 21, 1854.—Rev. John N. Bellows was installed pastor of the Unitarian Society in Wilton, N. H. Sermon by Rev. Dr. Bellows of New York.

JUNE 22, 1854.—Mr. Samuel Abbott Smith, lately of the Divinity School in Cambridge, was ordained pastor of the First Congegational Church in West Cambridge. Sermon by Rev. Dr. Peabody of Boston.

JUNE 28, 1854. — Rev. Stillman Barber was installed over the First Parish in Townsend. Sermon by Rev. Horatio Stebbins of Fitchburg.

JUNE 28, 1854. — Divinity Hall, the spacious and substantial ed-ifice erected at Meadville for the use of the Theological School in that place, was this day dedicated. Sermon by Rev. E. B. Hall, D. D. of Providence, R. I.

On the evening of the same day the sermon before the Senior Class of the School was preached by Rev. Henry Ward Beecher of Brooklyn, N. Y.

JUNE 29, 1854. — The Anniversary Exercises of the Meadville Theological School were held this day, and the following persons received certificates of the completion of their preparation for the Gospel ministry : — Henry B. Burgess, Lorenzo C. Kelsey, Tyler C. Moulton, John Murray, D. C. O'Daniels, C. C. Richardson, Charles Ritter, William G. Scandlin, Carlton Albert Staples, Na-hor Augustus Staples, George G. Withington.

JULY 2, 1854. — Mr. Carlton A. Staples was ordained pastor of the Unitarian Church in Meadville. Sermon by Rev. Dr. Hall of Providence, R. I.

JULY 16, 1854. — The sermon before the graduating class in the Divinity School at Cambridge was preached this evening, by Rev. Dr. Furness of Philadelphia.

JULY 18, 1854. — The Thirty-eighth Annual Visitation of the Di-vinity School in Cambridge took place this day, and the following gentlemen received certificates of having completed the prescribed course of study, viz. : — Moncure Daniel Conway, James Hackett Fowler, Marshall Gunnison Kimball, Calvin Stoughton Locke, Richard Metcalf, and Charles Henry Wheeler.

JULY 19, 1854. — The Commencement at Harvard University took place this day, when eighty-six were graduated Bachelor of Arts.

JULY 26, 1854. — Mr. Loammi Goodenow Ware was ordained pastor of Christ Church, Augusta, Me. Sermon by Rev. Dr. Bellows of New York.

———

AUGUST 30, 1854. — Rev. Robert P. Rogers was installed pastor of the Unitarian Society in Gloucester, Mass. Sermon by Rev. Dr. Dewey.

———

LORD BROUGHAM ON UNITARIANISM. — In a debate in the House of Lords, on the 4th of last August, on the subject of National Education, Lord Brougham advocated the establishment of schools open to all classes, in which no catechism should be taught, and no attendance at church required with respect to children whose parents objected to catechisms or to church attendance; but that due security should be taken that the religious instruction of children should be cared for out of school, while secular instruction was given in school. In the course of his speech he referred to Unitarians as follows: —

" He had often heard it said that Unitarians were not Christians, and some had gone so far as to call Unitarianism the half-way house to infidelity, forgetting that a half-way house, from the nature of the thing, might be either a half-way house towards infidelity or a half-way house from infidelity and towards Christianity. Assuming the difference that these misguided and fanatical men, with more zeal than knowledge, set up between the Unitarian and the Christian, he would ask, Whom did we cite as the highest authorities of Christianity? How often was it said, in arguing with an infidel on the question of the evidences, What better evidence would you have than that which satisfies the greatest masters of science, and the great masters of law? Who was a better judge of legal evidence than Lord Chief Justice Hale; of moral evidence than Locke; or of mathematical and physical evidence than Sir Isaac Newton? And yet Locke, having labored at one time under great suspicion of Unitarianism, which was groundless, was undoubtedly an Arian. It was undeniable that Newton was as thorough a Unitarian as ever attended Essex Street Chapel. If his noble and learned friend (Lord Campbell) had the least doubt,

as he seemed to have, he would refer him to Sir David Brewster;
and if he would consult that learned gentleman's work, or Sir
Isaac Newton's, he would find that, on examining the new manuscripts, which he had carefully done, he would see that there was
not a shadow of doubt of Sir Isaac Newton being a Unitarian.
Their lordships were not Unitarians. He doubted whether there
was in that house a Unitarian. [Lord Campbell. — "There had
been."] There had been, no doubt; but the errors of the Unitarians were not to be corrected by denying that Sir Isaac Newton
was a Christian, or that Dr. Lardner was a Christian, whose
work on the evidences of Christianity formed the groundwork of a
large portion of the celebrated work of Dr. Paley. It was not by
denying that men to whom Christianity and Christians owed such
a debt of gratitude were not themselves Christians, that they could
hope to correct that body of men of their errors. He hoped and
trusted that the notice he had taken of the grievous mistake into
which very well-meaning men — over-zealous and without knowledge in their zeal — had fallen, would have the effect of leading
them to remove this great abuse and grievance."

A Good Inference. — A late writer in the Westminster Review gives a half-playful article on the present " agitation for the
restoration of beards and mustaches to their historic position on
the countenance." He treats at length of the civil, literary, and
religious significance of the beard. He thinks that it is now in an
unnatural position in Europe. " Once the symbol of patriarch and
king (and so of the highest kind of order), it is now, it would seem,
that of revolution, democracy, and dissatisfaction with existing institutions. Conservatism and respectability (and after them, plau-
sibility and its companions) shave close. The mustache enjoys
military honor, indeed. But the beard itself is from sea to sea in
disfavor with power and order. It is hated at once by the king of
Naples, and by Mrs. Grundy. In England, too, public opinion
(which compensates with us for the smallness of our standing army)
is perhaps harder on the beard than it is anywhere else. All kinds
of offices discourage or prohibit it ; only a few travellers, artists, men

of letters, and philosophers wear it, and to adopt it places you under the imputation of Arianism or dissipation, or something as terrible, with respectable classes. Yet this opposition proves unable to stem the rising agitation. Pamphlets accumulate on the question ; and the curiosity about it has reached that degree of liveliness which authorizes us to pronounce it a movement." The reviewer then proceeds to trace the many allusions to the beard in classic and old English writers, in all of which he finds it was the acknowledged symbol of manliness, dignity, and honor. He closes with the following inference, which may be commended to the attention of young men : —

" But it will be observed, that the very reason which would induce us to sanction the wearing of the beard would also, in a vast number of cases, forbid its assumption. As certain dresses do not become diminutive women, and must, in order to display their wonted effect, be worn by those of noble stature, so the beard, identified as it is with sternness, dignity, and strength, is only the becoming complement of true manliness. If we are not mistaken, therefore, the cultivation of the beard is a perilous experiment for all degenerate sons of Adam, and may produce in the wearers the most ludicrous incongruity. We trust that the noble associations with the beard will never be degraded ; and we would advise all beard-loving aspirants to be well assured of their worthiness — physically and mentally — to wear it, before they venture to show themselves in a decoration so significant of honor. He who adopts it is bound to respect its venerable traditions, and to conduct himself with an extra degree of carefulness and propriety. For with beards as with other institutions, at bottom, it is the man that makes them respectable. To those who do venture to wear it, we would add : Let us have less hypocrisy ! Let us not hear that the healthy Jones wears a beard ' because he suffers so from tic,' &c. But let him who assumes it plant himself on what he conceives the sense and right of the matter ; his moral courage will then sustain him, until his friends, who may now amuse themselves at his expense, shall esteem him for his brave fidelity to his convictions."

THE EARL OF CARLISLE AT THE DINNER OF THE ROYAL AGRI-
CULTURAL SOCIETY. — At this season of the year, our attention is
frequently called in the newspapers to the anniversary meetings of
Agricultural Societies. We were surprised a few years ago at
the immense attendance at such meetings on the other side of the
water. Nobleman and peasant met together, for few things does
an Englishman love more than his land and cattle, and husbandry.
It so happened that we attended the annual Exhibition of the Royal
Irish Agricultural Society in Dublin : and we remember estimat-
ing at the time that it would take full eight of our Cattle Fairs to
equal that in the variety of productions and implements, and in the
number of visitors. The Society has permanent yards, stalls, and
museum, in the latter of which we examined with pleasure specimens of the grain that had taken the premium during the last
twenty years. The kernels were kept in glass vessels marked
with the proper year, and a handful of the stalk on which it grew
was placed by the side of it, so that we could see the comparative
size, height, &c., of the growth of many years. Drawings of
perishable premium articles, such as turnips, beets, &c., hung up
round the hall, with the weight and the year of production marked
on each ; and in this way the progress from year to year during a
whole generation could be seen, and its proof preserved. We
thought the plan worthy of imitation at home. By late English
papers we see that the Royal Agricultural Society of England assembled this year in Lincoln. It is stated that twenty-five thousand persons visited the show-yard in one day ; the receipts at the
doors amounted to over seven thousand dollars. At the dinner,
the Earl of Carlisle made a speech, and referred to his recent travels in Greece. We quote the following, as containing a curious
fact and a just reflection : —

" Though the inhabitants of those regions have shown of late
considerable prowess in military matters, and though they occupy
some of the fairest and most capable districts in the world, yet
their farming processes and implements do not certainly exhibit
much resemblance to those which are exhibited in the show-yard
of Lincoln, and I believe they have undergone little change since

the days of Homer. But I think we have no reason to despond even in this respect, for it did happen to me, — on a very extensive farm brought into cultivation by our enlightened and excellent consul, Mr. Calvert, — it did happen to me to see with my own eyes, on a farm in the actual plains of Troy, implements inscribed with the names of Garrett of Saxmundham, and Croskill of Beverley. And I believe that this is the real and true solution of the Eastern Question of which we hear so much, and that neither our fleets, however well manned, nor our armies, however valorous, nor our diplomatists, however skilful, can do so much as the plough, the spade, and the draining-tile, to revive exhausted provinces and to recruit a failing population."

ENGAGEMENTS.

On Sunday, June 11, 1854, the Secretary preached in Lancaster, to the Society of which Rev. George M. Bartol is pastor. In the morning a statement was given of the leading objects of the Association, with a more particular reference to the proposal for a Book Fund. Soon after this visit, a subscription-paper was passed round, and the sum, including the amount of a contribution at church, will be found acknowledged in the proper place. It was a pleasure to address the large and prosperous Society in this place ; and we trust a permanent connection will be maintained with the Association, by ties annually remembered and renewed on the second Sunday in June.

On Sunday, June 18, 1854, the Secretary preached in Bangor, Maine, to the Society which has Rev. Joseph H. Allen for its pastor. This is one of the largest Societies in our denomination, and the church which it has recently erected is a model for beauty and good taste, and a great ornament to this thriving city. For several years this Society has suspended its contributions to the Association. It was a satisfaction to find that interest was still felt in its purposes, plans, and hopes. By invitation of the pastor it was addressed in the morning upon the subject of the recent enterprise for the distribution of our religious literature, and an invitation was extended for earnest co-operation in this work. Expressions of hearty approval of this object were subsequently made, and a subscription-paper is now in circulation, with a promise of something worthy of the cause and of this spirited Society.

On Sunday, July 9, 1854, the Secretary addressed Rev. Dr. Putnam's Society in Roxbury. As the pastor himself had not long before preached in behalf of the Book Fund, and a contribution in its aid had been taken up at church, there was only a brief allusion, in the course of the morning sermon, to the general purposes of the Association in the position it now occupies and the opportunities it now enjoys. Gratitude was expressed both for the word that had before been uttered, and for the response that followed, while the belief was declared, that, if, after all our parishes have been heard from, there should be a deficiency in the sum proposed, we did not interpret the generosity of this noble parish too largely in supposing it would again extend to us a helping hand. It may here be added, that there is hardly another Society which has annually aided our Association with such unfailing regularity and promptness as the old First Parish in Roxbury.

On Sunday, July 23, 1854, the Secretary preached to the Society in Belfast, Maine. This is one of the oldest Unitarian Societies in that State. Rev. William Frothingham here had a long, peaceful, and successful ministry; and here, in 1847, his first successor, Rev. M. A. H. Niles, died within one week after his installation, disappointing many fond hopes which his ability and rare worth had awakened. Rev. Cazneau Palfrey, the present pastor, is in the seventh year of his ministry. The Society is strong and prosperous. It has happened that here also a connection with our Association has for several years been interrupted. Both forenoon and afternoon the Society was addressed upon the general subject of our position, duties, and plans. Notice was given that a committee of three ladies would be appointed to call upon the families of the parish, and to solicit their co-operation. The sum collected by them will be acknowledged, when received, in the Journal.

On Sunday, July 30, 1854, the Secretary preached in Glou-cester. The Society was then without a pastor; but it had given an invitation to Rev. Robert P. Rogers, whose installation took place on the 30th of August. The Society is an old one, and has had several pastors within our memory. Messrs. Hildreth, Hamilton, Waite, and Mountford have here been set-tled. In the reviving prosperity of this town, the Society has hopes of increased growth and strength. In the summer espe-cially the attendance at church is large, as few places furnish greater attractions for summer resort. The purposes and plans of the Association were presented in the morning's discourse, and an in-vitation was given to the Society to mark this last Sunday in July annually as the time for offering aid to our cause. Notice was given that a committee would immediately call upon the families of the Society for their contributions.

On Sunday, August 27, 1854, the Secretary preached in Exeter, N. H. A new Unitarian Society has recently been established in this ancient and beautiful town. It has obtained possession of a church in which a Universalist Society formerly worshipped. This Society, maintaining only a feeble existence, has been dis-solved, and the " First Unitarian Society in Exeter " has been formed, embracing, however, quite a number who have before called themselves Universalists, though including a larger number of Unitarians, who have heretofore worshipped in the other churches of the town. The step has been taken with great friendliness of feeling, and promises to be crowned with gratifying success. Preaching was commenced on the first of June last, and has been continued since to highly respectable audiences. It was a pleas-ing duty to welcome this new band of disciples into our broth-erhood of faith, and to extend to them the assurances of our fel-lowship.

In the last number of the Quarterly Journal a list was given of the places from which contributions were expected during the following three months, together with the date for each. As the plan here instituted becomes more generally understood, we feel sure that its importance will be seen and acknowledged. It is a great relief to the pastor to have an *annual* contribution for an approved object. The occasion presents itself, and requires no explanation, excuses, or justification. It is a great favor to the people, for they know when they will be asked to give, and will give with more cheerfulness. It is the unusual, uncertain, and un-prepared-for contributions that give trouble to the minister and impatience to the people. It is unnecessary to multiply words on this subject. The advantages of method and system must be apparent to all. By a careful observance for a year or two of the indicated time it will come to be known throughout the parish. Perhaps its recurrence may give the preacher a subject for his sermon on that day; or, if he proposes not to preach at home on that Sabbath, the contribution may be taken up in his absence.

The following Sundays are the annual times for collections in behalf of the Association from the societies placed against the dates : —

October 8.   Rev. Mr. Tilden's Society, Walpole, N. H.
October 15.   Rev. Mr. Bond's Society, Dover, N. H.
October 22.   Rev. Dr. Lunt's Society, Quincy.
October 29.   Rev. Mr. Stone's Society, Bolton.
November 12.   Rev. Mr. Stebbins's Society, Fitchburg.
November 19.   Rev. Mr. White's Society, Keene, N. H.
November 26.   Rev. Mr. Smith's Society, Leominster.
December 24.   Rev. Mr. Cudworth's Society, East Boston.

The future engagements of the Secretary are as follows : —

October 8th, at Scituate.
  "   15th, at Lancaster, N. H.
  "   22d, at North Andover.
  "   29th, at Pepperell.
November 12th, at Fitchburg.
  "   19th, at West Cambridge.

ACKNOWLEDGMENTS.

IN the months of June, July, and August there have been received the following sums : —

June	1.	From	friends in Barnstable, ...	$7.00
"	"	"	Christopher Woods, sale of books, . .	3.00
"	"	"	M. Wright, Indianapolis, . . .	2.00
"	"	"	Dublin, N. H.	13.00
"	"	"	Stow, Mass.	10.00
"	"	"	a friend in Francestown, N. H. . .	5.00
"	"	"	sale of books, ...	27.20
"	2.	"	Saco, in addition, ...	1.00
"	3.	"	sale of books at office, ...	48.91
"	"	"	two subscribers to Quarterly Journal, .	2.00
"	5.	"	a lady in Salem by Rev. G. W. Briggs,	5.00
"	6.	"	P. Putnam, Esq.	5.00
"	7.	"	a friend in Connecticut, . . .	20.00
"	10.	"	sale of books at office, ...	14.20
"	"	"	one subscriber to Quarterly Journal, .	1.00
"	12.	"	sale of books, ...	.37
"	16.	"	Concord, Mass., in addition, . . .	1.00
"	20.	"	sale of books at office, ...	8.20
"	21.	"	Rev. Mr. Cordner's Society, Montreal, .	36.25
"	23.	"	Auxiliary in Brooklyn, N. Y. . .	55.00
"	24.	"	" " Roxbury, Dr. Putnam's Society, . . .	100.00
"	"	"	sale of books at office, ...	8.00
"	26.	"	friends in Rochester, N. Y. . . .	30.00
"	28.	"	sale of books at office, ...	2.40
July	3.	"	" " " "	2.33
"	8.	"	" " " "	4.00
"	10.	"	two subscribers to Q. Journal, . . .	2.00
"	"	"	ten " " " (in Providence),	10.00
"	11.	"	two " " " . . .	2.00
"	12.	"	Hon. Samuel Hoar, Concord, . .	20.00

8 *

July	13.	From two subscribers to Quarterly Journal,	$ 2.00
"	"	" sale of books at office, ...	3.45
"	"	" friends in Buffalo, N. Y.	25.00
"	15.	" sale of books, ...	.50
"	18.	" " "	.30
"	"	" Miss M. Newman, ...	20.00
"	"	" friends in Bridgewater, by Hon. Artemas Hale, ...	40.00
"	26.	" Hawes Place Society, South Boston, .	100.00
"	27.	" sale of books at office, . . .	8.54
Aug.	3.	" sale of books at Salem, by Mr. Forman,	27.52
"	"	" " " office, . . .	1.12
"	11.	" John Avery, Lowell, life-member, . .	30.00
"	14.	" Samuel B. Buttrick, ...	1.00
"	"	" sale of books in Portland, . . .	10.00
"	15.	" " " by Mr. Forman, . .	75.00
"	16.	" Sterling, in addition, . . .	1.00
"	"	" sale of books at office, . . .	5.00
"	17.	" " " by John R. Howard, .	25.00
"	18.	" " " at office, . . .	1.87
"	19.	" . " " " . . .	23.18
"	21.	" Auxiliary in Fall River, in addition, .	8.00
"	22.	" sale of books at office, . . .	.82
"	24.	" friends in Lancaster, . . .	160.00
"	"	" one subscriber to Quarterly Journal, .	1.00
"	28.	" sale of books at office, . . .	17.03

A

CIRCULAR

OF THE

AMERICAN UNITARIAN ASSOCIATION

RESPECTING

THE BOOK AND TRACT FUND.

THE American Unitarian Association proposes to raise fifty thousand dollars, to be employed in the printing, distribution, and sale of religious books and pamphlets. Books for which there is a large demand, stereotyped or printed in large editions, can now be afforded at very low rates, compared with former prices. The Association would avail itself of this advantage in the circulation of large and small religious works, either by printing them in one of these ways, or by purchasing them in large quantities from the publishers, where this is more profitable. The whole fund, if it be necessary, may be employed as capital for this purpose. Some of these works will be distributed gratuitously; but it is intended generally to sell them at their cost. The Association proposes to establish depositaries for sales where there is a sufficient demand, and to employ travelling agents to sell them from place to place where this is most expedient. The money received from these sales will again be employed in printing and purchasing.

Supposing the cost of each work to average twenty-five cents (for though many will cost more, yet by far the greater number will be pamphlets costing much less), and supposing the yearly loss on the whole capital to be two per cent. ; before this capital is expended, *each dollar* will have circulated *two hundred works*, and the *whole capital* more than *ten millions*. Such a fund, as we have often seen, provides for its own renewal, by raising up so many more givers. More has been already given for our religious purposes in the Western States than we have ever expended there ; and it is reasonable to expect in this case a like result.

The voice of the speaker can reach but few even among his contemporaries. The best discourse is heard by a few hundreds only ; but when printed it reaches many thousands. A sermon of Dr. Channing's printed in his Works, if each copy has found but ten readers, has already been read by hundreds of thousands, and by how many more will it be read! The aggregate effect upon the public mind of the delivery of an oration even by Cicero or Demosthenes was little, compared with the aggregate effect of the same oration upon the millions who have read it since. At first thought it surprises us, that Addison, who could not speak, should have been Secretary of State ; but the House of Commons had then no reporters, and a pamphlet from his pen did more than the most powerful speech. And so it is now. A speech in Parliament or Congress does little, compared with the printed report of the same speech. The speaker really addresses the absent public, rather than the present assembly ; and in a few hours after his voice has reached the few, the press and the railroad send the report over the whole country, to millions of readers. He is not so much a public speaker as one who dictates to the reporters, as a writer dictates to his amanuensis for the public press. Let the same sermon be preached by a hundred preachers in the hundred largest churches in the hundred largest towns in our country, and let a writer sit down in his solitary study, and as he writes let a single press print at the rate of twenty thousand copies in an hour, and it will soon be seen whether it is the voice of the speaker or the pen of the writer and the type of the printer which move the world.

What has not been done, and what may not be done, by books? Of all that is known, in the world of science, literature, or art, of public affairs or domestic economy, of the land or sea and all that is in or on them, of the heavens above or of the earth beneath, of everything which concerns mind or matter, this world or the next, how small is the part which cannot be found in books! Why does the world advance so much faster now than it did in the early ages? Because each generation does not, as it once did, begin almost anew; but enters at once on a vast inheritance of the knowledge and experience of former generations, transmitted to it in books. Show us a Christian object which cannot be advanced by religious books, or a moral or religious evil which they cannot do much to remedy. Point out a spot in the wide land where they cannot do good. Name a class, profession, or any other body of men, who do not need them, or even a single soul whose state is so peculiar that there is nothing in them for him.

The Christian religion is founded on the histories and letters of the Apostles and their companions, — that is, on books. To prove the authenticity of these, we rely on the writings of Papias, Justin Martyr, Irenæus, Theophilus, Tertullian, and other early Fathers, that is, upon books. To settle the text of the Scripture, we examine ancient manuscripts and turn to books containing the reasons for and against their several readings. To determine their interpretation and ascertain their facts or doctrines, we study numerous books of commentaries. The early Church, and each of its successive generations, teaches us by books. The Christian mind and heart through eighteen centuries has intercourse and sympathy with our minds and hearts only by books. Of the great and master spirits of the Church, how few have ever spoken to us except by books! Christianity is especially the religion of books.

But the argument in favor of our present undertaking does not rest only upon the common uses of books in every period for religious or general purposes. There are reasons for the circulation of religious works at the present time, which never existed to the same extent before.

Much more may be done with the same sum now. The great improvements in presses, in the making of paper and ink, in binding and other things, have changed the whole matter. Twenty thousand large sheets can be printed on both sides by an eight-cylinder press and delivered in an hour. A good manuscript copy of the Bible formerly cost five hundred dollars, and a printed copy can now be purchased for twenty-two cents. A number of a monthly periodical containing one hundred and forty-four octavo pages, small type and double columns of original matter, with numerous wood engravings, is delivered to the purchaser for sixteen cents. Here we see what can be done by large editions. The more good we attempt to do, the less is the proportional cost.

The circulation of books in our country has increased rapidly during the last few years. The schools have filled the country with readers. Of Harper's Monthly Magazine

120,000 copies are sold every month. Other periodicals are pushing themselves forward towards a like amount. Channing's Works have had a circulation of more than 120,000 vols.; Prescott's Histories, 160,000; Webster's Works, 50,000; Bancroft's History of the United States, 30,000 copies; Sparks's American Biography, 100,000 vols.

Books do not now wait at the church or the library for the reader to come to them; they meet him in the steamboat and the car, at the hotel and the house where he visits; they penetrate the recesses of his home, and court his attention everywhere. They lie before him in his parlor and his chamber, on the table and the sofa, the bureau, the toilet, and the bed, to catch the slightest turn of his inclination and wait the exact moment of his leisure. The question is not, whether books shall solicit him to read them, but what books shall solicit him. And here also there is an improvement. The piles of high-wrought tales, ministering to the lowest tastes and the basest passions, bad in their details and worse in their general tendency, are growing scarce in the shop-windows, which they once filled; and there is room for better things to be read in their place. Christianity, patriotism, and even common humanity, have a deep interest in this question, What shall be read? and all the facts favor our attempt.

Other denominations see the importance of this advantage of a cheap literature and many readers. The American Tract Society employed 642 persons during the last year to distribute tracts and books in thirty of the States and Territories. The sum of the time spent by these distributers was 3,000 months, or 250 years. They visited 530,000 families, sold more than 487,000 books, and circulated more than 881,000. The sum expended was $385,000, of which $130,000 was for paper alone. The

Episcopal Sunday School Society expended $ 30,000 in Sunday-school books alone during the last year. The Methodist Book Concern in New York have $ 600,000 invested in their work, and an annual business of $ 250,000. The Branch in Cincinnati has $ 250,000 invested, and an annual business of $ 100,000. Methodist books and tracts to the amount of $ 50,000 are sold every year in Boston alone ; as much as the whole sum which we propose to raise. If we believed that we had no peculiar truths important to human souls, our share of the common duty to our common Christianity ought to make us unwilling to be left so far behind in its performance.

Besides these common advantages, Unitarians seem now to have an opportunity hitherto denied them for the circulation of books and tracts. Other denominations appear willing to receive and to read them, and they have been sold among them in quantities very much greater than formerly, even with our present limited means and efforts. The evidence of the change is very strong, even in places where it would be least expected. One hundred and fifty copies of Channing's Works have been sold in a single village in Central New York, to persons of all denominations. Nothing was done to urge the sale ; the books stood on the shelves, and those who wanted them asked for them. An experiment has been tried in several towns in Massachusetts to ascertain how far our books could be circulated, principally among those who differ most from us, and from one hundred to five hundred copies have been disposed of in each. In a town out of the State, where there was not, so far as is known, a single Unitarian inhabitant, three hundred volumes were *sold* in a day. In this place, the minister gave without doubt an honest opinion, when he said that " he did not believe that a copy could be sold." We could give a much better idea of these effects by extracts from the letters which we receive, but our limits do not permit it. We will state the substance of one letter, dated "Geneva, Kane County, Illinois, August 21, 1854." It mentions a Methodist minister who changed his opinions on some points by reading Worcester's last thoughts, — on the Atonement by reading Worcester's work on that subject, and on the Trinity by reading the Christian Layman; a Baptist clergyman who procured a copy of Channing's works solely to read his views on reforms, but at length ventured further, and with similar effects; both of these are now preaching for us; — two young graduates of Western colleges, who read our tracts and have gone to Meadville; — a Baptist deacon, who objected to his children's reading a primer which contained a hymn for a dedication of one of our churches, but who afterwards read Channing's and Ware's works, and has since contributed more than $1,000 to our objects within a short time, and whose present plans embrace the giving of as much more; — two young men converted from scepticism by Channing's works; one, a young merchant, gives liberally, the other has devoted himself to the ministry. Scattered instances like these of the success of a denomination may always be collected, but these are the results of books within a short time in the experience of one individual, communicated in a single letter. Believing that the progress of the Gospel is of more importance than the triumph of any particular form of it, we rejoice, nevertheless, in the advancement of what we ourselves believe to be Christian truths, and leave you to infer our duty on the present occasion, from the opportunities offered and the effects of our past limited efforts.

You will expect from us a more particular statement of

the facts respecting the need of these books, and of the purposes for which they are to be used.

FIRST *among these, we ask you to notice the state of many minds among us with regard to revealed religion.* Some entirely reject revelation and everything supernatural ; others are filled with doubts upon these subjects ; and a third class utterly ignore and refuse to consider them and all reasonings on either side concerning them. These states of mind have arisen from several causes still in operation, and which will continue to act and to add to the numbers of each class. Let us consider these causes.

One cause is the amount to which our minds have of late been occupied with matter, and subjects connected with matter, as distinct from mind. For many years less attention than formerly has been given to the moral and intellectual sciences, and less satisfactory progress has been made in them. But during this time the physical sciences have made great progress, and great discoveries have been made in them, and in the application of them to the arts, conveniences, and luxuries of life. Learning and thought have been absorbed in these subjects, to the neglect of intellectual and spiritual interests. Christian effort is necessary to counteract this tendency and avert its evil consequences, and this effort must be very limited without the aid of books.

A second cause is found in the effect of certain discoveries in astronomy, geology, and zoölogy, which appear to contradict the old and received opinions, as to what is taught in the Scriptures. The prevailing opinions among most sects concerning revelation and the Scriptures are such, that they cannot believe revelation and science both to be true, and which of them is false can be the only question with them. There are many individual exceptions among them ; but the masses, ministers and people, adhere to views which time and general consent seem to them to have consecrated, and with these opinions they can only meet the question by proving science to be false. The reason why this is not more generally apparent is because as yet they have only begun to agitate the question, and because in some cases superficial and insufficient solutions have been offered them, whose fallacy is not yet generally understood. These may postpone the real question, but cannot finally solve or evade it. With our views, we have nothing to hinder us from meeting the question on its true and proper grounds; and in order to prove revelation to be true, it is not necessary for us to prove science to be false. This gives us a great advantage in the discussion over some other denominations, and makes it the peculiar duty of our denomination to do all which we can to put an end to this supposed conflict between revelation and science, already dangerous to faith in many minds, and about to become so in many more. The danger must be met, not only by a more general discussion of the subject itself, but by every method of strengthening Christian faith in all within our reach. The discussion properly belongs to books, and besides this a great part of the persons to be acted upon can be reached only by books.

The third cause is found in the change which has taken place in the controversy respecting the age and authenticity of the Gospels. The principal question is, whether they were written by the Apostles and their companions, as they now stand, or whether they were written at a later period, either originally, or from some former history not transmitted to us. It is alleged that the miraculous element constituted no part of the original history or of the original faith of Christians, but crept by degrees into the common belief before these Gospels were written, and was thus introduced into them. According to this theory, they represent not what was originally true, but what was believed during the last part of the second and in the third century. This attack is made in much more decent and respectful language than formerly ; by some men who seem to say it because they believe it, and not merely from a feeling against Christianity. It is also supported by the German and other writers with much research and learning, and is beginning to be more noticed and sometimes openly or covertly favored to some extent in some reviews and books of general literature. We cannot shut our eyes to the fact, that it thus reaches the popular mind in a form, and affects it to a degree, dangerous to the faith of numbers in Christianity.

Norton's work on " The Genuineness of the Gospels " is the best answer in the English language to these questionings. Another work is just published by Professor Huidekoper, showing that certain opinions prevailed in the second and third centuries which would have been found in the Gospels if they had been of so late a date, and had represented the belief of those centuries. As no such opinions are contained in the Gospels, this is evidence of their having been previously written. These and some other similar works are specially intrusted to our denomination ; and it is our duty to circulate them, or such parts of them as may be most wanted for the defence of the authenticity of the Gospels, as well as to aid in the circulation of other books useful for this purpose.

The fourth source of infidelity will be found in the transition state of religious opinions, not indeed of long standing, but existing among denominations in New England, and spreading more or less through other parts of the country. When a dogma approaches the end of its reign, a

great indifference respecting it first springs up. This at
first is not doubt; men still continue to assent; doubt is not
yet perceived to be possible. But their reception of the
dogma is rather an assent than a belief. Formerly its
reasons were known, and seemed convincing; faith was
alive. Afterwards its reasons are laboriously and faintly
revived, feebly felt and obscurely understood, and it now
stands on authority only. It is still announced in consecrated
words, — words which were once full of spiritual life, kind-
ling deep emotion, calling up pious associations, and stirring
men's souls like the sound of a trumpet. Now the phrase
seems conventional in the speaker, and fails to arouse or
excite the hearer. Faith is feeble, and life departing. If
the grounds of the dogma are suspected, why are they not
re-examined? Partly because the doubter is too indifferent,
and partly because he still does not care openly to question
them. These remarks apply to much of the theology of
denominations around us. Sometimes a writer of the same
denomination does openly deny or question some point of
doctrine, explains it away, or limits it, until little is left.
Some parts of the writings of Dr. Bushnell, Mr. Abbot, Professor Stuart, and others, have done this. And although
Dr. E. Beecher did not so intend, his book has had the
effect upon his denomination of an attack upon old opinions,
as his method of escape from the difficulty has not been
accepted. Perhaps in similar cases some of the old clergy
are shocked and answer; but neither the attack nor defence
excites much interest. The dogma is approaching its end.
But truths underlie these dogmas, and, as we say, have been
concealed and buried up under them; and there is danger
that in many minds the truth will die out with the error.
We rejoice in any progress toward truth; but before a new
faith arises out of the ruins of the old, there is peril in the

9 *

period of transition.   Although we cannot address other denominations from the pulpit, facts show that their minds are
becoming more accessible to us by books.   We may thus
present to them these great fundamental and affirmative .
truths in their original and naked beauty and power, free
from the doubts, difficulties, and contradictions, which in
many of their minds encumber and·may strangle them.   For
instance, some of their own writers have rejected and aban-
doned errors in the doctrine of the atonement, which in the
Westminster Assembly's Catechism are made the most
essential parts of it; let us present to them the death of
Christ, free from these doctrines, but still the great central
fact of his religion, not to render God more merciful, nor to
bring God to us, but to bring us to God, and as Christ himself presents it to our hearts, the means by which he " will
draw all men unto him."   The danger of which we have
spoken already exists ; we understand its nature, but not its
future extent or duration.   Books are wanted to meet it and
to render this period of transition shorter and more safe.

. We have thus noticed four existing causes of scepticism.
But whatever may be its cause, our denomination has some
advantages over others in the conflict with it.   If a denomination undertakes to prove to a sceptic the truth of Christianity, it must prove the truth of every doctrine which it
holds to be fundamental ; and must tell him, that, if he does
not embrace all, he does not embrace Christianity.   This
produces two difficulties.   If the sceptic feels certain that
he can disprove one point, he is satisfied that he has disproved Christianity, and may decline to listen at all.   And
if he does listen, the difficulty of convincing him increases
with the number of points upon which he is to be convinced,
especially where these points differ from what he thinks
that he learns of God in nature and the government of the

world. From these and similar reasons, we succeed with sceptics where others fail. A single example will suffice. A few years ago, several intelligent and respectable gentlemen in a Western city, disbelieving some of the doctrines of the denominations around them, and supposing that a denial of these was a denial of Christianity, and that a refutation of them was a refutation of Christianity, were in the habit of meeting together, as free-thinkers, in a sort of infidel society. At one of the meetings a tract of the American Unitarian Association, found accidentally in a box of books, was read. They were deeply interested in it, and said, one and all, " This is reasonable, — this meets the wants of our nature, and is worthy of the Deity, as seen among the works of creation and in the government of the world. If these views are Christianity, we will be Christians." They at once procured a number of our tracts and books, and this led to the formation of a religious society in that city. Have not we particularly a duty to men like these, and in fact to all sceptics ? And with these advantages for the defence of Christianity, shall we continue to need the books which you have the means to furnish ?

SECONDLY. *There is a great want of books among the poor of cities and among seamen.*

Our ministers at large have informed us, that their labors are so great and so divided, that visits to each family must be short and few ; they cannot always be timed to their moments of leisure, nor protracted to answer all inquiries as fully as would do good. If they could leave a book or a tract, it might be taken up as opportunity permitted, laid down when occasion required, and reflected on during occupation. It might meet the eye of those whose out-door employments prevent any other communication with the minister. For such writings we have sometimes been obliged to depend on the kindness of other denominations. But our ministry at large reaches only a small part of the poor of our cities; and the number of our poor increases much faster than, with all our efforts, the ministry at large will increase. We cannot gather the great mass into our churches and chapels; but shall we therefore do nothing? Almost all the Protestant poor read; and much may be done by books among those whom the ministry never reaches, much to give them still a Sabbath day, and fill it with holy thoughts and occupations. But books must be obtained in sufficient numbers to do this.

The minister to seamen has told us, that he has constant applications for books and tracts among the thirty thousand seamen who sail from the port of Boston only. They have time on board and many of them are desirous to read. Some shipmasters carry old newspapers, rather than have nothing for them. When a crew have read the books and tracts given them, they sometimes throw them on board another ship spoken at sea, and in some instances receive another bundle in return. Sometimes these exchanges are made at the ports of destination, and repeated more than once, so that these writings have travelled round the world, going where nothing but a tract can go, and doing good over and over again in their circuit of Christian benevolence. The parish of these ministers is the world of winds and waves, and ports more dangerous to their flock than the ocean itself. On the wharf they take leave of them, and have nothing to send with them but their prayers, when, with your help, the Gospel might speak to them in their leisure hours and on their Sabbath day amid the silence and solitude of the ocean, and might still warn them among the mischiefs and temptations of a foreign port.

Seamen are more ready to pay than to receive gratuitously. The Book and Pamphlet Society once offered a supply, to which the seamen answered, that they would receive them gratefully, if they might form an auxiliary society, and thus aid the fund which supplied them. A crowded meeting was held for this purpose, and Rev. Mr. Taylor preached from the text, " Go and take the little book from the hand of the angel, which standeth upon the sea and upon the earth." About all seamen who were present signed their names as members, and wives pressed forward to sign the names of their husbands absent at sea. The evidence was sufficient to prove that, if good was not done in this way, it was not their fault, but our own.

THIRDLY. *In places in the West, and elsewhere, where there are as yet no churches, or only feeble churches, nearly all which can be done for religion must be done by books.* In neighborhoods too scantily settled to encourage the thought of maintaining worship at present, except by the occasional visit of a Methodist or Christian missionary (whose full value can only be felt in such places), it is often a custom to meet at some central house for religious worship. We, who abound in religious books and tracts, cannot estimate the want of them at such times and for such purposes. A young man, in writing some years since to the agent of the Unitarian Association for tracts, remarked, that " he had a sermon of Dr. Channing's, which he often read at religious meetings and valued beyond all price ; but was unwilling to lend it for fear it should be lost." He afterwards left wife and children, studied at Cambridge, and has been settled in the West. To this he himself was led by reading some tracts, and to this he would lead others by the same means. An old man came to the pastor of a Western church, who often received books and tracts from the Book and Pamphlet Society for distribution, and told him, that he had formerly obtained them and kept the Sabbath by reading them to his family and neighbors, the nearest church being several miles distant. He was about to go to Texas with his sons and their families and had now walked more than twenty miles to get some tracts, that he might have the means of continuing to keep the Sabbath in the land to which he was removing. He went away empty, as the clergyman had not been able to obtain a supply. The Book and Pamphlet Society has been since dissolved. "Send us," says a Western correspondent, "a good preacher, if you can; but if you cannot, send us some of those eloquent preachers, the books and tracts of your Association. It will be a great comfort to us to meet on Sunday and hear one of them read; it will remind us of the New England Sabbath and its ever-to-be-remembered instructions." Other neighborhoods, like those mentioned by the writers of these communications, are known to us. But through the extent of our Western country how many exist, of whom we know nothing, where as much good might be done by books and tracts, if we had the means! When we are assembled in our thronged and venerated churches, ought we not to remember the little circles of worshippers in the log-houses of the wilderness?

We hear by letters, and by our missionaries, of opportunities to gather societies; but we have no ministers to send to them. When they make an effort to support worship, a corresponding effort is expected on our part; and if the preacher does not come, the disappointment is proportioned to their previous efforts and sacrifices. All that we can do is to send occasional preachers, and, if you enable us, furnish a good supply of books and tracts, hoping for effects like those which we have mentioned; and thus we may keep the flock together until the shepherd comes.

And where we have *feeble churches* anywhere in the land,
unless we enable them to maintain worship constantly, the
need and benefit of religious books is almost the same as
we have found it to be where no churches exist. We have
not been so ready as other denominations to give aid in such
cases, except where it was probable that the society would
be able in a reasonable time to maintain worship without
assistance. We were unwilling to weaken the churches of
other denominations, and to use funds which were only sufficient for more promising undertakings. But if we do not
furnish aid to maintain a minister, their claim for every
other help is so much stronger. We are bound to supply
books and tracts ; and this has often sustained their faith
and aided their efforts until the prospect justified us in
assisting them to maintain worship, and has sometimes
planted the seed from which a prosperous society grew up.
When the Book and Pamphlet Society was in existence, a
pious farmer received from a friend some books and tracts
distributed by that society. He worshipped with a society
from whom he differed in modes of faith. At family worship on Sunday evenings he was in the habit of reading
these books with his family. Frequently a neighbor came
in and remained during service, and by degrees it grew into
a meeting of neighbors for public worship. The numbers
increased, until they were sufficient to form a society and
settle a minister, and will now contribute something to our
funds to supply books to others.

In other instances, when we have furnished books and
tracts, or pecuniary aid, societies have arisen, which were
soon able to support themselves, and have contributed to
help others. In 1835, a society, having just settled a pastor,
raised about $1,000 towards building a church, and $2,500
was contributed for this purpose in Boston. A small church

was built. It was soon too small and another was built, which was also soon too small; but before they left the last, the society raised $13,000 in one year, to pay off their debt and for the annual expenses and religious charities. About three years since they built a church, which cost $28,000. They have contributed liberally to aid other societies in the West, in one instance $3,000. They contributed $5,000 to the Meadville Divinity School, and offered generous aid to Antioch College. We understand that during the last year they have raised $45,000, and will probably unite with our other churches in aiding the Book Fund of the Association. We confess that this is an extreme instance of the fruit produced by the sowing of a little seed; but we might mention others, in which we have reaped an abundant harvest, if the facts already stated were not sufficient to show the need of books, and the good to be done by them among scattered neighborhoods and feeble churches.

FOURTHLY. *Beside the churches which bear the name of Unitarian, there are in the West fifteen hundred churches, and in the United States two thousand, who simply call themselves Christians, but who feel, act, and unite with us.* In concert with them we have established the Meadville Divinity School. Their ministers are earnest and faithful men, and, with the Methodists, have been the pioneers of the Gospel and borne the hardship of the day in a new country. May God reward them that they have kept it a Christian country until their own and other denominations could bring into it greater means and more organization. There are among them many full churches; but they want more books of Christian theology, — commentaries, treatises, answers to sceptics, and periodicals. They need what all Christians need, but they need it more, because, from the circumstances of a new country, they have been, like some other denominations, so insufficiently supplied. Besides the general benefit of good religious works, much may be done by placing some of our own publications in ministers' libraries and in circulation among the people. Other denominations have done much to circulate books and tracts in the West, while we have done little in that way. We may now do something to make up for our former deficiency. Our connection with the Christian denomination makes this our particular duty, and we produce the writings which are most wanted. It is impossible to tell how much a good book may do, sought, read, and circulated as it is, where books are scarce. Merely as Americans, we owe them a great debt, that feelings, habits, and principles have been planted in a wilderness, without which it would have been dangerous to the common prosperity. It remains for you to say, whether, as part of our present undertaking, we shall at once pay a common debt and also perform a particular duty. " Behold, I stand and knock," says the great Shepherd of all these flocks, Christian or Unitarian, strong or feeble, and of all the sheep not yet gathered into folds; — and shall we send him empty away ?

FIFTHLY. *A reason for our undertaking exists at the present time in the effects of the engrossing scene of worldly activity all around us.* Every kind of business has been pushed, apparently, to its utmost limit. All the gold of California, as it passed through our hands, all the money brought into the country by the sale of our stocks abroad, all the facilities of a greatly increased banking capital, have constituted an insufficient medium of exchange for its multiplied and extended transactions. All men seem more engaged than ever before in buying and selling, borrowing and lending ; making importations, which seem as if they would bankrupt the country, and paying for them by as extraordinary exports; contriving more ingenious schemes and undertaking mightier enterprises; building enormous buildings, and launching enormous vessels, to sail with a speed which but a few years since seemed impossible; introducing new manufactures, and new substances into old manufactures, and old manufactures into new uses; inventing new machines to sew our clothes and to reap our fields, to supersede human labor in every branch, and at the same time employing additional hundreds of thousands of laborers from abroad, while human labor was nevertheless scarcer and dearer than ever; with all this employment of machinery and labor, paying great rents and freights, because we cannot build houses as fast as they are wanted for dwellings, nor vessels enough for the transportation, nor warehouses sufficient for the sale of our merchandise; seeking to tunnel mountains for miles; laying down railroads until they cover the country like a net, and hastening over them in flocks which exceed all that has been told us of the migrations of birds, with a rapidity equalling the average of their speed, and on occasions rivalling the swiftest, and at the same time spreading in swarms over foreign countries; extending our settlements from ocean to ocean, and still coveting more land to make it the field of the same mighty action. Amidst such a scene of toil and business, hope and fear, pride and humiliation, inventings and contrivings, gettings and spendings, comings and goings, plans and disappointments, successes and defeats, struggles filling the day, anxieties breaking the rest of the night, and cares waiting for the morrow,—a game in respect to its changes; a race with regard to the rapidity and urgency of its progress; a competition for position, where no price is too great to be paid for superiority;

— amid such a scene, how difficult it is to teach those engrossed in it, that all this business is not the great business
of life ; that none of these ends are its great end, nor these
goods, evils, and interests its great good, evil, or interest ;
but that these great realities exclude the greatest reality.
The necessity of such teaching is greater in exact proportion to its difficulty.   Yet it is at such times, when the need
is greatest, that, by a natural consequence, the numbers of
the ministry are smallest. How, then, among all these
powers of this world acting intensely upon men, are we
to put upon them " the powers of the world to come " ?
A church that is a real and true church is bound not to
rest until it has found an answer to this question.

It is said, that with every evil comes a remedy.   When
the great material interests of which we have spoken began
to develop themselves, printing was invented ; but for some
time its power was little felt.   Books were scarce, and few
could read. The evil and the remedy were both in their
infancy, and grew up together.   Invention has increased
the power of presses, reducing at the same time the amount
of labor and the cost of paper, types, and ink.   Cheap
printing, large editions, and schools have filled the country
with books and readers, until the press has acquired a
power over the minds of men in some proportion to the
engrossing influence of the material powers which we have
just considered, and may be used to counteract them.   It
has been shown how extensively other denominations have
availed themselves of this advantage.   Here is the evil ;
here is the remedy.   Here are others stimulating us by
their example ; duty to God and love to man pleading with
us ; a decent regard to our own interest and reputation as
a denomination pressing us with lower motives; and all
throwing a deep responsibility on our decision.

SIXTHLY. *Unitarianism and Unitarians as such require a short consideration in relation to this question of the circulation of books.* It is for our interest, as well as for the interest of our common Christianity, that other denominations should know what we do in fact believe. Their hostility to us, which has done so much harm by exciting fears, ill feelings, and dissensions, has arisen greatly from a mistake as to what we believe. They had persuaded themselves that Unitarianism did not differ much from Naturalism, or would certainly lead to it, although we, like them, have repudiated and opposed it. A great part of them in New England, and some elsewhere, begin to perceive and acknowledge their mistake. By the circulation of our books among them we may do much to remove these errors. As we perceive among them the dawn of kinder feelings and a more just appreciation, and as the facts stated elsewhere in this circular show to what extent they are now willing to receive and read our books, it seems to be our duty and interest to avail ourselves of such an opportunity, and to provide the books.

Perhaps this may be the proper place to answer an objection which has generally been made by some Unitarians to all action by the denomination, and may therefore be made to this undertaking. The objection is, that this action necessarily carries forward the views of our own denomination; that this is a sectarian movement, and they are unwilling to do anything for sectarian objects. Some of them are willing to aid the action of other denominations, but not that of their own. Now, according to their definition, when the denomination, whom they aid, by its action carries forward its own views, it carries forward sectarianism; so that, after all, they do actually aid sectarian action. Practically, then, they do not object to sectarian action, but to the action of their own sect alone, and to that only because it is their own sect, — that is, because they voluntarily chose to connect themselves with it. They resemble soldiers enlisted in a regiment who should be willing to serve in any regiment, provided it was not the regiment in which they enlisted, and whose only objection to that was, that they had voluntarily enlisted in it, and had thus made it their own duty to serve particularly there. It is true, that each denomination propagates the Gospel by missionaries and books, as that denomination believes it. How else can it propagate it? And doubtless each member of it rejoices in its prosperity. But is this its chief object? Are not its great objects Christ and his Gospel and the salvation of souls? If each member should thus refuse to act with his denomination, the result would be, either that no one would act at all, or the views of a denomination would be carried forward by any body except those who believed them. The Unitarian would be carrying forward the Gospel as the Orthodox believes it, the Baptist as the Methodist believes it, and the Methodist as the Universalist believes it, the Universalist as the Episcopalian believes it, and the Orthodox as the Unitarian believes it. Would Christ and his Gospel and the salvation of souls be best advanced in this way?

The form of the objection is sometimes varied; the objector is willing to carry forward the common doctrines of all denominations, but not the peculiar doctrines of any. At present the Church acts only by denominations, each carrying forward its own views. He must persuade some denomination to exclude its own views from its own action, and then act with it, or he must act by himself, both of which are improbable, or he must not act at all, which is the usual result. And the objector must know and under the circumstances intend to do nothing, except to wish the circumstances different.

10 *

The Unitarian denomination rejects the greatest number of the peculiarities, and comes the nearest to his idea, and if he will not act with them, he must take the responsibility of disobeying precepts, and neglecting to perform duties, which have no such limitation in the Gospels.

Brethren, we have thus imperfectly spread successively before you the different fields of labor into which we propose to enter. These scenes have passed in review before us, in a succession like the unrolling of a moving diorama; and we hope that some of them will also resemble those dissolving views, in which winter by degrees changes to summer, and what was desolate and deserted brightens into fertility and beauty. By your help we will send into these fields laborers, all of whom are worthy, and some of whom have received, their hire; — Worcester, and Channing, and Norton, and the Wares, the learned father and the saintly son, and the Peabodys, and Noyes, and Whitman, and Dewey, and Bartol, and Eliot, and Sears, and all the writers of our tracts and in our periodicals. We will send them to a wider ministry than they have ever yet known. They shall indeed be ministers at large, for the whole country will be their parish. When they speak by their writings, they can preach on the same Sabbath in the humble log-house and the solemn temple; in the solitary wilderness and in the crowded city; on the shores of the Atlantic and the banks of the Mississippi. They need not be absent from one pulpit to be present in another; but their voice can be heard at the same moment, in every home throughout the land, and men's hearts will burn within them, as they talk with them by many way-sides.

Brethren, before you decide, think again of the Great West, which grows greater and wider, even while you read. Fathers and mothers, this Western world is to be the home of many of your children and your children's children. Sisters and brothers, one by one the companions of your infancy leave the family circle to find new homes among its prairies and forests. Will not your thoughts and your .anxieties follow them to scenes so different from any that you or they have ever known. Have you no fear, that year by year may wear away from their remembrance the moral and religious habits of New England. Have you no fear that a society without these restraints may spring up around them, endangering the best interests, both theirs and our own. Politicians and patriots, what will be the state of our country, when the power is in their hands? If you would prevent these evils, you must follow them with something more than your thoughts and anxieties. The mighty tide of emigration continues to roll on far beyond the sound of the church-going bell ; and in order that it may hereafter be heard there, the habits, feelings, and principles which belong to it must be preserved and maintained. We offer you the only means in our denomination of doing this, by sending books and tracts, " those silent and eloquent preachers," until the living preacher can come. So shall the Church and worship of God be established, and " unborn generations raise the long succession of his praise."

Our appeal is before you. If it is not in vain, give your name and assistance to the committee appointed in your parish. The works which you aid us to distribute will sometimes remove doubts from minds which will listen only to us, and defend Christian faith against attacks only more dangerous because conducted with decency and learning. They will do much to correct mistakes concerning our own opinions, and to conduct safely to the permanent truth and simplicity of the Gospel the existing transitions in the opinions of others. They will speak to men amid the solitudes of the ocean, and the scarcely less solitary retreats to which misery retires in the crowded town.   They will preserve individual principles until churches can be established, and make churches more intelligent, earnest, and spiritual, where they already exist.   They will often constitute the child's first lesson concerning God and heaven, and will comfort the chamber of sickness and smooth the pillow of death, when no other human aid and comfort is at hand.

THE

QUARTERLY JOURNAL.

VOL. II.   BOSTON, JANUARY 1, 1855.   No. 2.

LETTERS TO AN INQUIRER.

[The letters here promised are yet to be written, but in one sense
may be regarded as actual letters, addressed to actual persons. The
writer, like most ministers, has had many questions put to him of the
kind here intimated, and given many answers, orally or in writing.
Without attempting to recall any of these, he now writes in view of
such cases, and therefore prefers the form of personal address.]

I.

· My Friend, —

You ask for counsel and aid, as an honest but perplexed
inquirer into the truth of Christianity, the nature of belief,
and the character of the Unitarian religion. These are large
subjects. Volumes would not exhaust them, and no mind,
probably, would be able to satisfy yours, at once intelligent, confident, and sceptical ; — I mean in the better sense
of sceptical, as " doubting and inquiring," not in the bad
and vulgar sense of " infidel." I am not conscious of any
peculiar ability or qualification for the task you impose.
But if you ask it as a favor, and believe that I can aid you,

or be of service to any of the large class whom you represent, I have no right to decline the attempt. I give no
promise, however, as to the extent to which I may go, or
the exact course I may pursue. You must leave it all to
my convenience and preference, and you must not complain if I deal as plainly with you as you are apt to deal
with others.

You are in the habit of speaking, sometimes jocosely,
sometimes severely, of the discord and bitterness among
Christians, their many imperfections, and the wide distance
between their profession and practice. There is too much
truth in what you say : but how it proves, at the worst, the
falsehood or absurdity of the Christian religion, does not
appear ; nor is it evident that you yourself, or doubters
and reprovers in general, are any more consistent or more
perfect than the majority of believers.

But I will not begin with being an accuser. The honesty
of your doubts and the singleness of your motives I see no
reason for questioning. It is a narrow and pernicious
judgment that assumes all belief in religion to be virtuous,
and all unbelief sinful ; and though it were true and palpable, in the present instance, that the motives which actuate
you are not pure and single, there might be the more reason for making an attempt to reveal you to yourself, both
in your inconsistencies and your wants.

The first thing to be done, in all such inquiries, is to
agree upon the question itself, — to have a mutual understanding as to the point of the discussion. To give you
briefly my own view of it, I lay down the following proposition: " The Christian revelation is an historical fact,
resting upon the same basis of evidence as other historical
facts, and to be proved or disproved in the same manner."
The distinction of this assertion is to be seen in the word

fact. Christianity is not an opinion, a sentiment, a doctrine or system of doctrines, a theory or creed; but it is, or it is not, a fact, — the fact of a revelation, a new religion, — to be substantiated in the same manner as the life of Cæsar or the death of Socrates. If you object that the word " revelation " is vague and should be defined, I answer, that, without any attempt at a precise or complete definition, I use the word " revelation," as I design to use all words, in the ordinary acceptation, — denoting a " supernatural communication." It is easy to ring changes on the meaning of " supernatural," and to perplex yourself or another in regard to it. But I do not believe that any honest and humble inquirer ever felt any difficulty on this point, and I am not willing to spend time upon it. There is a strict and a loose sense in which men use the term " revelation." All truth, knowledge, science, may be said to be revealed. Reason is a revelation; Nature is a revelation; and many there are who affirm that their own nature, their intuitions, instincts, are as much a revelation as any other, and no other is necessary, or indeed possible. This brings the question back to a matter of *fact.* I do not choose to dispute about instincts or intuitions. I know nothing of yours, you know nothing of mine. There is no common ground between us. And if a man begin with asserting that his own knowledge is sufficient, that his conscience teaches him more than any one else can, even God, it is better to leave him to his own conceit. If he live long, or if he die early, he may find that there are some realities, out of himself.

The Christian revelation is a reality. As a divine communication, as a message from God to man given supernaturally, it is an open fact, for which no intelligible account can be given, without either admitting that which

appears upon its face, or branding the whole as a fabrica-
tion.   The Bible contains a revelation, distinct in kind and
mode from any revelation of nature or reason, or it contains a mass of falsehoods.   It is what it professes to be,
or it is a stupendous cheat, for whose origin, motive, and
continued success it is as difficult to account as for any
vast effect without an adequate or even possible cause.
Christianity proclaims itself to be a direct message from
God.   The messenger claims a miraculous origin, possesses and imparts miraculous powers, and appeals to
miraculous works.

Now, it is totally irrelevant to deny the possibility or
credibility of miracles, to offer a theory of miracles which
reduces them to natural incidents, or to say that they are
not necessary or not conclusive.   This is a false issue, and
it is surprising that so many sensible men and women are
carried away by it.   You may remember a discussion a
year or two ago, in the American Unitarian Association,
when the Executive Committee presented their Annual
Report, containing a " statement of belief."   Its adoption
was objected to by some present, and the discussion ran
off, I hardly know how, into a dispute upon " the value 'of
miracles."   The Report said nothing of the value of miracles ; nor is that the question at issue between believers
and unbelievers òf any class.   It is the *fact* of miracles
that is in dispute, and between the fact and the value there
is a wide difference.   You are welcome to estimate their
value as you please.   To different minds they have a
very different value.   Some Christians give them a much
larger place than others.   Some do not need them ; and to
many of us, probably to the great body of confirmed believers, the miracles of the New Testament seldom occur,
or are little dwelt upon, in comparison with the discourses

and character of Christ. So much the better. If the discourses and character of Christ so impress men that they need no other proof of his divine mission, and scarcely think of the miracles as such, it is one of the best evidences of the truth of Christianity. If this be all that you claim, or all that you stumble at, you need give yourself no concern. But if you go a step further, or many steps further, and *deny* the miracles, throw them out of the record, pronounce them fabulous and false, you impeach the veracity of that same Christ whose character so impresses you, and overthrow your own pretence. You say, " No, I only impeach, or rather I doubt, the truthfulness of the narratives, the soundness of their reasoning, or the fidelity of the transmitted record." Well, what proof have you, then, of any part of the record? Why do you believe the discourses which the same narrators give you, and on which you so insist as conclusive? How came those false witnesses, or, at the best, very-credulous and weak-minded men, to conceive of such a being as Christ, and so delineate his character that you pronounce it divine? Do you see no inconsistency there? It is at best an appeal to your own consciousness, your own sense of right and wrong, as the *only* tribunal whose decisions you accept or can trust. Nay, it is worse than this. You would impose those same decisions, those convictions and intuitions of your own, upon others and all. Your own mind, and in its present state, is to be the criterion of every mind. If you do not need the evidence of miracles, no one does. If you prefer other satisfaction, so must every one else, and at the same time distrust this ; yea, deny the reality of this. For to that again does it come, or the argument amounts to nothing. If you question the *reality* of miracles, if you reject them as matters of fact, and would tear them out of

11 *

the record, say so, and then we understand each other.
On the other hand, if you admit their truth, you may hold
your own theory in regard to them, and attach to them
such relative value as you think belongs to them among
the evidences of Christianity, without impairing, in my
judgment, your title to the name of believer.   There is all
the difference in the world between the explanation of a
miracle and its rejection, or between the place assigned to
it in the scale of evidence and the question of its truth or
falsehood.   And it is a very childish thing to attempt to
decide this question by a reference to mere feeling.

Still you say, and many insist, that no outward evidence
can prove that to be true which is not felt to be true, and
that which is felt to be true needs no other proof. Both
parts of this common assertion are questionable in point of
fact, and feeble as argument. It is more than questionable, it is certainly false, that no outward evidence can
avail without inward conviction, or against it. Of course
we cannot believe that which we *know* to be untrue. But
half our knowledge rests upon evidence which has nothing
to do with feeling, and no relation to consciousness. Judging by my own consciousness, or my sense of right and of
fitness, I should doubt the reality of many events which I
knew to have occurred, and many characters which I knew
to have existed. I read of wonderful men and wonderful
deeds in time past, — am I to judge them genuine or spurious, according to my own notions of propriety and probability?   Then would many a fact become fiction, and
fiction fact.

There are facts which are not only independent of consciousness, but directly opposed to it, — opposed to the testimony even of the senses. Such are some of the facts of
science. We *see* the sun rise and set; we know it does

neither. We *feel* that the earth is still, yet know it is always revolving. What is the nature of this knowledge, and the ground of a conviction, so in defiance of universal observation? It is of the nature of faith, and it stands upon the testimony of competent men. Without any questioning, with no demonstration, and no capacity in many cases of following the demonstration, men believe that which they do not understand, and act through life upon the truth of what seems to them incredible! And what becomes of your favorite criteria, — intuition and sensation?

Come back to the question of fact. This is the proper question, the only fair question, and a fair inquirer will not attempt to evade it. It is all that I propose to establish in the present letter. Yet it is not merely preliminary, but a part of the discussion, and essential to the whole. For unless we know what we are talking about, it is useless to talk; and when we do know, a great part of the work is done; — especially in this case, where the first question of all, and one that affects all, is this, By what kind of evidence is Christianity proved and accepted, and by what kind of evidence is it disproved and rejected? Or take it thus, and bring it home to your own case, How will you know when you have proved Christianity to be true or false? Have you asked yourself this question, my inquiring friend? Have you looked closely at the *nature* of the inquiry? There are many who do not, I know; many unbelievers, and nearly as many believers, it may be. It is true, doubtless, as you say, that multitudes accept Christianity without knowing why. Through inheritance, education, custom, policy, indolence, dread of heresy and the odium of dissent, they find themselves believers, many of them real, many only nominal. But even with the latter, if the religion be true and a blessing to society, they share the blessing, though they may deserve no credit for their belief, and would be stronger and better men if it stood on the true basis, on intelligent and firm conviction. But does this prove anything against the religion, or anything in favor of doubters and rejecters? Are you sure that they are any more consistent or intelligent in their unbelief? If the question were made to turn upon intelligence, or upon moral character, Christianity probably would have nothing to fear. But this would not be a fair test, nor would it be possible to make a just comparison. I assume nothing as to character in favor of one class or against the other. Christians have done harm enough, by imputing to unbelief in the abstract, and to all unbelievers, depravity of motive or life. Let us shun these allegations, leave all comparisons, whether of morals or mind, and come to the single, fair question. And let me make it clear, though with repetition.

Christianity is a fact. As a revelation strictly, as a special communication from God to man through Jesus Christ, with both natural and supernatural confirmation, it is an historical fact, to be investigated, sifted, proved, or disproved, like other alleged facts, institutions, or revelations, dating their origin at a remote but defined period. And this we further aver: the life and death of Christ, the faith and fate of his early followers, the fall of the Jewish state and the establishment of the Christian, by the force of means not common or merely human, are facts as capable of demonstration as the acts of Nero, the great persecutor, or the arguments of Celsus, the first noted objector. And starting from this point, I will simply ask, at present, how we know anything about the persecutions of Nero or the arguments of Celsus? Note it, as a curious circumstance, lying at the threshold of such an inquiry, and offering instruction as to its merits, that men take for granted, without proof or question, all that is told of Nero and Celsus, particularly the objections of the latter, who wrote in the second century, and those of Porphyry in the third, and Julian in the fourth, — they take these for granted, and turn them against Christianity, while they deny or doubt the very characters, writings, faith, and life of those contemporaneous with these assailants, composing the very persons and facts which they assailed, and coming down to us through the same testimony. In truth, the writings of the assailants themselves, their quotations from the Gospels, and various admissions, contain no small or unimportant part of the facts to be proved. To proceed strictly in order, therefore, if one means to demolish the whole structure of Christianity as it stands in the Gospels, he should begin with demolishing Celsus, Porphyry, and Julian ; and having conclusively proved that no such men ever existed, or that they said nothing about the Christian heresy, and evidently knew not its existence at that early day, he may then be ready to strike at the foundation, namely, the pretended fact, that the Gospels were then in existence, and were the same as those we now hold.

Please bear in mind that this is the question before us now ; and believe me yours, in good faith.

H.

" It is putting catechisms and confessions out of their place to look on them as magazines of truth. There 's some of your stout orthodox folks just over ready to stretch the Bible to square with their catechism ; all very well, all very needful as a landmark ; but what I say is, do not let that wretched, mutilated thing be thrown between me and the Bible " — *Dr. Chalmers.*

AN ORDINATION CHARGE.

[At the ordination of Mr. Charles Henry Wheeler as pastor of the Unitarian Church and Society in Danvers, on the 4th of October last, the charge was given by his father, Rev. Amos D. Wheeler, of Brunswick, Me. Something more than the parental relation gave peculiar interest to this performance. We have asked and received permission to insert it in our Journal.]

WHEN the Apostle Paul, after a long experience in the duties and responsibilities of the Christian ministry, had introduced the youthful Timothy into the field of ministerial labor, and constituted him the pastor of the church at Ephesus, he addressed him as his " own son in the faith," and gave him a *written Charge*, which is preserved to us in the two Epistles bearing his name. The example of Paul has been followed in the Congregational churches upon all similar occasions; and there is a very obvious propriety, as well as utility, in adhering to the time-hallowed usage. In accordance with your expressed desire, and with the concurrence of this Ecclesiastical Council, I am present, at this time, to perform such a part; and if I cannot speak to you with the authority of Paul, I may certainly claim the right to advise you, in virtue of a relationship which is even more intimate than that of an own son in the faith.

The present occasion is one of no ordinary interest both to you and to me. To you, it is the commencement of new cares, duties, trials, and responsibilities: to me, the fulfilment, in part, of my long cherished hopes, with reference to your aims and pursuits in life. I know your views, feelings, and principles too well to permit even a momentary doubt, that, in entering upon this new sphere of duty, you will commence with a conscientious purpose, and with a faithful endeavor to do what you can for the advancement of Christ's kingdom upon earth, and for the moral and spiritual welfare of those among whom, in the providence of God, you are called to labor and to live. At a time so solemn, — at an hour when all trivial thoughts must be banished from your mind, — at the commencement of a relation upon which consequences so momentous may depend, — the studied ornaments of diction would be out of place ; and I shall be compelled to use great " plainness of speech." Another will admonish the people of the duties which they owe to you ; my part will have been performed, when I shall have reminded you of the duties which you owe to the cause of Christ and to them.

You will, of course, understand, — and all present will understand, — that there is no one upon this Council who claims any right of dictation, or of unauthorized interference, in relation either to your duties or to the affairs of this religious society. It belongs to you and to them to determine all questions of relative duty or interest among yourselves. We claim to be Congregationalists, in the strict and proper sense of the term, and we adhere to the fundamental principle of Congregationalism, that every church has a right to manage its own affairs in its own way, and that no authority can properly be exercised upon it, which does not originate within it. We do not admit that the Apostles, in any such respect, have ever had any successors in the Church. We are present to aid and encourage ; not to control. We desire to be helpers of your joy ; and not to " have dominion over your faith." In everything of this nature, you will be answerable, not to us, but to conscience and to God. But I would not have you regard these services as unmeaning ceremonies. They have a deep significance, and they ought to exert a salutary influence, and one that will continue to be felt long after this occasion has passed away.

You have now, my son, — my son also in the faith, — been solemnly consecrated and set apart to the work of the Gospel ministry. You have become an overseer in Christ's vineyard, an under-shepherd to receive the care of Christ's flock. And it devolves upon me to say to you, in the words of Paul to Archippus : *Take heed to the ministry which thou hast received in the Lord, that thou fulfil it.*

First of all, remember that you are to stand in a Christian pulpit, that you have received a Christian ordination, and that you have been invited among this people, in order that you may fulfil the duties of a Christian minister. If you have come with any other motive, or aim, or expectation, your position is a false one, and no time should be lost in setting the matter right. I need not attempt to define to you what constitutes a Christian, or a Christian minister, for there is a common understanding in regard to this subject, which sufficiently defines it for the purpose which I have in view. When the disciple, in his own estimation, becomes greater than his master, — when he deems himself qualified, by reason of his intellectual or moral endowments, to sit in judgment upon his doctrine or character, and to show in what respect they might have been improved, — when he is disposed to regard as mythical everything that is recorded of Christ, save only such things as may agree with his present experience, and those moral sayings which Plato or Socrates might have uttered as well, — then it is time for him to pause and consider whether he can honestly retain a position, the relations and duties of which are so differently estimated in the public mind. He may be a Christian in character, and he may be able to do good in his way; — God will be the judge of that; but if he feels constrained to preach " another gospel " from that which Christ and his Apostles preached, and consequently that which, in reality, is no gospel at all, he should be willing to forego the use of a name which no longer expresses his true convictions, and which he has therefore no right to retain. I am not seeking to withdraw you from your allegiance to the truth; for it was the truth to which Jesus himself bore witness, and the truth is important above all things else. What I mean to say is, that if, in the fluctuations of human opinions, and in the different phases of religious belief which all are liable to experience, you should ever come to the conclusion that the words of Christ possess no higher authority than your own, then your proper place will be out of the Church, and not in it. I do not, however, anticipate any such result; for I have reason to " hope better things of you, and things which accompany salvation, though I thus speak." While, therefore, you continue to hold the office of a Christian teacher, I admonish you to reverence his authority, and give heed to his words. Receive his doctrines unquestioned, and substitute no other in their stead. Convince yourself, in the first place, with respect to what Christ really taught, and then let the fact that *Christ has said it* be to you the end of all controversy, the solution of all doubts. Drink deep into his spirit, remembering always what is written : " He that hath not the spirit of Christ is none of his." Exhibit in all your intercourse with others, and in all the daily walks of life, the gentleness and forbearance of him who never " broke the bruised reed," nor " quenched the smoking flax." Let the same tender compassion be shown to the erring and guilty. Let the same ready forgiveness be extended to the penitent. Let the same kind words of comfort and encouragement be whispered in the ear of the tried and tempted. Let the same voice of friendship and sympathy be heard by the suffering and sorrowing. Preach-Christ to your people. Go to them, — not as a mere lecturer upon morals ; not as a mere polemic upon subjects of theological controversy and sectarian strife ; but as the bearer of a heavenly message, addressed personally to them, and one which they cannot reject but at their peril. Preach Christ from the pulpit ; preach him in the domestic circle ; preach him by the way-side ; preach him always and everywhere, by word and by deed, whenever you can find a willing listener, wherever you can quicken the germ of a religious life. Point always to Jesus as the Lamb of God that taketh away the sin of the world, — as the Saviour of men, as the conqueror of death.

You will endeavor, of course, to maintain the true independence of the pulpit. You will not allow your judgment to be warped, nor your action to be impeded, by any improper interference with your own sphere of duty. You will not be restrained from giving utterance to what you may deem important truth, from any unworthy motives of fear or favor. You will not keep back from your hearers anything which would be profitable to them, from any considerations of personal detriment or advantage. But, at the same time, you will be careful not to sacrifice the substance for the shadow, the reality for the mere name. You will not deem it necessary to say and do things which you would otherwise regard as inexpedient, from the mere desire of being thought independent, thus reducing yourself to bondage on the pretence of being free. You will remember, moreover, that others have rights as well as you, and that you are bound to respect those rights ; that others have *consciences* as well as you, and are under the same obligations to obey them. Absolute independence nowhere exists, and the liberty of the pulpit must of course have its limits. A Christian congregation would certainly be justified in refusing to sit patiently under the ministrations of one who should avail himself of the advantages of his position to inculcate immoralities, or the principles of undissembled atheism. The only difficulty is in deciding just where the limits should be fixed. There are many causes operating at the present time to render the duties of the Christian minister embarrassing, and to interpose obstacles in the way of his success. And perhaps there never was a period when he needed more the wisdom of the serpent and the harmlessness of the dove. I am aware that mere considerations of prudence have but little weight with many, and that questions of mere expediency are deemed improper to be entertained. I know that it is a maxim with some, that whoever has a word of truth is bound, under all circumstances, to utter it, whether men are prepared for, it or not. But I know, too, that Jesus always imparted the truth to his followers as they were able to bear it; and that his chosen Apostles, imitating his example, were accustomed to feed with " milk " those who were unable as yet to endure " strong meat." Let it never be forgotten, that there is not only a best thing to be said and done, but also a best time and manner for saying and doing it; that there is a time to be silent, as well as to speak; and that he who is unable to discern the difference is hardly to be trusted in " rightly dividing the word of God." He will involve himself in perpetual difficulties, without accomplishing any great amount of good.

Undoubtedly there is much evil in the world that can and ought to be removed. There is much that is faulty in human institutions. There is much that is wrong in the administration of human governments. There are prevalent social vices, and habits of personal immorality, worldliness, and sin. And there is that in the common instincts and propensities of mankind, which, in its natural operation and tendency, leads to them all. The minister of the Gospel ought, therefore, by the very nature of his office, to be the foremost among reformers. The character and condition of the world are to be changed; and this work, if accomplished at all, must be accomplished through human instrumentalities. Christ came in order to " make all things new," and the preachers of his Gospel are bound to labor for this result. But " no man is crowned unless he strive lawfully." No improper means should be resorted to, even for the purpose of doing good. Carnal weapons are never to be employed in a spiritual warfare. The minister of Christ should be a true and earnest reformer; but he ought never to become a bold and reckless innovator. All motion is not progress. All changes are not improvements. The true spirit of reform, as exemplified in the Gospel, is always united with a wise and moderate conservatism; and true conservatism will always give place to prudent and safe reforms. " Prove all things : hold fast that which is good," — is the most correct rule in principle and the best in practice. Let it not be forgotten.

The proper sphere of a minister's duties is within the limits of his own parish. I do not say that he is never to pass beyond them, — that he is never to perform labors for the benefit of others than those who attend upon his ministry. He is the servant of Christ, and is to go where Christ directs, and to do what Christ commands. In a certain sense, he is a debtor to all men, and should do good to all as he may have opportunity. He has a right to such occasional relief as may be afforded by ministerial exchanges. He has a right to such seasons of relaxation and rest as his health may require, and as will tend to render him better fitted for the ordinary routine of parochial cares. But he has no right to seek labor and profit abroad, to the neglect of duties at home. Remember that you have entered into a moral and legal contract with this religious society, and that you are under obligations to fulfil it. Next to God and to Christ, your best powers and your highest intellectual efforts should be consecrated to those who employ you. And doubtless it is better thus. There is a benefit in a division of labor, when every one performs his allotted task. The husbandman who sends laborers into his field would derive but little profit from their industry if they were to work without order, or to leave their tasks to be performed by others, while seeking employment somewhere else. The keeper of vineyards would be but little benefited in cultivating those which belong to others, if he neglected his own.

You will meet with difficulties, and your success in overcoming them may not equal your hopes. But do not allow yourself to become discouraged. Do not be impatient to witness immediate results. Persevere, and in due season you will reap, " if you faint not." When the seed is cast into the earth, we do not expect at once to gather in the harvest ; for we know that it requires time for the blade to appear, and the ear to fill, and the fruit to ripen. We know that days and weeks must pass, that moons must wax and wane, and that much care and labor will be required before the field is ready for the reaper. "Four months, and then cometh the harvest," is the law in the natural world. Learn from it what you are to expect in the moral and spiritual.

12 *

Jesus taught and toiled and performed his miracles of mercy, yet made but very few converts during the whole period of his ministry. And of those who enrolled themselves at first in the number of his disciples, from motives of worldly policy, a very large proportion, as soon as they learned that their desires were not to be gratified, " went back and walked no more with him." And with a feeling of sadness, though not of discouragement, — for he still trusted in God, — he addressed that pointed and expressive inquiry to the Twelve, " Will ye also go away ? " Learn patience from his example.

These services will soon be ended, and your cares and responsibilities, with reference to this people, will have commenced.

Go, then, my son ; enter upon your field of toil, and perform your allotted labors. Go, and carry with you the best wishes of all who have taken an interest in your ordination ; and a father's prayers and blessing. Go, and " be thou faithful unto death " ; and Christ shall " give thee a crown of life." Sow the good seed with'unsparing hand, and wake and watch, lest the enemy sow his tares. And though some should fall by the way-side, where the fowls of heaven may pluck it up, and some on stony places, where it will perish for lack of earth, and some among thorns, which will spring up and choke it, yet all will not be lost ; for some also shall fall upon good ground, and bring forth fruit, thirty or sixty or an hundred fold.

Give yourself wholly to your work, and leave the event with God. The ignorant are to be enlightened ; the careless and indifferent to be aroused ; the dead in sins to be made alive again ; the lost to be sought and found. The Gospel which you preach may prove, indeed, to some " a savor of life unto life," and to others " a savor of death unto death"; but let the result be what it may, no stain of guilt will be found upon you.

Go visit the flock now waiting for their shepherd. Feed the sheep and feed the lambs. Lead them into green pastures. Lead them beside the still waters. See that none of them wander astray. See that none of them are left to perish without the fold. " Preach the word ; be instant in season, out of season ; reprove, rebuke, exhort with all long-suffering and doctrine." Toil on, " in the labor of love and in the patience of hope," looking unto Jesus, and walking in his steps. Then, when *he, the chief Shepherd,* shall appear, you shall receive a crown of glory that fadeth not away ; when the Lord shall make up his jewels, he will say to you, and to those who have been guided by you in the narrow way of life, *Come, for ye are mine.*

THE MONTREAL CONVENTION.

THE proceedings of the Convention of Unitarians held in October last in Montreal were fully reported in the newspapers of the day, and need not be reprinted here. It was an occasion of much interest to the large delegation that assembled in the church of our faith in that city ; and we hope it will not be without its influence upon the society which invited and generously entertained the Convention, which has at least, we think, had proof of the freedom of thought, and earnestness of speech, and unity of Christian spirit, and sincerity of fraternal fellowship, enjoyed by their brethren in the States.

As we propose to give only such a notice of the Convention as may be of some use as a permanent record, we shall simply state its organization, and indicate the general course of its proceedings. Rev. Samuel K. Lothrop, D. D., of Boston, was chosen President, who was sustained by three Vice-Presidents, — Benjamin Workman, M. D., of Montreal, Hon. Albert Fearing, of Boston, and Rev. Joseph Allen, D. D., of Northborough. The Secretaries were Rev. Joshua Young, of Burlington, Vt., and Rev. Ephraim Nute, Jr., of Chicopee, Mass.

Following the example of last year, the Committee of Arrangements had invited three persons to read essays on the subjects proposed for discussion ; and accordingly Rev. John H. Morison read an essay on the " Limitations of Christian Liberty"; Rev. John Cordner read an essay on " The Necessity of a more complete Co-operation of the Laity with the Clergy in Church Action and General Christian Effort "; and Rev. Joseph H. Allen read an essay on " The Church as a Social Power."

These essays will be found below. Before turning to them we may add, that, besides the discussions to which they led, discourses were preached by Rev. Dr. Lothrop and Rev. James F. Clarke ; the holy ordinance of the Lord's Supper was administered, Rev. James W. Thompson, D. D., and Rev. Andrew P. Peabody, D. D., officiating ; and prayer-meetings were held in the morning, which were very fully attended, and were among the most satisfactory exercises of the week. On Wednesday evening there was a delightful gathering in St. Lawrence Hall, where the members of Mr. Cordner's society gave a public reception to their guests, Hon. John Young, M. P. P., in the chair. The occasion was marked by a refined and graceful hospitality, and by the interchange of cordial Christian greetings. Resolutions, commemorative of friends who, during the past year, have left the scenes of earth, were passed at one of the sessions of the Convention ; as were also other resolutions, expressive of thanks that Canada had so often afforded a safe retreat to those who were seeking a liberty dearer than life.

THE LIMITATIONS OF CHRISTIAN LIBERTY.

By Rev. J. H. Morison.

I have been requested to prepare an essay on the Limitations of Christian Liberty.

If a revelation from God has been given to us, we are bound by its authority. What it declares to be truth, we must accept as such. What it commands to be done, we must do. We have no right to question its authority or to resist its claims.

If a revelation from God has been given to man, except by a perpetual miracle there is only one way of transmitting it from age to age; namely, committing it to writing, and in written documents handing it down substantially unchanged from generation to generation. No one, we believe, not even the Roman Catholic Church, pretends to the existence of a perpetual miracle of this kind. If, therefore, a divine revelation has come down to us from any remote period, it must be through written documents, which documents are likely to be the only authentic records of the revelation.

Now, we receive Christianity as a revelation from God, and we recognize in those who place themselves under it no right to call its authority in question.

But further than this, we know nothing of Christianity as a revelation from God, except through certain written documents transmitted to us from the times of the Apostles, and professing to give an account of the life and teachings of Jesus Christ. These writings we accept as faithful records, and the only authentic and original records, of what Jesus actually taught and did. No one pretends that there are now in existence any other historical accounts of Jesus which are entitled to any consideration whatever. If, therefore, we give up these records as unworthy of credit, we give up the revelation itself, since it is only through the writings that we have any knowledge of the revelation. To be sure, the records are not the revelation, and are not to be confounded with it. Neither is the cask imported from a distant continent to be confounded with the wine which it contains; but if on that account those having it in charge should think it of so little consequence as to have its hoops loosened and its seams opened, they in the simplicity of their hearts may exclaim, "It is only the cask that we are throwing away, not the wine; we would not waste a drop of that." But all their professions would hardly convince us of their discretion. The writings of the New Testament are not of themselves the revelation of God in Jesus Christ; but they contain that revelation, and we cannot seriously impair *their* trustworthiness without also impairing *its* authority. It is only through them that we can know of it as a revelation from God. If, therefore, we reject them as unworthy of credit, we at the same time reject it as a divine revelation.

When, therefore, we receive Christianity as a revelation from God, we must at the same time admit the authority of the New Testament writings as faithful records; for it is only through those records that we can know either what Christianity would teach, or whether it is a revelation from God. We receive, then, these writings as truthful records. What they plainly declare that Jesus said and did, that we receive as said and done by him. Without stopping here to discuss those minute points of criticism which enter into the treatment of all historical testimony, but which cannot essentially modify our conclusions in this matter, we may say, in general terms, that we accept the accounts given in the New Testament of what Jesus said and did. We accept those accounts on the authority of honest and competent witnesses. We read them as such. We apply to them the tests which we apply to other original and authentic historical writings. We apply to them the same rules of interpretation. We expect to find in them the same apparent discrepancies in unimportant matters, the same substantial truth in all weighty and important facts.

But, without dwelling on these particulars, we may here say, that, in receiving the religion of Jesus as a revelation from God, we receive it as we find it in the New Testament writings. We bow before the authority of Christ and his religion, as we find them in the writings of the New Testament. Here, then, in this direction, are the limits of our Christian liberty. What Christ in the Gospels has taught for truth or enjoined as duty, that we, as Christians, hold ourselves bound to accept and obey. Our Christian liberty, while it allows us to walk with perfect freedom through the wide domain of Christian truth and Christian duty, and through the whole realm of thought and life that does not interfere with them, here establishes its bounds, and forbids us to go one step beyond. We know nothing of Christianity as a revelation from God, except what we learn from the Gospels. The Christianity that we have in them is the only Christianity, as a divine revelation, that we can have. As far as that goes, so far our Christian liberty extends; by one step beyond, we go beyond the limits of Christianity itself, and of course beyond the limits of Christian liberty.

We receive Christianity as a divine revelation, and the Gospels as truthful records of that revelation. But who shall determine for us precisely what that revelation is, — precisely what it teaches respecting the nature of God and Christ, of man, his duties and his destiny ?

There are three ways in which written documents like those which make up the New Testament may be taught and enforced. There may be a distinct order of men raised up from age to age with a miraculous power to explain and enforce the doctrines and precepts of Christ, and to make such additional regulations as the altered circumstances of the world from time to time· may require. The Roman Catholic hierarchy claim to be such an order, and the Mormon priests, I believe, make a similar claim. The Roman Church claims to be the sole depositary, interpreter, and administrator of the religion of Jesus. We reject these claims, because we find neither in the sacred writings which the Romish Church has preserved, nor in other historical documents, or the writings of the early Christians, any grounds for the assumption and exercise of such an authority.

Secondly, there might be a divinely instituted order of men, without any special miraculous inspiration, set apart from time to time, like the judges of a court, as the only authorized expositors of Christian faith and practice. The English and perhaps the Presbyterian Church, each of them, claims to have such a divinely instituted order of men. We reject these claims on precisely the same grounds as those on which we reject the more imposing assumptions of the Catholics. Neither in the Scriptures nor in the writings of the early Christians, nor on any just principles of reasoning, do we find good grounds for allowing to them such an authority as they would assume.

In the third place, there are those who allow that Christ addresses himself to the individual soul ; that the Scriptures are the only external and sufficient rule of faith and practice; and that every man, in the best exercise of the faculties which his Maker has given him, and responsible to God alone for his fidelity, is to search the Scriptures for himself, and learn for himself what Christ has revealed. This, the ground nominally assumed by the early Protestants, is the ground on which we profess to stand. We do not claim the liberty to overthrow, to set aside, or to ignore the least of the commandments of Christ, or to teach others to do so; but we do claim the liberty to read, to study, and to apply to our own hearts and lives, the great precepts of his religion, to learn for ourselves what he has taught as the great and essential doctrines of his religion, responsible in our researches and our conclusions only to him and to our Maker. As we honor Christ too much to allow any one to break down his authority in any case under the pretence of extending the limits of our Christian liberty, so do we honor him too much to allow any one under any pretence whatever to circumscribe what he has established as the broad limits of our Christian liberty.

" You are perfectly free," say many who profess to believe in the sufficiency of the Scriptures and the right of private judgment, — " you are perfectly free to study the Scriptures for yourselves. It is your duty so to do. But then every man who reads the Scriptures with an unbiased and prayerful mind will find in them the great doctrines of Total Depravity, the Trinity, and a Vicarious Atonement. If you do not find them there, it is evident that you do not go to the Scriptures in a right spirit, and therefore you cannot be recognized by us as Christians." But what sort of liberty is this? We are perfectly at liberty, nay, it is our duty, to study the Scriptures for ourselves; but unless we find in them just what you find, then we are not entitled to the Christian name! You put into our hands, perhaps, the Westminster Catechism, and tell us to study the Bible ; but tell us also, that, unless we find the Catechism in the Bible, we do not read the Bible aright. Which is the master here, the Catechism or the Bible ? The doctrines of the Catechism are enthroned as the doctrines of Christianity. Nothing is allowed to modify or repeal them. If the Bible does not teach just these doctrines, then it is no Bible to us. We may accept every word in the New Testament, and say we believe them. "But how do you believe them ? " is the question. " Do you believe them in the sense of the Westminster Catechism ? If not, you do not believe them right, and cannot be recognized as Christians by us." What is this but to give the Westminster divines authority over the Bible, and, while professing the profoundest reverence for it, to bind it down by their peculiar metaphysical opinions, as able men have sometimes got possession of the person of their sovereign, and, with every outward mark of homage, have constrained him to affix his signature and seal to their decrees, and thus employ his very name and authority to annul and pervert his commands ?

We have a right to study the Scriptures for ourselves, and to abide in perfect simplicity and good faith by the results of our investigations. But the moment we erect our views into a standard of faith to be enforced as a test of the faith of others, that moment we raise our authority above the authority of Christ, we usurp a power which he never granted to any man or association of men, and, without authority from Christ, curtail the liberty which he has left to all his followers.

But there is danger, it is said, if we leave these matters of Christian doctrine open to every one. Very well. Suppose that there is danger. What then ? If Christ has left this whole ground open, and not given either to you or me, or any body of men, authority to build up walls around as much of Christian truth as we can comprehend, mingled probably with our own individual errors, and to denounce as unchristian all who will come within those limits, — if Christ has delegated to us no such authority, then in exercising that authority we are wanting in reverence to him, we are setting up our individual or associated opinions over his word, and substituting our limited and imperfect notions in the place of the glorious liberty of the children of God. You honor and reverence Christ as the Son of God. How dare you then allow a human tribunal, however august or venerable, to interpose its authority between him and your own soul ? You honor the Bible and would have it free. How dare you then allow any human articles of faith to bind down its meaning, and force its free and glowing inspiration into their cramped and lifeless forms ? We can trust Christ to speak for himself, to come with his words of life and power directly home to each individual soul. We would study the Scriptures with earnest and prayerful hearts, bringing to our studies all the helps that lie within our reach. And, having carefully drawn from them what we believe to be the great doctrines of salvation, we would teach them to others. As they come with life-giving efficacy to us, and are dear and precious to us, we would teach them to our children, and do what we can to extend their influence through the world. But we dare not draw them up in the form of a creed, and impose them on others as essential to salvation and as the whole Gospel of Christ. We believe that in his words and his life lie truths more deep and vast than any we have been able to define, — truths to be reached by the great pioneers of religious thought in the more advanced stages of Christian experience. While we teach to our children and those whom our words may influence what we cherish as Christian truth, we always bow to the authority of the Scriptures, and beseech those who listen to us to accept our views only as they shall find them harmonizing with the words of Jesus. We would remand them with perfect freedom of thought to the Scriptures, to learn there for themselves the will of God from the only authentic revelation that we have of his will. The liberty that we ask for ourselves, we give also to them.

In doing this we fall back on the rights of the individual soul, but we also fall back on the authority of Christ, on the power of divine truth, on the ever-living and protecting presence of Almighty God. The Jesuit loses his own individuality and falls back on the power of his order, feeling strong in that. We in all humility and faith fall back on the authority of one greater than any order or association of men, even Christ, and feel strong in him. The Episcopalians fall back upon their Church, and all the respectability and power that are associated with it. We may have no such marks of earthly dignity connected with our Church, but we fall back on him who alone gives sanctity and power to teach, and who has promised that, wherever two or three are gathered together in his name, there will he be in the midst of them. The Catholics may look back to the glorious memories of the past, to its ancient rites and prayers, bearing on their wings the odors and sanctities accumulating from the devotion and fears of the devout for fifty generations ; we fall back on the Ancient of Days, our dwelling-place in all generations, who will not forsake those who put their trust in him. Thus, while other denominations fall back on human instrumentalities and submit to them, we, in the larger liberty that we claim, feel ourselves upheld and carried on by the ever-living power of Christ and his word, the sanctifying presence of the Holy Spirit of God and his almighty and perpetual care.

But there are those to whom even this seems a poor sort of liberty. "Why," they ask, "shall we submit to any authority but that of the human soul?" Because the soul is not sufficient for itself. Because the soul, left to itself, with no authoritative instruction from abroad, would indeed be helpless and enslaved, though the whole universe should lie open before it. Its own powers and capabilities, its destiny, the highest laws of its being and the loftiest and most inspiring truths, must be revealed to it, before it can enter on the enjoyment of the highest liberty for which it has been created.

There are strange ideas abroad respecting liberty of thought, as if it consisted in being set free from every species of restraint. The bird that obeys no law must flutter helplessly on the ground, the slave of its own extravagant ideas of liberty. But when it learns to obey the laws of aerostatic motion, and in obedience to them spreads out its wings and librates them in the air, it soars aloft, it sails abroad through the unresisting element, it faces the tempest and forces its way through, or soars above the storm, and by obedience to law moves almost with the freedom of an incorporeal spirit. So the human soul, not knowing or not obeying the great laws of spiritual thought and life, grovels helplessly upon the earth, the slave of its own ignorance or waywardness. But when it obeys these laws, it rises into higher realms of thought, it moves with a larger liberty, and soars away into a wider and nobler sphere of being. Christianity, in revealing to us the highest laws of life and the highest truths on which the human mind can be engaged, prepares man for the largest liberty

13*

of which his nature is capable, if he will only submit to those laws and accept those truths. For here, as everywhere else, the maxim of the great master of modern thoughts, Lord Bacon, holds true, that by obeying we govern and control.

Still, the very word *authority* is distasteful to us. We cannot submit to it. We must have unbounded liberty. We will not consent to be led even by the Son of God, forgetting that it is only through obedience to the highest authority that we can be led out into the largest liberty. It is a foolish and slavish notion that many have on this subject. A company of prisoners, who have been bound for years in the centre of an inextricable labyrinth, by all their private efforts have hardly succeeded in loosening a single chain, or in advancing a single step through the dark and intricate way that leads out from their dungeon. But one who knows all about it, and who has keys to unlock their chains and open every door, comes in and kindly offers to lead them out, if they will only put themselves implicitly and entirely under his direction. "We submit," they reply, " to no man's authority. We claim to be free, and shall consent to be guided only by those ideas of absolute truth and absolute liberty which unfold themselves spontaneously to the soul." And so, from their peculiar notions of liberty, they remain in their dungeon, and cling to their darkness and their chains with a proud sense of personal independence.

For more than a hundred generations men had been confined in the labyrinth of human life and destiny, slaves, to a great extent, and victims of ignorance and sin, unable to set themselves free, but rather groping more darkly, and after each new effort sinking down more helpless and hopeless, in the blind and inexplicable maze. A being from above, who has threaded its dark windings and in his own person shown that he can go through it all and break loose from its bondage, offers to lead us out and set us free, if we only will put ourselves under his guidance and follow him. But, like the Jews of old, we deny that we have been in bondage. We cannot submit to the authority even of the Son of God, that he may make us free, because, as a condition of perfect freedom, he exacts of us now what we choose to regard as a blind submission to his authority. He would lead us out into larger fields of thought, and into that perfect liberty of heart and life which is to be attained only by obedience to the highest laws of our being; but we will not consent.

Thus it is that, though the very limitations of our Christian liberty, submission to the authority and obedience to the commands of Christ, are, when rightly understood, the means of securing our spiritual enfranchisement, we refuse to accept the truths which Christ has revealed by what we call a blind faith in him. " It narrows," we say, " and shackles our freedom of thought." As well might we say that we will not consent to be cramped in our views of the sky by a narrow and enslaving instrument like the telescope. We will use only the independent powers of vision which God has given us, and with them freely expatiate through the universe." But they who submit to the restraints of the instrument expatiate more freely, and range with their enlarged vision through worlds and systems of worlds which otherwise had been closed against them by intervening realms of space too wide for their unassisted powers of sight to traverse. So, by submitting to the authority of Jesus, through faith in him, we are allowed to move on beyond what we could reach before, through realms of thought encompassing this span of life, and stretching out beyond all that we could guess before, into the domain of man's immortality, the infinite perfections of God, the consummation of Christ's kingdom, and the reign of righteousness in regions of eternal bliss. These august disclosures of truth which we receive through faith in Christ, and which open to us such boundless fields of intellectual activity and freedom, melt away into unsubstantial mists before the earnest gaze of those who reject the authority of Christ, and seek in their own unaided minds the sole grounds of their belief.

And as the fields of thought through which our minds may range in perfect liberty are infinitely enlarged by our submission to the authority of Christ, so still more that inward consciousness of freedom, which grows out of the emancipation of the soul from every sinful and unhallowed passion or restraint, is infinitely enlarged by our subjection in Christ to the highest laws of spiritual life. As, bowing in profound humility before God, our souls are thereby lifted up into the purest heights of devotion, as, submitting to death on the cross, our Saviour rose triumphant over death ; so, by the entire submission of ourselves to Christ, we are brought into perfect harmony with the purest laws of our spiritual being, are conscious of no restraint, but, in the free action of heart and thought and life, attain unto the glorious liberty of the children of God.

I have spoken of the limits of our Christian liberty. We claim the right, each one of us, to study the Gospels for ourselves ; we recognize our obligation to abide by their instructions. Here is the extent that we claim, and here are the limits that we recognize, of our Christian liberty. But, precise as this language is, it leaves a large border of territory that cannot always be distinctly defined. It is not easy to point out the limits of the earth's atmosphere, and

show precisely where its thin particles give place entirely
to the thinner ether that pervades the planetary system.
Yet such limits do exist.   It is difficult to mark the boundaries of the sun's illuminating influence, and to indicate
the exact limits within which its rays shine, and beyond
which they are lost in the brighter radiance of other and
brighter orbs.   The freest elements, even in the physical
universe, are shaded off in their extreme limits by such insen-
sible gradations, that it lies not within the reach of man's
faculties to point out the precise boundary where their
feebly pulsating motions are, ánd where they cease.   It is
still more difficult to define the yet freer elements of our
moral nature, and to show precisely where man's liberty is
dissolved in the all-pervading laws and providence of God, or
where the light of man's intellect is merged in the higher
illumination that comes to meet it from the Divine intelligence.   These are subjects on which general principles
may be established, and useful rules and precepts laid down ;
but on which precise definitions, marking off the exact boundaries between what is human and what is divine, can never
be given.   Yet such boundaries unquestionably do exist.
So, in the treatment of the subject before us, having laid
down general principles respecting the authority of a divine
revelation and the extent of our Christian liberty, it is not
easy to say, in any particular case, precisely where the one
melts away before the higher light and influence of the
other.   Still, the distinctions are plain enough.

We say, that we must submit to the authority and the
words of Christ, as we find them in the New Testament.
But there is a large field for free inquiry in determining
precisely what constitutes the genuine text of the New Testament.   We cannot say precisely what amount of emen-
dation and rejection in the received text will exceed the

just limits of Christian liberty, and throw a man out of the pale of Christianity. But we do know, that there is all the difference in the world between one who rejects altogether the genuineness and the authority of the Constitution of the United States, and one who, admitting both, would avert certain obvious misprints in the copies of that instrument which he and his neighbors happen to have. So there is all the difference in the world between one who recognizes the authority of Christ and of the Scriptures, though he may doubt about the genuineness of particular passages, or the authorship, for example, of the Epistle to the Hebrews, — all the difference in the world between such a man and one who denies altogether the authority both of Christ and the Scriptures. It is idle to say that they occupy the same position. It is a violation of the principles of either common honesty or common sense. They not only stand, one within and the other without the limits of Christian liberty, but in regard to Christianity itself they stand in entirely different attitudes.

So with respect to articles of faith. They may be drawn up as helps in our religious inquiries and instructions. It is not easy to see just where they cease to be helps in the study of the Scriptures, and begin to interpose their restraints and authority between the individual soul and the words of Jesus. But it is perfectly easy to see the difference between one who teaches what he believes, urging others always to examine for themselves, and one who holds up his articles of faith and declares that all who do not find them in the Scriptures must be shut out from the privileges of the Christian Church here, and its hopes hereafter.

NECESSITY OF A MORE COMPLETE CO-OPERATION OF THE LAITY WITH THE CLERGY.

BY REV. JOHN CORDNER.

THE Committee of Arrangements have requested me to introduce, by a brief essay, the second topic which they propose for the consideration of this body. It is stated thus : — " The Fitness and Necessity of a more complete Co-operation of the Laity with the Clergy in Church Action and General Christian Effort." I comply with the request, because I scarcely feel at liberty to decline, although I must be permitted to say, that, considering time, place, and circumstances, I should have greatly preferred to hear some other voice offering the first remarks on this subject.

It cannot fail to strike any one who looks beneath the surface of things, that in Christendom there are two distinct and conflicting ideas at work concerning the Church and its organization. One of these we may indicate at once, as the sacerdotal idea; which is exclusive and narrow. And for the other I know no more fitting term than the democratic idea, which is inclusive and comprehensive. The one has reference to a class, and would make that class the Church. The other has reference to the whole, and would make that whole the Church. Through the action and prevalence of the one idea, the Church becomes a corporation of priests. Through the action and prevalence of the other idea, the Church becomes a body of people. The sacerdotal and exclusive idea produces the limited Catholicism of Rome. The democratic and comprehensive idea produces the wider catholicism of Protestant Christianity.

In its relation to Christianity, sacerdotalism is traditional. Judaism and Paganism had each its priestly class. This class had special functions and special privileges, by which it was distinctly separated and set apart from the body of the people. In paganism we recognize it as the natural result of man's tendencies and wants wrought out under peculiar conditions.

Humanity must have a religion, and if, through wilfulness and sin, it wander away from the true God, and lose sight of him, it will create an object of worship out of its own conceptions, which it will enthrone, in some form. Though created out of itself, this object will be invested with attributes which deter from close and immediate intercourse, and hence the necessity of some mediating agent between the worshipper and the god. Thus comes the priest, who receives the sacrifices in the name, and offers them upon the altar, of his deity. Privileged with a direct and peculiar intercourse with the god, he will consequently stand marked and distinct from the body of the people. In Judaism we recognize in the priestly class an integral part of a great and divinely appointed institution. The Mosaic ceremonial was, for its time, an instrumentality of God to conduct the Hebrew nation and the human race to a higher plane of religious culture and a clearer sight of himself. Of its necessity and fitness we need not speak here. This were beside the present question. Enough for us, that such ritual existed, and that its priesthood was a fact. This priesthood received the sacrifices of the congregation, and offered them upon the altar. It had access to the holy place and to the holy of holies. The high-priest only could enter behind the veil, and there, in presence of God, appeared in behalf of the people. And standing before the people, habited in his vestments, he appeared as the messenger of the Lord, and the visible depositary of divine truth and knowledge.

We see, then, how sacerdotalism appeared in Pagan

forms of worship, and we see that it was an essential part of the Hebrew ceremonial. And from these Christendom' has inherited it as a tradition. The early converts, both Jewish and Gentile, were familiar with it, and though not authorized by the teaching of Christ or his Apostles, yet in the organization of the Christian ideas into an institution it came to be accepted, and was given a prominent place. Hence the priesthood of Christendom was considered as a separate and privileged class.

While sacerdotalism is traditional, that which I have called the democratic idea is essential to the Christian religion. This religion recognizes no respect of persons. In the overthrow of the Hebrew ritual, it sees the overthrow of all privileged and authoritative human priesthoods. The New Testament reveals Christ as the Prophet, Priest, and Prince of the Church. The Christianity of the New Testament levels all national and other outward and accidental peculiarities by which one man is raised or privileged above another. God is the Father, and all are his children. Jesus Christ is the Master, and all his disciples are brethren. In the great structure of the Christian Church, every individual soul is, or may become, a living stone. Every Christian man is called on to become a priest before God, and offer up his own sacrifice.

Protestantism stands on what I have called the democratic or comprehensive idea. It was in virtue of this idea, asserting the right of the individual soul, that Protestantism sprung into existence, and sought to disengage Christianity from the grasp of the priesthood and the corruptions of Rome. If any section of Protestantism still clings to sacerdotalism, it does so in violation of the principles which gave it birth and being, and if it adheres strictly and consistently thereto, it must renounce this principle of its birth. Hence it comes to pass in our own day, that the way of Oxford, logically and legitimately pursued, lands the pilgrim in Rome.

Protestant Christianity in its essence, then, is democratic and comprehensive, not sacerdotal and exclusive. It regards the Church as a body of people, a popular body, not a corporation of priests or clergy. Anglican Episcopacy, I suppose, lies nearer Rome, and has stronger sacerdotal tendencies and tastes, than any other portion of Protestant Christendom. But its Protestant character is asserted in its constitution by the presence of the crown, representing the nation at large. Presbyterianism has been styled the republicanism of Christianity, and in the forms and usages of Congregationalism we find a still wider recognition of popular rights claimed and conceded.

The comprehensive idea which levels all class barriers in the Christian Church, and asserts the rights of all disciples to the highest privileges connected therewith, is held and cherished by us all in this body, and by far more besides. What an excitement we should have, if any claims were seriously put forth for special Christian privileges on behalf of a priestly or clerical order! But the Christian medal whereon we find stamped the charter of our rights has its reverse, whereon is stamped the corresponding and correlated duties, and we cannot separate the one from the other. If we accept either, we must accept both. We think we are free from the tradition of sacerdotalism. Perhaps we are. But possibly we are not. Some traditions cling long even after our confidence in them is shaken. At any rate, the language sticks to us, constantly inviting the presence of the ideas. The terms *clergy* and *laity* are still commonly employed among us. These I regard as of sacerdotal origin. If I remember right, Dr. Channing has somewhere expressed his wish that they were out of use. But

I suppose we mean nothing more by the terms respectively, than ministers and people. Whatever the evil be, however, which the employment of such terms indicates, it lies far deeper than the mere use of words.

Go into any, into the average of the Protestant congregations that met together on last Sunday, and what, think ye, was the prevailing feeling among the masses of the people? The Catholics, we know, gathered that they might see the visible sacrifice offered which none but priestly hands can touch. Within the rails of the altar stood the priest mediating between them and Heaven. They look upon him as apart from them, of a different order, and performing an office for them which they have no right to perform for themselves. And they witness his rites with what adoring thoughts they may, without feeling any responsibility for the service. It is his, not theirs. Now it would be instructive if we could discover to what extent the great mass of the Protestants differed from the Catholics in shifting the responsibility of the service on their minister. What multitudes come into the pews of all Protestant churches entirely passive, and waiting to be acted on by the pulpit. They do not feel any responsibility in having their own minds quickened by previous devotional thought, so that they might help themselves, and help the minister too, by their sober and devout presence. Then, again, in matters of church action and general Christian effort, which go beyond the fixed services of public worship, how are the pews commonly represented? Does the minister find himself aided and sustained in such matters by the body of the congregation, as their common idea of a comprehensive church would properly require, and naturally lead him to expect? It is the rare exception when he does. Generally, if he finds the proportion

of one layman in ten who shows a living and active interest in such affair, he feels encouraged. Do I exaggerate
the state of the case, when I say that nine tenths of the
people show no interest at all ?

The Church is the grand want of the world, — the
Church as we understand it, inclusive and comprehensive,
— the Church as a living, spiritual body of people. It is
expedient that we have pastors and teachers to-day, as in
the early times. But such pastors and teachers do not
stand in theory, and ought not to stand in practice, in the
place and stead of the body of the people, to do the work
of the Church. The Christian rites and privileges of the
people are on a par with those of the pastors. And in
every department of Christian activity the duties also of
the people are on a level with the duties of the pastors.
The Church was active and aggressive at the first, and it
requires to be active and aggressive still. There were
error, ignorance, and sin against which it waged war
eighteen hundred years ago, and there are error, ignorance, and sin against which it is called to wage war to-day.
The existing state of society, in the Old World and the
New, shows its terrible want of the divine remedies of the
Gospel. The Church has a great and pressing work to
perform, as an agent of renovation and redemption. I
need not remind you of its twofold obligation to those
within and those without its own pale. In every department of obligation, pastors and people, laity and clergy,
are co-ordinately responsible. The minister is called on to
be interested in the wants of the people whom he serves,
and to meet such wants, temporal and spiritual, as best he
can. But the people are equally called on to be interested
in each other, and minister to mutual necessities. This
must needs be involved in the idea of the Church as a fra-

ternal communion. The wants and woes and wrongs of society around him demand the Christian minister's attention and exertion; but there is not an argument or appeal in such a case valid to him, that is not equally valid to all Christian people.

If Protestant Christendom had been true to its ideal of a comprehensive Church, and practically recognized its duties as well as its privileges, another and a far higher order of things would now be visible in the world. Instead of having only a small section of the Church — a single member, so to speak, of the general body — actively interested in the Church's work, it would have had the whole body, and all the members thereof, — head, feet, eyes, hands, — earnestly and hopefully engaged. Such general co-operation as this would have kept the warmth and strength of a living body in the Church itself, and its effect upon the world of men and things outside its pale would have been with marked power in every generation. God would have worked visibly in it and through it; Christ would have been the animating soul thereof, and it would have accomplished greater works than miracles. I gladly concede and gratefully accept all that it has done. The Church has effected much, even in its maimed and partial state of working; and here I see proof of the wonderful power of the divine ideas which it has in its keeping, and of the holy sympathies which its crucified Founder has awakened in human hearts. But if so much has been accomplished by the Church in its maimed and partially efficient state, what might have been accomplished if the whole body had been alive and at work, — if every Christian disciple had felt himself in some sense a Christian missionary, and had worked for the promotion of the Gospel spirit and life all around him ?

14 *

By the late laboriously compiled census of religious worship in England and Wales, it appears that there were in
that country, on a given Sunday, between seven and eight
millions of persons who attended the public services of the
Christian Church.   The entire population is quite close
upon eighteen millions.   If we subject a third, which is a
large allowance, for extreme youth and extreme age, we
have left about twelve millions without any physical hindrance between them and public worship.   It is clear,
therefore, that a very large proportion of the people neglect
the ordinary ministrations of Christianity.   And such neglect indicates a great deal in respect to the moral and
social condition of a nation.   But if the Church, in the
comprehensive sense already indicated, were alive and
active, the people and pastors alike filled with the spirit of
Jesus, and disposed to Christian labors, how long could
such neglect, and the social and moral unsoundness which
it indicates, remain ?   We hear of crying evils in the social
state, — bondage of mind and body, side by side with li-
centiousness of mind and body, — but how could these
things last if the seven or eight millions of persons who
attended Christian worship on that day felt a personal responsibility in the matter ?   If the occupants of the pews
and the occupants of the pulpits individually and alike
felt a weight upon their own souls concerning this wrong ;
if they felt for those who suffered as suffering along with
them ; and if they exerted themselves accordingly, as the
visible and working body of Christ, the evil would be removed ; and the multiplied barbarisms which disfigure and
disgrace our present civilization would disappear before the
next century of the Christian era had dawned full upon our
world.

Here the ideal of a perfect and effective Christian con-

gregation rises before my mind, and I see the vast field
of effort which lies around it on every hand. I see the
blessed Gospel seed which it might scatter, and I see the
harvest of good fruits which its faithful husbandry might
produce. In contrast with this, the actual state of many a
formally organized Christian society rises up also, and I feel
grief and shame for the lack of earnestness and power, the
lack of fidelity to great and sacred trusts, which such a
state presents. Here illustrations spring up, tempting to
farther comparison of the pulpit to the pew, of the laity
with the clergy, so far as regards responsibility for such
failure and want of power. But I must desist. Here I
must stop. My remarks are already too lengthened. And
yet they are too brief. The call made on me was to introduce the subject, not to exhaust it. I now leave it to the
consideration of the brethren here assembled.

ABSTRACT OF AN ESSAY ON THE CHURCH AS A SOCIAL POWER.

BY REV. JOSEPH H. ALLEN.

THE Essay commenced with defining the true position
of the Church to society as a "spiritual power," i. e. "a
power dealing *directly* with men's motives, beliefs, principles, and moral discipline, and only *indirectly* with those
external facts and institutions which make the domain of
the temporal power, or the State."

The need of such a power was next set forth, as "seen
in the lamentable controversies that distract the peace of
Christendom; in the existence of frightful social evils,
which the State makes scarce an effort to remove; in the
anarchy that prevails as to the first principles of morals, and

the absence of any great common interest or faith pervading the forms of our social life," — showing that " there is still lacking an intelligent, thorough, and commanding, organization of the profoundest moral conviction of men, such as may correspond to our complete notion of the Church of Christ, with forces proportioned to its work."

The phrase " spiritual power " was further defined as including, " not only the charge of worship, religious culture, and moral discipline, but also the organization of charities, the whole field of education, and the advance of truth, ethical, religious, scientific, and social; in a word, all the intellectual, moral, and religious interests of human soeiety." The Roman Church of the Middle Ages being the most complete example of such a power, its foundation was exhibited as consisting in, — 1. The Deity of Christ, with the denied dogmas of the Real Presence, and Apostolical Succession; 2. The Augustinian religious fatalism, making men helplessly dependent on church offices; 3. The doctrines of Hell and Purgatory, which made the first of ecclesiastical discipline; as well as the great social services rendered by that Church.

The Church was next assumed as " even less a teacher of truth, than a social fact and a social power "; and the conditions of that power were next inquired into, as adapted to the present age.

The Church was further defined as (in the mystical language of the Testament) " the spiritual body, corresponding to the exterior and visible body, whether of the parish, the State, or the Christian world "; or as " the aggregate of those living religious agencies which we methodize and incorporate in our associated religious life." Its office was next set forth : first, as dealing in personal spiritual culture, and next with needed charities and existing wrongs. And the first essential want in the construction of that power was stated to be " a clearly recognized basis of authority on which it may rest, — an authority as absolute and independent as that of the Roman Church, but suited to a set of conditions wholly different and new ; authority so broad and clear and firm as to redeem the mind from feebleness and fear; so generous as to win, by pure, spiritual persuasion and the omnipotence of truth, the willing reverence of men ; so strong as to hold in check an age of passionate and wayward liberty."

The authority of the Gospel among us " is a sentiment of personal loyalty felt in the sphere of personal religion ; but for social ethics, or the religion of humanity, it needs to be stated in another form. . . . . The last word of the scientific mind and social experiences of man must be its authentic exposition. The seat of the only authority to which an age like ours can appeal is in the educated sense and conscience of men, — generalized, indeed, in the ethical maxims of Christianity, but to be reconciled with the largest and latest experience, and freest mental tendencies, of the human race, — science and faith to be perfectly blended into one."

For this we require, first, " a more intellectual and scientific treatment of social wants and evils than has been prevalent hitherto. Social ethics, however earnest practically, must submit itself to the dictate of intellectual conditions, as to the directions which it shall take. It is by a steady search for *truth* that we shall, by degrees, lay the foundation of that authority to which we must submit.

" Secondly, the Church has it in hand to organize the conscience and life, as well as utter the interpreting forms of thought. Every church within its limited sphere must realize, as it may, the full pattern of a true social life."

And this both by its general culture and by its special agencies. " Christian charities present a field coequal, in grandeur and importance, with that of Christian culture ; a field that should be more thoroughly surveyed and occupied.

" It is not so much the change of present instruments, or the multiplication of them, we need, as a clearer consciousness that, by means of them, we are working to so glorious issues, and with so goodly a fellowship ; that in proportion as a thought or a deed of ours corresponds with a real want, or is in league with an eternal truth, we are working towards the building up of the vast Christian structure of the future, which shall realize, to another age, the kingdom of God on earth, in a larger, and holier, and truer sense than the structures of the Christian civilization of the past."

The Congregational body of New England, and especially our own denomination, were then stated as standing nearest to a right apprehension and realization of such power. " The *Church feeling*, based on affectionate loyalty to God and Christ, is deepening among us year by year ; let it be followed up by a larger and truer apprehension of the function of the Church as a consecrated divine agency in human life. Then it shall be our commission to lay deeply and broadly the foundations of that spiritual house which must embrace the cultured understanding, the disciplined conscience, and the rich fruits of religious experience, that in no single element it may fail to embody the purest and noblest life of humanity."

DIVINE PROVIDENCE AND PHYSICAL LAWS.

AT the Anniversary, August 1st of this year, of the Porter Rhetorical Society in Andover Theological Seminary, George I. Chace, Professor of Chemistry in Brown University, delivered an Address on the above subject. The *fact* of God's providence he regards as " too clearly revealed in the Bible, and too strongly supported, also, by great and wide-spread analogies, to admit of question or doubt." But inquiries may arise as to the *mode* or *extent* of this providence. So far as it relates to " human agency, there is no difficulty. Besides having formed men, God immediately operates upon their hearts by the influence of his Holy Spirit. He has only to touch here the springs of feeling and desire and action, and these flow out in accordance with his most perfect will." But " shall we suppose the elements of nature, like the hearts of men, to be immediately acted upon by God ? Touching with the finger of his power these sources of all material phenomena, does he cause the latter to flow out in subservience to his moral purposes ? Back of the chain of antecedents and consequents, by which physical events are bound together, may we not suppose an influence exerted, moulding and determining their character, without at the same time disturbing the order of their succession ? Behind the machinery of second causes, which alone meets the eye, may not the great First Cause be continually operating, and evolving the changes of the physical world in harmony with the moral ? This view of the subject, although frequently presented, is, I think, attended with grave difficulties."

These difficulties are found, first, in " the stability and

perpetuity of the existing order of things"; secondly, " in
the clearest and most unquestioned teachings of physical
science "; and thirdly, in the fact that experience affords no
evidence favoring the above-named view.   There are three
ways in which the power of the Divine Being, within the
forms of manifestation to which he has confined himself,
may be exerted in directing the course of human events;
— " remotely and indirectly, through the organization
and physical arrangements of the outward world; more
nearly, through the constitution and endowments of each
human being, whether immediately conferred, or transmitted
by hereditary descent from the original progenitor of the
race; and yet more nearly, by the direct influence exerted
upon the hearts and consciences of men by his Holy
Spirit."   Through this last mode, especially, God's provi-
dential care may adapt itself to individual exigencies,
though the physical laws do not bend to circumstances.
" Although the avalanche pause not in its precipitous descent, the traveller may be removed from the place over-
whelmed by it.   Although the tempest sweep onward,
abating not a jot its fury, the vessel may be turned from its
track, and reach in safety the desired haven."

As to the *extent* of the Divine Providence, Professor
Chace thinks it is wisest to hold that it relates to the great
ends proposed by human probation, to the real and essential in the government of the universe, and not to the thousand collateral results which constitute the outward and
variable allotment of individual life.   The line of distinction cannot be very precisely drawn " between what we
may suppose to have been designed, and what to have
arisen from the action of general causes, without being
specially ordered.   Nor is such discrimination necessary.
All that is really important is, that we should avoid, on the

one hand, restricting the Divine Providence to a narrow-
ness of range incompatible with its controlling influence, in
nature and human society; and, on the other, extending it
so as to take in actions and events of too little moment to
be regarded as ends in the constitution and government of
the world, without offence to the dignity of its Author."
" To imagine every one of my bodily or mental acts,
however humble, and every occurrence of my life, however trifling, the subject of a Divine purpose, is absurd and
derogatory to the character of God."

Professor Chace maintains that the general views of God's
providence which have now been indicated meet the teachings of the Saviour, are friendly to just and noble conceptions of God and to an exalted piety, and save us from an
error on this subject which " vitiates the practical judg-
ments, dwarfs the intelligence, and tends to the formation
of a narrow and egotistic type of Christian character."

Perhaps our readers have seen sharp, and in some cases
sneering, notices of this Discourse. It was not very palatable
to our friends in Andover, and it has been severely criticized
in other quarters. For ourselves, we will take the liberty
to say that it is much easier to censure than to refute it.
We think the author has allowed as much scope for a prov-
idential interposition in human affairs, as is claimed by the
common sense of Christians. After all, his theories of the
precise degrees and limits of that interposition are of little
consequence. They are modestly stated as his view of the
case. The subject is beyond the limits of human knowledge. The only advantage of the philosophical speculations suggested, is to turn the mind from the superstitious
and fanatical aspects of the subject which have become
somewhat common. For this purpose, the practical tone
of this Discourse is admirable. In this lies its chief influ-

ence and worth.   It is a bold and noble lesson to give to Andover, and we wish it could be given to, other places which we might name.   Especially has it interested us as an evidence of the independent and fresh way of treating religious subjects in quarters where we have been accustomed to look only for stereotyped and traditional thoughts. We shall conclude our notice by enriching our pages with a few paragraphs, which we quote the more freely, as but few of our readers, it is probable, have seen the Discourse itself.

" Against this general method of inquiry concerning the Divine Providence, it may be urged, that, as the fact of such a Providence is made known to us only in the Scriptures, we should look.to them exclusively for a knowledge of its mode and its limitations ; that Revelation being in its subject-matter above the reason, it furnishes no appropriate field for the exercise of that faculty ; that although we are unable to conceive how the stream of physical events can in any instance be turned from its proper channel, without disturbance of natural laws, or how these laws can maintain constantly the order and stability of the universe, and at the same time lend themselves everywhere as pliant instruments in its moral government, both may nevertheless be entirely possible. Our powers of conception, it may be added, are extremely limited. What seems to us difficult or impossible even, may be perfectly easy to God.   It becomes us, therefore, to submit our weak and puny intelligence to his higher wisdom, and receive with an unquestioning faith whatever his word reveals to us.

" In the presence of an audience such as I have the honor to address, I need not say that this is mere whining and cant and drivel, utterly unworthy of the book in support of whose claims it is offered, — utterly unworthy of the head or the heart of any true man or good Christian.   As if, forsooth, it were possible to have any higher authority than the clearly pronounced decisions of the reason ! *   As if this were not the only faculty — I include the

* " A well-attested revelation must command our belief in matters above the reason, as well as where, from the *complexity* of the data,

moral as well as the intellectual endowment — by which we are able to distinguish between right and wrong, — between truth and error! As if the Bible itself did not everywhere recognize it, and constantly appeal to it, and derive, in the last analysis, all its sanctions from it! As if, granting the possibility of a revelation independently of the reason, such a revelation would be of the slightest value to us! As if, after having received it, we should be anything but a vessel having a chart indeed, but without rudder or compass to steer by. Let us ever beware of the sin and folly of disparaging the reason. It is the only high and God-like endowment possessed by us, — the only attribute in which man still bears the image of his Maker. Seek not to degrade and humble it; but bow in willing submission to its rightful authority. It is the voice of God speaking within you. Every one of its utterances carries with it the Divine sanction. Whatever we learn from other sources is at best but knowledge at second hand. It has authority, and demands our reception and confidence only as it comes with credentials recognized by the intelligence. Veil this light within, and you have nothing without but mist and obscurity. Extinguish it, and you are at once and for ever enveloped in profound darkness. Disparage the reason, — deny its paramount authority, and you cut off the only arm by which you hold on to the plank of truth floating upon a boundless ocean of possibilities. From the free air and sunlight of day, you go down, down into the gloomy depths of a fathomless, bottomless scepticism.

" Employ the moral scalpel upon the human heart as freely as you choose. Fearlessly lay bare its quivering fibres of sentiment and belief. From that which is sound and healthy, dissect with an unflinching hand whatever is of morbid or abnormal growth. But destroy not the heart itself. Let that, healed and regenera

---

although singly comprehended by the reason, its decisions are hesitating and doubtful. But on subjects coming within the proper sphere of the reason, no revelation, however strongly attested, can command our belief in opposition to the clear and distinct affirmations of that faculty. Only doubt and uncertainty can emerge from the conflict of two equal and opposing authorities."

still send forth to every part of the frame the streams of life and sensibility. Throw into the intellectual cupel every form of opinion. Raise the heat and press the blast until the pure golden truth, freed from the dross of error, shines forth with dazzling brightness. But preserve entire and unharmed the cupel, or all your labor will be in vain. Defend, with a strong arm, the oracles of God. So far as they are intrusted to your keeping, guard them with a jealous care. Suffer them not to be corrupted by the deceits of a vain philosophy. Uphold them against the oppositions of science, falsely so called. Meet with indignant and withering rebuke the jests of the profane and the cavils of unbelief, when directed towards them. But set them not at variance with the intelligence. Bring them not into collision with the plain teachings of common sense and common experience. If your faith be in conflict with the clearly ascertained laws of nature, or the well-established principles of science, — which are only the inductions of a larger experience, — you will do well to modify it. If you continue the unequal contest, you are sure in the end to be beaten. The ever-active spirit of investigation, and the continually growing developments of knowledge resulting from it, cannot be restrained by the fetters of a creed. As well might you hope to bind leviathan with threads of gossamer, or stop the fiery steed to which the car has been harnessed by modern invention, by placing your hand upon it, or by simply looking at it. Interpretation has always, in the end, yielded to the demands of advancing science, however long it has struggled against them ; and it always must yield. Nor are the interests of piety and religion in danger of permanently suffering from it. The truth, although for a time depressed, it may be, at length, detached from the leaden weight of error that bore it down, is seen floating still more buoyantly upon the surface. Resist not progress in any of the paths of human inquiry. There is surely everywhere need enough of more knowledge. If the light pain you, it is because your eyes are weak or diseased. Give the necessary attention to them ; but do not attempt to put out the sun. In your zeal for the interests of Christian truth, do not exalt the Scriptures at the expense of the reason. Remember that the latter is the elder daughter of Heaven.

At least, pay her equal honors. ' Exalt her, and she shall promote thee. She shall bring thee to honor when thou dost embrace her. She shall give to thy head an ornament of grace ; a crown of glory shall she deliver unto thee.' " — pp. 40 – 44.

" There is another reason why we should not voluntarily suffer any form of error to attach itself to the doctrines of Christianity, and go forth under their sanction, to which I would briefly allude. However harmless, or beneficial even, such error may for a time appear, it is sure in the end to work mischief. Like the little book of the angel in the Apocalypse, though sweet in the mouth, it will make the belly bitter. Even though its direct influence on the heart and the life be not prejudicial, it will prove an obstacle in the way of the general reception of the doctrine with which it is associated. To the sincere and earnest inquirer after truth, it becomes a stumbling-block, while to the enemies of our holy religion it serves as a mark for the direction of their shafts. The Christian minister, who, by his eloquence and fervid zeal, spreads erroneous doctrines through the churches, does more to harm Christianity than a hundred infidels. Besides furnishing its adversaries with their most potent weapons against it, he is himself scattering broadcast the seeds from which scepticism and unbelief will, sooner or later, spring up. Indeed, blows aimed at Christianity through the false views connected with its teachings, not unfrequently render it an actual service. The error is detached from the truth by the vigor of the stroke, and the latter goes forward, unclogged and unencumbered, on its heavenly and divine mission." — p. 51.

" I think it not difficult to see how generally received error, here, may exert an influence upon thoughtful minds greatly to be deprecated. Let us suppose a man, whose ideas of the character and government of God have been formed chiefly from the observation of his works. He has seen that in the natural world events occur in a definite and fixed order, so that any antecedent being given, he may with certainty infer its consequent. He knows that it is upon this fundamental fact, or law, that the sciences, relating to such events, are built up ; and that without it, the most

15 *

enlarged experience would have no value as a guide to action. He can, therefore, no more doubt the wisdom and benevolence of the law as a part of the Divine government, than he can doubt its reality.

" He has further observed, that, in the bodily organization of man, the structure and endowments of the several parts obviously have in view the good of the individual. Disease and suffering, it is true, are incident to the general plan upon which he is constituted; but these nowhere appear as the object of contrivance and design. On the contrary, their occurrence is guarded against by numerous checks and hindrances, and when they have actually arisen, the evil is met, as far as possible, by remedial provisions. The wisdom and benevolence of the Creator are, therefore, here equally apparent.

" He has further observed, in the intellectual and moral constitution of man, features which look beyond the mere securing of happiness, to the higher ends of virtue and goodness. As in the preceding case, these ends are not, in every instance, realized; or in any, indeed, so perfectly as could be desired, or as might beforehand have been deemed possible. He sees, however, in the endowments of our nature, manifest provisions for their attainment; while the liability of failure in respect to them, so far as he can understand, is necessarily incident to the conditions of moral action. He concludes, therefore, that the Author of the Universe is characterized by a love of right, and a disposition to promote it, as well as by the attributes of wisdom and benevolence.

" Now let such a man be told, that, although God has subjected the natural world to fixed and invariable laws, He nevertheless everywhere shapes the events arising under them so as to meet the requirements of His moral government. Let him be further told, that everything which transpires in our world is immediately ordered by God, and in perfect accordance with His will, — that evil is as really provided for, as much the object of contrivance and design, as good, — that suffering and sin spring as directly from the constitution of things, and must have been as truly intended, as happiness and virtue. Carry these ideas of God's Providence to their legitimate consequences, by unfolding to him, as found in books of systematic theology, and as still occasionally presented from the pulpit, the doctrines of foreordination, election, and reprobation.[*] Tell him that the object of the Divine Being, in creating the world, was the illustration of His own attributes, and not the good of His creatures ; that He forms and makes use of them, in whatever way may best subserve that end, wholly ignoring any claim which they might be supposed to have upon Him as their Creator. And, to complete and give consistency to this view of the Divine character and government, add a discourse on the glory of God, and the joy of His saints in the sufferings of the finally lost, — sufferings which He had predetermined, and rendered escape from impossible. Let all this, I say, be told to a man such as I have supposed, and what effect would it be likely to have upon him? If he received it as the simple teaching of the Scriptures, might it not lead him to question their authority? Would it be strange if his confidence in them, as a revelation from Heaven, should be shaken by it? " — pp: 53-55.

" Let us ever cling to this great central truth of Christianity, — this corner-stone of all faith and all religion, — the perfect moral integrity of God's character, — his simple, impartial, unselfish goodness, — his sacred regard for justice and right, — his love to all his creatures, demonstrated and made manifest by his unsparing provisions for their welfare. It is the Alpha and Omega of the Scriptures, — the beginning and the end of their teachings. Every sentiment of our moral nature responds to it; while the innumerable voices which come from without us all unite in its affirmation. Disguise or cover over in any manner this truth, whether by the idea of a Divine Providence immediately determining every human action and event, or by the supposition of their equally universal PRE-determination, — whether by abstract reasonings as to what God might have done, or by erroneous conceptions of what he actually has done, or of the motives which prompted it, — and you diminish by so much the power of the Gospel. Shut out

---

[*] ". The foreordination of evil, not as necessarily incident to the plan of creation, but as voluntarily incorporated in it. Election and reprobation, not as *determined by* character, but as *determining* character."

of view this truth, by substituting for the requirement of true, spiritual worship, the mere observance of outward forms and ceremonies, and you take from our holy religion all that distinctively belongs to it. But let the doctrine of God's moral perfections have the pre-eminence which the Scriptures everywhere give to it, — let it bend to the requirements of no creed, — let it yield to the demands of no human infirmity, — let it be held up, as taught in the Bible, and more especially as illustrated and exemplified in the provisions of the Gospel, — and Christianity shall go forth conquering and to conquer, without stay or hindrance, until this revolted world shall be brought back to God, — until ' the heathen shall be given to his Son for an inheritance, and the uttermost parts of the earth for a possession.' " — pp. 60, 61.

THE SYRACUSE DISCUSSION.

THEOLOGICAL tournaments have of late years passed out of fashion. The public mind has been interested in other matters more than in questions of dogmatic divinity. Occasionally a zealous Universalist disputant has provoked a controversy on the points of his creed ; but the old issues between Trinitarians and Unitarians have for a long while been undisturbed. We do not regret this. There are questions in the realm of religious thought which concern us all infinitely more than theories about the derivation and rank of the Ambassador sent from heaven. The fact of his appointment, the certainty of his authority, the terms of his message, the necessity of conformity to his spirit, — these are the points of everlasting and universal interest ; and on these, as it is grateful to reflect, there is more unanimity among all professing Christians.

We do not, however, regard Trinitarian errors as harmless. They diminish the essential credibility of the Gospel. The struggle against them, begun in the third century of the Church when these errors first appeared, renews itself in every generation. The latest public discussion in regard to them was that of which we propose to give a brief notice.

On the twenty-eighth day of last February, Rev. Luther Lee, a Wesleyan minister, and Rev. Samuel J. May, a Unitarian minister, appeared before an immense audience in the City Hall in Syracuse, N. Y., and during eleven evenings, with an increasing degree of public interest, they discussed the doctrines of the Trinity. A reporter was present, and the speeches on both sides have been published at the Wesleyan Book-Room, in a pamphlet of one hundred and sixty pages, now before us.

The discussion was opened, after prayer and the appointment of a moderator, by a speech from Mr. Lee, who avowed his purpose to defend the doctrine of the underived Deity of Jesus Christ; and for this purpose he quoted many of the texts usually relied upon by Trinitarian divines.

Mr. May, in his reply, said he should undertake to prove that God alone is God, and that the notion of a Trinity was introduced into the Church by the Platonizing Christians, in the third century of the Christian era.

We do not propose to follow the discussion, which took up in succession the criticism of texts, the authority of creeds, the divine attributes ascribed to Christ, the alleged two natures in the Son of God, the personality of the Holy Ghost, and the faith of the early Christians. It appears to have been conducted throughout with dignity, gentlemanly courtesy, and mutual Christian affection. Much irrelevant matter was introduced, as was natural in a discussion before a popular assembly; and there was so little in common between the speakers in their philosophy of religion and principles of interpretation, that oftentimes much talking failed to bring their minds *en rapport* with each other. We propose to give a specimen of the debate.

We select the topic of the alleged two natures in Christ. This is the vital point of the Trinitarian scheme. Mr. Lee undertook to prove it, — 1. By showing that the Scriptures call Christ both God and man ; and for this purpose he selects one class of texts and arranges them by the side of another ; 2. From the fact of Christ's pre-existence ; 3. By passages which assert his Deity and humanity in the same clause. And here we will quote from his second speech on the fifth evening : —

" Take for instance, if you please, this passage.

" ' For unto us a child is born, unto us a son is given ; and the government shall be upon his shoulder : and his name shall be called Wonderful, Counsellor, The mighty God, The everlasting Father, the Prince of Peace.' Isa. ix. 6.

" It cannot be maintained that this is all true of any one nature.

" It cannot all be true of a being wholly divine, because he could never have been a child. It cannot be all true of a human being because he could not be called ' The mighty God,' — nor could it be true of an angel, for no angel was ever ' child born.'

" But Mr. May remarked upon this text, that it was only said he should ' *be called* ' the Mighty God, not that he *was* the Mighty God.

" The reply is, he was so called by inspiration. So called by Divine appointment.

" Again it is said, Matt. i. 23, ' Behold, a virgin shall be with child, and shall bring forth a son, and they shall call his name Emmanuel ; which, being interpreted, is, God with us.'

" ' God with us,' — God and man. ' God with us,' — God united to us, clothed in our nature.

" ' If David then called him Lord, how is he his Son ? ' Matt. xxii. 45.

" Now here is a question asked by our Lord, which no one in heaven nor on the earth can answer if Jesus was not possessed of two natures, — 'If David then called him Lord, how is he his Son !'

" This question can be answered only by admitting the two natures of Christ." — pp. 66, 67.

 Mr. Lee's fourth argument is that " the office and work of Christ required that he should combine a divine and human nature in one person." Under this head he proceeds as follows : —

" The necessity of an atonement I am prepared to defend the moment it is explicitly denied. For the present it is assumed.

" The work of making an atonement for the sins of men required it.

" 1. No mere human being could atone for sin.

" If Christ was a mere human being, which he must have been if he did not possess two natures, he was under the same law to God that all other human beings are, and could not atone for the sins of other human beings.

" In order to an atonement, there must be something engaged on which the law had no claim.

" Every created being is bound to devote all his powers to the Creator, during the entire extent of his rational existence.

" But Christ has made an atonement for the sins of men. This I am ready to prove if it be denied.

" 2. None but a human being could make an atonement for men.

" To redeem human nature, right reason says human nature must be the offering.

" For this we have the opinion of St. Paul: ' Forasmuch then as the children are partakers of flesh and blood, he also himself likewise took part of the same; that through death he might destroy him that had the power of death, that is, the devil.'

" Death was the penalty of the law, and the death of the body was one of the consequences involved.

" Christ took our nature and died and rose again to redeem us from the power of death.   —

" The fact that he was a human being, our brother, allies us to him, and through him to God. The two natures were necessary to render him a suitable mediator between God and men.

" ' There is one God and one Mediator between God and men.' I Tim. ii. 6.

" ' Now a Mediator is not a Mediator of one, but God is one.' Gal. iii. 20. .

" ' He ever liveth to make intercession for them.' Heb. vii. 25.

" ' Christ is entered into heaven itself, now to appear in the presence of God for us.' Heb. ix. 24.

" Humanity is there, and he represents us in the court of heaven, with one hand on the throne, and the other upon us, his poor kinsmen.

" V. The doctrine of the two natures of Christ may be urged from the fact that no other account can be given of his nature and character.

" The Scriptures declare him to be God and man, but they pronounce him nothing else.

" If he is not God and man, what is he?

" It will be said that he is the Son of God.

" But what is the Son of God? Is he a God? or is he a man? or is he neither?

" I press the question, What is he?

" If it be said that he was God and not man, then God was once born a child, and grew, and lived, and died.

" If it be said that he was a man and not God, then we have only a human Saviour, a human Redeemer, and a human Intercessor, whose arm is but an arm of flesh.

" It is written, ' Cursed be the man that trusteth in man, and maketh flesh his arm.' Jer. xvii. 5.

" But of Christ it is said, ' Blessed are all they that put their trust in him.' Now put that and that together.

" If it be said that he was neither God nor man, what was he? Was he an angel? No, for angels cannot die.

" But admit that he was God and man, and all is plain, and we have a Saviour worthy of everlasting trust. One to whom we can commit our souls without distrust or fear of being confounded. Beneath his protection we may rest secure, though the universe be moved. For he upholdeth all things by the word of his power. This is our Saviour, — this is our Christ. In him we now trust, and shall for ever and for evermore." — pp. 67, 68.

The reply of Mr. May is as follows : —

" In algebra it is difficult to solve an equation of which the terms are all unknown quantities. But the moment you get a known quantity into one of the terms, the trouble is over. Upon that you can base a process of reasoning that shall bring out the solution sought after. Just so it is in the case before us. I could not disprove my brother's first proposition respecting three infinite persons, perhaps, excepting so far as I could show that the parts of it contradicted each other. But in the one now before me, I discover a quantity that is known to me. One term is a man : and if I know anything, I know what a man is, at least so far as to perceive that the other parts of this proposition of two natures, God and man so united as to be one and the same person, cannot be true. ' If I have any idea of God, it is, that he is an infinite Spirit, who has existed from all eternity, uncreated, unbegotten, underived, without beginning or end, incapable of change, possessed of all wisdom, all power, all goodness, without a visible body or material members.

" My idea of man, if I have any, is that of a finite being, clothed in flesh and blood, who began to exist a longer or shorter time ago, whose powers are limited, who knows but little compared with what is to be known, and can do but little, by his own unaided strength.

" Now is it possible so to compound these ideas as to make of them one and the same idea ? What can be plainer to the human mind than that a finite being cannot be also an infinite being ; that a person who could do nothing of himself was not the veritable Creator of the Universe ; that a being of limited knowledge cannot know everything ; that a being who commenced his existence (as this complex person, second in the Trinity, certainly did)

eighteen hundred and fifty-four years ago, had existed from all
eternity ; that a person who, according to this doctrine, at the commencement of the Christian era incarnated himself, and superadded
to his deity perfect manhood, is not the being who has never
known the shadow of a change? These questions answer themselves.

"But they do not bring us to the end of the contradictions, inconsistencies, impossibilities, involved in the doctrine which Mr.
Lee has pressed upon me●

"Now, sir, I have another very-grave objection to this doctrine,
which I wish to submit to your consideration before I examine the
slender proofs on which my opponent is willing to rely for its
support. This doctrine of two natures implicates the moral character of our Saviour, impeaches his veracity, and attributes to
him deceit, equivocation, falsehood. For according to this doctrine, Jesus sometimes spoke and acted in his human, and sometimes in his divine nature, without admonishing his hearers in
which of his natures he was speaking or acting. Thus on more
than one occasion he declared that he could of himself do nothing,
but if he were God he could at that very moment do all things,
and yet he did not tell those who heard him that he meant that *as
a man* he could do nothing. On another occasion he declared that
he knew not the day nor the hour of judgment. Now according to this doctrine of his two natures, he was ignorant of that
great event only *as a man*, although he knew it perfectly as God,
and yet said nothing to guard his hearers from misunderstanding
him.

"Once more, when he forbade the young ruler to call him
good, because ' there is none good but *one*, that is God.' If he
meant only that goodness should not be ascribed to him as a man,
while it should be ascribed to him, in its highest conceivable measure, as God, why did he not intimate that this was his meaning?
And when he forbade his disciples to pray to him, to ask anything
of him, but to ask all things of God in his name, how can it be
explained, if he knew himself to be God, that he did not guard his
hearers, and those who may now read the narratives of his life,
from dangerous error, by intimating that he meant no one should

worship him or pray to him *as a man*, while as God the whole universe should do him homage? If the doctrine of the two natures be true, if Christ was God as well as man, then he was guilty of what in the mildest term we call equivocation. If a king or president should declare that he had no power to pardon an offender, meaning that he had no power to do so as a man, while at the same moment, as the supreme ruler, he could set him at liberty by a word, he would equivocate. If Sir Isaac Newton had been asked to tell some earnest inquirers by what forces the planets were held in their orbits, and had replied, he did not know, meaning that he did not know it as a common man, while as the discoverer of the great law of gravitation he understood it very well, all would say that he equivocated, deceived, said what was not true. So, if Sir John Herschel should now be interrogated, by persons who wished to know in what year Encke's comet will appear again, and he should answer that he did not know, meaning all the while, that he did not know that distant day *as a man*, while he did know it as an astronomer, he would be guilty of deception. No one would ask him or Sir Isaac Newton such questions as common, unlearned men, but as men who had studied these subjects, and were fairly presumed to know vastly more than those who put to them the inquiries I have supposed.

"And more, if Archimedes, the philosopher of old Syracuse in Sicily, had been applied to, to move a ton's weight, and had answered that he had no power to do it, — meaning that by his own unaided physical strength as a man he had not power enough for such an undertaking, — he would justly have been accused of lying, especially by those who had heard him say, in his scientific lectures, that with the power of the lever, if he had a suitable fulcrum and a place to stand on, he could move the world.

"Such duplicity, such deception as this, the doctrine we are considering virtually imputes to Jesus Christ, when his disciples made inquiries of him respecting the day of judgment. They approached him as an uncommon person, — as one who they were persuaded knew more than most men, perhaps more than all men ; they appealed to him to tell them on this important subject what he knew more than they did, — more than other men knew. If, therefore, in any way, in any character, or in any nature, he was able to answer their question, he deceived them by replying as he did.   So likewise in the other cases to which I have referred.   If words have any meaning, Jesus Christ expressly disclaimed the possession of any of the attributes of Deity.   He disclaimed omnipotence, when he declared, ' I can of myself do nothing.'   He disclaimed omniscience when he declared, ' Of that day and that hour knoweth no man, neither the Son, but the Father.   He disclaimed supreme and infinite goodness when he said, ' Why callest thou me good?   there is none good but one, that is God.'   This is plain language ; there is no mystery or obscurity in it.   The terms ' I,' ' me,' ' my own self,' as every one knows, always denote an individual or person; and they include the whole of that person ; they comprehend all which goes to constitute him what he is, viewed as an individual or whole.   In this sense our Saviour must have used them, or he must have been guilty of manifest prevarication.

" Then consider further, — no one who witnessed his wonderful works supposed that of his own power, as an ordinary man, he did them ; but some suspected that he might be a being of a higher order than human.   To. that apprehension in his disciples it was that he spoke when he disclaimed omnipotence, omniscience, and attributed his power and wisdom to God, who gave to him all of either of those attributes that he had manifested to their admiration.

" But again : If there be any part of Christ's example which is more valuable to beings such as we are, in the midst of trials and temptations, it is his confiding and submissive piety.   What words nerve so powerfully our resolution to withstand the wrong, as his ' Get thee behind me, Satan,' or rather the spirit which they evince !   And oh ! what words come to us with such a sustaining power, when our hearts are ready to sink under a bitter disappointment, or sore bereavement ; what words, in the hour of overwhelming affliction, help us to say so exactly what should be said by all dependent beings, and in the very utterance of them awaken a faith and a submission kindred to that which inspired them.   I say, what words were ever spoken so full of the spirit of filial trust and pious resignation as his, 'The cup which my Father hath given me, shall I not drink it? Father, not my will, but thine, be done.' But if this doctrine which Mr. Lee affirms be true, it takes away all reality from Christ's acknowledgment of dependence, his supplications for aid, and his expressions of entire acquiescence in the Divine will. If he were God, how could he have really suffered as he appeared to do in the garden of Gethsemane. If in him 'the Godhead and manhood were joined together, never to be divided,' what are we to make of his cry upon the cross, 'My God, my God, why hast thou forsaken me!' If he were the Eternal Jehovah, how could his death upon the cross have been anything more than an appearance? His resurrection and ascension too, what evidence would they be of man's immortality? If Christ were God, to whom could he have offered prayer? If he were himself the Highest, Holiest One, to whom could he look up with reverence? If he were the Infinite God incarnate, his prayers must have been offered to himself; and thus his devotions become utterly unintelligible; and we are deprived of the strengthening, comforting influence of his example in our days of trial, in our nights of affliction.

"In conclusion, sir, let me say that the use which this doctrine requires us to make of certain expressions of Scripture *mystifies the Bible*, and destroys all confidence in the meaning of its language. If, for the sake of supporting a system of doctrines, devised centuries after Christ's ascension, we are required to set aside the plain, obvious meaning of Christ's declarations respecting himself, and assume that he meant something very different from what he certainly said; — why, if this be the use we are to make of the Bible, there can be no dependence placed upon its teachings; we had much better go directly to the creeds of the churches, and not trouble ourselves to look for any truth beyond them; or, better still, go back again into the bosom of the Roman Catholic Church, which boldly assumes and frankly tells us that we cannot be trusted to read the word of God for ourselves, but that the true interpretation of the Bible is committed to the Church, — nay, more, that certain doctrines of higher significance than those which are recorded in Scripture have been transmitted

16 *

in the unwritten word of Apostolic tradition, and can be learned only through the teaching, and on the authority, of the consecrated ministers of the ' Holy Catholic Church.' " — pp. 70 – 72.

Towards the close of the discussion, Mr. May states the reason why he had engaged in the debate : —

" Here some may be ready to inquire, why I am so outspoken and earnest in my opposition to their doctrine of the tri-one God ? I answer, first, because, unscriptural, irrational, and utterly unintelligible as that doctrine is, they make more account of it than of all Christ's preaching and character. They regard a man's belief of this doctrine, or assent to it, as a better evidence of his soundness in faith, than the -most upright conduct, and the most benevolent affections, manifested by him in all the relations and intercourses of life. They throw distrust upon the only test of a true faith, which Jesus proposed, when he said, ' By their fruits ye shall know them ' ; and set up a test of admission into the Christian Church, and of acceptance with God, which was nowhere prescribed by Christ or his Apostles, and which is no evidence of righteousness of life or holiness of heart.

" The second reason for my opposition to this doctrine of the three-one God is, that it is made the basis of a system of doctrines, which has as little resemblance to Christianity as anything that can be found in the theologies of the heathen world ; — a system of doctrines, in which the character of God is fearfully misrepresented, the nature of man frightfully distorted or caricatured, and the destiny of the greater part of the human race is declared to be far worse than that of ' the brutes which perish ' ; — a system of doctrines which has alienated from Christianity many of the best minds of every age, if it has not driven them into blank infidelity, discountenanced the personal, independent, thorough study of the Scriptures for one's self, and made religion to be too generally considered a supernatural condition, that is, superinduced upon the favored few, ' the elect,' the number of which was determined before the foundation of the world ; and represents that even they are to be saved, not because of any faith or good works in them, but wholly in consideration of the righteousness of Christ imputed to them, or in some inexplicable manner transferred to them; — so that this system of theology has made the righteousness of men (their individual and joint efforts to do the will and accomplish the purposes of God) of little or no consequence compared with their acceptance of this dismal creed of the churches. The Gospel of Christ has been supplanted by this theology of the Christian Fathers of the third and fourth centuries, and the work of the Lord has been everywhere hindered. .

"I rejoice to acknowledge that many, who have been entangled by their education in the intricacies of this labyrinth of inconsistencies, have yet been so affected by the divine precepts and the perfect character and simple doctrines of Christ, that they have listened to the responses of the spirit in their own hearts, and have become likewise the dear children of God, true Christians. But the number of these is everywhere far less than it would have been, if all of Christianity and nothing of Calvinism had been everywhere preached and inculcated. The dark system of theology, however, still stands dominant in most of the churches, and diffuses a baleful influence throughout Christendom.

" Within the last sixty or seventy years, this system of terrible error has been more vigorously assailed than ever before, in England and this country; and, aided as the assault has been by improvements in the education of the people, and changes for the better in man's notions of civil government, an impression not to be effaced has been, made upon this citadel of orthodoxy. Man's attention has been directed more than ever to the practical requirements of Christianity. And just within the period I have named more has been done directly than ever before, since the primitive age of the Church, to enlighten and save mankind. And, sir, in the only part of the world where Unitarianism has ever attained anything like the ascendency, there, just there (in Boston and its vicinity) more plans have been devised for the relief of suffering humanity, and more has been done in their behalf, than anywhere else.

" Nevertheless, sir, the system of Calvinism so called still remains, upheld by all the power of the Papal Church, domiciliated as the dependencies of that Church are in every part of the world ;

upheld by the Church of England, sustained as it is by that mighty
monarchy ; upheld in our country by the offspring of the English
establishment, — the Episcopal Church ; and upheld by the venerable Presbyterian Church, and by the Methodist and Baptist
Churches, that give it a qualified support.   True, Professor Mau-
rice of England, and Professor Crosby of New Hampshire, and
Dr. Bushnell of Hartford, and Professor Fitch of New Haven,
and Doctor Beecher of Boston, and others, have each and all, from
within, made great breaches in the foundations of this system of
error.   Still it stands ; and so long as it stands in the holy place
where the Gospel of Christ alone should be enshrined, so long
ought the ministers of Christ to assail it.   My brother frankly
acknowledges to me, that the creeds of the Presbyterian and Episcopal Churches are stated in language which has become obsolete.
' No Trinitarian,' to use his own words, ' can be found, who, if he
were called upon to state his views, would state them in the exact
language of either of those creeds.'   Why, then, should those
creeds be retained a day or an hour longer?   Let them be laid
away among the *things of the past;* and let the people, all the
people, be encouraged and assisted to study the Bible and the
volumes of Nature and Providence, ' remembering,' in the words
of the venerable John Robinson in his parting charge to the church
that came to Plymouth, ' that there is more light yet to break out
from them all ' ; and assured that he who shall learn from them to
love truth and hate error, to dread all wrong, and try to practise
all righteousness, to recognize impartially all the rights of all his
fellow-men, to abhor oppression and cruelty, and love justice and
mercy, — in a word, he who shall have so learnt as ' to deny
ungodliness and worldly lusts, and to live soberly, righteously, and
godly in this present world,' he, and he only, has learnt that
which has made him wise unto salvation, let his theological opinions be what they may."— pp. 151, 152.

The conclusion of the discussion deserves to be quoted,
for the sake of the picturesque scene at which the curtain
fell.   The closing speech was made by Mr. May, whose
final paragraphs are as follows : —

" When I first heard of you, brother Lee, it was as a man who had generously espoused the cause of the poor and wretched slaves in our country. I heard of your battling manfully with the Goliah sin of our nation, that has wellnigh subjugated to its base purposes the Church and the State, the religion and the politics of the country. I heard how faithfully you were dealing with that terrible iniquity, as you found it secreted and protected by the great Methodist organization, to which you then belonged. I learnt how nobly you, with a few other faithful ones, came out from that corrupted body and set up an altar upon which you might, in godly sincerity, offer the daily sacrifice of prayer to the God of the oppressed. I honored you for your fidelity to the right.

" Since you came to this city, I have heard of your kindnesses to the outcasts, — the fugitives from our American despotism, — how you have sheltered them under your roof, fed them at your table, and helped them on their way 'to the land of the free and the asylum of the oppressed.' My soul has been drawn towards you as a good son of God.

" I cared not much to know what your theological opinions might be, to enable me to form an estimate of your Christian character, so long as I could see the fruits of the spirit of charity in your life. And now that I have found, in the course of this discussion, what your opinions are ; although they appear to me very unscriptural, very irrational, very inconsistent with themselves and self-contradictory, still I will not withdraw my confidence from you as a man and a Christian, so long as I see that you abound in love and good works. And here, brother Lee, after all our disputing, is my right hand of fellowship, if you are willing to receive it.

" Mr. Lee said : I take your hand, and fellowship you as a man and a philanthropist, but I have no fellowship with your theology.

" Mr. May. — Nor I with yours ! I suppose that your theology is just as unlike to mine, as mine is to yours.

" Then (turning to the audience) he said : I thank you, fellow-citizens, for your long-continued and patient hearing of what we have had to say. I have only to beg of you to read what we have said, and consider it well that you may understand; compare our doctrines and arguments with each other as impartially as you may be able, and both with the teachings of the Bible, and judge for yourselves which of the two is nearer the right." — p. 160.

LIBRARY OF THE AMERICAN UNITARIAN ASSOCIATION.

IN the Rooms of the Association, at 21 Bromfield Street, provision has recently been made for the accommodation of a library which the Executive Committee desire to collect. It seems important on many accounts, for the convenience of present use, but more for purposes of future reference, to form a library of all Unitarian publications. The Rooms of the Association seem to be the appropriate place for such a library, and the officers of the Association the proper persons to have charge of it. In this library all works included in the following classes should be found : —

1. Those which relate to the history and development of Unitarian Christianity in any part of the world. Books which explain its rise, spread, and present condition in Switzerland, Poland, Transylvania, Holland, Germany, France, England, should here be brought together. These are indispensable to any historical view of the Unitarian doctrine.

2. Those which indicate and unfold the earliest tendency in this country to Unitarian modes of thought. Undoubtedly that tendency showed itself at a much earlier period than is generally supposed. The controversies that attended the Whitefield excitement made a rapid develop-

ment of a liberal theology.   Before the Revolutionary war pamphlets were published which, as we turn to them now, seem to have singularly anticipated the arguments and strifes of our day.   Copies of these, we suppose, may be found in the attic collections of many old families.   As bearing on this particular point of illustrating a tendency to liberal modes ôf religious thought in New England, they are of inestimable value, and all means of collecting them should be carefully improved.

3. All reports of literary, charitable, missionary, philanthropic, and reformatory societies, managed by liberal men.   These will some day be referred to with interest, as illustrating the spirit and power of the denomination.   Such documents, after they are once read, constitute to most persons the works of least value on their shelves; but to a historian they are often beyond price, as showing the form and pressure of the times to which they relate.

4. One copy at least of every book published by a Unitarian author.   No other denomination, in proportion to its size, furnishes more authors, nor authors whose books are more acceptable to the general mind of the country.   It would show a varied and fertile literature were we to enumerate all the works which during the last twenty-five years have appeared from the Unitarian press.   In the department of sermons, especially, this literature exhibits a marked peculiarity.   A new style of preaching was introduced by the eloquent Buckminster.   He was among the first to depart from the formal and antiquated style which had long resounded in the pulpit, and to adopt a more natural and fresh mode of address.   Perhaps he shares the honor of introducing the change with Mayhew, who preceded him, with Freeman, his contemporary, and with Channing, Thacher, Abbot, Kirkland, Ware, and Green-

wood, who with such great popularity succeeded him in the same line. At any rate, it was the Unitarian pulpit which gave fresh interest and life to New England sermons. Some of the volumes of discourses published by our liberal divines have had the merit accorded to them of being the best models of pulpit address which the country has afforded. They have had considerable circulation among various denominations of Christians, and have done much to influence the general pulpit style. Books of this class, and many of them of great excellence, are frequently offered to the public, and the library of the Association should by all means have a copy of each.

5. Complete sets of every periodical work devoted to the interests of the denomination. There should be one place where the inquirer will be sure to find every work of this kind. We have had many periodicals which, though for the most part they have sustained but a brief existence, have been conducted with much ability, and have rendered good service. Beside the Christian Disciple and the Christian Examiner, we need name only the Unitarian Miscellany, at Baltimore, the Western Messenger, in Louisville, the Unitarian Advocate and Scriptural Interpreter, in Boston. Entire copies of these, and of every periodical we have published, should be here carefully preserved. Each sheds an important light upon the modes of thought, feeling, and activity in the denomination, and will hereafter be of great value for purposes of historical reference.

When, from this brief description of what the library of the Association ought to be, we turn now to a passing notice of the books already procured as the nucleus of the desired collection, we are reminded how much is to be done before our wishes can be realized.

We have a complete set of the Disciple and Examiner, —

the work which is the richest product of our periodical literature, and long may it be as vigorous and fruitful as it now is, — a complete set of the Western Messenger, Unitarian Miscellany, Liberal Preacher, and Scriptural Interpreter. We have also a complete set of the Tracts of the Association, — a series which, for the freshness, earnestness, and ability of discussion of religious subjects, it would be difficult to match by any similar publications. The works of Norton, Channing, Dewey, Palfrey, Ware, Greenwood, Follen, Livermore, are also on our shelves, together with a hundred volumes from that large class of authors who have published but a volume each. We have also forty-two bound volumes of the Letters received by the Secretary in each year since the organization of the Association, — a work of great value to the future historian of Liberal Christianity in New England.

But our enumeration of what we possess is intended chiefly to reveal our wants. We shall be grateful to any friends who will assist us in the object we have in view. From all authors in our denomination, we hope we may receive a copy of their works. Sets of periodicals from libraries of deceased ministers will be of essential value to us, for which we will gladly exchange recently published and popular books. Even partial sets may enable us to complete imperfect copies now on hand. Reports of Societies, and old pamphlets in controversial divinity, will also be gratefully acknowledged. We do not suppose we shall form a large library at once. But by keeping our eye upon this matter through a series of years, we trust we may accomplish results which may hereafter be valued.

UNITARIAN LITERATURE.

WE were led the other day, by a short sentence in a letter, to reflect upon the character of the literature which we are circulating. The writer was a stranger to us, and, living in a remote part of the country, a Tract of the Association by chance fell into his hands. "At first," he writes, "I turned away from it, almost in disgust, remembering how distasteful to me the very word *tract* had become, in consequence of the hortatory drivel and mawkish sentimentalism with which I had so often found that publications under that name were filled. But something in the appearance of this tract called my attention to it; and when I read on, page after page, admiring alike the fresh, manly style, the clear, good sense, the reasonable views, the unaffected piety, of the little work, I was sorry that I so soon came to the end. I assure you I never before had the slightest idea that such valuable writing was ever put forth under the name of a tract; and my object in this letter is to order the entire series of your publications."

This sentence suggested a comparison between the works we issue, and those published by other Tract and Book Associations. In regard to these last, we should not express ourselves as did our correspondent. He probably had seen but a few of their works, and these, it so happened, were not at all to his taste. We have no disposition to underrate their merits. We cannot entertain the least doubt that the publications of the American Tract Society, for example, have done immense good. Some of them are written with great beauty and power, and with a richness of religious experience which give them a worth far above all mere rhetorical and artistic finish. Even in the larger works on religious subjects at the present time circulated among our Orthodox brethren, such as the works of Emmons, Edwards, Baxter, Woods, and others, we doubt not that thousands find rich nourishing food, in comparison with which our publications would seem to them to be only husks and straw. We freely admit this in justice to one side of the case.

But there is another side too. There is a large class of readers to whom these publications appear in the light which our correspondent somewhat strongly indicated. To them such a work as Sears on Regeneration is a voice of to-day; it is fresh, earnest, full of beauty and power; and with a magic divining-rod opens fountains of sensibility and faith which all those Orthodox workers in this field of theology, with their shovels, crow-bars, and tremendous powder-blasts, could not approach. To them Dewey is a most awakening and suggestive writer, and, judging by the frequency with which his sermons have been preached in Orthodox pulpits, a similar estimate, we suspect, is made in other quarters of the value of his writings. To them Channing is an author with whom they love to commune, for they are drawn captive by the beauty of his mind, the child-like fervor of his faith, and the fine humanity of his spirit. To them Ware seemed, by the eminently devout and practical manifestation of his character, worthy to be placed in the highest calendar of saints; and from no other book have they drawn so many useful suggestions as from his "Formation of the Christian Character." To them the argument of Norton in his Genuineness of the Gospels furnishes a rock for their faith, it is so clear and convincing, so candid and manly, and is built up with such a scholarly and massive strength. We all know, likewise, the pleasure and profit with which they will read such a book as Clarke's

Doctrine of Prayer, or such a one as Eliot's Doctrinal Lectures, or such a one as Burnap's Rectitude of Human Nature, or such a one as Peabody's Sermons of Consolation, or such books as Livermore's Commentaries and Discourses. The bare names of these publications remind us of the richness of our literature. What would be done with these books, if, with their taste, scholarship, ability, they had been devoted to the defence of an orthodox faith? They would have been printed and distributed by millions of copies. The truth is, we are not aware of the value of the instrument for the diffusion of a pure Christianity which Divine Providence, in our fresh and able literature, has put into our hands.

MEETINGS OF THE EXECUTIVE COMMITTEE.

September 11. The members of the Board were all present, except Messrs. Clarke and Callender. Much conversation was held on the expediency of sending a missionary to Kanzas. The immense emigration to that territory, the spiritual destitution of the new settlers, the importance of founding religious institutions in the very beginning of the growth of towns and villages, and the great good which suitable men would exert in the establishment of schools and distribution of books, as well as by preaching the Gospel, — these were points which came up for earnest consideration. They led to inquiries relating to the probability of procuring the right kind of men to engage in this work. The Secretary presented some information he had obtained in regard to this point. It was finally voted to lay the subject upon the table for the present, in the hope that we may hereafter see some door opened through which we may enter successfully upon this work. The chief obstacle in the way of undertaking some useful service at once is the want of means. No one can be expected to set out on such a missionary excursion without some guaranteed compensation. Crippled by the state of our funds, we hope the time will come when, through the Christian generosity of our friends, we may no longer be compelled by our empty treasury to suffer golden opportunities of usefulness to pass by unimproved. Some missionary service, worthy of our position and influence as a denomination, we hope we may soon undertake.

The Secretary suggested at this meeting the importance of establishing a library in the Rooms of the Association. Some of the considerations then presented may be found stated at length in an article in this number of the Journal. The subject of procuring suitable accommodations for such a library was referred to the Business Committee, with full power.

It was voted that the Secretary prepare and publish the Annual Unitarian Congregational Register for 1855, and that it be sent to auxiliaries and subscribers to the Quarterly Journal.

Letters were read from our faithful and devoted missionary at the West, Rev. Peter Betch ; and it was voted to supply him, at his request, with one hundred and twenty-five sets of Channing's Works, twenty-five of which to be a gift to him in acknowledgment of his most useful services.

From Rev. Leonard Whitney, of Keokuk, Iowa, interesting letters were received, giving an account of his labors in that place, and of the prospects of the diffusion of Christian truth, and the promotion of a spirit of vital piety, in the region where he lives. Some members of the Board stated

17 *

that they had had the pleasure of a personal interview with Mr. Whitney, and had been deeply interested with the history of his change of opinions, with the evidences of his earnest spirit, and the tokens of success in the work in which he was then engaged. It was voted to give Mr. Whitney two hundred dollars' worth of books to be sold in Iowa and neighborhood, the proceeds to be appropriated towards the erection of a church in Keokuk; and the Secretary was directed to transmit the books accordingly.

Upon the representation of the state of the Society in Belvidere, Illinois, of which Rev. William Bradley is pastor, it was voted to appropriate two hundred dollars towards sustaining public worship in that place.

A request, from some members of the Federal Street Society, that they may use the Rooms of the Association for the purposes of a Vestry, for one evening a week during the winter, was referred to the Business Committee.

October 2. At the meeting this day all the members of the Board were present, except Messrs. Fairbanks, Fearing, and Briggs.

The special committee to whom the subject had been referred made a report, that they had effected a purchase of the unsold copies of Professor Norton's Genuineness of the Gospels. The Secretary was directed to have a portion of them bound and kept on sale. We take pleasure in recording this purchase. It will be an important service to the cause of Christian truth, to give a wide circulation to this work. It is not a work that will have a popular sale. But for ministers' libraries, for public institutions, for students in divinity, and for the instruction of men of liberal culture, no work can be more valuable. The Association has purchased on terms which will admit of a considerable deduction from former prices ; and we confidently look for the sale of many copies.

The Secretary stated that he had received a letter from one of the Professors of Union Theological Seminary, N. Y., asking for a donation of our publications for the library of that Institution. He said he took pleasure in reading a correspondence marked by Christian courtesy and kindly feeling. It was unanimously voted to forward to the library of the above institution copies of all our books, and the Secretary was directed to send them.

The following letter from Rev. J. G. Forman, resigning his situation as missionary and book-distributor of the Association, was read : —

"*Boston, September* 29, 1854.

"Rev. H. A. MILES, D. D.: —

"My dear Sir, — A devoted attachment to the life and labors of a settled pastor, and the difficulty of pursuing the interests of the Association, as its Missionary and Book Agent, without frequent interruptions and loss of time, arising from home cares, the imperfect state of my wife's health, and the education of my children, prompt me to resign the situation I hold in your service, that I may accept a call I have received to become the pastor of the Unitarian Society in Sandwich.

" During the time I have been in the employ of the Association, I have experienced your kindness and reasonable allowance for loss of time in pursuing my labors, to a degree for which I am duly grateful. In my final settlement, as on a former occasion, a proper deduction will be made for this loss of time.

"In whatever situation I may be, I shall continue to feel a deep and abiding interest in the prosperity of the American Unitarian Association. I believe it is engaged in a most noble and Christian enterprise, and I trust is destined to send the living and printed word of Gospel truth to all parts of the earth, by means of its future operations as a Missionary Tract and Book Association.

" During the five months of actual service which I have rendered, I have not only obtained numerous subscriptions to the Book Fund, and the Quarterly Journal, but have sold over *one thousand volumes* of Unitarian books, in a few towns here in New England, by personal calls upon families, mostly of our own household of faith. Of these I think about two thirds have been the Life and Writings of Dr. Channing. I mention this fact to show what reasonable ground of expectation there is that the Association, by means of its Fund, as capital, and its agents in the field, may circulate not merely *thousands*, but *millions* of our best religious books throughout this land.

"I cannot take my leave of my present situation, as an agent of the Association, without expressing my confidence in its future plan of operations, and wishing it a hearty God-speed in its hopeful and promising enterprise, nor without expressing the wish that the wealthy churches and laymen of our denomination, whom God has blessed with a liberal store, will make the Association what it ought to be, an effectual and well-provided 'Unitarian Book and Tract Association.'

"With sentiments of respect and friendship towards yourself and the members of the Executive Committee,

"I am, very truly, your servant in Christ,

"J. G. FORMAN."

The resignation of Mr. Forman was accepted, with the expression of thanks for the services he had rendered, and with wishes for his usefulness in the new field of labor upon which he enters.

After due inquiry and consultation, Rev. George S. Ball, of Upton, was unanimously appointed to the situation which Mr. Forman had resigned.

November 6. All the members of the Board were in attendance.

A letter was read from Rev. James F. Clarke, commending to the notice of the Association the missionary labors of Rev. B. F. Stamm, who for some time has preached and distributed books in Wisconsin, and bearing witness to the earnestness of his spirit and the success of his labors. It was voted to appropriate one hundred dollars in aid of Mr. Stamm.

Interesting letters were read from Peoria, Illinois, informing the Committee of the prospect of establishing a hopeful society in that place, under the ministry of Mr. McFarland, a graduate of the Cambridge Divinity School. It was voted that the Secretary open a correspondence with the committee of the Society in Peoria, and express our interest in their condition, and wishes for their success.

At this meeting still further conversation was held in regard to sending a missionary to Kanzas. The names of several persons were proposed as suitable to become missionaries in this enterprise. The whole subject was referred to the Secretary, with instructions to make further inquiries, and prepare matured arrangements for the subsequent action of the Board.

The importance of publishing a Book of Prayers for Family and Private Devotion was presented for consideration. Calls for such a book have often been made, both at our Rooms and of our book-distributors; and though we have several works of this kind, which have been highly acceptable and have had a ministry of good, it was thought that a new work might create some fresh interest, and meet wants now not supplied. Measures were adopted towards securing the preparation of such a work. We shall have occasion to refer to this subject again.

The Committee attended to certain proposals from Mr. John Wilson of Boston, tendering to the Association the publication of a work of which he was the author. It was referred to the Committee on Publications, with full power.

Final action on the proposition to print a volume of Selections from the Christian Examiner was referred to Messrs. Lincoln, Briggs, and the Secretary.

It having been stated that Tracts Nos. 24 and 25 are out of print, the Secretary was authorized to reprint them as an article in the January Quarterly Journal, and to have five hundred extra copies published in the form of Tracts.

EXTRACTS FROM LETTERS.

A LADY in the interior of the State of New York who, through her great interest in the circulation of religious books, had sent to us for a supply, writes : — " The Tracts you sent have been all distributed, and are doing their work, in some cases ' with observation,' and in others, I doubt not, silently ; and I should be glad to distribute more if I had them. In one case those I laid on a hotel-table were read and re-read by a lady of the Methodist Church, who was so much interested in them that she came to me to beg for more, or to ascertain where they might be procured. The books have sold readily. I see you have lately published a small book containing Dr. Dewey's Discourse on Retribution. I should be glad to get it, for never did any sermon impress me like that, and it has been my habit to give away whatever copies I can procure."

One of our clergymen in a town in Central Massachusetts, who has engaged in this work of book-distribution with great spirit and success, writes : — " The prospect is good for disposing of all the books on hand within a short time in this village. Many more within the limits of the town I hope to send forth on their beneficent mission. Time for the service is the only thing wanting. In the course of my operations thus far, I have met with many encouragements,— enough to assure me that this is a work of great good. Many of these silent preachers are making themselves felt in the ever-widening circles into which they have been introduced. In some instances they are recognized and acknowledged by those who bear another name than ours, and who have been taught to look upon us with unfriendly prejudice. Some have testified their delight to me in the most enthusiastic terms. These books of Clarke and Sears are doing a good work. They have given me many openings for religious conversation, and saved some pastoral visits from being barren and unsatisfactory. The twenty-five or thirty copies of the Memoir of Mrs. Ware are well-read books in any sense of the term, — doing service like the volumes of a circulating library, preaching from house to house, giving to the wives and mothers of our Israel impressive lessons of true womanhood. I am more than ever convinced that this book-movement is a timely measure. I have learned much in distributing the works you sent me. The comparative efficacy of the printed page and the living voice in this reading era is not what it once was ; and we Unitarians have too long neglected to adapt our action to the change. God speed the work in which you are engaged, to a result infinitely better than the triumph of a party, to the diffusion of a true evangelical religious life in hearts now so cold and barren."

From another clergyman we hear as follows : — " Amid many signs of indifference and discouragement in the field of labor assigned me by Divine Providence, I was induced, by reading of similar efforts in other places, to undertake to see all the families in my parish supplied with one or more of the fresh awakening books you have lately published.

I have reason to bless the day on which I resolved to do this.   I met with a hearty response where I little looked for it.   The book gave me opportunity to talk with my parishioners.   Their readiness to purchase has imparted a new interest to my mind, and their reading has increased their interest in my preaching ; so that, on the whole, I think things are looking better with me than they have for years. At any rate, a good book in every family library in my parish is seed from which I may hope for something by and by."

. A clergyman informs us of a new mode of book-distribution which was adopted by his parish.   He made the importance of such distribution the topic of a sermon, which was followed by a contribution.   Sufficient money was raised to purchase a large number of books, and these were placed on a table in the entry of the church, and-the congregation were invited to take such as each would like to read.   More than five hundred volumes were taken. Some advantages were undoubtedly reached by this plan. By purchasing in large quantities, the books were obtained cheaper, and the contributions of the more favored placed good books in the hands of those who could hardly afford to purchase them. ·

An earnest book-distributor in Western Pennsylvania writes : — " Having come to the conclusion to devote my time again to the work of circulating books, and knowing none which I think better than those published by your Association, I must supply myself anew.   Within a week past I sold seven sets of Dr. Channing's Works to a Presbyterian, who has disposed of them among his friends.   During the . past year, I have supplied him with no less than thirty sets. Every few weeks he has come round to get from five to ten sets.   He tells me he often sells them to Baptist preachers. You may send me one hundred sets of Channing's Works during this fall, and I will try to sell them as fast as I can."

Another friend writes from the State of New York : — " First and last, I have sold scores of your publications. Some of the books you send me are invaluable. I may mention Sears on Regeneration, and Clarke on Prayer, especially. For myself, I do not care much for merely doctrinal or controversial works, and would much rather circulate books having some positive spiritual *pabulum* in them, than such as merely antagonize a dead dogma."

From Iowa we have received a letter from which we make the following extracts: — " Here is a State of 50,000 square miles, and a population of over 300,000. I wish to become your colporteur, to visit all our principal towns, among which I hope to sell a thousand dollars' worth of Channing's Works. Where are they more needed, where are they likely to be so welcome, and to do so much good, as among that portion of our people here who have no preachers to set before them the truth? Had not the silent but powerful voice of your writers preceded me in my field of labor, there would never have been occasion for my voice. They had gone before to prepare the way ; and, before any living preacher was on the ground, had spoken words of courage and hope to many an inquiring soul beyond the Father of Waters. And could the works of those men be carried into every county and important town in our great and rapidly growing State, — could they be placed in the libraries of every lawyer, physician, and minister, — I believe they would do more to make the cause of truth known and respected, more to prepare the way for an intelligent and stable faith in the Lord Jesus Christ, than could be effected in any other possible way."

The Society in Rockford, Illinois, has received aid from our New England churches towards the erection of a house of worship. From a letter lately received, we learn that " the Society there is in a growing and prosperous condition, and is full of zeal. They are now building a neat stone church, in the early English style. It is to cost $ 7,000, and will comfortably seat three hundred and fifty people."

One who has recently completed his preparation for the ministry, and to whom the new Territory of Kanzas offered a promising field of labor, writes as follows : — " As I am going on a mission of peace and good-will with a company of emigrants, I will tender to you my services as a colporteur in Kanzas. Much good may be done there by the circulation of books of the right kind. They both prepare the way for the preacher, and supply in a measure his place. But give us books of the right stamp. Give a literature freighted with the spirit and life of the Saviour, that shall probe deeply the sores of sin, and that shall present to us a living, present Jesus to heal and to save, not a philosopher to palliate and beguile, and I will do what I can to circulate it, so that life and freedom may be given to Kanzas. Our colony is made up of a mixed multitude from all the sects of Christian believers. They are intelligent, though not many are much acquainted with books, but all are inquisitive. I go as their minister. We shall need hymn-books, prayer-books, and Sunday-school books. You will see at once what we need, and your judgment will be a better guide than my direction." It afforded us pleasure to send a box of books, and we shall be glad to hear of the success of the enterprising and devoted missionary.

The Rev. J. R. McFarland, a native of Virginia, a graduate of the Cambridge Divinity School, who is acceptably known to many in Boston, where he preached for several months, has gone to Peoria, Illinois, to establish a Society in that growing place. In a letter, he says : — "Having chosen my field with deliberation, my mind is at ease. I shall enter upon it cheerfully and with confidence ; for with such a cause, when did ever faithful, patient, prayerful, and persistent devotion fail of success ? To me it is clearly and simply a question of faith and patience. I shall not be trammelled by precedents or antecedents. I shall have a fair chance. In a subjective point of view, the inducements that this field present are still greater. I covet the discipline of working there in my Master's cause, and with my Saviour's words to encourage me ; though I remember that it is not of him that willeth nor of him that runneth, but of God that giveth the increase." The sympathies and best wishes of many hearts accompany our brother to his new sphere ; while we feel assured that the spirit with which he undertakes his ministry is a hopeful augury of success.

The extracts from letters above given are of a hopeful and encouraging nature. Such is the spirit of most of the letters we receive. Occasionally we are addressed in other words, as will be seen by the following extract, which we select in order that our readers may see both sides of the case. A book-distributor in one of the Middle States writes : — "The Unitarians are here classed with unbelievers, and are generally alluded to in the pulpit as infidels and atheists. Among the Quakers it is different, but by some of the other sects I experience far from civil treatment or common courtesy. They tell me, and especially the Old School Presbyterians, that they cannot consent that their families should read Channing, although he was a good sort of man in his way, and a very moral character. You have little conception how great here is the want of that liberality of religious views which prevails so much in New

England. If you have any amount of funds placed at your
disposal for the conversion of the heathen, I think you cannot do better than to send a missionary here. Ignorance
and superstition abound, and want and vice go hand in
hand."

As an offset to the above, we may quote a few words
from another letter, received from one whose mind has been
quickened and blessed by the distribution of our books : —
" I have read every word of those publications, some parts
of them a second time. On my knees have I thanked God
for them. I express all the gratitude of a thousand ac-
knowledgments in the simple sentence, I thank you."

NOTICES OF BOOKS.

Life and Character of REV. SYLVESTER JUDD. Boston : Crosby,
Nichols, & Co. 1854.

WE never understood Mr. Judd during his lifetime. And yet
it was our privilege to meet him, in many well-remembered interviews, at his own church, and in his own house. Still it was
only one aspect of his nature that we saw, the rounded and full-
orbed view of which a vein of eccentricity and apparently of ped-
antry concealed from us, though it is now presented in this deeply
interesting biography. We thank the writer for it. Led on by
her admiration and love for her subject, she has done her work
uncommonly well. Abstaining from words of eulogy, she has
brought out Sylvester Judd himself, in the simplicity of his life,
in the freshness and richness of his genius, and in the sincerity
and fervor of his piety ; and he lives before our eyes, and takes
possession of our heart as we read these charmed pages. In
common with all who met him, we had regarded him as a man of
mark and power ; but the reader who surveys the totality of his life

and writings will see unmistakable signs of greatness, which would have placed him in the first rank of eminence had his life been prolonged. The sketch given of the *White Hills, an American Tragedy*, proves that he had rare genius in a department of composition with us seldom entered. But it is the religious aspects of this biography with which we are now chiefly concerned. No young man can carefully read it without receiving the best instruction. How many gifted minds may at this moment be passing through that same fearful trial of a revolt against a Calvinistic Christianity! What a help to them may be the revelations of this book! What a service both to the peace of their minds, and to the uncorrupted beauty and glory of our Redeemer's truth, to give this biography a wide circulation through the land!

Ida May; a Story of Things Actual and Possible. By MARY LANGDON. Boston: Phillips, Sampson, & Co. 1854.

THIS book comes out just as we go to press, and the eagerness with which the first copies are called for gives promise of an almost unprecedented sale. Through the politeness of the enterprising publishers we had a copy before the work was sold; and to the deep interest awakened by the book itself was added the pleasure of thinking of the thousand home-circles in which it will help beguile the hours of the winter's night. Comparisons will naturally be made between this work and that of Mrs. Stowe. But with the exception of the aim with which both were written, and of the fact that both picture "life among the lowly," they have nothing in common. Ida May is no imitation. Its course of events, description of character, and management of dialogue, are so fresh and original, that we should not be surprised to learn that the conception was formed before "Uncle Tom" was given to the world. Nothing in that world-renowned story surpasses some scenes in Ida May. If the latter has less variety of incident, less genius in the delineation and portraiture of original characters, and less power to fill the reader's imagination with horrible pictures, we are not sure that it would have been less effectual in the cause for which it was written had it enjoyed the advantage of priority.

The absence of all signs of partisanship, and the suppression of all personal feeling, are remarkable. But another thing helps it more. The race to which Ida May belongs brings her fate home to ourselves, to our own domestic circles, to our own children. Herein lies its power. In the artistic management of the story, perhaps it was a mistake to have the origin and name of the beautiful child discovered so soon. It was almost impossible after that to prevent a decline in the interest of the tale. The work breathes a deeply religious spirit, and brings out in many beautiful and affecting expressions the devout hopes and trusts of those whose hard lot it depicts. Its perusal makes us thankful that another pen of commanding power is devoted to the formation of a just, earnest, and we hope omnipotent public opinion.

The Epistle of Paul to the Romans, with a Commentary and Revised Translation, and Introductory Essays, by ABIEL ABBOT LIVERMORE. Boston: Crosby, Nichols, & Co. 1854.

ANOTHER important service in the promotion of a popular comprehension of the Scriptures has Mr. Livermore here rendered. This book follows in the line of its predecessors. It does not propose to discuss the many different problems in metaphysics, philology, and theology, which the contents of this Epistle have started. The work is designed for popular use, as an aid in Sunday-school instruction, and in the domestic reading of the Scriptures. With excellent judgment and taste the author has adhered closely to this purpose, and has produced a book which will be welcomed by thousands of the " Liberal Christians in the United States " to whom it is dedicated. In two or three examples only, among many which we have examined, we find an interpretation given to a difficult passage different from that which we have been in the habit of expounding, and the current argument and sense of this Epistle, which readers oftentimes altogether fail to receive, we believe is here accurately and clearly unfolded. We have read the preliminary Essay, entitled "The Bible Inspired and Inspiring," with a renewed admiration of the wisdom and strength of its positions, and of the eloquence of many of its paragraphs. We think Mr. Livermore did wisely to retain, in the revised translation, so much of the phraseology of the Common Version. It is among our sincerest wishes, that his health and strength may be spared to enable him to extend his critical labors through the other Epistles of the New Testament.

———

An Offering of Sympathy to the Afflicted, especially to Bereaved Parents. By FRANCIS PARKMAN, D. D. A new Edition, with Additions. Boston and Cambridge : James Munroe & Co. 1854.

No work ever more perfectly answered its design, and many a sorrowing heart has here found comfort and hope. In a pastoral experience of years, which made us acquainted with many homes of affliction, we often gave this book to a bereaved family, and never without thanks for a direction to these tender and sympathizing words. Beside the brief Memoir of Dr. Parkman, from the pen of Dr. Farley, we have in this edition new articles from Messrs. Bellows, Dewey, Huntington, Hedge, Osgood, and others, which have added to the value of the book.

———

Sermons, by THOMAS T. STONE, *of Bolton.* Boston : Crosby, Nichols, & Co. 1854.

WE have here twenty-four original sermons, from one whose devout, spiritual style of preaching has been greatly admired in our churches. Several of them are occasional sermons, suggested by interesting dates in the author's ministry, or some instructive public event. Not often does a small rural congregation have the opportunity of listening, Sunday after Sunday, to sermons so earnest and fresh, and so carefully prepared and finished.

———

The City Side, or Passages from a Pastor's Portfolio. Boston : Phillips, Sampson, & Co. 1854.

THIS little book is written, as the Preface informs us, to counteract the common impression that the ministry has nothing but dreary spots and shady sides, and to show that it has oftentimes "its allurements and attractions." Some of the scenes described are taken from actual occurrences, which transpired under our observation. We do not know the authoress, who has told her story very fairly, though we think we have had quite enough of this sort of literature.

———

Mile-Stones in our Life-Journey. By SAMUEL OSGOOD. New York: Appleton & Co. 1854.

MR. OSGOOD has made a wide circle of thoughtful readers again indebted to his graceful pen. Not many authors are admitted to those sacred privacies where we gladly welcome him, — at the hearth-stone, and at the points of solemn commemoration in our life's pilgrimage. He writes with a gentle and tender spirit, as if he felt the privilege of this intimacy, and with a loving and thoughtful purpose would make our reflections subservient to holy ends. We hardly know the other books which so well illustrate the union of brotherly counsel, pastoral affection, and graceful scholarship. "Sermons in *stones* " he helps us to find ; and to all young friends asking bread, we shall give it in giving stones, if they be Hearth-stones or Mile-stones.

———

A Parisian Pastor's Glance at America. By REV. J. H. GRAND PIERRE, D.D. Boston : Gould & Lincoln. 1854.

WE frequently met the author during his visit to the United States, and were agreeably impressed with his quiet and dignified manners. On his return to Paris, he gave an account of religion and religious institutions in America, in a series of articles, in a paper of which he was the editor ; and these now form this book. They seem to be in the main very fair and appreciative in their statements, though it is evident their author had been misinformed as to the former condition of Unitarianism in this country.

———

Kanzas and Nebraska. With an Account of the Emigrant Aid Companies, and Directions to Emigrants. By EDWARD E. HALE. Boston: Phillips, Sampson, & Co. 1854.

IT is no small service to a good cause to supply, at a few weeks' notice, a valuable book, which exactly meets a pressing exigency; and it is a proof of no small courage, industry, and command of resources, to be able to render that service with promptitude and ability. Great credit is due, on both accounts, to the author of this book, who has done much to give imm ate impetus to a noble cause of philanthropy.

———

Martin Merrivale. His ╋ Mark. BY PAUL CREYTON. Boston: Phillips, Sampson, & Co. 1854.

THE reader of this title must not pass the book by, supposing that it is one of the flashy works of the day. Purporting to trace the career of two young men who came to Boston, in the lowest condition of poverty, to try their fortune, one in mercantile pursuits, the other as an author, it contains a great deal of effective satire upon the manners, thoughts, and customs of the day, and resembles the works of Dickens more than any other book written among us, in its minute observation of ordinary life. A pure, healthy moral tone pervades these pages, and the story is managed with the ease and interest of a practised hand. It is an illustrated work, got up in the good style of its publishers.

———

Hymn-Book for Christian Worship. Boston: Crosby, Nichols, & Co. 1854.

THIS new collection of seven hundred and sixty-one hymns appears without preface or name of author; but it is generally understood, we believe, that it was prepared by the pastor of the Second Church in Boston, for the use of his Society. All who know him will expect a work of good taste and judgment, nor will an examination of this book disappoint them. The continued multiplication of hymn-books proves, we suppose, that no one yet meets the wants of all; but the sure repetition in each of about two hundred hymns, which are universal favorites, and are almost always read and sung on every Sabbath in our churches, proves also that either of our hymn-books may reasonably satisfy any congregation. For this reason we think the difference between their merits is much less than what is generally supposed; and as to the adaptation of a hymn to a particular subject of discourse, we esteem this point of little comparative importance. A hymn breathing a spirit of devotion is appropriate to all subjects suited for pulpit discourse, and will do more to promote the end of public worship than any ethical rhymes. We believe that this is the view which is generally taken of this matter; and that, with a great variety of *books*, the devotions in our churches are aided by a remarkable uniformity in the use of *hymns*. Still, it may be well that scope be given to preferences in the matter of arrangement and various readings, and we welcome this last contribution to the songs of the sanctuary. We regard it as among the best in use, and there will be pastors and churches that will give it the preference.

———

A Liturgy for the Use of a Christian Church. Boston: Crosby, Nichols, & Co. 1854.

THIS is prepared by the same skilful hand that gathered the hymns in the book above noticed. It is the fifth book of the kind used in our churches, beside the King's Chapel Liturgy, which they all more or less resemble. The desire for a liturgical service is evidently increasing, though it is not likely such a service will ever be universal in our body. The Liturgy now under notice has the two great merits of retaining much of the venerable phraseology of the Books of Prayer in the great elder churches of Christendom, and of providing for alternate reading of the Psalms by the pastor and people.

———

Books for Young Reader.

PARENTS, teachers, and friends of the young have much reason to be grateful to Messrs. Crosby, Nichols, & Co., for the industry and enterprise they show in publishing books for the instruction and amusement of youthful readers. Not confining themselves to American publications, they look over the field of foreign works, and procure translations of the best French and German tales. Two works of this kind have just come from their house. They are, *Popular Tales, by Madame Guizot, translated from the*

French; and *Children's Trials, translated from the German.* They are both illustrated works, and are published in an ornamented and beautiful style. If not equal to American works of the same class, they have the interest which always belongs to foreign customs, manners, and modes of thought, and they inculcate good lessons, and breathe a pure spirit.

⁎⁎⁎ So many books are published merely for the amusement of the young, that we may notice a mode of entertaining them in which a little book has called to its aid the sister arts of design and painting. We refer to the divertisement lately published by Messrs. Crosby, Nichols, & Co., entitled *Fanny Gray, a History of her Life.* A pretty story in rhyme is illustrated by six graceful figures, which the little hands of children delight to put together and to take apart. Nothing can exceed their exquisite finish. Already it has become a great favorite with the young, who love to read, and place visibly before them, the varying fortunes of "lovely Fanny Gray."

RECORD OF EVENTS AND GENERAL INTELLIGENCE.

SEPTEMBER 6, 1854. — Mr. Tyler C. Moulton was ordained pastor of the Unitarian Society in Austinburg, Ohio. Sermon by Rev. Dr. Hosmer, of Buffalo, N. Y.

SEPTEMBER 20. — Mr. Nahor A. Staples was ordained pastor of the First Congregational Church and Society in Lexington, Mass. Sermon by Rev. F. D. Huntington, of Boston.

SEPTEMBER 26. — A conference of Unitarian Christians in Connecticut was held in Bridgeport, and interesting services were conducted in the Unitarian church in that place.

SEPTEMBER 26. — The annual meeting of the Maine Association of Unitarian Churches was held in Augusta, in that State. The reports from standing committees were read, which led to interesting discussions.

SEPTEMBER 27. — Rev. Edmund Squires, formerly of England, was installed pastor of the Unitarian Church in Hallowell, Me. Sermon by Rev. F. D. Huntington, of Boston.

SEPTEMBER 27. — Rev. Frederic Newell was installed pastor of the First Congregational Society in Littleton, Mass. Sermon by Rev. James F. Clarke, of Boston.

OCTOBER 4. — Mr. Charles Henry Wheeler was ordained pastor of the Unitarian Church and Society in Danvers, Mass. Sermon by Rev. Dr. Peabody, of Boston.

OCTOBER 4. — A convention of the teachers and friends of Unitarian Sunday Schools was held in Worcester, Mass., w en a report was made upon the subject of a new organization of a Sunday-School Society, which it was resolved to form, and of which the following persons were elected officers, to wit : — Hon. Albert Fearing, *President;* Rev. W. G. Eliot, D. D., Rev. E. B. Hall, D. D., *Vice-Presidents;* George Merrill, Esq., *Treasurer;* Rev. F. T. Gray, *Secretary;* Hon. Samuel Hoar, Rev. A. Hill, D. D., Rev. F. D. Huntington, Thomas Gaffield, Esq., and Rev. Calvin Lincoln, with the above-named officers, *Directors.*

OCTOBER 10, 11, 12. — The Autumnal Convention of Unitarians was held in Montreal, Canada.

OCTOBER 18. — Mr. Richard Metcalf was ordained pastor of the Unitarian Church in Bath, Me. Sermon by Rev. Dr. Hall, of Providence.

OCTOBER 25. — Rev. J. G. Forman was installed pastor of the First Congregational Church and Parish in Sandwich. Sermon by Rev. F. D. Huntington, of Boston.

NOVEMBER 1. — The semiannual meeting of the Middlesex Association of Sunday-School Teachers was held in Cambridge. Sermon by Rev. Mr. Woodbury, of Lowell.

NOVEMBER 2. — The Unitarian church in Concord, N. H. was entirely destroyed by fire. The Rev. A. B. Muzzey, pastor of the Society, had lately been settled. Preparations had been made to hold evening services, and for this purpose gas had been introduced into the church. Some defect in the pipes led to the conflagration. The house was built in 1829, and was a convenient and attractive edifice. We sympathize with our friends in the loss of their church ; but do not doubt there will be ability and zeal to replace it in this enterprising and spirited Society.

NEW UNITARIAN PREACHERS. — The Unitarian clergy of England have lately received three important accessions to their number, in the persons of the Rev. John Panton Ham, Rev. William Forster, and Rev. John Barling, who are recent converts from the Orthodox Dissenters.

TELEGRAPH BETWEEN AMERICA AND EUROPE. — A right has been given to M. T. P. Shaffner, the American agent, to construct an electric telegraph from North America, over Greenland, Iceland, and the Faroe Islands, to Norway and Copenhagen. — *English Paper.*

THE POPE'S WAY OF ARRESTING THE CHOLERA. — The Cardinal Vicar of Rome has just published an edict, in which, attributing the cholera to the sins of the Romans, he directs that the finger of St. Peter, the arm of St. Roc, the heart of St. Charles, and other relics, shall be exposed to the adoration of the faithful, in order to avert the wrath of the Almighty. — *London Guardian, October* 4.

INFLUENCE OF UNITARIAN LITERATURE IN ENGLAND. — Rev. James Martineau made a speech not long since at the anniversary of the Warwickshire Unitarian Tract Society, in which he expressed the opinion that the operations of Unitarian Associations " should not be continued within the limits of former years," and that it would be well to publish works that would promote general relig_ious reading and inquiry. Our readers know that the importance of a like change in associated operations has been felt on this side of the Atlantic, and for the same reasons which Mr. Martineau proceeds to give. "If our societies," said he, "do not greatly increase in numbers, our literature has powerfully leavened the great mass of the population. He once heard a minister of powerful in_fluence say, 'I can't get great numbers to hear me, it is true; but I prevent a great number of ministers in the neighborhood from speaking a great deal of nonsense.' The fact is, Unitarians are a sort of theological police over the world."

UNITARIAN CATHEDRAL IN LONDON. — At a recent meeting of the London District Unitarian Association, the project of erecting a Unitarian Cathedral in London was considered; and a writer in a late number of the *London Inquirer* urges attention to the suggestion. He thinks it would give a fresh impetus to the denomination, if they placed conspicuously before the world a visible symbol of their faith. "Different minds are differently constitut_ed and differently impressed. The Unitarian Church should in externals adapt herself to each and all; and draw men to pure Christianity, not by their reason only, but by their whole being, — their hearts, their sympathies, and their affections." He thinks that by cordial co-operation it would not be difficult to raise the three hundred thousand dollars which will be required in order to commence the undertaking, and suggests that no Pagan nor Romanist architecture should be employed, the former reminding us of the Pantheon, the latter breaking out into the trefoils and trifoliations of a Trinitarian faith. It is easy enough to say of this whole plan, that this money "might be given to the poor." May it not be given to both? And in the answer once returned to this objection, is there not something implied which seems to justify the occasional resort to "very costly" means as a testimonial of affection?

OPENING OF ESSEX STREET CHAPEL, LONDON. — It is just

eighty years since the first avowedly Unitarian place of worship was opened. The event took place April 17, 1774, in presence of Dr. Priestley and Dr. Franklin.

———

CHANNING'S WORKS. — At the anniversary, last September, of the Southern Unitarian Society, at Poole, England, Rev. W. J. Odgers spoke upon the importance of using the press more vigorously and extensively for the promotion of Christian truth, and mentioned the present plans of the American Unitarian Association as " giving a most encouraging example." In the course of his remarks he illustrated the importance of book distribution by the following fact : — " A physician, on being recently asked if he had ever read Dr. Channing's Works, replied, ' O yes ! Dr. Channing's writings made me a Christian.' This gentleman had been brought up as a member of the Church of England ; but when, in maturer life, he was led to reflect upon the doctrines taught in the Church, and to perceive the inconsistencies presented by its creeds and articles, he felt that, if Church-of-Englandism were Christianity, he could not receive it. At length the perusal of Dr. Channing's writings presented to him the Christian faith in a form which was not opposed to the best dictates of his nature, and he was thus led thankfully to embrace it. There is a large number who can be saved from infidelity only by Unitarian Christianity."

———

ANECDOTE BY REV. WILLIAM JAY. — In the recently published Autobiography of Mr. Jay, among the reminiscences of distinguished contemporaries, he gives some anecdotes of John Ryland, the celebrated Baptist preacher ; one of which, for its charitable lesson, we quote : — " Mr. Ryland was intimate with Mr. Whitefield and Mr. Rowland Hill, and much attached to many other preachers less. systematically orthodox than himself, and labored, as opportunity offered, with them. He was, indeed, a lover of all good men ; and while many talked of candor, he exercised it. Though he was a firm Baptist, he was no friend to bigotry or exclusiveness. He warmly advocated the cause of mixed communion, and republished Bunyan's reasons for the practice, with the addition of some of his own. And this brings to my mind the fol-

lowing occurrence. I was one day to dine with him at a friend's
house ; the company was large : and while waiting for the dinner,
a minister asked him his opinion concerning strict communion, and
excluding pious men from the Lord's table. He replied thus :
' You decide the thing by calling it the Lord's table. Suppose,
sir, when I entered this room, I had taken upon me to say, " Mr.
Such-an-one [naming him], you shall not sit down at this table,
and Mrs. Such-an-one [naming her], you shall not sit down at this
table," what would Mr. D., the master of the house, say ! " You
are not the owner of this table, but the master is. The table is
mine, and I have a right to invite them, and I *have* invited them ;
and is it for you to forbid them ? " So in the Church ; the table is
the Lord's, and all who are called by his grace are his guests, and
he has bidden them ! ' "

From the *Bibliotheca Sacra* for last October we gather a few
items of intelligence, which may be of interest to some of our
readers. — In the public library of Geneva a work has been found
of much interest to Protestant Christians. It is a manuscript history of French Protestants in the various places to which they fled
for refuge. It was composed about a century ago, by Pastor An-
toine Court. He was an ardent friend of the Protestants during
the reign of Louis the Fifteenth, and died in 1781. After his
death his manuscript was lost sight of, and has only recently been
discovered, among other papers deposited at Geneva. — The sixth
volume of the Encyclopædia Britannica, just published in London,
contains, among other articles, a sketch of the life of Channing, by
Dr. W. L. Alexander. — Of the theological works lately published
in Europe, a very large proportion relate to ecclesiastical history.
There is a marked revival of interest in this branch of investigation. — There seems to be of late a considerable development of
literary activity in the various departments of theology among
the Catholics of France, as well as elsewhere in Europe. This
has become necessary, in order that Catholicism may maintain itself in some of its old homes. — We take the opportunity of this
reference to the *Bibliotheca Sacra* to express our sense of the
great ability with which this work is conducted. It is edited by

Professors Park and Taylor of Andover, assisted by ten or twelve of the ablest theologians in the country, with Drs. Davidson of England, and Alexander of Scotland, for foreign correspondents. The October number appears in new type and in a neat and attractive style. The prospectus states " that it will aim to meet the demands and to increase the power of the pulpit, by examining a wide range of topics, and furnishing illustrations of Christian truth from the various departments of science."

ENGAGEMENTS.

SUNDAY, September 17, 1854. Preached in Burlington, Vt., to the Society of which Rev. Joshua Young is pastor. This Society has for many years steadily and ably upheld the cause of a liberal faith, though it is the only representative of Unitarian views in that part of the State. It has been favored in its pastors. Rev. Dr. Ingersoll here had a ministry of many years, and Rev. O. W. B. Peabody was here taken by death in the midst of his work, and departed leaving many precious memories behind him. No parish has a more beautiful site for its church. It stands in the centre of a large square, and is embowered by trees, while around it are the streets and dwellings of one of the most beautiful towns of New England. It is furnished with clock, organ, vestry, parish library, and all the appurtenances of a prosperous church organization. The present pastor has been there but about two years, and is laying the foundations for a successful and useful ministry. The Society was addressed in the morning upon the need of co-operation in the promotion of what we agree in regarding as the true Gospel of our Lord Jesus Christ, and a contribution was taken up, the amount of which will be found stated in its proper place.

Sunday, September 24, 1854. Preached in Medfield, Mass. Rev. Rushton D. Burr is the pastor of the Unitarian Society in that town. His parish is composed of an agricultural people, who live a little one side of the great lines of travel; and their town

19 *

has not been visited with the increase of numbers and enlargement of business which have marked other places. The Society, however, is not only willing to give a cheerful support to its own religious institutions, but is disposed to do something to extend these blessings to others. Mr. Burr, to other means of usefulness, has added attempts to promote the circulation of books.

October 8, 1854. Preached in Scituate, to the Society over which Rev. Fiske Barrett is settled as pastor. Every mariner sailing out of Boston remembers the church which forms so prominent an object on the South Shore. As its color has recently been changed from white to slate, it does not so quickly as before strike the eye, — a fact of which seamen have made complaint. This outward change is not the only one which the church has lately undergone. During the last season it has been repainted inside, frescoed, newly carpeted, supplied with organ and clock, and there are few rural churches which have a more attractive appearance. At the invitation of the pastor, the Society was addressed upon the position in the religious world occupied by our denomination, and the duties which that position involves. Many years have passed since this Society has given any aid to the Association. Perhaps there has been some prevalent misunderstanding as to the measures, aims, and spirit which the Association seeks to cherish. Time may fully correct this. If the Association undertakes a Christian work, which can be accomplished in no other way so well as by the co-operation of our churches, — if it seeks to prosecute that work in the spirit which the Gospel of Jesus Christ enjoins, and actually accomplishes some desirable results according to wise plans and in an earnest and hopeful faith, — it will not believe that any Society, when all this is well understood, will withhold its sympathy and aid. It was pleasant to see the signs of prosperity among our friends in Scituate, and confidence is felt that it will co-operate with other churches of our faith in doing something to send forth the blessings of truth, freedom, and peace.

October 15, 1854. Preached to the newly formed Society in Lancaster, N. H. Rev. George M. Rice is at present the officiating pastor. Unitarian worship has been sustained only for a few months. The Society meets in the County Court-House, which is centrally situated, and not ill situated for the uses of public worship. The day proved very rainy, and but a small portion of the Society was in attendance. An opportunity was had, however, to converse with several of them, and a zealous and determined band of believers they compose. It was a pleasure to see what a privilege and satisfaction they considered attendance upon Unitarian preaching, and what a noble spirit of self-sacrifice they manifested in order that it might be continued. Nestled amid the hills of Upper New Hampshire, and almost under the shadow of Mount Washington, in the simplicity and fervor of a true faith does this Society worship one God the Father. We commend them to the good wishes and friendly aid, if needed, of our friends in other places; and we hope especially that those of our clergy who, visiting the White Hills, may find it convenient to pass a Sunday in Lancaster, will make proof of Lancaster hospitality, and give Lancaster Unitarians an opportunity to hear the word of truth from their lips.

October 22, 1854. Preached to the Society in North Andover, of which Rev. Francis C. Williams is pastor. In the morning the history, position, and plans of the Association were the topics of discourse, and the intended visit of Rev. Mr. Ball, the newly appointed book-agent, was announced. His purpose is to call upon every family in the parish, to afford opportunity to all to obtain religious books from him, subscribe for the Quarterly Journal, and contribute towards the Book Fund. Visiting a parish immediately after a full statement of the objects of the Association from the pulpit, he goes, not as a stranger, but as an expected cooperator in a good cause; and his presence and conversation and explanations in the homes of our friends give assurance of a practical and earnest work. The Society in North Andover is one of our old and prosperous parishes. It worships in a neat and attractive church, and is highly respectable for numbers and character. The relations of Christian courtesy and respect which it sustains to other denominations, and which are manifested towards it by them, are worthy of a grateful notice.

October 29, 1854. Preached in Pepperell, to the Society of

which Rev. Charles Babbidge has been, for more than twenty years, the pastor. The Unitarians of this place have been called to bear burdens which would have crushed most parishes. Few in numbers, and not abounding in means, they have been strong in their union, their courage, and their attachment both to the cause to which they have been pledged, and to him who has upheld it as their spiritual guide. When the days of greater ability to assist in sustaining Christian enterprises shall come to this Society, in proportion to its means it will not be behind any in its generosity. Mention was made of the work of book-distribution in which the Association is now engaged, and the pastor, by his consent, was named as agent for promoting the circulation of the Journal.

November 19, 1854. Preached in West Cambridge. The young pastor of this Society, Rev. Samuel Abbot Smith, has a full church, and one of the most united and prosperous societies in the neighborhood of Boston. It was addressed in the morning upon the subject of fidelity to our Saviour, the object being to show what loyalty to his cause and obedience to his words require at our hands. Allusion was made to the present plans of the Association, and a contribution, towards which the pastor had on the previous Sunday bespoken the favor of the congregation, was taken up. On another page its amount will be found acknowledged, as also the generous gift of a parishioner to make himself and his pastor life-members of the Association.

The following are the Sundays in January, February, and March, for the annual collections in the Societies here named : —

January 14. Rev. Mr. Nichols's, Saco, Me.
" 21. Rev. Mr. Bradlee's, North Cambridge.
" 28. Sterling.
February 11. Rev. Dr. Newell's, Cambridge.
" 25. Rev. Mr. Saltmarsh's, Canton.
March 4. Rev. Mr. Hall's, Dorchester.
" 11. Rev. Mr. Pike's, "
" 19. Rev. Dr. Hall's, Providence, R. I.
" " Rev. Dr. Hedge's, "

ACKNOWLEDGMENTS.

In the months of September, October, and November the following sums have been received : —

Sept. 4.	Sale of books at office,	$ 11.43
" 12.	" " "	1.00
" 15.	" " "	22.70
" 17.	Contribution at Burlington, Vt.	51.63
" 21.	Sale of books at office,	2.45
" "	Friends in Lowell,	6.00
" 23.	Sale of books at office,	.77
" 24.	Contribution at Medfield,	19.78
" 25.	Sale of books at office,	2.00
" 28.	" " "	20.00
" "	A friend, by Rev. Dr. Newell,	10.00
" 30.	Sale of books at office,	28.07
Oct. 2.	Contribution in Mr. Hall's Society, Dorchester,	76.00
" 4.	Friends in Cambridge,	100.00
" 5.	Subscribers to Quarterly Journal,	5.00
" "	Sale of books at office,	1.50
" 7.	" " by J. R. Howard,	10.00
" 8.	Contribution in Scituate,	16.86
" "	" " Uxbridge,	13.00
" "	Subscriber to Quarterly Journal,	1.00
" 10.	Sale of books at Chicopee,	50.00
" 19.	Subscriber to Quarterly Journal,	1.00
" 20.	Subscribers " "	5.00
" 21.	Sale of books at office,	49.07
" "	" " Templeton,	9.73
" 24.	Subscribers to Quarterly Journal,	2.00
" "	Sale of books at Chicopee,	25.00
Nov. 1.	" " at Barnstable,	5.20
" 3.	From Eben Conant, Esq.	5.00
" 4.	Sale of books at Ware,	15.00
" "	Subscribers to Quarterly Journal,	2.00
" "	Sale of books at office,	29.49
" 6.	" " Medfield,	8.17
" 7.	From a friend, Miss L. E. P.	2.00
" "	" " Hon. I. W. Beard,	4.00
" 9.	Sale of books at Brookfield,	15.00
" "	" " at Lunenburg,	10.00
" "	From friends in Taunton,	240.00
" "	" " Church of Disciples, Boston,	50.00
" "	Sale of books at Waltham,	35.00
" 11.	" " "	65.00

Nov. 11. Quarterly Journal, ... $1.00
"   13. From a friend, W. H. D. . . . 30.00
"   " Sale of books at Calais, Me. . . . 7.00
"   14. "   "   at Portland, Me. . . 5.40
"   " Subscribers to Quarterly Journal, . . 2.00
"   " A friend in Waltham, ... 50.00
"   17. From J. R. Howard, sale of books, . . 15.00
"   20. " Contribution in West Cambridge, . 67.75
"   " " Subscribers to Quarterly Journal, Wal-
            tham, ... 25.75
"   " " Friends in Worcester, by Rev. E. E.
            Hale, ... 110.00
"   21. " Sale of books in Portland, Me. . 5.00
"   " " Subscribers to Quarterly Journal, . 2.00
"   " " Mr. James Brown, to make himself and
            Rev. Samuel Abbot Smith Life-Mem-
            bers 60.00
"   22. " Friends in West Roxbury, . . 30.00
"   " " Subscriber to Quarterly Journal, . 1.00
"   23. "   "   "   " . 1.00
"   " " Hon. David Joy, through Rev. R. Ellis,
            for Book Fund, ... 25.00
"   24. " Sale of books in East Bridgewater, . 8.30
"   25. " Subscribers to Quarterly Journal, . 8.25
"   " " Sale of books in East Cambridge, . 7.00
"   " " Subscribers to Quarterly Journal, . 2.00
"   27. " Contribution in Keene, N. H., a part of
            it the final payment by a lady in that
            town to make Rev. W. O. White a
            Life-Member of A. U. A. . . 56.25
Nov. 27. From sale of books in Springfield, . . 2.75
"   28. "   "   "   Charleston, S. C. . 10.00
"   29. " West Roxbury, in addition, . . 8.72
"   " " North Andover, ... 30.00
"   30. " Friends in Bridgewater, Book Fund, 100.00
"   " " Benjamin A. White, of Milledgeville,
            Ga., for Book Fund, . . 20.00

WESTERN DEPARTMENT.

[Under the editorial care of Rev. W. D. HALEY, of Alton, Illinois, to whom all communications for its pages are to be addressed.]

By request of our Western churches, a Western Department is permanently added to the Quarterly Journal. The importance of a faithful history of our cause in the West is much felt, and it is conceived that such a record can be made only by men whose lives are spent amongst the stirring elements of Western experience. We feel that the warm impressions of their daily contact with Western life will be beneficial to our Eastern churches ; and, on the other hand, that a frequent interchange of thought and experience, in the pages of the Journal, will benefit them, by causing an identity of purpose to be recognized in the toiling and self-sacrifice of both East and West. There are many items of intelligence, passages of missionary experience, and much valuable statistical information, which would not only be interesting, but valuable. Unitarianism has taken a start in the West, the results of which will only be limited by the labor bestowed upon it ; and we are sanguine enough to believe, that very few years will elapse, ere our liberal faith will make such conquests in the West as our Eastern churches can have no conception of. If this should prove to be a true prophecy, — or if it should not, — a published history of the early struggles of our first Western churches will be of great worth. At present the history of each church can be written without much labor, and with great accuracy ; in most cases the founders of the various churches, or their immediate successors, are the present pastors. We wish to make this Western Department the record of the origin and success of every one of our Western churches, and we hope all our Western ministers will feel willing to perform their share of the labor. In the present number, we furnish an outline of the history of our churches at Buffalo and St. Louis, — the extreme east and west bounds of our Western Conference. There is much in both narratives "to point a moral," but without stopping to consider this, we will only suggest our earnest desire, that each of the intermediate churches will furnish a record of their origin and progress as early as possible. May we venture to hope that Detroit, Louisville, and Keokuk will send in their cheering experiences by March next? Further than this we have only to say, by way of introduction, that we look to the ministers of the Western churches to make the pages of this Department rich, if not with sentiment, at least with facts. A short experience of Western life has convinced us that there is much to be told which needs narrating, and that the common experiences of Western ministerial life would be interesting to Eastern readers, and cheering to us of the West, as evincing the unity of our efforts and of our desires. Our Eastern brethren have their frequent exchanges and ministerial association meetings; separated only by townships, they can have frequent comparison of thought and experience. But here in the West whole States divide us, boundless prairies stretch between us, and mighty rivers begin and end their flow, ere we can greet each other: these pages, however, may afford us the same privileges, or at least a substitute for them, as those enjoyed in the East. Let this Western Department be our ministerial association, or rather, let it be a quarterly session of our Western Conference, full of that spirit which makes our annual gathering so refreshing and heaven-like.

HISTORY OF WESTERN UNITARIAN CHURCHES.

No. I.—ST. LOUIS, MO.

To Rev. W. D. Haley, *Alton, Ill.*:—

You ask me to give a brief statement of the past history and present condition of the church and congregation under my care. To make such a statement interesting, it would be necessary to go into details inconsistent with brevity. But as brevity is the first condition imposed, I must confine myself to a few general facts, which may serve to give a tolerably good idea of our present standing.

We are now just at the close of twenty years since our first meeting, which was held in a small school-room, November 29th, 1834. After two or three months' trial, we organized a Society, in which seventeen persons enrolled their names. Of this number there are now but five continuing with us. The smallest congregation on Sunday, to which the pastor has preached, numbered eight persons, upon a very pleasant day in March, 1835. Once, however, he declined preaching, as there was but one person present besides himself and the sexton, and that one was the gentleman with whom he lived.

Our first house of worship was built at an expense in all of seventeen thousand dollars, of which three thousand were received as a free gift from our sister churches in the Eastern States; a timely gift, without which we must have failed. It was dedicated in October, 1837. When we entered it, we were eleven thousand dollars in debt, of which one half was liquidated by the first sale of pews. In 1844 this first house of worship was enlarged to give room for the growth of the Society, at an expense of four thousand dollars. In 1847, we found ourselves encumbered by a per-

manent debt of nine thousand dollars, besides debts on open
account of nearly two thousand more. The payment of
interest on so large an amount was ruinous, and we determined to pay the principal. The interest fell due on the
1st of January, and the effort was begun early in November. By the 1st of December, the whole amount was
raised, chiefly by free gift, and on the 1st of January we
were completely out of debt. We regard this as the first
permanent establishment of the Society. Before that period
we were weak, but then became strong. Our advice to all
young societies would be, *Do not incur debt.* But if unavoidably incurred, as I think it was with us, let them seize
upon the first moment to pay it. Make the sacrifice, whatever it may be, and have done with it. No Society can
prosper with an interest account to be annually settled.

The effect upon us was very marked. Our growth became rapid, and in two years we began to talk of a new
church. By the end of four years, the talking began to
"take the name of action," and in December, 1851, our
new house of worship was dedicated. It had taken two
years in building, and the whole cost, inclusive of furniture,
was over ninety-nine thousand dollars, which was one third
more than we intended or were prepared to meet. We
were of course again largely in arrears, but no part of what
we owed had yet assumed the form of a permanent debt,
and we determined that it should not do so. On the 1st of
October, 1852, notice was given to the congregation that an
effort would be made to settle all demands, so as to go into
a new year unencumbered. This effort was successful, and
on the 29th of November, our Anniversary Sunday, we
were able to congratulate each other upon being free. We
may say, therefore, of our present building, that no debt
has ever rested upon it. It was, in fact, not quite finished

at the time of which we speak, and the day on which the
" building account" was first balanced was that on which
the full payment of all demands was arranged. It was
done at a great sacrifice on the part of fifteen or twenty
persons, but we believe that not one of them now regrets
it. There were instances in which individuals gave from
one twentieth to one tenth of all they were worth to accomplish the result.

A few statistics may here be added. Since the formation of the Society there have been *three hundred and sixty*
baptisms, of which *sixty* have been of adults. *Seventy
couples* have been married. *Three hundred and fifty-seven*
have been regularly admitted as members of the church.
Two hundred and sixty deaths have occurred in the congregation, or under its pastoral care. At present, about
two hundred and fifty families belong to the congregation,
and there are over two hundred active church-members.
Our church will hold, comfortably, twelve hundred persons,
or, if crowded, fifteen hundred, but is of course very seldom
full. The average attendance is about in the usual proportion. The Sunday School has two hundred and thirty
names, with an attendance of one hundred and fifty, under
the care of a superintendent who has not been absent, voluntarily, once in sixteen years, and of thirty teachers who
are very diligent in performance of their duties. At the
anniversary celebration last week two hundred children
were present. There is also an afternoon school for colored persons, to which about fifty scholars belong, and
which is taught partly by our members, and partly by those
of another church, — to one of whom its establishment is
due.

From time to time we have attempted to establish a Ministry at Large ; — at first under the Rev. Charles H. Dall,

and then of Rev. M. De Lange, and now, after several years' intermission, under the care of the Rev. C. G. Ward, who has lately entered upon the service, and we have reason to believe will accomplish a good work.

The Society has been from the first under the ministry of the same pastor; but in the year 1847, during his absence, the Rev. William O. White, now of Keene, N. H., filled his place with great acceptance, and for nearly two years, beginning in October, 1849, he was aided by the valuable and faithful services of an associate pastor, the Rev. Robert Hassall, now of Mendon, Mass. It should also be here mentioned, that in the year 1830 the Rev. Mr. Pierpont preached twice in the Market-House of this city to a large audience. The Rev. John Chapman followed him, in June, 1833, and preached three times in the hall of the National Hotel, then first used.

Yours truly,

W. G. E.

St. Louis, November 22, 1854.

No. II.

BUFFALO, N. Y.

In 1831, Rev. John Pierpont visited Niagara Falls, and while he was there, Mr. Noah P. Sprague, having consulted with a few friends, called upon him for counsel respecting the formation of a Unitarian Congregational Society in Buffalo. On his return to New England, having been unable to preach himself, he induced the Rev. Thomas R. Sullivan, of Keene, N. H., to go to Buffalo, and preach three Sabbaths. The services were held in the Court-House on Washington Street; and on the second Sunday a meeting was appointed for the organization of a Society, which took place on the 2d of December, 1831.

During the summer of 1832, Rev. Jonathan Whittaker preached two Sabbaths to the Society in Buffalo, and Rev. Alanson Brigham officiated once; the services being still held in the Court-House. On the 2d of November, in the same year, Rev. William Still Brown, from Bridgewater, England, commenced his labors as the regular minister of the Society. His first services were held in a hall occupied by the Universalist Society, on the corner of Pearl and Mohawk Streets; afterwards the Society worshipped in a room in the *fourth* story over No. 200 Main Street, until they removed to a room which they fitted up as a place of worship on Main Street in Ellicott Square; in this latter place they held their services until the church was built.

During the year 1833, steps were taken to erect a church edifice. In June of that year, the sum of $ 2,925 was subscribed toward the object; and in July a lot was purchased for the sum of $ 2,000, on the corner of Eagle and Franklin Streets, and a church was erected on it at a cost of $ 7,000, exclusive of the lot. The new church was dedicated in November, 1833, Rev. John Pierpont preaching the sermon. An organ was presented to the Society by Noah P. Sprague; it was used until 1836, when it was presented to the Unitarian Society in Meadville, Penn., and the fine instrument now in use was purchased, at an expense of $ 2,000. The sale of slips in November, 1833, only resulted in the disposal of fourteen, at the aggregate of $ 2,919, fifty-four pews remaining unsold. These were days of discouragement, and yet the friends of the Society were undismayed; they believed they were contending for the " faith once delivered to the saints," and they hoped. How well founded was that trust is best seen in the present

20 *

prosperous and highly encouraging condition of the Society.

The Society continued to prosper from the dedication of the church, so that in 1845 the church was enlarged at an expense of $ 2,000. Twenty slips were then added, and other improvements have since been made from time to time, until the present very comfortable place of worship has been secured. The building, although rather larger than true architectural taste would dictate, is otherwise very tasteful, and conveys the true Puritan idea of worship. The present pastor, Rev. G. W. Hosmer, D. D., was installed October 16, 1836. At the time he took charge of the interests of our liberal faith there, Buffalo was in the " Far West "; he left a united parish at Northfield, in the beautiful valley of the Connecticut River, to minister to a congregation usually numbering about one hundred and fifty persons. The results of his faithful pastorate, extending over eighteen years, are most gratifying. The present condition of the parish is prosperous in the highest degree ; the slips, of which there are ninety, are all taken ; the number of communicants is seventy-five, and of Sunday-school scholars one hundred. They have a Ladies' Benevolent Association, and meetings during the week for worship and study of the Bible. The Society has always been self-sustaining, except a loan of $ 1,000 for the erection of the church. During the last four years, the sum of $ 4,000 has been annually raised. The work upon which the energies of the Society are now mainly directed is the purchase of a parsonage. A very pleasant residence has been secured, and a large portion of the amount paid over. The effort is an important one, as it is securing an income of $ 400 per annum toward supporting worship in all time to come, and doing this in a way far preferable to any merely pecuniary endowment. The pastor gives a great deal of attention to the common schools, a work which is second to none in importance. Within the last three months he has visited thirty schools. We rejoice to hear that a very kindly feeling prevails between our brother and the other ministers in Buffalo; would that it were universally so in the West. In his communication detailing some facts connected with this sketch, he states that he meets the Universalist minister on the one hand, and the Orthodox on the other, and wishes he may become a sort of *unifier* of the two; we desire that he may, but we know of some instances in which the prevalence of Unitarianism has "unified" the most opposing elements into an ungenerous opposition to our efforts.

The Society at Buffalo is one of the strong buttresses of Unitarianism in the West. Ever ready in word and deed to advance our divine religion, ready to sympathize as its early struggles have prepared it to sympathize, it is actively, by its generosity, and passively, by its triumph over difficulties, encouraging weaker bands to emulate its career. In its fellowship is more than one precious example of the devoted, *Christian* Unitarian layman; whose names almost slip from us while we write, and are only withheld because we know they

> " Love to do good by stealth,
> And blush to find it fame."

May our common faith still cheer and encourage both pastor and people, and the influences they are sending forth return with benediction upon their own heads.

ITEMS OF LIBERAL CHRISTIANITY IN OHIO, AND THEREABOUTS.

FIRST Congregational Church in *Cincinnati*, A. A. Livermore, Pastor. Families, 130; church-members about 50; Sunday School, 96 pupils, and 12 teachers; congregation from 250 to 350. Cause slowly advancing, and hope of erecting a new church when the pressure of the present hard times is past.

Antioch College, established by the Christian Connection, and aided by the Unitarians, has the second year about 400 pupils, male and female, and 14 professors and teachers. The President, Hon. Horace Mann, writes, " We are having the best term we ever had, for diligence, order, and examplariness of conduct."

This institution is, however, much embarrassed for want of funds to discharge its debts and complete its buildings. Both the Catholics and Methodists stand ready to buy the buildings, it is said, and they may even hope that, like ripe fruit, it is just ready to drop into their hands; but we earnestly hope and believe that every liberal Christian will do his part to prevent this noble enterprise from coming to any such disastrous end.

Just now another cloud rises in the horizon of Antioch College. Besides the misfortune of the hard times to embarrass its finances, there is added the question of slavery. A Christian Elder, writing from Graham, N. C., says : " The action of our Convention (the Christian Convention in Cincinnati, in October) on this question has deprived Antioch College of several thousand dollars; as the South had done nothing, and several wealthy men were waiting to see the result of the General Convention in Cincinnati. One of them told me the other day that he had one thousand dollars in bank, which he intended to give to the College, and send the money by me when I returned. Two others had done the same. Now they refuse to give one cent, and say, ' Every man to his tent, O Israel! ' " If then the Southern brethren give less for the cause of Liberty, we hope the Northern ones will give more.

At *Columbus, Ohio*, Unitarian services were held on October 22, and fifty or sixty were gathered together. There are several families there very much interested in our views. It is hoped that the Rev. W. H. Knapp, now Steward of Antioch College, formerly Unitarian minister at Nantucket, Massachusetts, and afterwards at Newton, may be able to officiate at Columbus during the present winter. One hundred and fifty dollars in these hard times have been raised for preaching, and an equal sum, it is hoped, may be secured from the Western Unitarian Conference, or the American Unitarian Association. In time a good Society can be formed in this flourishing capital of the State, if all parties do their duty.

At *Cleveland*, Rev. A. D. Mayo, formerly of Gloucester, Massachusetts, is officiating to a liberal society, lately organized, who assemble in a new and beautiful hall, belonging to our friend, H. M. Chapin, Esq. Salary for one year's engagement, one thousand dollars. The prospects of success are encouraging.

At *Austinburg, Ohio*, Rev. Tyler C. Moulton is ordained as pastor, and the cause of Liberal Christianity is hopeful and progressive.

At *Berlin Heights*, and *Berlinville*, *Ohio*, Rev. H. D. Andrews, formerly of Meadville, and also of Lane Seminary, has preached to small audiences of liberally disposed hearers. He continues his services at the latter place, and has organized a Sunday School, Temperance Society, Prayer Meeting, and proposes to establish a Parish Library, — a measure of great value and moment to many of our Western churches. No regular church or society has yet been organized.

Nahum Ward, Esq., of Marietta, has given one thousand dollars to Antioch College, and Charles Stetson, of Cincinnati,. has given five hundred dollars to the same institution. Both gentlemen have been chosen members of the board of Trustee , which consists of thirty-four in all.

Individual Unitarians are also to be found in many other towns and cities of Ohio, besides the above; viz. Lancaster, Marietta, Dayton, Blanchester, Yellow Springs, South Charlestown, New Vienna, Springfield, Glendale, Springdale, Toledo, Sandusky, Jefferson, and Avon.

During the last six months, the following books and tracts have been distributed and sold from the Book Depository of the Western Conference in Cincinnati, Messrs. Truman & Spofford, Main Street, between Third and Fourth Streets, and by the pastor of the church.

150 Unitarian Views, Judge Pirtle's and Rev. Mr. Fuller's Reports.

100 Hall's Dedication Sermon at Meadville.

100 Minutes of Conference at Louisville in May last.

100 Quarterly Journals of A. U. A. for July.

13 Bible News.

12 Meadville Circular, to induce young men to enter the Christian Ministry.

68 Eliot's Discourses.

50 Miles's Gospel Narratives, a gift to the Conference by Rev. B. Parsons, of New York, and distributed among the elders of the General Christian Convention at Cincinnati, in October.

35 copies of Keene edition of Priestley's Corruptions of Christianity.

Also several copies of Channing's Works and Memoirs, Livermore's Discourses, and Commentary on Romans, Sears's Regeneration, Clarke on Prayer, Christian Views, Sunday-School Manuals, Offering of Sympathy, Religious Consolation, Livermore's Commentary, 3 vols., and Lectures to Young Men, Marriage Offering.

13 volumes to the Library of Antioch College.

At *New Albany, Indiana*, Unitarian services have been held three Sabbaths, this fall, by Messrs. Heywood and Livermore. About fifty men were present in the Court-House, attentive to hear and eager to read our tracts. A Jewish Rabbi, who speaks eleven languages, and is now a convert to the Baptist Church, but who believes in the Sonship of Christ, and disclaims the Trinity, was present on more than one occasion. He says, what we have always believed, that Unitarians could make more converts to the Gospel from the Jews, and we may add from the Mahometans too, than all the other bodies of the Christian world, because we hold the simple Unity of God. Does not this view suggest an important duty, especially when taken in connection with the late communications of Rev. C. T. Brooks, touching our missions at Madras and Calcutta in the East Indies?

The Quadrennial Christian Convention met in Cincinnati, October 7 – 11. About fifty Christian Elders, and many laymen, were present. Rev. Dr. Stebbins of Meadville, Pa., President. The meetings were highly interesting, and were promotive of the great common cause of Liberal Christianity through the whole country.

A. A. L.

THE

QUARTERLY JOURNAL.

VOL. II.   BOSTON, APRIL 1, 1855.   No. 3.

TRACTS OF THE ASSOCIATION.

THE American Unitarian Association have lately stereotyped those tracts of their series which were out of print. Of the three hundred tracts published between the years 1825 and 1853, nearly one hundred were stereotyped when first issued, or soon after. Of about one hundred others, the Association have copies in their depository. The remaining one hundred have been out of print, thus depriving us of the use of some of the best tracts that have been published, and preventing our answering calls, not unfrequently made, to supply the entire series.

The stereotyping of these is now completed; and though it has been attended by an expense of nearly two thousand dollars, it was felt that in no other way could a part of the Book Fund be more judiciously expended. We have no literature more able and popular, more replete with sound learning, and more deeply penetrated with an earnest religious spirit, than that furnished by these tracts. The seal of the confidence and approbation of our friends has been

stamped upon them.   They are, for the most part, as fresh
and effective to-day as they were when first published.
We have no works more often called for.   The singular
variety of topics they discuss enables them to meet all
points of the great theological controversy, and adapts them
to all stages of inquiry and progress.   Had they not been
written, we could do nothing better than to employ, if
possible, their authors in furnishing this identical matter.
A list of the names of the writers of these tracts is the
best guaranty of their excellence, and that is a favored
series of works to which Henry Ware, Jr., Orville Dewey,
William Ellery Channing, James Walker, Convers Francis,
Samuel Barrett, Alvan Lamson, Noah Worcester, F. W.
P. Greenword, Alexander Young, N. L. Frothingham, John
G. Palfrey, Samuel Gilman, William H. Furness, George
R. Noyes, Ezra S. Gannett, W. B. O. Peabody, and many
others of like eminence, have contributed.   It is sometimes
said, We cannot understand what Unitarianism is.   We
may direct all such persons to this series.   Though it is
the work of eighty writers, it is the best treatise *De Unitate
Fidei* we possess ; and we think that no one who reads it,
observing the old Catholic rule, *Quod semper et ubique et
ab omnibus creditum est,* would fail to gather from it a
clear and consistent statement of our belief.

We take this opportunity to give notice that the Association is now ready to furnish complete series of these tracts,
in twenty-six handsomely bound volumes.   They are sold
at cost, and will make an ornamental and most useful addition to the library of any clergyman or public institution.

We have also bound up these tracts in volumes according to subjects.   The stereotyping of tracts out of print has
enabled us to recommence the plan, and include many before omitted.   We have made the following volumes : —

1. *The Unitarian Faith Established*, including tracts by Dr. Henry Ware, Jr., Dr. Barrett, President Walker of Harvard College, Dr. Dewey, Dr. Brazer, Dr. Gilman, Dr. Young, Rev. William Ware, Dr. Hall, Dr. Noyes, Dr. Channing, Dr. Lamson, Dr. Gannett, Dr. Burnap, Dr. E. Peabody, and others.

2. *The Trinitarian Faith Examined*, containing tracts by Dr. Noah Worcester, Dr. Lamson, Rev. George Ripley, Dr. Henry Ware, Jr., Dr. Noyes, Rev. James F. Clarke, Rev. S. G. Bulfinch, Rev. Bernard Whitman, Samuel Eddy, late Chief Justice of the Supreme Court in Rhode Island, Dr. Farley, Dr. Eliot, Rev. John Cordner, and others.

3. *The Doctrine of the Atonement*, containing tracts by Mrs. Barbauld, Dr. Francis, Dr. Carpenter, Rev. John Pierpont, Dr. Hall, Dr. Noyes, Dr. Gannett, Dr. E. Peabody, Dr. Thompson, Dr. Burnap, Rev. James F. Clarke, Rev. J. I. T. Coolidge, and others.

4. *The Saviour*, containing tracts by Dr. Greenwood, Dr. Barrett, Rev. Bernard Whitman, Dr. Lamson, Dr. A. P. Peabody, Rev. Mr. Simmons, Dr. Hedge, Dr. Dewey, Dr. Lunt, Rev. G. W. Briggs, and others.

5. *A Good Life*, containing tracts by Dr. Barrett, Rev. William Ware, Rev. Cazneau Palfrey, Rev. John Pierpont, Dr. H. Ware, Jr., Dr. A. P. Peabody, Dr. Greenwood, Rev. E. L. Sewall, Dr. Dewey, Dr. Hall, Dr. Lamson, and others.

6. *Aids in Reading the Bible*, containing tracts by Dr. Allen, Dr. Farley, Dr. H. Ware, Jr., Rev. A. A. Livermore, Dr. Noyes, Dr. Dewey, Rev. Samuel Osgood, Dr. Miles, and Dr. Eliot.

7. *Religious Culture*, containing tracts by Dr. Francis, Rev. Mr. Muzzey, Dr. Noyes, Dr. Worcester, Dr. Peabody, Dr. Putnam, Dr. Channing, Rev. C. W. Upham, Rev. F. T. Gray, Dr. Dewey, and others.

8. *Motives and Examples*, containing tracts by Dr. Channing, Rev. Sylvester Judd, Dr. Hill, Rev. George E. Ellis, Rev. Chandler Robbins, Dr. Frothingham, and others.

9. *Fresh Thoughts on Old Themes*, containing tracts by Dr. Dewey, Dr. Channing, Dr. Furness, Dr. Walker, Dr. Putnam, Dr. Peabody, and others.

The above volumes, neatly bound, will be furnished at cost.

A FEW THOUGHTS ON THE BOOK OF REVELATION.

A FRIEND asks us, in a letter lately received, to give some general views explanatory of this book, which has greatly perplexed him. We would remind our correspondent that he is far from being the only one who has been tried in this way. A large library would be collected, if all the Commentaries on the Apocalypse were brought together. And what a monument it would make of fruitless speculation and foolish conjecture! The Pope, Cromwell, Bonaparte, the Reformation, the French Revolution, the Second Advent of Christ, — all these have been found in these chapters. There has never been a religious opinion so absurd and monstrous, but what, if no other parts of Scripture yielded it support, it might be kept in countenance by some text found among these strange scenes and visions. Once, at the funeral of an old minister, it was said in his praise, in the lack, perhaps, of other things, that he never attempted to explain the Revelations. Would our correspondent cruelly cut us off from the chance of receiving a like eulogy ?

But is there no key to this book which the best scholars generally use to unlock its hidden meaning ? There certainly is such a key, and we will do our best to present it to our friend, if he will first attend to a few preliminary considerations.

It was a belief of the Jews, that every great transaction which took place in this lower world was first symbolically represented before the inhabitants of heaven. The Omnipotent Father, angels and archangels, cherubim and seraphim, saw the scenes of earth pass before their eyes ere those scenes were known among men ; and this dramatic representation of coming events, it was supposed, formed a chief part of the employment of the spiritual world.

They believed, further, that a glimpse of the signs and symbols used in heaven to foreshadow the events of earth was sometimes accorded to the vision of Prophet or Poet. In a state of trance, a time of highly wrought mental excitement, when the soul of the Prophet or Poet was absorbed and carried away in the contemplation of the coming events of Providence, it was supposed that his spirit for a little while left the body, was caught up into heaven, and had a momentary view of its prophetic scenes. We need not look upon this supposed fact as a violation of all the known and familiar experiences of life.   How easy to bring it within the sphere of what every good man has himself felt !   In moments of devout thought and spiritual fervor he feels confident that he knows something of the intentions and purposes of God.   No doubt this knowledge and confidence were stronger in the case of the inspired Prophets ; but their inspiration, we may conclude, was according to the same laws by which anticipations and convictions are revealed to us.

The greater difference between them and us lies in the manner of expressing these anticipations.   We think in *words*, because we are familiarly used to written and printed words.   But the Prophets of the Old Testament, of whom we now speak because the language of the Apocalypse is drawn from them, were not used to abstract words. The earlier method of expressing thoughts by *pictures* and *signs* was then better known.   Words were beginning to take the place of picture-writing, but had not yet superseded it.   Hieroglyphics still had a preponderating influ-

21 *

ence, and would naturally keep it longer in all matters connected with religion than anywhere else. The Prophets thought by pictures, and represented their ideas by pictures, and such pictures were then as certainly and readily understood as words are now. This single fact sheds a strong and most interesting light over all the prophetical writings of the Scriptures. We are carried back to a time long preceding alphabetic writing. The image of a man out of whose mouth came a two-edged sword, denoting commanding authority; the image of a man who held the stars in his hand, denoting a far-reaching power; the image of a book that no man could open, denoting the unknown decrees of God; the image of a child leading a lion, denoting ferocity subdued by gentleness; the image of a lamb in the midst of the throne, denoting that the tender compassion of the Son is an alliance with the omnipotence of the Father; — no one can doubt that these are translations into words of ancient hieroglyphic pictures.

We may illustrate the difference between our mode of expressing thought and that used by the Prophets, by an example drawn from modern history. Before our Revolutionary war, and while the Declaration of Independence was yet under discussion, it is well known that one of the patriots who took part in that high debate, expressed his strong confidence in their final success. The words of John Adams are familiar to all: " I see clearly through the events of this day. Our poor names may perish, but our cause will succeed. God will raise up for us friends; the Declaration will give us respectability in the eyes of the world, and the day on which we make it shall in after ages be celebrated by bonfires and illuminations, and the shouts of a great and free people."

If we suppose a Hebrew Prophet foreseeing the result

of our war of Independence in the same way that Adams foresaw it, only with a degree of certainty which raised the anticipation above a guess, how would He have expressed his prediction? Not by abstract words, but by hieroglyphical signs and symbols. Taking perhaps the animals on the national coats of arms to represent the two nations, we may imagine a Hebrew Prophet setting forth his prediction of our success by such pictures as these: "Then the Spirit caught me, and showed me in a vision of heaven what must shortly come to pass. I beheld, and lo! a lion, fierce and terrible. And he saw afar off the young eagle, to which he sprang for a prey. I looked again, and lo! the lion returned bleeding to its den, and the eagle soared in triumph. Then the hills clapped their hands, and all the trees of the wood rejoiced."

We will now apply these preliminary considerations to the case before us. In his banishment on the Isle of Patmos, the Apostle John, now in his old age, revolves in his mind the promises of Jesus that his kingdom shall triumph over all its enemies. He casts these promises into the language of the old Hebrew Prophets, and weaves the grand and majestic poem called the Revelation. Summoning the principal churches nearest him on the shores of the Mediterranean to hear his words, he represents himself as having a view, as through an open door, of the scenes then passing in heaven, which were symbolical of what was soon to take place upon the earth. "Behold a door was opened in heaven." And as we, using the Apostle's eyes, look through that door, what a multitude of strange images do we behold! Thrones, and elders, and beasts, and spirits, and harps, and vials, and horses, and horsemen, and burning mountains, and falling stars, and flying dragons, and pearly gates;—how can we find any plan and any meaning in these wild and confused scenes?

A little careful study will reduce this seeming chaos to some degree of order. We find the great drama of the Apocalypse divided into three acts. The destruction of Judaism, signified by the symbol of Jerusalem; the over-throw of Paganism, indicated by the symbol of Rome, here called Babylon; the general establishment of Christianity, symbolized by the descent of the New Jerusalem; — these are the three great events around which all the interest in this book is made to revolve, while subordinate symbols are chosen to shadow forth the prominent circumstances by which each of these events was attended.

We will cast a glance at each of these three acts. In plain and simple words, John might have said, " It is decreed in heaven, and the decree has been revealed to me, that after wars, and famine, and pestilence, and troubles from sedi-tious Jews and Roman armies, from which all true believ-ers in Christ shall be gathered out and saved, Judaism shall be overthrown." But the Apostle had been a Jew, and was writing to those who had been Jews, and both to him and to them the imagery of the old Hebrew Prophets had a charm, vivacity, and power exceeding all other words whatever. Accordingly, he proceeds to clothe the thought we have here stated in that diction. Through the open door, which gave him a view of heaven, he saw first of all the great throne, and the book of decrees which none but the Lamb could unseal; and there passed before his eyes the white horse of *war*, the red horse of *victory*, and the pale horse of *famine;* and when the number of those who are sealed is known, he saw swarms of locusts, represent-ing devouring armies, and flying horsemen, denoting the Roman cavalry, till at length Jerusalem is cast down, and the Temple of God is removed into heaven. This first act in this pictorial prophecy extends to the close of the eleventh chapter.

In setting forth the second great event above named, it would be agreeable to our mode of narration to say, "that the infant Church, while in great danger from being destroyed by Paganism, would yet be preserved until Paganism itself, though upheld by the power of Rome, should be overcome and subdued." But how has the Poet and Prophet John set forth these truths, from the twelfth to the twentieth chapters inclusive? Caught up in spirit again into heaven, he saw a great dragon ready to devour a new-born child. But Michael and his angels, rescuing the child, banished the dragon to earth, where it united itself to the beast that had the ten horns and ten crowns, i. e. the Roman government and its numerous provinces. But by a series of woes which came upon them, both the beast and the dragon were destroyed, and all heaven sang glory and praise to God.

The third event is the future triumph of Christianity. We all know what descriptions of that triumph our abstract words would furnish. But John, in the twenty-first chapter of the Apocalypse, sets the same thought forth under the image of a great and rich city, coming down from heaven to earth, with its gates of pearl, and streets of gold, and God its glory, and the Lamb its light, and the nations walking in its peace, and nothing entering that defileth, or worketh abomination, or maketh a lie. The whole picture is beautiful and animated, and the frequency with which its imagery has been used in all devotional poetry is a proof of the deep hold it has taken upon the imagination and sensibilities.

In the statements we have now given, our purpose has been to present a general view of the approved method of interpreting this book, without any pretence to critical exactness. We would recommend any one who wishes to

understand the Apocalypse, to read first the prophecies of
Ezekiel and Daniel. All the imagery of the Revelation
is taken from those earlier writings. The chief merit of
the Apostle John consisted in the skilful adaptation to his
purpose of materials already in his hand. He originated
but little, either in ideas or style. His predictions of the
coming fortunes of Christianity are only those beforehand
given by Christ, as recorded by Matthew and Luke ; and
these predictions the Apostle clothes, as we have already
said, in the drapery of the old Hebrew Prophets. Thus,
for example, all the essential features of the description of
the Son of Man, Revelation i. 13 – 16, are quoted from
the prophecies of Ezekiel and Daniel. We would particularly refer to this description as a more full illustration of
the remark before made, that the imagery of this book
carries us back to the earliest attempts at picture-writing.
Representing the seven leading churches of Asia as seven
golden candlesticks, and Christ in the midst of them, denoting his true position in the Church, the Apostle goes on to
say, that in the midst of the seven candlesticks he saw
"one like unto the Son of Man, clothed with a garment
down to the foot, girt about with a golden girdle ; his head
and his hairs were white like wool, as white as snow, and
his eyes were as a flame of fire, and his feet like unto fine
brass, as if they were burned in a furnace, and his voice as
the sound of many waters ; and he had in his right hand
seven stars, and out of his mouth went a sharp, two-edged
sword, and his countenance was as the sun shining in his
strength." No one can doubt that this is a description in
words of a hieroglyph, which represented a royal person-
age of great power and authority. The long garment and
golden girdle were worn by kings, the white hair was the
symbol of authority ; the eyes of flame denoted his piercing

knowledge; the brazen feet, his power to crush his foes; the voice as of many waters, his command heard above every other sound; the two-edged sword out of his mouth, his power to slay merely by a word; his countenance as the sun, his splendor and majesty. If we make a picture of a person as thus described, we have doubtless a hieroglyph which was well understood long before the invention of letters, before the Pharaohs and the Pyramids.

But the Apocalypse has an interest altogether above and beyond this. We cannot read its descriptions of the great multitude of people who were redeemed out of all nations, and kindred, and people, and tongues, the thousand and ten thousand and thousand times thousand, without seeing, at once that the Apostle John was no believer in a Calvinistic Deity, who dooms the larger portion of his children to terrible and hopeless woe. Amid all the conflicts between good and evil which it represents, there is ever a cheerful and hopeful tone pervading it, as if, though dark and dreadful woes should for a while visit the earth, yet truth and mercy would in the end be victorious, and multitudes that no man can number shall go to join in the song of praise to God and the Lamb.

There are other important doctrinal hints to be derived from this book. In that glimpse of heaven which the Apostle represents that he obtained, he saw God the Father on the throne, and by his side stood Jesus Christ. Of course, then, the Apostle did not believe that they were one and the same person. Our Trinitarian friends tell us, that, of all the Evangelists, John most certainly taught the supreme deity of Christ, affirming in the first chapter of his Gospel that Christ is the Almighty God himself. "The Word was with God, and the Word was God." As Unitarians we accept these words as true. We joyfully believe that the Word was Divine, dwelling with God, and a part of God himself, since Christ was filled with God's spirit without measure, and is to us a manifestation of the Father.   But if the words in John's Gospel are to be understood in the bald and literal sense sometimes given to them, if he intended to teach that Christ is the Almighty God, and there is no Almighty God but Christ, as has been said, how surprisingly strange it is that this same Evangelist John, writing many years later, and giving an account of what he saw in heaven, did not represent Christ as on the throne of the universe !   John saw him only at the right hand of the Father.   There is no Trinitarianism in the Apocalypse.   If John was a Trinitarian in his Gospel, he is a Unitarian in the Revelation.   The earlier book must be interpreted by the later.

But we will read this wonderful book for a higher than a doctrinal purpose.   We will pause over its varied and beautiful imagery, so as to make future glories seem realities ; and while we journey on towards the celestial city, we will pray that we may be prepared to sing the song of Moses and the Lamb.

RELIGIOUS CONDITION OF GENEVA.

DURING the last summer, Rev. J. J. Tayler, Principal of Manchester New College, London, spent a few months in Switzerland.   In a series of three letters, recently published in the London Christian Reformer, he gives an interesting account of the religious condition of that land. From his third letter, relating to Geneva, we propose to give our readers a long extract. We feel sure, however, that they will not regret its length. It is some time since the Unitarians of America have had any full and exact information in regard to the situation of their brethren in Geneva. The following statements, coming from one of the most honored Unitarian ministers of England, and as the result of his personal observations in Switzerland, will be read with great interest. The article has much valuable information on many points, and we thank the friend who kindly called our attention to it.

"I think that the situation of Geneva is unreasonably depreciated. Visiting it once more after an interval of thirty years, even from this grander end of the Lake, I thought the approach to it, under the brilliant light of a summer's evening, very striking. Yet I should hardly have recognized it again. Revolution had been busy everywhere. The old fortifications had almost entirely disappeared, and large piles of handsome building, to me quite new, lined the quay which borders the end of the Lake. I was fortunate enough, during my stay, to become the guest of a very amiable family, occupying a delightful *campagne*, or country-house, a short distance from the city, on the shores of the Lake, and in full view of Mont Blanc and the Savoy mountains; who exhibit an admirable specimen of the old Genevan society, combining cultivation and refinement with great simplicity of manners and an inexpensive, unostentatious mode of life. They regretted to me the gradual decline of the old Genevan manners, and the inroads of luxury and the love of display. I found two sentiments strongly predominant in the minds of these estimable people, whose views on subjects of religion and society were liberal and enlightened: dislike of the principles and means by which the extreme radicals had effected the late revolution, and a dread of the moral influence they might exert on the future character of Genevan citizens; and next, a deep conviction of the necessity of renewed religious earnestness and activity to meet these evils, and encounter on one hand the prevalence of a Voltairian unbelief, and

on the other the efforts of Catholic proselytism among the less instructed classes. Men of long-established influence and character,
wise and enlightened liberals, friends to progressive reform, had all
been displaced from the Council and the government, to make
room for parties whose chief recommendations to office were their
readier yielding to every blast of the popular will. My host and all
his old political associates were out of office, and expected ever
to remain so. I must do my friends the justice to say, that these
sentiments did not seem at all to proceed from disappointed ambition, as they cheerfully admitted the good intentions of the more
honest radicals then in power, successors of the more ambitious
and less scrupulous men who had inaugurated the revolution.
An old friend, whom I had known in England twenty-five years
before, a stanch and intelligent liberal, had become, I found, a
strong conservative in Genevan politics; not that his principles
had undergone any change, — they were essentially the same; but
he had to deal with very different men. He told me that, when
he left business and came to settle in his native town, Geneva was
the happiest and most prosperous community in the world. Industry and art were flourishing; the different classes of society
lived in harmony with one another; the public finances were well
administered, and the public instruction perhaps unrivalled in
Europe. But men are sometimes ruined by the restlessness
which uninterrupted prosperity engenders. An unprincipled and
ambitious man of ruined fortune and most profligate habits, aided
by revolutionary influences imported from without, working on
the envious and repining discontent of a certain portion of the
population, upset this state of things, and introduced a government of ultra-radicalism. All the institutions of the republic
were affected. Even the Academy did not escape. Men of an
European reputation for science and letters retired in disgust; and
persons of extreme principles, avowed Atheists, whose governing
maxim was, Let us eat and drink, for to-morrow we die, were
fetched from every part of Europe to fill their place. Such was
my friend's account; and he is one on whom I could rely; for his
inmost heart is liberal, and he measures his words before he
speaks. In one respect, the chief of the Genevan revolution is

less open to censure than M. Druey, at Lausanne. He has left uninfringed the principle of religious liberty, — has rather given it a greater breadth than it had before. His own interest and right principle coincided in this instance. He was glad to strengthen himself by the new suffrages of the Catholics. Geneva, by throwing down its ancient fortifications, seems, as it were, to have opened itself to the whole world, and to have lost its exclusively Protestant character. I saw several Catholic priests walking in full costume on the quays, and for the moment fancied myself in Belgium. In the city of Calvin, of the five members of the Council of State, three, I believe, are at this moment Catholics, and of these three one is President. But they are strongly opposed to the pretensions of the priests, and the religious liberties of Protestants are, I was assured, perfectly safe in their hands. Good comes out of evil, though it may be tinged with a little prejudice. There is nothing like antagonism for putting men's faculties in action and quickening progress. The dread of Catholicism has roused all the latent religious earnestness of Geneva. Lectures have been delivered to crowded audiences on the principles of the Reformation. The instruction of the young and of the humbler classes has been prosecuted with a new zeal. Invitations have been given, and opportunities afforded, to inquiring Catholics to make themselves acquainted with the Scriptures and the leading Protestant doctrines ; and the result has been — not in this, as in so many cases, to be ascribed to interested motives (for in Geneva, at the present time, there are as many worldly reasons against as for quitting the Catholic faith) — a continual accession of converts to the Protestant Church.

" Geneva has many points of resemblance to what I have heard and read of the city of Boston in the United States. There is the same union of religious earnestness with intellectual cultivation, of republican simplicity of manners with a marked predilectionfor historical traditions and distinguished names; the same prominence given to religious interests; the same respectful consideration and high social position of the clergy, — not from their wealth or worldly greatness, for their salaries, I believe, are moderate, but for their office and mental culture and intimate relation to the moral condition of society, connected as many of them are by intermarriage with some of the leading families of the republic. Geneva abounds with religious associations and religious agencies of every description, especially since the reaction to which I have referred. The ladies are particularly active in these good works of benevolence and piety. They have set on foot recently, in addition to the older institutions, Sunday Schools and Infant Schools for the religious instruction of the children of the humbler classes, and founded Reading Societies and Visiting Societies for the circulation of sound instruction and a wholesome literature. There is a system of religious agency of this description established in every parish in Geneva, in which the pastor takes a leading part, and is the natural head. I found the ladies, in the excellent family where I was a guest, deeply interested and working heartily in the promotion of these benevolent objects. The daughter of Professor Cellerier was the originator of many of them, and is regarded as the animating soul of this philanthropic movement. There is certainly much to encourage us everywhere in the religious aspect of the times, amidst much apparent discord and dissolution; a silent leavening of society, through the agency of all sects and churches, with the true spirit of Jesus Christ. An inestimable Italian family, with whom we are here residing *en pension*, tell me that institutions resembling our Ragged Schools have recently been set on foot in the kingdom of Sardinia, chiefly through the exertions of benevolent and devoted ladies of the educated class; and that the better portion of the Catholic clergy look on them with favor, and give them all encouragement. One of the most important of the Genevese societies is that for the assistance of Protestants dispersed in Catholic countries (Société Génevoise de Secours Religieux pour les Protestants Disséminés), closely allied in its general object with the ' Gustav-Adolph's Verein' in Germany. I have the ' Rapport' of this society for 1853, given me when I was in Geneva. This, with the ' Annuaire Religieux de la Ville de Genève pour 1854,' containing an account of all the religious services and institutions of the city, I will put into your hands on my return. A short analysis of their contents might interest the readers of the Christian Reformer.

"I arrived at Geneva at an interesting season, on the eve of one of the four annual celebrations of the Lord's Supper, when the young people of the several parishes, having completed their course of catechetical instruction (which is full and prolonged, and very properly much insisted on in this Church), are admitted to communion for the first time. You know, dear sir, what importance I have long attached to this pastoral work; how anxious I have been that we should introduce some regular system among ourselves; and with what satisfaction I found the same idea entertained and enforced by our excellent friend, Mr. Kenrick. I was truly glad, therefore, to have an opportunity of being present at this ceremony. I accompanied the friends with whom I was staying, at an early hour, to the church of St. Gervais. It is an antique-looking edifice, with huge projecting galleries, and possessing no architectural beauty whatever; but it is of large dimensions, and was crowded in every part. My friends assured me there could not be less than twenty-five hundred people in the church, of which at least a third were men. This last was an unusual circumstance, and considered a good omen, — a sign of reaction towards a more healthy state of public feeling. The gentlemen who accompanied me took me to an excellent place, just fronting the pulpit, in the benches appropriated to the magistracy of the city. I had of course no business to be there, but as these *messieurs*, my friend observed, were mostly *incrédules*, he was sure we should not be disturbed. Before the service commenced, I had time to look about me. Just over my head, on an adjoining pillar, was the following interesting inscription: 'Souvenirs du Jubilé de 1835 (the tercentenary of the Reformation). Les Citoyens de St. Gervais à leurs descendants de 1935.' But I was at length diverted from such observation and its accompanying reflections, by a voice from the pulpit. A young man with long bands, a theological student from the Academy, had opened the service (the usual practice here) with reading the Scripture lesson for the day. The ministers of the city preach in rotation at the different churches, a printed list of services being circulated among the parishioners at the close of every week. It so happened, that I had heard the sermon on

22 *

this occasion the preceding day in the cathedral of St. Pierre,
where there had been a preparation service on the Saturday afternoon. I was able, therefore, to follow it very well. It was
good, particularly in the earnest exhortation at the close; but
to my taste it was too rhetorical, and its delivery far too theat-
rical, and evidently studied. I was stupid enough to prefer the
quiet, simple earnestness of the good pastors of the ' Eglise
Libre ' at Montreux. However, it certainly produced effect,
for the people were very attentive. To the right of where I sat,
in a bench appropriated to them by an inscription on its back,
were three members of the ' Venerable Compagnie des Pasteurs,'
all of them young or middle-aged men, who were to take part
in the approaching ceremony. At the close of the sermon, these
gentlemen, with the officiating minister, took their station by
two long tables with the bread and wine, covered with a white
cloth, on each side of the pulpit, two ministers at each table.
Having first communicated themselves, they distributed the elements to the congregation, as it defiled successively in front of
the tables, one minister giving the bread and the other the cup,
each act accompanied by the appropriate words of Scripture.
In the other Genevan churches, the men communicate first and
the women afterwards; in St. Gervais, the two sexes partake of
the bread and the wine indiscriminately, as they happen to sit
in the church. This peculiarity arose from the following circumstance. During the frequent wars with Savoy which followed the establishment of the republic after the Reformation,
a female citizen of the parish of St. Gervais distinguished herself
by some acts of uncommon valor in a sudden attack on the city
by the Savoyards. When all was over, and the magistrates
wished to signalize her patriotism by some mark of distinction,
she asked, in preference to everything else, that the women of
her parish should henceforth be allowed to communicate at the
same time with the men. This good lady had evidently a pre-
vision of our modern associations for asserting the rights of women.
What I may call the material part of this ceremony was a little
too long and fatiguing; though, from its novelty, and the sight
of such a crowd, it interested and affected me. I prefer our more

frequent and quieter communion. I thought it an omission, too, that there was no particular recognition in any part of the service of those who then communicated for the first time. They were lost in the crowd, and communicated along with the rest. An opportunity of most solemn impression seemed to me thus lost, which, in any efforts of ours to build up a similar kind of service in our churches, I do trust we shall keep steadily in view. In this respect, the Lutheran confirmation, at which I remember to have once assisted many years ago at Göttingen, seems to me a more impressive and edifying ceremony than the ' grande communion ' of Geneva. In the afternoon, I attended worship at the Madelaine, the largest church in Geneva, and interesting as being the first in which the doctrines of the Reformation were preached. Owing to my distance from the pulpit, and the preacher's dropping of his voice at the close of his sentences, I caught very little of his discourse, which I much regret, as he is considered one of the best of the young preachers.

" In regard to preachers, I was rather unfortunate, the best and the most eminent, particularly MM. Munier and Martin, having discharged their parts in the services of this annual celebration during the previous week. I was particularly sorry not to hear the last-mentioned gentleman, and what I saw of him in society one evening increased my regret. He is a very interesting man, full of animation and originality in his discourse, of a truly catholic spirit in his theology, heartily rejoicing in the exemption of the Genevan Church from a dogmatic creed, and expressing his full conviction that the intercourse of Christians at the present day should be guided rather by the sympathies which unite, than the speculative points which divide, them. He inquired with some apparent interest after the state of Unitarianism in England. His history is remarkable. In his youth he served in the army of Napoleon, and fought at Waterloo. He has published, without his name, some interesting reminiscences of the scenes of his military life, in a charming little volume, entitled, ' Voyage d'un Ex-officier: Fragments d'une Correspondance Familière. Paris, Cherbuliez, 1850.' His preaching, I am told, is distinguished by its earnestness and simplicity, — its vivid apprehension of the realities of human life, — its profound conviction of the necessity of religious faith for the consolation and guidance of the human soul. When he entered the Academy to prepare himself for the ministry late in life, his first compositions, so one of the ancient professors told me, were distinguished by the same character of reality and earnestness. I have no doubt he owes this, in some measure, to his own living experiences. I have often thought some discipline of the same kind would be a capital termination to the academic studies of our own ministers, — I do not exactly mean by slaughtering men, but by some living contact with the positive realities of life, teaching them how to translate the ideal *abstract* of the college into the *concrete* of the world as it actually is. It is an excellent practice of the Academy of Geneva to send its young men, on the completion of their studies, before they enter on a regular pastoral charge, to act for some time as missionaries in connection with the ' Société de Secours Religieux,' of which I have already spoken.

" The Theological Faculty of the Academy of Geneva is the only institution of the city which the radical storm hitherto has not touched. There are five Professors, who divide the different branches of theological instruction between them. Of four only I have any knowledge : Dr. Chenevière, who is the Rector, and Professor of Dogmatic and Controversial Theology ; Professor Munier, who undertakes Hebrew and the Exegesis of the Old Testament ; Professor Châtel, whose department is Ecclesiastical History ; and Professor Cellerier, now retired from the functions of a teacher, who has the superintendence of the bursaries, and of the young men who study by aid of them, in connection with the Academy. M. Munier, to whom I brought a letter of introduction, was unfortunately in the country during my short stay. I caught a glimpse of him for a minute one day, as he was hastening with his carpet-bag to the steamboat. Dr. Chenevière received me with great kindness and courtesy. I brought him a letter and some books from a friend. He is a fine-looking man, past sixty, I should conjecture, with a spirited manner and dignified bearing. I am inclined to think that he has strong sympathies with what we call the older Unitarian school. I found from conversation, that he was a most determined anti-Calvinist, and I suspect is a somewhat sharp controversialist. He spoke with a kind of horror of the spirit of Calvin. 'He would burn you,' said he, 'if you did not think as he did. *Ce n'est pas aimable, cela.*' He did not seem to me to speak very encouragingly of the prospects of his theology at Geneva just now. 'Do your opinions make progress?' I asked. '*Pas beaucoup*,' was his reply. He very obligingly presented me on my departure with a copy of his essay, 'De la Prédestination et de quelques Dogmes Calvinistes combattus par la Raison, la Sentiment, et l'Ecriture.'

"M. Cellerier, the author of the 'Introduction to the Old Testament' translated by Dr. Wreford, and of the 'Sermons' published in Dr. Beard's Selection, is a venerable old man, now in infirm health, but of the most benignant aspect and manners, living with his amiable wife and daughter in a delightful *campagne* about a mile out of Geneva. He now only preaches occasionally. His eloquence, I am told, is distinguished by a sweet persuasiveness. Singularly enough, the parties who have chiefly urged him to publish sermons are the clergy of the Anglican Church and the Unitarians. He told me he was busy preparing a popular edition of his 'Introduction to the Scriptures.' I just now mentioned that M. Cellerier has the superintendence of the bursaries attached to the Academy of Geneva. It is a curious fact, that these bursaries are the proceeds of a foundation created by our own Queen Anne, and augmented, I believe, by William and Mary, for the education of French Protestant ministers, during the bitter persecutions which followed the revocation of the Edict of Nantes. This fund has been exposed to frequent and imminent perils during the revolutions of the last century, and there have been periods when its very existence was kept a profound secret. Happily, it has been preserved untouched to the present day. I regard it as a most fortunate circumstance — of auspicious omen to the future interests of a genuine Protestantism — that so many of the men who fill the Protestant pulpits of France, and often rise to positions of great social influence in such cities as Mar-

seilles, Lyons, Paris, and Frankfort, should have passed in their
early years through the liberalizing, enlightened, and truly spiritual discipline of the Academy of Geneva. Of the fifty or sixty
theological students who habitually resort to it, thirty or forty
come from the South of France, supported by bursaries (averag-
ing, I believe, about twenty-five pounds per annum) of English
origin ; and these students are distributed *en pension* among respectable families, where they are judiciously watched over, and
advised and counselled with paternal solicitude, by the benevolent
Cellerier. My friend, M. Châstel, assured me, that among the
ministers educated at Geneva, whatever might be their theological
tendencies in other respects, there was generally the strongest appreciation of the right and privilege of free Scriptural inquiry,
and the firmest determination to resist the imposition of a creed,
— a possibility, strange to say, not so utterly remote and out of
the question as it might once have seemed to be. The theological
course in the Academy of Geneva embraces four sessions, each, I
believe, of nine months, like our own. During this course, while
general scientific culture and theological learning are considered
indispensable, especial attention is paid to the cultivation of the
gifts of preaching and of pastoral influence. They complain, as
we do, of the frequent imperfection of the scholastic preparation of
the candidates for admission into the Academy. The French, in
particular, are often very superficially grounded in the rudiments
of learning; though such is their natural quickness, that they
frequently make up for these deficiencies by the ardor and assidu-
ity of their subsequent application.

"I had much pleasure in the society of M. Châstel, the Professor of Ecclesiastical History, and passed the greater part of
one morning with him. We had strong points of sympathy in
our common studies, and still more, as I was rejoiced to find from
conversation, in the close affinity of our views respecting the nature, influence, and proper work of Christianity. He is extensively read in German theology, and, with the retention of a profound
faith in Christianity and a spirit truly devout and serious, knows
well the established and unassailable points of theological science,
historic and dogmatic. I knew this excellent man four-and-

twenty years ago, when he spent a day with me in Manchester. In the interval, I found he had risen to eminence and distinction in his peculiar department of learning. Two of his works have procured him a wide celebrity. One obtained the prize offered by the French Academy of Inscriptions and Belles Lettres, in 1847, on the following subject: 'Histoire de la Destruction du Paganisme dans l'Empire d'Orient.' The other, which received a similar distinction from the ' Académie Française ' in 1852, is entitled, ' Etudes Historiques sur l'Influence de la Charité durant les premiers Siècles Chrétiennes, et Considérations sur son rôle dans les Sociétés Modernes.' My friend presented me with both these works, and I anticipate instruction and delight from reading them. M. Cellerier spoke of them in high terms, and assured me they were really ' savant.' M. Châstel, who himself formerly filled the office of Librarian, took me over the Library and Museum of the Academy. The foundation both of the Library and of the Museum is due to the celebrated Bonnivard, whose place of long captivity in Chillon, celebrated by Byron, is before my eyes as I write. The Library of Geneva is one of the interesting places in the world. You cannot enter it without seeming to breathe the very air of religion and learning. The space above the shelves is filled from one end to the other with the portraits of eminent men, illustrious for their writings and their labors from the era of the Reformation to the present day, who have all had a connection, more or less direct, with this great focus of Protestant intellect and energy, — Calvin, Farel, Erasmus, Turretin, Scaliger, Budæus, Grotius, &c., &c., De Candolle terminating the noble series. Among these, no one can pass over a most striking and characteristic portrait of Des Cartes, anything but handsome, yet full of intellectual expression, representing, one feels sure, the very life of its extraordinary prototype. I had no time to inquire into the special value of this large collection of books ; but it is rich, as most libraries of similar date and origin are, in the learning of the great controversies of the sixteenth and seventeenth centuries. It contains some very beautifully illuminated manuscripts, and interesting specimens of the handwriting of many distinguished men ; among the rest, a large collection of the letters of Calvin, and a great number of sermons and homilies delivered by him in the churches of Geneva. The former (the letters) have been transcribed, and will be included in the entire correspondence of Calvin, Latin and English, which is now in course of publication by a French gentleman resident at Clarens, M. Bonnet, with whom I have the pleasure of being acquainted, and which will prove a valuable accession to our knowledge of the time of the Reformation. Perhaps the most curious and valuable relic among the manuscripts of the Genevan Library is a collection of religious pieces in prose and· verse of very ancient date, but breathing the spirit of the future Reformation, — written in the old Vaudois dialect, and containing, along with the rest, the *Nobla Leyczon* which is supposed to be as old as 1100 A. D., and of which I remember to have read some extracts translated in Raynouard's Specimens of the Poetry of the Troubadours. A curious anecdote is connected with the history of this manuscript, whch I had from one of the former librarians, and which may amuse the lovers of literary rarities. Under the empire, Napoleon sent a request to Geneva that some of the treasures of their Library, among the rest this Vaudois Manuscript, should be sent to Paris to enrich the imperial collection. The librarians made, I believe, no difficulty about the other works, but signified their wish to retain this., Napoleon, in true imperial style, wrote back, that it was not a matter of *s'il vous plait*, but of *je le veux*, and that he must have the manuscript. Forthwith they hid it, where it could not possibly be discovered; and when the imperial messengers arrived, they told them they could not immediately find the work, but that they would search with them for it in every hole and corner of the Library. Of course it was not found, and so it was retained.

" M. Châstel, like M. Chenevière, spoke with some despondency of the prospects of liberal and undogmatic Christianity just at present. Hitherto, the predominance of radicalism had not at all aided them, but rather produced the contrary effect. Fear of Catholicism had stimulated a reaction towards the dogmatic formulas of the time of the Reformation. Under the old system of ecclesiastical management, the ' Company of Pastors,' including the theological Professors of the Academy, after due attestation of competency, appointed ministers to the vacant pulpits of the city; but it was always an understood thing, that the wishes of the congregation should be consulted and attended to; so that no instance of collision between the ' Compagnie ' and the congregation, at least of late years, had been known to occur. There is a wide difference between a whole parish taken promiscuously in a civil point of view, and the earnest members of a Dissenting congregation intent on one object, as with us. M. Châstel assured me, that the throwing open all at once the choice of their pastor to men uninterested in and unprepared for such an act, had not been followed by any beneficial effect. Few attended on the day of election, which left an easier course for intriguers and partisans who wished to carry their own objects. Hitherto such elections have been decidedly against what we should call liberal views. M. Châstel evidently dreaded the consequences of persisting in this system, and decidedly expressed his apprehension that an effort might ultimately be made to reimpose a dogmatic creed.

" The society formed recently at Paris, and called ' L'Alliance Chrétienne Universelle,' to which my attention had been directed by my friend Mr. Kell of Southampton, before leaving England in the summer, has excited, I am glad, some interest and sympathy in Geneva. This society, as you perhaps know, makes the essentials of Christianity to consist of three principles : ' The Love of God, the Creator and Father of all men; the Love of all Men, as immortal creatures and the children of God ; the Love of Jesus Christ, the Son of God and the Saviour of Men.' Perhaps the great *moral* principle of Christianity, the *transformation* of the inward man by the power of faith and love, is not expressed with sufficient distinctness, though it is implied, and may certainly be inferred, in this scheme. It is, however, a noble, catholic utterance of genuine Christianity, which deserves the sympathy and open recognition of our body, and to which I hope you will not fail to draw the attention of your readers. On my return, I will place in your hands the first two ' livraisons ' of the publications of this society. In the second of them, you will find a letter announcing the adhesion of some distinguished members of the Genevan Church, and a most admirable reply by the 'Alliance' itself to their brethren of Geneva, signed by the President and Secretary, which contains a most full and satisfactory exposition of the views and principles of the society, supplying, I think, some of the deficiencies which I had noticed in the general announcement. I really think you would render good service to true Christianity, if you would publish in your pages the Geneva letter and reply, with a translation. Among the names subscribed to the Geneva letter, I find those of many pastors, two of the professors of the Academy, MM. Châstel and Munier, some jurists, and General Dufour, who was commander-in-chief of the federal forces during the war of the 'Sonderbund.'

"My dear sir, I strongly feel, on the eve of my departure from the Continent, that there is a great stir and agitation coming over the religious mind of Europe, which cannot but issue to the service of truth, if we are only each of us, in our respective positions, faithful to our convictions, simple-minded, and large-hearted. We want bravery and confidence; we want the encouragement of sympathy and co-operation; we should multiply our relations as much as possible, abroad and at home, with all such societies as will receive us as brethren, and will work with us in the simple love of truth and the fervent spirit of humanity. I believe there are thousands who would hold out the hand of welcome to us, if they only knew more of us than our obnoxious name. We are frozen to death by reserve and insulation. A grand warfare is going on, under different names, between the religion of Love and the religion of Fear, — the religion that is in harmony, and the religion that is at war, with the noblest inspirations of our common humanity. I have long made my choice and taken my part; and with such feeble weapons as God has intrusted to me, I will fight on against Jesuitry and uncharitableness, till I am bidden to retire from the field. Of the final issue of the contest I have no doubt, dark and discouraging as may seem for the moment its present aspects; but when the triumph comes, as in God's own hour it must, it will be shameful to feel that we have lost all claim to participation in it, through our own inaction and pusillanimity.

J. J. T."

RICHARD HERTFORD AND JAMES M———.

HISTORY gives no record, since the early ages of the Christian Church, of a period which is so marked in its influence upon the destiny of man, or which did so much to advance his highest interests, as the first half of the sixteenth century. Rendered memorable by the learning of Erasmus, the zeal of Luther, and the piety of Melancthon, there is no period to which the eye of the thoughtful student or the Christian scholar turns with so deep an interest. The intellectual calm which had so long brooded over Europe was broken. A new impulse was given to human progress. The discovery of another hemisphere and the invention of the art of printing were the important links in the chain of events which seemed leading to great results. Old trains of thought, old modes of action, were passing away, and new channels were opening to engage the mind and occupy the labors of man.

By the side of these discoveries, another, but seemingly a far humbler one, may well be placed. From the moment when, heaven-directed, the humble Augustine monk discovered on the dusty shelves of the library the long-neglected volume, error began to sink and truth to rise in the ascendant. We follow him in imagination, as he turns with wondering delight the sacred page; again and again he repairs in secret to the spot which contains his treasure, and breathes the earnest wish that it were indeed his own. From his cell is gleaming forth a light which is to widen and glow, brightening all succeeding ages, cheering the pathway of duty and pointing to a glorious future. Before the name of Luther, those of the statesmen and conquerors of that day have all grown pale, as the stars of night are dimmed by the light of morning. The great result of this conflict was to prove to man that he was responsible only to his God for the honest convictions of his mind. The thunders of the Vatican, once so formidable, were henceforward to be powerless. Not the will of the Roman Pontiff, but the word of God, was to be the infallible rule of faith and duty.

From the German Reformer we turn to the English monarch, who then exercised a sway over his people far more despotic than had been claimed by his predecessors. The key-note of freedom falls harshly upon his ear, for he knows full well that freedom from spiritual bondage is but one step towards general emancipation. If man's spiritual fetters are broken, he learns to feel his rights as a child of the common Father, and civil despotism cannot long continue. Henry the Eighth enters the field of controversy, attempts to silence Luther, and earns for himself the pompous title of " Defender of the Faith,"— of that faith which he is so soon to discard, when it refuses to gratify his lusts. England was preparing for a change. The activity of the Anglo-Saxon mind could not easily be bound down by authority. There were causes at that time in operation favorable to the reception of new light. Wycliffe, the " morning star of the Reformation," had not lived in vain, and the whole genius of the nation, even then, tended to a dissolution from Rome and its head. Henry did not for a moment dream of enfranchising his subjects from spiritual dominion; he intended only to transfer the supremacy from the Pope to himself; and when, by an especial act of grace, he gave permission to the laity to read the Scriptures for themselves, the concession was accompanied with the clause, that it was by the favor of the sovereign, not as the right of the subject.

Soon, however, the suspicious mind of the monarch saw danger resulting from his liberality. In 1543 the permission was revoked, and it was enacted, "that no one should read the Bible to others in public; that it should be read in private to families only by lords and gentlemen; personally and in secret, only by householders and women of noble or gentle birth; while every artisan, laborer, apprentice, or woman, except the above named, who *should presume* to open the sacred volume, should be liable, for the first offence, to a month's imprisonment." The monarch believed his will was law, but he had only poorly weighed the power of a conscientious purpose, the might of a determined will.

To us who live under the most favored circumstances, where the liberty to "search the Scriptures" is our very birthright, it is a task of no small difficulty to realize the position here described. Such a privation seems impossible of endurance. Perhaps it is only by these strange contrasts that we duly appreciate our own blessings, and the fearful responsibility resting upon us for their right improvement.

Among the honest and toiling artisans of the metropolis, Richard Hertford had always ranked among his associates as a man of sound understanding, great sincerity of purpose, and unbending integrity; "his word was a bond." It chanced that, in consequence of his business relations as a mathematical-instrument maker, he had been brought into connection with some foreign merchants, who were possessed of a copy of Luther's translation of the Bible into German. His interest had been powerfully excited, and he was among the first to avail himself of the royal permission to study the sacred page. The little room in the rear of his shop was the constant resort of a few friends, who, when the labors of the day were over, deemed it their

23 *

greatest privilege to assemble in Richard Hertford's humble home, to dwell upon the great themes of hope, of pardon, and immortality. Sadly indeed did the new edict fall upon them. Their little meetings were to be dissolved; the labors of the day were no longer to be crowned with the hopes of heaven.

Some, while they mourned over the privation, could yet return to their former current of life, and soothe their disappointment with hopes of brighter days. Others, again, became engrossed with their daily gains, — with their goods and merchandise. Not so with Hertford. He was a thoughtful, almost a solitary man. One daughter, Janet, was his only earthly tie; and the father and child were united by more than an earthly bond. Together they cherished hopes of heaven; they could not yield to an unjust decree; there was a Heavenly King who claimed their highest allegiance, and to this duty they could not prove false. The nightly assemblage of friends had ceased, yet in private they continued to explore that mine of truth which was more precious to them than gold.

Their motions were watched. Information was given, and Richard Hertford, with his child, was dragged to prison, as warnings to all who should hereafter presume to violate the royal command.

The dark winter day was closing in upon the streets of London as they left their cheerful home; a prison was now their abode. In vain did Janet beg to be allowed to remain with her father. They were separated, and in silence and solitude, in the gloom of their cells, this night, and many successive nights and days, passed on. But they were not alone; the Father's eye was upon them, his felt presence was ever around them; the gloom of a prison was cheered by many well-remembered words they had read in the holy book; and England's monarch, a slave to his own passions, was far less free than his captive subjects.

The days and weeks passed on; the period for their release arrived. But Richard Hertford's resolution was formed. He could no longer remain in a land where, without crime, he had been made the inmate of a prison; where he might again suffer a similar penalty; where he must forego the duty and privilege he believed so justly his own.

The shop was closed; the room once so bright and cheerful had other inmates; while the father and child left all, competence, home, the associates and companions of their daily life, the cherished memories of the past, all were resigned for conscience and for God, to seek a shelter and a new home in Switzerland, where the charter of their eternal hopes should not be wrested from them.

Three centuries have passed away. Time and change have been busy with the works of man. New actors have successively arisen and disappeared from the world's great theatre. The arts have been perfected, civilization has advanced; many a mad career of earthly ambition has been run; kingdoms have declined, and others have arisen in their places; the very names of many who then acted a conspicuous part in the great drama of life are now forgotten. But while earthly glory has faded, and the pride and pomp of this world have passed away as the dream of the night, the word of God has remained, unchanged and glorious, and towering above all transitory interests. It has the same claims upon our highest reverence, the same power to strengthen and sustain, it is still the same light to guide and direct the sincere inquirer, as when the liberty to study its holy promises required the sacrifice of home, and kindred, and country.

ere those .... : :
matic .... : ...
formed a ... . :
world.

They believ.. ....
symbols ....
was sometimes .... — .
In a state of ....
excitement, when the .. . . —. : .
absorbed and ....
coming events of .... —. .
spirit for a ... .
heaven, and had a ....
We need not look ....
all the known and .... : . :
to bring it with the ....
himself felt! In ....
fervor he feels ....
intentions and purposes of ... .
and confidence ....
Prophets; but ....
cording to the same ....
victions are revealed .. ..

The greater ....
manner of expressing ....
words, became .. .. — . . :
printed words. But .. .... : .. .. .
whom we now speak ....
lypse is drawn from ....
The earlier method of ....
signs was then ....
take the place of ....
seded it. Hence ....

... all the better
... evolt. Doubts
... rying aspects;
... goodness of a
... lod of revela-
... rent a lesson?
... this revelation
... ich distinguish
... enable him to
... gnify the one
... sult of inquiry,
... Shall he disap-
... and darkness
... creeping over
... e chosen min-
... He stands on
... to advance or
... h to save him.
... He exhorts
... nbiased mind,
... The sincere
... nced that this
... consideration;
... may lead him,
... ke the dearest
... thly hopes; for
... ther more than
... he teachings of
... very fountain-
... lt of his investi-
... s no contradic-
... and, and, while
... on and authority

Among the most important events since that period is the birth of a new nation, founded upon the spirit of that holy book, widely as it may have since departed from that spirit, — a nation great in power and resources, where all are free to read and judge for themselves. Shall any obstacles here be placed upon the impartial judgment of the individual mind?

In a quiet village of our own New England, a few years since, might be seen, in his retired study, a young man apparently about twenty. His brow was calm and intellectual, but a shade of sadness and even of gloom told of an internal struggle, — spoke of stern mental conflict. On his table before him lay his Bible, but it was unopened. If he is mourning over the blighting of cherished hopes, if he is perplexed and uncertain where to take his stand upon life's great arena, why does he not seek for guidance and direction there, where he may find an unerring rule? No regal power, no statute of his native land, forbids.

James M—— had been early taught to reverence the Bible; his parents were conscientious and devout. Their fondest wish was, that their son might stand in the holy place, a minister to others of those truths so precious to their own hearts. James had, accordingly, been educated in the strictest principles of the Genevan Reformer; he had passed through his collegiate course with honor to himself and pride to his parents, and had now entered a seminary for the completion of his theological studies. The Bible is before him; he is encouraged to read and study the sacred page, but from that study he is expected to draw only certain conclusions; he must move only around a fixed centre, and find no other doctrines than those contained in the creed to which his assent is required. But these are doctrines which he finds it impossible to comprehend, before which his reason must be passive, at which all the better feelings and nobler aspirations of his heart revolt. Doubts arise; he looks upon Nature in all her varying aspects; they speak with one voice of the power and goodness of a Father. Is not the God of nature also the God of revelation? Why, then, do they teach so different a lesson? Did not the same merciful Being who gave this revelation bestow also those noble reasoning powers which distinguish man from the lower orders of creation, and enable him to receive those revealed truths? Shall he magnify the one gift by degrading the other? He fears the result of inquiry, lest it should involve him in further doubt. Shall he disappoint the hopes of his parents? All is doubt and darkness before him. He feels a lurking scepticism creeping over him. Shall the child of so many prayers, the chosen minister of good to others, become an infidel? He stands on the very brink of a precipice; he fears to advance or recede, when a helping hand is reached forth to save him.

A friend of his childhood comes to his aid. He exhorts him to "search the Scriptures" with an unbiased mind, with the single aim of discovering the truth. The sincere and conscientious mind of James is convinced that this only can save him. He banishes every other consideration; he must follow duty and truth wherever they may lead him, even though they may require him to forsake the dearest earthly friends and forego the brightest earthly hopes; for Jesus has said, " He that loveth father or mother more than me, is not worthy of me." Laying aside the teachings of men, he turns to the study of the truth at its very fountainhead; light dawns upon him, and the result of his investigations is a form of belief which involves no contradictions; which sees everywhere a Father's hand, and, while it reverently acknowledges the divine mission and authority

of Jesus, and believes that the Father and Son are one in
purpose, design, and affection, still hears the words of the
Saviour himself, "My Father is greater than I." Freed
from doubt, unshackled by time-worn opinions, his mind
expanded to the influences of that light which ever dawns
from the sacred volume, and he became a powerful and
effective advocate of that faith which had come to him in
his hour of need, and had saved him from the horrors of
infidelity. Though many hopes of usefulness were blighted
by his early death, yet his eloquence, his zeal, his piety
and devotion to the cause which he espoused, have left an
impress upon his age which cannot pass away.

Is the history of James M—— a solitary instance?
Are there not many who can bear testimony to the power
of the Unitarian faith to rescue from doubt and indifference? And have we not all, upon whom this glorious
light has dawned, a responsibility resting upon us? The
humble Christian in the private walks of life, the Sabbath-
school teacher, as well as the minister of the Gospel,—have
we not all a duty resting upon us to do something for our
precious faith? Shall we not, while cherishing the largest
charity and love towards those who differ from us, ever be
true to our convictions, and help to spread before all minds
what may give them a knowledge of this unspeakable gift?

AGITATION.

THE writer of this article is not an agitator; neither is
it the design of the article to recommend or encourage
agitation. By nature and habit he is unfitted for such a

work, and his tastes and his inclinations would lead him in a different direction. But he regards the existence of agitation as unavoidable, in the present condition of human society; and as designed to accomplish similar purposes in the moral world to those which are effected by storms and convulsions in the material.

We do not prefer the tempest and the tornado. We do not pray for the commotion and strife of the elements, — the winds that rend the mountains, the earthquake that shakes a continent, the lightnings that terrify and destroy. But we know that these things are necessary, and that in the operations of Providence, whatever partial and temporary evil they may produce, they will result in good. The atmosphere would soon become vitiated and pestilential if there were a perpetual calm. The waters would become stagnant and destructive to health and life, if they were never disturbed. Nothing could long survive, unless in their appointed seasons " the rains descended, and the floods came, and the winds blew." These are the great purifiers in the works and operations of nature, and they are necessary to the production of such results. They come, and often before their fury many a house may fall, and life may be destroyed, and desolation spread around; but a new and fairer scene shall arise from the ruins, and more than an equivalent shall be rendered back as a compensation for the loss, — fields clothed with fresh verdure, health glowing upon the countenance, strength and activity displaying themselves in mind and limb. Thus will the waste be repaired, and the calamity prove a blessing in the end. In like manner, we do not desire, for their own sake, moral convulsions and civil commotions; and there may be much to apprehend from the unsettling of those habits and principles upon which the order of society is based; but it is sometimes necessary that these things also should occur, so that a new and better order may succeed. And therefore, although we do not pray for such things, nor labor to bring them about, yet there is no reason to despair in regard to the issue, but very much reason to hope.

It is recorded in the Gospel of John, that at certain seasons an angel descended into the pool of Bethesda and troubled the waters, and that then "whosoever first stepped in after the troubling of the water was made whole of whatsoever disease he had." Whether this was designed to be merely a statement of the popular belief with reference to this matter, or of an actual occurrence, it will serve equally well as the symbol of an important truth. The waters did not possess their healing properties until after they had been stirred. And thus the agitation of the social and moral elements is often necessary to health and soundness. Thus, too, the descent of the angel may be regarded as symbolical of the workings of Providence in all these events. Society, in all its forms and phases, requires occasionally to be put in commotion. Without interruption at times in the flow of human affairs, governments, religious systems, and public morals have a tendency to degenerate, and to become oppressive and corrupt. Let everything settle down into a state of long-continued and undisturbed repose; let there be neither parties nor sects, nor political, nor religious, nor any other excitements; let there be no longer any opposition to recognized principles, nor to existing institutions, nor to the general course of action and the measures adopted in Church and State, and how long does any one suppose that either of them would remain in as healthful a condition as at present? Let there be no attempt to reform the manners and habits of society, and how long does any one imagine they would continue to be as good even as they are?

No great and permanent good has yet been attained,
no extensive and lasting improvement has yet been made
in man's social condition, no important change has ever
yet been produced in the moral and religious, or even
the political, state of communities and nations, without a
greater or less degree of agitation and excitement. Revolutions, whether they have reference to laws and institutions or to the moral and social habits of a people, can .
seldom be effected without debate and strife. The interests
of men can never be seriously disturbed without exciting
their passions. The prejudices which strike their roots so
deep, and which intertwine themselves so closely with the
intellect and the heart, can seldom be removed without
difficulty and danger. In our efforts to pluck up the tares,
we are very liable, in most cases, to pluck up the wheat
with them. In attempting to bind "the strong man," even
if our object be to save, and not to "spoil his house," we
can hardly expect to succeed without a contest.

It required a very general and powerful convulsion to
unsettle the feudal institutions of Europe, and to bring
about the changes of modern civilization! It may require
another convulsion, equally extensive and powerful, to
overthrow existing despotisms. The moral diseases which
have always pervaded society, the inveterate abuses which
have always existed in connection with everything good
in human character and condition, have never been cured
or corrected without a conflict with them, and possibly for
a season augmenting and aggravating the evil. And "the
thing that hath been, it is that which shall be; and that
which is done, is that which shall be done," with reference
to all effects of such a nature. The Spirit of God may
descend, it is true, with gentleness like the dove; but when
Satan falls, it will be as lightning. The kingdom of God may

grow up in the heart, as it has extended itself in the world, like the seed which springs forth from the soil, unfolding itself gradually, " first the blade, then the ear, and after that the full corn in the ear." But the kingdom of Satan can be destroyed only by the most energetic and unceasing warfare.

These general statements may be illustrated by a reference to various and numerous historical facts.

. The religion of the Gospel is a religion of peace. Its mission was to proclaim " peace on earth and good-will to men." The Author of it is accustomed to be styled " the Prince of Peace." He was so gentle, that he would not break " the bruised reed "; so earnest and anxious to save, that he would not quench " the smoking flax "; so loving, that he would willingly do harm to none ; so forgiving, that he was always disposed to reward evil with good. He came " not to destroy men's lives, but to save them "; not to inflict injuries upon men, but to bless them. And such a cause, and such a spirit, if it were possible in any case, should have encountered no opposition. But he was a reformer, the most thorough and radical that the world ever saw ; for he aimed at no partial reforms, no putting of new wine into old bottles, or of new cloth into old garments, no patchwork system of the rotten and decaying with the fresh and strong. His purpose was to " make all things new "; to supersede the institutions of Moses by better institutions of his own ; to change customs and laws ; to put an end to pagan idolatries ; to remove errors and superstitions grown hoary with age ; to renovate society in all its grades ; to banish from the earth all vice and crime, oppression and wrong; to impose restraints upon the passions and appetites of men ; to present before them better motives and higher aims ; to enkindle within them new hopes and aspirations ; and thus, through the influence of the religion which he taught, and the train of causes which he put in operation, to regenerate the world; and thus to hasten the day when, in the prophetic language of the Scripture, "the heavens shall pass away with a great noise," and there shall appear "the new heavens and the new earth, wherein dwelleth righteousness."

And he well understood, that in the accomplishment of such a work there must be opposition, and commotion, and strife; that the waters in order to impart healing must be stirred to their very depth. For in referring to the consequences of his mission, clearly foreseen, he asserts in the most direct and positive manner, that he "came not to send peace upon the earth, but a sword"; to set parent at variance with child, and child with parent, and to make a man's foes "those of his own household." And such were the effects produced. He was regarded by his countrymen, and especially by the chief priests and the rulers of the people, as an innovator and a disturber of the public peace. They accused him of "stirring up the people throughout all Jewry." They said, "We have found this fellow perverting the nation, and forbidding to give tribute unto Cæsar." And it was upon charges such as these that they were able at length to prevail upon the Roman Procurator to put him to death. There can be no doubt but that tumults and excitements arose among the people in consequence of his doctrines and his efforts in promulgating them, and that many were disposed to charge upon him the very disturbances which they themselves had produced.

The Apostles also were engaged in carrying forward the same works of reform, and they were regarded and treated in a similar manner. Paul and his fellow-laborers, in the way already indicated, were agitators of the most zealous and determined kind. They gave themselves no rest.

They travelled from city to city, from province to province, from clime to clime, always laboring for the accomplishment of the same great object; always bearing about with them the marks of the Lord Jesus; always intent on performing the work which had been given them to do, so that they might finish their course with joy, and the ministry which they had received of the Lord Jesus, "to testify the Gospel of the grace of God." They attacked sin in its strong-holds. They carried on an unceasing warfare against spiritual wickedness in high places. They hesitated not to speak boldly of prevalent errors and vices. They spared neither Pharisaic hypocrisy nor Gentile immoralities, neither Jewish intolerance nor Pagan superstitions. And rulers trembled in their presence, and heathen temples shook, and idols were dethroned, and the fire ceased to burn upon their altars.

Of course there was excitement, for such effects could not be produced without it. There were tumults and riots, for men are seldom inclined to surrender quietly the means by which they have their wealth, and in such a state of feeling they are not always obedient to law. Some said, " These that have turned the world upside down have come hither also." Some said, " This fellow persuadeth men to worship God contrary to the law." The men of Jerusalem affirmed, " This man ceaseth not to speak blasphemous words against this holy place and the Law, for we have heard him say that this Jesus of Nazareth shall destroy this place and change the customs which Moses delivered unto us." The men of Ephesus, all with one voice, shouted " for about the space of two hours, Great is Diana of the Ephesians ! " and the whole city was filled with confusion because Paul had said, " There be no gods that are made with hands," and had succeeded in turning away much people, and thus had brought their craft into danger. The Jews cried out, " Men and brethren, help! This is the man that teacheth all men everywhere against the people, and the Law, and this place."

Such were the circumstances in which Christianity was first established, and such was the estimation in which the first Christian teachers were held. What should we have known of the important truths of Christianity, what should we have enjoyed of its consolations and hopes, if there never had been any agitation? Where would have been this greatest reform which this world has ever witnessed, but for those fearless and noble-hearted men of a different age, who began the work and yielded up their lives in the defence of their cause?

We prize our Protestant liberties. In the lapse of centuries ecclesiastical tyranny had gained possession of the Church, and spiritual domination had been exercised so long, that it had ceased to fear or to expect resistance. The waters had been undisturbed for so great a length of time that they had become corrupt, and the period had at length arrived for the angel to descend and trouble them. Then the Reformation broke out, and a host of agitators appeared. There were controversies, and excitements, and tumults, and convulsions, and persecutions, and bloody strife. And upon every side men's hearts failed them for fear. But healing came out of them. The Church was vitalized. Intellect was stimulated. Abuses were corrected. Religious freedom was secured. Even Romanism was benefited by the movement which threatened its overthrow. These, too, are the good results growing out of a period of agitation.

Those were stormy times which preceded and comprehended the American Revolution. Few can desire their

return. There were fears, and jealousies, and heated controversies. There were alienations, and evil surmises, and
mutual recriminations among those who had been neighbors and friends. There were accusations, and betrayals,
and seizures, and expulsions of all who were believed to
be in favor of the opposite side. Then " horrid war " with
its scenes of carnage and desolation, oft repeated, and prolonged through sad and weary years; war, with its many
thousand victims, and its millions of expense. These were
great and fearful evils, and it is by no means strange that
many shrank from encountering them. But out of them grew
our national independence, and after them came peace,
plenty, and public prosperity, such as no nation within so
brief a period has ever before attained. Had it not been
for this season of controversy, strife, and peril, where would
have been those peculiar privileges of which now as a
people we are accustomed to boast ?

It would be easy to extend these illustrations, but more
are not needed. The statements which have been made
are statements of fact. No one will deny that in these
instances, at least, agitation has resulted in good.

But to what purpose these remarks ? Not to encourage
agitation, as it was stated at the beginning, nor yet to
oppose it. Whether we approve of popular excitements or
disapprove, whether we endeavor to promote or to prevent
them, it matters but little. They will come. As certainly
as the tempests disturb the waters of the ocean, just so
certainly will there be swellings and heavings, and tumults
and commotions in the great deep of the human intellect
and passions. There is a law in one case as well as in the
other, and there is a gracious Providence watching over all
and working in all. What, then, is to be done ? Despair
not under any circumstances, but always be hopeful. The

condition of society is still far from being perfect. There are still evils to be eradicated, and wrongs to be righted. Some of these, perhaps, may be near the surface, and some of them very far below it. They must be reached before they can be remedied. And, wisely or unwisely, the attempt will be made. It must be confessed that mistakes are often committed. It must be acknowledged that all movement is not progress, and that men may agitate for evil purposes as well as good. But, making all proper allowances for things of this nature, one thing appears certain. Important reforms are never accomplished without agitation. The spirit in which they are attempted, and the spirit in which they are received, may doubtless be faulty, and may need to be improved. But the law of progress cannot be changed. Then, if it must, let it come. Let the waters be troubled, if God so wills ; not superficially, but to their lowest depths. Let there be discussions and controversies upon all subjects, both sacred and profane, and good shall come out of evil; the truth shall be brought to light, and the just cause shall triumph. Who can doubt the issue ? The lover of truth will not fear. The friends of justice and right will have nothing to apprehend. The bad cause alone can be endangered ; and who would wish it to succeed ?

W.

WHAT SHALL I DO ?

THIS question is often asked by parents, amid the anxieties and perplexities of parental discipline. How can I teach my children obedience, and train them up to good affections and useful lives ? · A few hints on these points

are here submitted, in the hope that they may lead at least
to some thought.

"You have a remarkable government over your child,
madam," said a gentleman to a young mother, whose little
child, creeping across the floor, had turned its course from
the fender in obedience to its mother's uplifted finger.

It need not be remarkable, if all mothers, instead of
making mere playthings of their infants, would take a little
pains to teach them that what they require of them must
be done. Then, as they grow older, there would not be
such scenes as this, which are now too common.

"No, Lucy, you must not go out to play now ; it is too
warm."

"Yes, mother, *do*." (In a drawling tone, and leaning
persuasively across her lap.) "I want to."

"No, dear."

"O p-l-e-a-s-e !"

"No, darling, I had rather you would not."

"O yes ! I want to."

"No." (Very gently, and looking half ready to yield.)

"Yes ; I shall ! I want to ! I must ! (In a decided
tone.)

"No, love, don't go. Mind mother, now."

"Yes ; I 'm going. I *am !* "

(No notice taken of it.)

(Again.) "I am, mother. I *am* going."

"No, Lucy ; mother has told you no. You cannot go."
(A little more firmly, yet not decidedly.)

Then follows a little crying ; then a bribe from the
mother, which avails nothing ; and so it goes on till a victory is gained on one side or the other, (and it really
makes little difference which, for after such a questioning
of authority, the parent's influence for the future must be

very weak,) and the mother turns to her guest, who has perhaps witnessed with astonishment the whole scene, and, as if half ashamed of her weakness, apologizes: "Lucy is so nervous that it is impossible to govern her like other children."

It is no uncommon occurrence to hear a parent speak in this way. "I let Johnny sit up till we go to bed. It is n't good for him, I know; but the poor child is so nervous (he inherits it from his grandfather) that it would make him really ill to force him to go before. He 's never fond of being alone."

What a poor preparation for a struggle with the rough world, the world which makes no allowance for nerves and delicate feelings! What an insufficient foundation for self-conquest! If such a father and mother be permitted to look discriminatingly upon their son's manhood, will there not be bitter regrets that he was not early hardened and strengthened against himself?

But too great severity is as hurtful as over-indulgence. Authority may by this means become of no avail. No mother who is really anxious about the welfare of her children will require more than is absolutely necessary of them while they are too young to understand right from wrong; but it is equally undesirable at any time in their lives to draw the rein too tightly.

I have seen such petty commands so constantly issued by faithful, well-meaning parents, that the children, though possessed of a large share of affection, have at last ceased to regard them at all; not from any feeling of disrespect, or desire to disobey, but merely through force of habit, and having found it impossible to answer all the demands, and becoming gradually hardened to disregard all alike.

Exact from children of any age as little *disagreeable*

obedience as possible, and it will always follow, of course, that what is required will be too important not to be enforced, and therefore firmness on our side and ready obedience on theirs will be the consequence.

Although constant care and watchfulness is more than ever necessary, a perceptibly close government must not be held over young men and women, particularly at that age when they feel their importance most. It is especially annoying to them to be directed and ruled in trifles.

That girl of nineteen must feel a strong affection for her mother, and possess a sweet disposition indeed, who will, with perfect good temper, bear to be told day after day to make trifling alterations in the arrangement of her dress. And that son must have a high appreciation of his father's regard for his welfare, who, at the same age, will stand meekly to be catechized, whenever he has arranged his dawning moustache, placed an eye-glass before eyes guiltless of defective vision, and without permission gallanted a fair friend to an evening concert.

But by forbearance and gentleness, win their love, with their respect. Show yourself companionable notwithstanding your difference in age ; and though they may naturally desire a little harmless freedom, they will come to you for advice, and bring home a frank account of their pleasures and pursuits abroad, for the children of such parents will rarely have anything to conceal.

If they occasionally take to themselves hurtful freedom, do not scold them ; nothing is so galling to youth as being treated like wilful childhood. Appeal to them as rational beings, capable of affection and discernment ; or, still better, as men and women, who have a position to attain and retain in the world. A call upon the nobler parts of human nature very seldom fails of meeting with response.

I have heard a grown-up daughter rudely told to hold her tongue, because, naturally interested in the subject, she had ventured a remonstrance or remark while her excited father was scolding one of her brothers or sisters. Such cases are not, I hope, of common occurrence, for they only serve to alienate the affections of the reproved, and derogate from the dignity of the reprover. No after indulgence from the parent will entirely heal the wound thus made.

Come clearly to the conclusion whether a desired indulgence is proper for a child or not ; if so, grant it without delay ; if not, gently but firmly deny it. It is best to say simply, " Do this," or " Do not do that " ; be sure that he thoroughly understands your commands, and then, if possible, leave him to act freely. Should he choose to disobey, say but little to him at the time ; but when next he seeks some favor of you, refuse it, giving him to understand your motive. If the child be too young to carry his reasoning powers so far, place him, as soon as he has disobeyed, in a corner of the room, for a longer or a shorter period, according to the nature of the offence.

If it be absolutely necessary to prevent his disobedience, as, for instance, playing with fire, it is well to substitute some amusement which shall divert his mind, and make him forget his intentions.

Avoid, if possible, corporal punishment, which may seem to produce, and that very quickly, the desired effect. It may intimidate the child so that he will not dare to repeat the offence, but at the same time it too often exasperates him, and, by injuring the temper, does far greater harm than would balance the benefit derived from a prevention of the fault.

Industry possesses a much larger share of the world's good opinion, than many qualities which full as much merit regard. But it indeed well deserves consideration ; for the child who has learned to prefer occupation to idleness will never *seek* forbidden pleasures, and often *avoids* them when thrown in his path.

" Satan finds some mischief still for idle hands to do," is no empty jingle, and there is no better way of diverting a child from injurious tastes and pursuits, than that of procuring for him some agreeable occupation, — something that he will consider useful.

A great share of the secret of success, if secret it can be called, lies in that word, useful. A well-known writer says : " There is no greater pleasure you can give children, especially female children, than to make them feel that they are already of value in the world, and serviceable as well as protected."

There are many ways of inculcating, or endeavoring to inculcate, industry. It is among the most common things in the world to hear it said, " Do get your sewing ; how can you be so idle ! You never do anything but lounge about." Or, " Come and sit here beside me, and don't get up until you have finished hemming that handkerchief." Or, to the boy deeply engaged in watching the motions of a fly on the window-pane, " Get a book and read ; how much time you are wasting ! " Perhaps the words take effect for the moment, but I do not believe that one single instance was ever known where habits of industry were thus formed.

There are some children so constitutionally languid and inert, that no such plan would succeed with them. I should appeal to the affections and sympathies of such. Give them something to do for a sick or poor person, let them receive their expressions of gratitude themselves, and a pleasant association will be connected with the effort they make. This repeated once or twice will call from them voluntary offers of assistance. Your little girl will soon wish to give up an hour's play to assist you in making a child's frock, and your little boy will before long ask to be permitted to carry a bundle to a poor woman, that he may merit some share of the pleasure caused by their comfort and gratitude ; but at the same time care must be taken that too frequent calls be not made upon this feeling, for fear of wearying their good-nature, or causing a taste for flattery to take the place of a sincere desire to do good.

We must vary the motive. " Finish this neckcloth before father comes home, it will surprise him so "; or, " I wonder whether you could fill this basket with chips before I finish this seam," — will often wonderfully quicken the fingers; and many faults in temper may be attributed to having nothing to do. The child is thrown back upon his own wearying thoughts, or, what is worse, seeks amusement, if it is permitted him, in exciting entertainments which cannot be continually supplied ; and in the interval he becomes fretful, peevish, and even violent, if his inclinations are thwarted.

There is not much to be feared of a child who loves to read; for, occupied with his book, he will feel little desire for other amusements, especially those inconsistent with his parents' wishes, and an interesting story will often induce him to leave his comrades when their noisy sports break into quarrels and become distasteful to him.

This love of reading is not altogether a natural taste. Though many children possess it without pains on the part of others to impart it, and though no two possess it in an equal degree, in many cases, if not invariably, it may be inspired by judicious management ; such as reading aloud to the child before he is able to read for himself, or leav-

ing a story in its most interesting part for him to finish, if
he is able; and it will almost invariably happen, that, if he
can persuade no one else to do it, he will finish it himself
rather than lose the story; but we must not leave too
much for him, as, unless he can read fluently, it fatigues
him, and much of the interest is lost.

It has been found very useful in imparting such a taste,
to place a little bookcase in his room, filled with books
which he can call his own, made attractive by pictures and
neat bindings. The pleasure derived from their possession
will induce him frequently to take them down for examination; the pictures attract him, and the next inducement is
to find out what they represent. By a little such management, provided always no deceit is used, a love of reading
has been and can be inculcated, and the taste will prove a
source of the greatest enjoyment through life, and a safe-
guard against dangerous temptations.

I have used the general term *reading*, but I do not call
the perusal of the empty printing (I cannot call it literature) of the present day reading; that requires the exertion of no single faculty, and it would be better that children
should utterly waste day after day than fill their minds with
thoughts that should never be there, and prepare them to
be disgusted with this commonplace world, which all who
live in must be more or less fettered to, — unfitted for the
duties which must be required of them, deprived of the
power of appreciating the beauties with which the world is
filled, and causing them to repine even while partaking of
the bounties spread out around them. Look to it, mothers,
that you set your children no example in this. Instil into
their minds, if possible (and possible I think it is), a true
taste for reading; — for poetry, that the commonest things in
nature may appear beautiful, that the loveliest qualities of

the mind may be stirred within them ; for the biographies of great, and especially good men, that the noblest aspirations of their hearts may be awakened. For instance, what young girl could rise from a faithful perusal of the life of Mrs. Ware, and not feel that there was some place for her in the world, — some mission to fulfil, — not feel refreshed and invigorated, and ready to begin life as it were anew, looking on its common duties as precious opportunities ? How different this feeling from the languid desire to shut out all the world, — the feeling with which she would close a common novel over which she has wasted hours !

Temper is the most common of all faults, shared alike by rich and poor, high and low, moral and immoral ; even those who pride themselves on their exemplary character are as liable as any to fall into the snare. It is the cause of more unhappiness in the world than misfortunes, illness, and death together. The parent is often too subject to passion to be able to conquer it in a child. A box on the ear from an exasperated father never cooled an angry son, a violent shake from an excited mother never drove away angry feelings.

Ordinary punishments too often tend to the same result. A child knows, though he may not express it, that when he is violently whipped or petulantly slapped, it is done more in revenge than for punishment ; and the words, " Go to bed without your supper, miss ! " spoken in a loud, angry tone, will only through fear prevent a repetition of the offence ; no sense of duty will be awakened, no feeling of filial regard.

Just as inefficacious are unexecuted threats, spoken in the heat of passion. " Don't you ever do that again ; if you do I will whip you ! " — produces no good result. The child repeats the offence partly to test the effect, the parent is in a different mood, and no notice is taken of it.

If corporal punishment must be resorted to, be sure that the child clearly perceives that you are not angry with him, only grieved. Then let the punishment be proportioned to the real repentance of the culprit, not to the offence ; for you wish to forget those things which are behind, and push on to those things which are before. You only punish to prevent a repetition of the fault, and if that end is already gained, where is the benefit of punishment ?

In these great matters of temper, example is all important ; a loving, gentle, forbearing disposition, exhibited by a father or mother, will go further to foster the same disposition in a child, than volumes of precepts and a life spent in correction.

Of all kinds of temper, obstinacy is the most difficult to manage. Any trace of it in the preceptor is almost sure to influence the pupil ; and yet firmness is absolutely indispensable in government of any kind ; the line of separation is very faint. Prevention in this case is certainly better than cure. Obstinacy is almost invariably taught by forcing a child to divert his mind instantly from what engrosses it. " George, stop whistling ! " If we are not instantly obeyed, we impatiently repeat the command, when perhaps he cannot at once banish the tune from his mind. He is called obstinate, when perhaps we are at this very time teaching him the first lesson. " Georgie, you may look at the pictures in the great book, if you will be very careful," or " Come and look at this pretty little flag," or anything to divert the mind, and suggest a new train of thought, would have worked wonders. Nothing is harder than to eradicate that obstinacy. Punishments may for a time repress the difficulty, but when all restraint is removed, as it must be sooner or later, two hydra-heads take the place of one. Rewards are scarcely more efficacious ; they appeal to the lower qualities of human nature, and if submission is once bought, a higher price will be set upon it a second time. An appeal to their noblest feelings answers the best purpose. First, be sure that the child is not in the right ; convince him that you have no self-interested motives in desiring him to yield ; show him his fault ; appeal to his sense of duty, his love of God, and if each fail, his affection for yourself ; and the child must be hardened indeed if you do not succeed.

In some children there is a natural truthfulness, which makes it unnecessary even to point out the wickedness of falsehood ; while in others there seems to run a crooked vein of deception, tinging everythng they do or say. In these latter your example, your *real* abhorrence of deceit in every shape, will be very effectual. Convince them also how great an aversion God feels towards anything but perfect truth ; that he sees their inmost thoughts, and judges all by what they really are, not what they seem. And by all means remove from them every obstacle in the way of fear ; for if a child is never afraid to tell the truth, one half the inducements to falsehood are gone.

In very young children their imagination often runs away with them. They will tell of events which never took place, and accurately describe as their own toys which they never possessed. This is not falsehood, but will soon lead to it if not checked. By all means do not encourage them, however entertaining they may be ; but, according to their understanding, show them the difference between a fancy sketch, understood beforehand not to be true, and an assertion that every one is to believe. An infinite amount of anxiety in after life may thus be saved.

In many families selfishness is the predominant fault ; a

25 *

rank weed choking many fragrant flowers. Mothers are self-sacrificing creatures, and yield to their children too often for their real good. It would seem that here a good example fails in its effect, but if it is an example of self-sacrifice for every one, instead of for a darling child, it will not be in vain. Every really distinguished act of which a child is witness leaves an impression on his mind, which may grow fainter, perhaps very faint, but can never be effaced. It is much better that these silent influences should surround him, and cause very gradually, almost imperceptibly, the desired effect, than that constant commands and exhortations should be resorted to, which always weary and seldom improve him, because they tend to turn his thoughts towards himself, and annihilate the greatest charm of childhood, and indeed of every age, self-forgetfulness. Seek as much as possible to prevent his thoughts centring on himself.

A popular authoress says : "Let us be content with nature, or rather let us never exchange simplicity for affectation. Nothing ruins young people more, than to be watched continually about their feelings ; to have their countenances scrutinized, the degree of their sensibility measured, by the surveying eye of the unmerciful spectator. Under the constraint of such examinations they can think of nothing but that they are looked at, and feel nothing but shame or apprehension, and they are afraid to lay their minds open lest they should be convicted of some deficiency of feeling. On the contrary, the children who are not in dread of this sentimental inquisition speak their minds, the whole truth, without effort or disguise. They lay open their hearts and tell their thoughts as they rise, with a simplicity which would not fear to enter even the palace of truth."

This power of self-forgetfulness is often utterly destroyed, at an early age, by that pernicious practice of giving the opinion of other people as an inducement to do right. " What will.grandmother say if you do that ? " or, still worse, " You must always tell the truth ; nobody loves a naughty girl who does not tell the truth. What would Mrs. Grundy say, if she heard you tell such a story ? " Thus doing a double injury, substituting, instead of the noble desire of doing right, a thirst for the praise of others, and leaving, in the place of a lovely self-forgetfulness, a temptation to hypocrisy which will embitter the whole life.

I have spoken of what I consider the most important points in the moral education of a child, and all the illustrations I have made use of are facts which have come under my own observation. There are many things which here must be entirely left out of sight, but which in practice will of course be attended to, if the three great requisites are regarded ; namely, a distinct and permanent idea of God ; a hold on their affections ; a good example.

It is not to be expected that certain rules systematically laid down can be infallible in the government of children, because no two are alike, and there are many beside home influences which tend to form the character. They cannot be kept entirely from the world. They must have friends and companions who are comparative strangers to the parents, and it is better that it should be so. Who would choose that a son or daughter should live and die in perfect *innocency*, even if possible ? How much more glorious to fight the good fight, and, resolutely conquering temptation, go down to the grave like a warrior, covered with honorable scars of victory, and meriting one word upon our tombstone, — Virtuous ! Virtue stands above innocency in God's kingdom.

A parent's influence extends far, but it still has limits,

and the most faithful mother possible cannot be sure that her son will be a perfect man. Still, no effort on her part is ever entirely wasted. The good seed may lie long dormant, but it never wholly dies, and we may be sure that every parental precept and example takes effect, though that effect may not equal the expectation.

James Montgomery relates the following anecdote in regard to himself.

"Not long since, some rascals broke into my house, whilst I was delivering an address at a chapel in Sheffield, and stole, among other things, a silver inkstand, which had been presented me by the ladies of Sheffield. A few days after my loss, a box came directed to me, and on opening it, lo! there was the missing inkstand, and a note in which the writer expressed his regret that he had entered my house and abstracted it. The thief said that his mother had taught him some of my verses when he was a child, and seeing my name upon the inkstand, he first became aware whose house he had entered, and was so stung with remorse that he could not rest until he had restored my property, hoping God would forgive him."

Montgomery adds: "This was the greatest compliment, in my opinion, that I ever had paid me." But it seems to me rather a tribute to the mother who taught the verses, than to the man who wrote them, and could that mother have known of the deed, she would not have felt that *all* her early lessons were lost.

OPPORTUNITIES OF RELIGIOUS INFLUENCE.

A SMALL volume, recently published by a lady of strong Calvinistic principles, contains many valuable suggestions under a title similar to the one I have chosen for these thoughts. The writer deems it very important that professors of religion should bear about with them, under all circumstances, a sense of their responsibility as such, and omit no opportunity for sowing the seeds of wisdom and truth. Now, while I would by no means advocate the indelicacy with which many persons obtrude their peculiar views upon those of an opposite faith, I think that too great diffidence in the matter often causes us to neglect those golden opportunities which are afforded to us so directly from the hand of Providence, and which, if rightly improved, might have tended to the arrest of some sinful fellow-being, and, possibly, to his ultimate restoration to life and peace. Shall we dare assume so fearful a responsibility, and be called to answer in the last day the momentous question, " Where is thy brother? "

I fear that Christians scarcely realize the importance of manifesting, under all circumstances, by *precept* and *example*, a *sincere* respect for subjects of a sacred nature, — for the Scriptures, for the Sabbath and its holy services, and for the Sunday school, with its influences so full of hope for the Church. Especially is this watchfulness incumbent upon us Unitarian Christians, surrounded as we always are by those who receive their own opinions rather from tradition than conviction, and by others who are accustomed to look upon us with righteous horror, and to watch carefully for defects in our armor. With all such persons let us prove our fidelity to the precious inheritance which

God has given us; ever maintaining its strictly Scriptural character and its entire sufficiency for the regulation of the life that now is, and the solemnity of its teachings with regard to the life " beyond the vale."

There is also a class of persons whom we often meet, who, deeply interested in all these lofty themes, are desirous to make them the subject of *conversation*. Here, too, is an *opportunity* which we may not lose. Let us listen candidly and respectfully to the expression of their feelings and hopes, and rather invite than discourage a free interchange of thought, and be ever ready to meet them in a fair argument. In all such encounters, while we may not hope to convince by proofs drawn from Scripture those who are accustomed to read the Bible by the light of their creed, and to substitute for reason the time-hallowed phraseology of their catechism, yet we may and should always leave an impression upon their minds that our religious opinions are the result of deep thought and an honest examination of all the evidence in the case; and, moreover, that they constitute our most precious treasure, — one for which we are cheerfully willing to labor and to make such sacrifices as its promotion may require.

I have sometimes been pained to witness the reluctance which Unitarians manifest on occasions of this kind, when it really seemed as if they felt that an apology was demanded from them for daring to differ in opinion from their Trinitarian brethren, and as if withal they felt a little mortified at belonging to a sect which could not number so many adherents as that of their opponents. If these things are common among our denomination, we cannot be surprised that it should be approached, in some instances, with contempt, and that the sincerity of our profession should be questioned. Possibly the prevalence of this lukewarm and hesitating spirit in some quarters may account in part for the fact, that those courageous and powerful expositions of our theology which are given to the public from time to time by our most eminent clergymen have earned for them the enviable title of "Orthodox" men, altogether in advance of their denomination in piety and zeal; in fact, quite separated from it and identified with those who had previously monopolized those Christian graces.

To the female members of our body, as well as to their fathers and brothers, is allotted, I think, an important work in the vineyard of the Master. In view of this, let them improve the opportunities for religious culture with which we, as a sect, are so highly favored, and hold their faith so intelligently, that, in the chances and changes of life, it may not be so easily relinquished as it too often has been. Said a young friend who had found a temporary home among Trinitarians, "I never knew what religion was until I embraced the faith of these friends, and I have recently made a public profession of it." For this state of things I could find no apology, for I knew that she had sat for years under the ministrations of one of our most distinguished clergymen, who devoted himself most assiduously to the instruction of his people upon points of doctrine, as well as to exhortations to practical fidelity. Other instances I have known of young females, who have left their homes to be employed as teachers, and have yielded themselves up as ready converts to the various Trinitarian sects by which they were surrounded. These things could not have occurred, it seems to me, if they had examined for themselves the foundations of the faith to which they had been accustomed in their early years, and had given to religion only the same degree of attention which they devote to other subjects of inquiry.

In view of such cases as I have adverted to, and especially of the vast numbers in our country who have never heard of our views of truth, I heartily rejoice in the enterprise recently commenced of establishing a " Book Fund," by means of which works may be cheaply published and extensively circulated which shall explain our interpretations of the Gospel of our Lord and Saviour.   I am glad to learn that so cordial a response has thus far been made to our appeal for funds for this great object, and trust that the work will never be allowed to languish for want of that support which we can so readily give, if we rightly appreciate its importance.

J.

LETTERS TO AN INQUIRER.

II.

My Friend, —

If in my first letter I succeeded in showing that the question between us is, first of all, a question of fact, and that the evidence by which it is proved is of the same kind as that which sustains other historical facts, the next step will be to exhibit that evidence.   In doing this, I shall make no attempt at completeness, nor go much into details.   If you wish, or are willing, to examine systematically the evidences of Christianity, you can easily go to those great storehouses, — the works of Lardner, Paley, and the like.   And if you want something more fresh, — as in these days of novelty and taste few have the patience to go very deeply or thoroughly into such matters, — I would refer you to the admirable Lectures of President Hopkins of Williams Col-

lege, and Dr. Palfrey of Cambridge, delivered before the
" Lowell Institute," in Boston, a few years ago, and since
published. Nor should any fair inquirer fail to read Mr.
Norton's volumes on the " Genuineness of the Gospels."
But if you think it too much trouble to read such large
books, while I warn you of the peril of slighting so momentous a question on account of the trouble or time it may
cost, I will endeavor to set before you a few simple facts
which cannot be denied, and yet cannot be admitted without admitting a great deal more.

In the first place, Christianity, as it stands in the New
Testament, is a present reality. It exists, and its existence
is to be accounted for. As a palpable fact, as a vast institution, as the professed faith of civilized nations, as the
established religion of a great part of the world, and the
cherished trust and inward life of countless multitudes of
men, the existence of Christianity is a present reality.

In the second place, this religion is a reality of the past, as
well as the present. You know very well that, in the form in
which we hold Christianity, it is at the very least, and positively, fifteen hundred years old. I name that period as taking us back without dispute to Constantine, who enthroned
Christianity, as the religion of the Roman Empire, about
three hundred years after the alleged time of Christ. Here
is a fact as unquestionable as any belonging to the past.
And it is not a fact of mere names and dates. It proves not
only that the religion then existed, and was deemed of sufficient importance to be allied with the power of an empire,
but it proves also that it was the same religion, in all respects, that we now have in the Gospels. For the historian
Eusebius, a contemporary and trusted friend of Constantine,
gives us in his writings, still extant, the entire canon of the
New Testament, as it was received in his day. He enu-

merates the books, speaks of them as known to all the
churches, and quotes from them enough to show that they
are the same as now; that is, essentially the same. The
differences are slight, and weigh nothing in comparison
with the agreement of the large number of manuscript
copies of the Greek Gospels still in existence, and easily
compared both with each other and with the printed version.

This last is an important as well as unquestionable
fact, and one which few sceptics appear to know or consider. Have you ever considered it yourself, or known it?
I mean the fact, that there are in existence more than six
hundred, if not seven hundred, manuscript copies of the
whole or portions of the Greek text of the Gospels, made
at different periods, in different countries of Asia, Europe,
and Africa; and, beside these, many manuscripts of ancient versions of the Gospels entire, written in the different
languages of those different countries; and, still more, many
manuscripts of the Christian Fathers, containing large quotations from the Gospels, with ancient commentaries, such
as those of Origen in the third century, and Chrysostom in
the fourth. Have you considered that all these different
copies of parts or the whole of the Gospels, so early, various, and unconnected, give us the same essential text?
This proves incontestably, beyond the proof that you can
find for the authority and integrity of any other ancient
writings, that these writers and copiers must have drawn
from one original manuscript, one and the same Gospel.
Mr. Norton says: "As far back as our knowledge extends, Christians, throughout all past ages, in Syria, in
Alexandria, at Rome, at Carthage, at Constantinople, and
at Moscow, in the East and in the West, have all used
copies of each of the Gospels which were evidently derived

from one original manuscript, and necessarily imply that such a manuscript, existing as their archetype, has been faithfully copied."

Here is historical and moral evidence, not only of the antiquity, but also of the identity and purity, of the Gospels, as we now hold them. Nay, you may almost call it mathematical proof. For while these Gospels existed only in manuscript, as they did for centuries, it was utterly impossible for any single transcriber heedlessly or intentionally to alter *all* the copies, or any large number. And the fact, which we ourselves can verify, that no material alteration or variation does exist in any of them, but that all essentially agree, though made without the possibility of collision or even comparison, is absolutely conclusive of the existence and wide prevalence of our identical Gospels as early as the second century.

Take this one fact, and attempt to account for it on any other supposition than the reality of the events themselves recorded in the Gospels as having occurred at the time alleged. In other words, suppose that no such being as Christ existed, taught, wrought miracles, died, and rose again, as the Gospels say, but that the whole, or the most vital part, was invented, — a fiction or forgery. This forgery, then, was committed, or this fiction written and circulated, east and west, as early as Constantine and Eusebius. Those men and their times were about as far removed from the alleged time of Christ and his Apostles, as we are from the alleged time of the Protestant Reformation. Do you believe in the reality of that Reformation? Do you feel sure, and can you prove, that such men as Luther and Melancthon ever existed? Suppose them not to have existed, do you think it would be easy to invent them, and palm them and their accompanying fictions upon the credulity of the world at this time? The idea is absurd. You feel insulted by the very suggestion, that you or others could be so cheated in regard to facts interwoven with the whole history of the last three hundred years. Then you ought to feel equally insulted, and know that you may insult others, by a suggestion of the possibility that the Gospel history could have been *invented* within two or three hundred years of the alleged time of its origin; or could have then existed in the form it did, and been received in places and countries widely separated, as a genuine, authentic record of facts, unless it were genuine and authentic.

Carry it up now another hundred years, and there stands Origen, as we have intimated, born only one hundred and fifty years after the death of Christ, living to the age of seventy, the most learned man of his day, and leaving writings from whose still extant pages can be shown, not only the existence and wide prevalence of the books of the New Testament, but their harmony with ours in all essentials. Indeed, if the Gospels themselves should be now lost or destroyed, it would be easy to restore nearly all of Matthew, Luke, and John, from the large quotations that Origen made, together with his added comments upon difficult passages and mooted questions. How much nearer was he to the times and characters of which he wrote, than is our own historian, Prescott, to those which he describes! Does any one doubt the latter, either the honesty of the man or the reality of the events recorded? The cases are not parallel, but they are enough alike, as to evidence, to strengthen our faith in the Gospels, especially when we remember that Origen does not give us merely his own opinion, but the concurrent opinion of the whole Christian community, and many communities, in his day. And then, as another step in the line of testimony, his master, Clement, takes us thirty or forty years nearer still to Christ; and with him, Tertullian and Irenæus, the last of whom was a pupil of Polycarp, himself a disciple of John the Evangelist. These writers also quote 'freely from the Gospels, enumerating and describing them, and showing their identity with our own.

Take, then, another easy illustration. Irenæus stands at about the same distance from the first preacher of Christianity, as that which separates us from the period of the American Revolution. As we have talked with men who were familiar with the leaders of that Revolution, so Irenæus had conversed with one who was intimate with the beloved disciple; and his testimony, in the treatise that has come down to us, is direct and ample in favor of the existence and authorship of the Gospels, and of the sacred regard in which they were held at that early day.

It is unnecessary to go further in this testimony, though Justin Martyr and Papias were still nearer Christ's time, and both refer to the Gospels in a way that confirms and completes the proof. The proof is cumulative and conclusive. You can bring no stronger evidence, I think none as strong, for the authenticity and integrity of any other ancient writings. Indeed, it is conceded by all, as matter of historical verity, that in the second century, when their truth or falsehood could be surely known, the Gospels which you now read in the New Testament were universally read in the churches, and held sacred by at least three millions of persons, as genuine productions of those whose names they bear, and true records of the facts they state.

And now let me ask you, my friend, if you know how much is proved when this fact is admitted. It is one thing to demand proof, another to know when you have it. And though you may think that that is a poor sort of evidence

26 *

which is not perceived and felt, I must remind you that it requires some knowledge of the nature of evidence, and some habit of reasoning, as well as docility and candor, to see and admit the force of many arguments in common life. No faculty is so much neglected, even in the best systems of education and courses of instruction, as the logical faculty. Every year we meet young men and young women, not of the ignorant but of the educated classes, who think themselves very adroit reasoners, and love dearly to *argue*, but seem scarcely to know what argument means, and, when fairly and completely refuted, return to their positions again and again, as if nothing had been brought against them ; and this, not always from pertinacity, or pride of opinion, but seemingly from ignorance of the very laws of reasoning. There is here both a mental and moral habit, to be well considered. And without bringing allegations, — a very unfair way of answering an opposer or inquirer, — I only call your attention to the fact, and beg you to be sure that on no subject, least of all in religious investigations, where the young and confident are most prone to this weakness, you take up objections hastily, or fail to consider what is really proved, and all that is thence to be inferred and admitted.

Here, for example, is a fact clearly established ; not a theory, dogma, assumption, or superstition, nor yet the assertion and opinion of one man or several, but a great historical fact, attested by all the early churches and oldest Christian writers, confirmed by Roman and Jewish authors, whose prejudices were all against it, and proved also by the opposers and assailants of Christianity, whose very objections and quotations show the existence then, and general acceptance, of the same Gospels that we hold. And this is the fact itself, — that these books, whose statements, incidents, miracles, and revelations you cannot accept or credit, were accepted, believed, and followed by multitudes at a time when to invent them was impossible, as the truth of their assertions could be easily proved or disproved. This fact is admitted. You admit it yourself, I presume, as all do who know anything about it. Why, then, do they not admit, and why do not you admit, the truth of the religion, the reality of the revelation, contained in the books they received and revered? " O, that is another matter," you say. No, my friend, it is not another matter; it is this matter, and no other, and no less. If these Gospels, with the events they record, and the characters they portray, particularly that of Christ, in his life, death, and resurrection, were so early received, and the events believed, yea, *known* to be true, it is as conclusive evidence of their truth, and as absolute demonstration, as history, fact, or human nature admits. Believe this, and, if you are consistent or at all reasonable, you will believe the divine origin of Christianity, the supernatural character of Jesus Christ, his delegated and indisputable authority, his exercise of power such as no man can have except God be with him in a more than ordinary sense, the fulfilment of his own and many former predictions, the certainty of his resurrection and ours, the necessity and availableness of repentance and obedience, the accountableness and immortality of every soul of man.

You admit all these truths, provided the Gospels are true. And that the Gospels are true, I repeat, you have all the evidence that the nature of the case admits, all, therefore, that you have a right to ask. The truths alleged are not rumors, guesses, or possibilities; they are certainties, if the facts are certain. And the facts are certain, if anything can be known of the history of the past. They are as sure

as human testimony can make them ; and he who rejects
human testimony rejects the whole past.   They are as
sure as the destruction of Jerusalem by Titus, or the burning of Rome by Nero, or the infidelity of Celsus, the apostasy of Julian, and the conversion of Constantine.   You
read with interest Josephus's History of the Jews, so insep-
arable from the history of early Christianity ; you enjoy the
ability and ingenuity, perhaps the sneers, of Gibbon, whose
attempt to explain the spread of Christianity assumes and
asserts the truth of the most material facts in question.
Then by what reasoning or pretence can you reject or
doubt the truths of the New Testament history ?   It stands
upon evidence which all the principles of sound logic and
common law require you to admit, and which eminent
lawyers and impartial judges, coming to the examination
as they would to a law question, often with prepossessions
unfavorable, have again and again sifted, weighed, and
pronounced conclusive.   On far lighter grounds, on evidence of a kind and degree that will not bear a moment's
comparison with this, remote events are believed by all ;
theories and stories, new marvels and incredible statements,
are accepted as indubitable ; the most momentous verdicts
are rendered, under oath, on merely circumstantial testimony ; property is staked, risks encountered, life exposed,
and many lives legally taken away.   If you have little confidence in professional theologians or interested ministers
of the Gospel, you may have faith, or at least respect, for
the judgment of such a mind and character as those of
Mr. Greenleaf, late Professor in the Cambridge Law School.
In a large volume, which he published while there, on the
Harmony of the Gospels, &c., he thus speaks of the weight
and value of the evidence on which they rest : " If it were
the case of a claim to a franchise, and a copy of an ancient

deed or charter were produced in support of the title, under parallel circumstances, on which to presume its genuineness, no lawyer, it is believed, would venture to deny its admissibility in evidence, nor the satisfactory character of the proof."

But I have said enough, perhaps more than enough, on this one point. To one I have confined myself in this letter, and, believing it essential, have been willing to repeat myself until I could make clear that which many minds, believing as well as doubting, appear to see darkly and hold loosely, if at all; namely, that the evidence on which we rest the genuineness of the Gospels is the same in kind as other evidence, and in degree superior to that which upholds any other system of truth or train of facts so remote. Weigh this evidence well. Scrutinize it as much as you will; summon the witnesses and question and cross-question them to any extent; subject the whole to the severest test you can invent, so that it be reasonable and just; — then, in the fear and love of God, with the thought of your fallibility and accountableness, and the stupendous consequences, to yourself and to all men, of receiving or rejecting such truth, *if it be truth*, make up your own decision; or, if not able to do that, persevere in getting all the light you can, and especially in seeking the wisdom that cometh from above.

Yours, in sincerity and hope,

H.

THE NATURAL MAN AND THE SPIRITUAL MAN.

THE Apostle observes, that " the natural man receiveth not the things of the spirit of God, because they are spiritually discerned." The word *natural*, which here occurs, is

the same in the original which in two other places in the
New Testament is rendered *sensual.* The Apostle James
speaks of the wisdom that is not from above as being
" earthly and *sensual.*" The Apostle Jude speaks of
those " who walk after their own lusts as *sensual,* having
not the spirit." The natural or sensual man is one enslaved to appetite, earthly and vitiated in his temperament
and inclinations, having no relish for subjects of a spiritual
and elevated character. Spiritual truth requires a spiritual
taste, or capacity to discern it. It must be viewed through
a medium not discolored or distorted by any selfish, sordid,
or worldly influence.

That the things of the spirit of God are to be spiritually
discerned in order to be appreciated, involves no mystery,
nothing that need discourage any one in his religious convictions ; they are those eternal and immutable truths which
the inspiration of God has given to the world. When
willingly received and faithfully applied, they breathe into
the soul a spirit of holiness, and produce a spiritual life.
Truths proceeding from a spiritual source will be of a spiritual temper, and lead to a spiritual result.

The inquiry naturally arises, how this spiritual discernment of spiritual subjects is to be acquired ; how this
love for the pure, heavenly, and divine is to become the
prevailing attribute of the soul. We say, generally, as
other important attainments are made. The person that is
devoted to the study of philosophy discovers great beauty
in the subject. His whole heart is in it. It occupies his
entire mind. Everything around him he beholds with a
scientific eye. To him everything in the material world
is philosophically discerned. As he is continually inves-
tigating the works of Nature, to him she unfolds her mysteries, which are not perceived by the common mind. The

person devoted to the study of mathematics discovers beauties in the science which escape common observation. With enthusiastic pleasure he studies his diagrams, and draws therefrom some new, mysterious truth. The person devoted to the fine arts will discover beauties or blemishes in a piece . of statuary, or a design on canvas, that would entirely escape ' the notice of the common observer. He could see where the chisel or pencil could have given more prominence to a feature, or more life to the expression. It was by consuming days and nights in his *studio* that he acquired this exquisite taste and accurate discernment.

These illustrations are sufficient to show on what conditions we may reasonably be expected to be experimentally acquainted with religious themes. If we are as devoted to religion as men are to other subjects, which absorb their thoughts and control their affections, we shall doubtless become spiritually capacitated to understand it, and to know something of its vitality and power. God, the inspirer of all good impressions, will assist our humble inquiries, and strengthen all good purposes. He will make that plain to the inquiring mind, which will be dark to those who neglect their moral and religious culture. As a man by a long attention to philosophical study, has acquired a peculiar taste for it, so by an habitual acquaintance with spiritual truth we contract a fondness for it, and fully understand that it is the true bread which the soul requires for its nourishment and growth;—as our Saviour observes to his disciples, "It is given unto you to know the mysteries of the kingdom of heaven"; and this was owing to their devoted attention to his instructions. They were teachable and free from prejudice; and this prepared them to understand these parables, which were hid from the stupid and prejudiced multitude. Thus to understand the mysteries of the Gospel,

we must cultivate a docile temper, and " receive the kingdom of God as a little child."

How, it may be reasonably asked, can we be expected
to attain to a spiritual apprehension of divine truth, unless
we give it a devoted attention ? How can we know the
joy and peace of believing, unless the proper subjects of
faith are familiar to our minds ? To one person a passage
of Scripture appears without interest, and he derives no instruction from it, when to another, who has made the Bible
his study, it is full of force and meaning. There is nothing
unaccountable in this. In the one case an ignorance of
the sacred volume disqualifies him from discerning the
precious pearls that lie hid within it ; and in the other case
a familiar acquaintance with it enables him to trace the
golden thread which runs through its inspired pages, connecting passage with passage and truth with truth.

There is no mystery that mankind should be so opposite
in their tastes and acquirements in regard to spiritual subjects. It is to be accounted for on well-known principles,
which, in the above remarks, have been shown and illustrated. How is it possible, that those who ignore the Gospel and shun its influences should know how to admire the
divine perfections or a Saviour's love ? How can those
living in the practice of sin know " the beauty of holiness " ?
How can those whose whole souls are absorbed in worldly
care know anything of spiritual happiness ? We must
not look for the fruit and enjoyment of religion where its
seed has not been planted and cultivated.

We live in a world full of instruction, if we will only
open our minds to receive it. The outward universe is
ever telling us something of God. The book of nature
seems to speak to us of our obligation to love and obey its
Author; and the volume of revelation is ready to teach us

those deep things pertaining to the method of his mercy on which the light of nature is silent. But both of these sources of instruction will be sealed to us unless we repair to them in the spirit of earnest inquiry.

In proportion as we give to religion our attention and trust will it reveal to us its divine reward. "For whosoever hath," faithfully improves what he hath, " to him shall be given, and he shall have more abundance." A devout frame of mind will prepare us to make still further attainments in knowledge and virtue. Obedience to the Gospel will enable us to understand its essential truths and requirements. It is the great law of our spiritual being, that the more we seek, the more shall we be capacitated to find.

Let it not be that we have eyes and see not, and ears and hear not, because our hearts are too gross, too earthly and sensual, to apprehend those spiritual relations which God, in his infinite kindness, has set before us in order to become the true riches of the soul. Let us, above all things else, study to understand our higher nature, its capacity, its wants; then God will not have spoken to us in vain; Christ will not have labored and suffered for us in vain ; we shall not have lived in vain.

P. S.

THE DIVINE PROCESS OF RECONCILIATION.

THE whole process of man's reconciliation with God is obviously set forth in the parable of the Prodigal Son. We have a right to say this, because no reader can doubt that our Saviour intended to present in this beautiful picture an ideal of a good parent; that he himself entirely approved the conduct he ascribed to the prodigal's father; that he meant it to be understood as indicating the course that a wise, kind, and just parent would take. No reader ever imagined that it was intended as a picture of parental weakness, or suspected that Christ put his own sentiments into the mouth of the elder brother, who thought the penitent was received back on too easy terms.

The process of reconciliation, thus illustrated, is simple and intelligible. The picture presented to the imagination is complete. It satisfies at once the conscience and the heart. Every parent feels that he ought thus to treat a penitent child, and every child feels that he would most honor his parent by expecting from him such treatment. And as this parable is obviously designed to illustrate the dealings of God with his sinning and repenting children, if any other element were essential to our reconciliation it would have been introduced. But the introduction of another element would mar the beauty of the picture. We should then have an ideal of a parent more perfect than our Father in heaven.

The prodigal was received and forgiven on the sole ground of his repentance, and desire and purpose of reformation. The father demanded no satisfaction for insulted parental authority, no expiation for a violated law, no reparation for wasted goods. Neither did he wait till the son had proved the reality of his penitence and reformation by a long course of goodness, but immediately took him back into the family, and permitted him to complete the process of restoration under a father's care, and with a father's encouragement and help.

There is a certain amount of retribution from which no human love can save a penitent. It is a necessary result of our moral constitution. The prodigal must have experi. enced it, — notwithstanding his free pardon and his imme.

diate restoration to the privileges of the filial relation, — in bitter regrets for wasted time and property, in self-incurred moral weakness, in long and arduous struggles with depraved tastes, inflamed appetites and passions, and evil habits strengthened by a long course of sin, and it must have been long before he enjoyed the full peace of confirmed goodness.   And as an earthly parent cannot, so our Heavenly Parent does not, deliver his children from these consequences of transgression.   Yet does the true penitent immediately become an object of God's complacent regard, and in all his conflicts with the manifold difficulties and disabilities consequent upon his past sins, he may know that the favor, blessing, and aid of his Father are with him.

It is observable that in this illustration of the great reconciliation no mediator appears.   In the course of his own silent meditations the prodigal " comes to himself," and resolves to arise and go to his father, and he goes immediately into the presence of the father, without an advocate or intercessor.   Yet is this parable in fact full of Christ. The place of his mediation in the process of reconciliation is indicated by the fact that it is he who gives us this touching exhibition of the father's pardoning love.   This fact also indicates the nature of Christ's mediation.   It consists, not in suffering in his own person the penalty of our sins, or doing anything whereby it is made possible or right for the Father to do what else he could not or would not have done ; but he reconciles man to God by melting the heart of man in penitence, and filling it with faith in the Father's love, which has been ever the same, and ever waiting to receive, pardon, bless, and help the penitent.

This parable ought to be considered the leading passage in the New Testament on the subject of man's reconciliation with God, or, as it is popularly called, the Atonement.

Its instruction is clear, complete, and decisive. It would seem that other more obscure passages, instead of reflecting darkness upon this, should be permitted to borrow light from it. We might safely leave the doctrine where the parable leaves it. Any objection to the doctrine of the free pardon of sin, on the sole conditions of sincere repentance and return to God, is in fact an objection against this parable itself. Since, however, such objections are made, we will subjoin a few remarks.

Placability makes an essential part of our idea of a complete moral character. One who rigorously exacts every due that justice permits him to claim, and who demands full reparation for every injury that is done him, is not a good man. Our moral judgment condemns his character. We see that he is wanting in that compassion and disinterestedness that enter into our conceptions of high excellence. That virtue of justice which all men are obligated to practise consists in faithfully rendering to others all that they can justly demand of us, but it does not oblige us to demand of others all that we can equitably claim of them. Justice requires that we pay to our neighbor the debts we owe him, but certainly we can forgive him the debts that he owes us without a violation of justice. Our rights are our own, and we can forego the enforcement of them whenever we please, and benevolence will often require us to refrain from enforcing them. There are many cases in which we should do wrong to insist upon them. The assumption that God could not consistently with justice pardon the sinner without full satisfaction for his sins, seems, therefore, to have been made unwarrantably, and without regard to the first principles of justice. Was any man ever deterred from indulging an inclination to forgive a poor debtor his debt by the belief that it would be a sin against justice?

It is sometimes said that no government could be maintained by the principle of freely pardoning offenders on repentance alone; that it would be subversive of all civil authority; that, when an offence has been committed against the law, it is necessary, to vindicate the majesty of the law, that the offender should suffer. But this objection is founded on imperfections in human government, which must not be imputed to the Divine. The reason why it would be subversive of civil order in a state to proclaim free pardon to all penitent criminals is, that the magistrate cannot look into the heart to determine the sincerity of repentance, but would be continually liable to be imposed on by hypocrisy, and to let loose upon society men who were still disposed to disturb its peace. Still, however, the fact that in all governments the power of pardon is lodged somewhere for occasional use, shows that even human government is not wholly a stranger to this principle, and that the offender can sometimes go unpunished without injury to the sanctity of the law. But suppose that the magistrate could look into the heart, and that he should see with certainty that an offender had truly repented, that his evil propensities were completely subdued, and that he was prepared to become a peaceable, honest, useful member of society, can any good reason be given why the penalty of the law should not be remitted? Would not the infliction of further punishment be unnecessary and gratuitous evil?

Objections to the doctrine we have here maintained are drawn from analogies of civil government, rather than of domestic government. But the whole tenor and spirit of the Gospel lead us to look to the family rather than to the state for illustrations of this subject. Domestic government is much more perfect and discriminating in its adaptations to the characters and conditions of individuals than civil

27 *

government, and therefore more nearly resembles the government of God. The ruler cannot know all his subjects as the parent knows his child. He cannot adjust the course of his government to individual cases. He is obliged to enact general laws, to annex one unvarying penalty to transgression, and to inflict that penalty whenever the law is violated. But the discipline of the parent admits of being accurately adapted to the circumstances and moral condition of each child. The ruler does not afford the subject any direct help in obeying the law under which he is placed, but the parent can aid and encourage his child, and, by the influence he may exert over him, breathe into him moral strength to perform what is required of him. Civil government can take no cognizance of repentance, but the parent can judge of the effect of punishment on his child, and can remit it as soon as it has produced sincere contrition, or forbear to inflict it at all when it has been made unnecessary by a quick repentance. In all these respects, how much more effectual is family government than civil government. We repeat, it is from the analogy of the family, and not of the state, that the Gospel invites us to form our conception of God.

We have lately seen it asserted, that, if God *can* forgive sin on the sole condition of repentance and reformation, he has nowhere declared that he *will* do so. We can only express our unfeigned astonishment that any attentive and candid reader could bring away such an impression from the perusal either of the Old or the New Testament; and will subjoin a few passages in which the free pardon of sin that is truly repented of and forsaken is most explicitly declared or necessarily implied.

Isaiah lv. 7. "Let the wicked forsake his way, and the unrighteous man his thoughts; and let him return unto the

Lord, and he will have mercy on him, and to our God, for he will abundantly pardon."

Jeremiah xviii. 7, 8. "At what instant I shall speak concerning a nation and concerning a kingdom, to pluck up and pull down and to destroy it, if that nation against whom I pronounced turn from their evil, I will repent me of the evil that I thought to do unto them."

Ezekiel xviii. 21, 22. "If the wicked will turn from all the sins that he hath committed, and keep all my statutes, and do that which is lawful and right, he shall surely live, he shall not die. All his transgressions that he hath committed, they shall not be mentioned unto him; in his righteousness that he hath done, he shall live."

The case of Nineveh. The prophet is sent to that very corrupt city to announce, without any qualification, that within forty days Nineveh should be overthrown. This announcement alarms the king and the people; they humble themselves before God, and resolve to turn away every one from his evil way, and from the violence that is in their hands. It might be argued upon this case, that their penitence and obedience could not expiate their past transgressions; that the majesty of the Divine law had been insulted, and satisfaction must be made by a quantity of suffering; that God's word had gone forth, and his veracity was concerned in the execution of the sentence. The prophet himself was displeased and angry at the event; but we read, " God repented of the evil which he said he would do unto them, and he did it not."

From the New Testament, it would be enough to refer to the parable on which we have already commented.

In another parable, in which the doctrine of forgiveness is illustrated, it is said, " I forgave thee all that debt *because thou desiredst me;* shouldest not thou also have had compassion on thy fellow-servant, even as I had pity on thee ? "

In the Lord's prayer we are taught to pray, "Forgive us our debts, as we forgive our debtors." And how are we required to forgive our debtors? "If thy brother trespass against thee seven times in a day, and seven times in a day turn again to thee, saying, I repent, thou shalt forgive him."

From that petition in the Lord's prayer it follows that the principle on which God forgives, and the principle on which man is required to forgive, is the same. Either man is not required to forgive till after strict reparation of an injury, or else God forgives on the sole condition of true repentance.

P.

MEETINGS OF THE EXECUTIVE COMMITTEE.

A REGULAR monthly meeting of the Executive Committee was held December 4, 1854, at which all the members were present, with the exception of Hon. Albert Fearing.

The President, as chairman of the Committee on Publications, made a report in favor of printing a manuscript, submitted at a former meeting, by Mr. John Wilson of Boston. The Committee had carefully examined this work, and were unanimously of opinion that it was the fruit of extensive and painstaking research, and that it would exert a strong influence in favor of Christian charity and truth. Mr. Wilson has collected from a wide range of Trinitarian authors the testimonies they furnish in support of the cardinal principles of Unitarianism. It is not a reprint of his well-known work, entitled "Concessions of Trinitarians." That work was chiefly devoted to an examination of *texts of Scripture.* This, on the other hand, relates to principles of interpretation, the proper exercise of reason, the duty of candor, and inquiry, and mutual courtesy and respect, the characteristics of true Christianity, &c.; and the title which it had been proposed to affix to the work is the following : *Unitarian Principles confirmed by Trinitarian Testimonies.* The value of such a work must depend upon the number and high standing of the authors from whom the *testimonies* are quoted. Judged by this rule, Mr. Wilson's book will be one of great importance, and can hardly fail of exerting a deep and beneficial influence. It will prove that the chief principles for which Unitarian Christians contend have at times found strong assertion from the highest Trinitarian authorities. Some delay may unavoidably occur in the issue of a book of the size and importance of this, but we hope it may, at some future time, be given to the public. The whole subject of contracting for the publication of the work was referred to the Committee on Publications, with full power.

The Secretary made a report in regard to the preparation of a Prayer-Book. In answer to a circular, he had received between seventy and eighty forms of prayer, and nothing remained now but to arrange them in some proper order for publication. From the examination bestowed upon them, it was believed that they would make a valuable book for domestic and private devotion, and that, as the composition of so many different clergymen, it would be peculiarly acceptable to the public. The Committee on Publications were authorized to proceed with the materials on hand, and publish a Prayer-Book in such arrangement and form as they may judge best. This is the work whose publication is announced in another part of this Journal.

The Secretary stated that he had received an application

from the " Lawrence Athenæum," in Lawrence, Kanzas, for a gift of all the publications of the Association, for the library of that institution. As an opportunity of forwarding them presented itself at the time the application was received, he did not wait for the approval of the Executive Committee, but had made up a package of books and had sent them to Kanzas. It was voted to approve of the action of the Secretary, and to give the books forwarded to the " Lawrence Athenæum."

The chief part of the time of this session of the Committee was occupied in the discussion of some plans, submitted by the President, in regard to the extension of our publishing business, and to the commencement of a *series of Libraries*, into which all our religious literature may be gathered. After a free interchange of opinion upon this subject, the whole matter was referred to the Committee on Publications, to report at a subsequent meeting.

January 8, 1855. At the meeting of the Committee this day, the whole Board was present, with the exception of Hon. Stephen Fairbanks and George Callender, Esq.

A letter was read from the new Unitarian Society in Exeter, N. H., giving a brief account of its rise, condition, prospects, and wants, and concluding by soliciting some assistance from the Association. It was voted to appropriate one hundred and fifty dollars in aid of that Society.

Proposals from Mr. Channing, in regard to the publication of another edition of Channing's Works, were submitted to the Committee. It was stated that but a few copies are now on hand, and that a thousand copies had been sold during the last year. The importance of continuing to supply this work at the lowest possible rate was acknowledged by all; and the Business Committee were directed to conclude a bargain for one thousand copies, on the most favorable terms.

The Secretary made a full statement in regard to the condition of the Tracts. The Association has long been unable to supply complete sets, as many of the tracts are out of print. For the same reason, a plan, commenced during the last year, of binding volumes of tracts, selected according to *subjects*, has been suspended, because many of the most valuable of these publications cannot now be supplied. The facts in regard to the entire series were briefly these. Of the three hundred published, we have the stereotype plates of about one hundred; we have some copies, enough for a present supply, of another hundred; while of the rest we have either no copies at all, or at best but very few. It was a subject of great regret that the whole series had not been stereotyped as fast as they were issued. But then no one expected they would be called for to the extent to which they have circulated, and another edition, it was thought, would meet all future wants, though in some cases these editions have been multiplied to the number of twelve. These successive issues could have been furnished at small cost, if the Association had possessed the stereotype plates. The time, it was believed, had come when a new policy should be adopted, and we should begin to stereotype all the old tracts as fast as they are wanted. The plan of doing this requires us to look to the probable extent to which these tracts will be called for in future years. We see no reason to doubt that they may still have a wide circulation. They constitute one of the best products of our religious literature, and the controversial tracts, which may have done their work in this part of the country, are needed in remote places, where Unitarianism has more recently arisen. In view of the facts of the case, it was voted that it was expedient to stereotype at once one hundred of the tracts now out of print, under the direction of the Committee on Publications.

It was voted to publish a book, entitled " Early Piety ; or Recollections of Harriet B——." This little work has since appeared from the press, and a notice of it will be found in another part of this Journal.

. The Treasurer brought to the notice of the Committee the fact that the sum of five thousand dollars, a part of the Permanent Fund, might soon require to be reinvested, in consequence of the change of hands through which the Indiana Street Church has passed. It was voted that this subject be referred to the Business Committee, with full power.

The Committee on Publications, to whom had been referred the suggestions of the President in regard to embodying our literature in a series of libraries, made an extended written report. It recommended the adoption of the plan with reference to books to be hereafter published by the Association ; and that the first library of the series be called *The Devotional Library*, the first number of which shall be the Prayer-Book, soon to be published. It recommended, further, that other libraries be called *The Biblical Library*, including works explanatory of the Scriptures, such as a Commentary on the New Testament, which it is hoped we may ere long be able to publish ; a Bible Dictionary, if a suitable work can be found ; Bible Atlas, &c. ; — *The Theological Library*, including all our best standard books on theology ; — *The Biographical Library*, in which department our literature is singularly full and valuable ; — *The Christian Youth's Library*, embracing works adapted to the young. It was further recommended, that we should endeavor to obtain original works in all these departments, by offering to pay a liberal compensation to authors ; but that in all cases, whether by the adoption of books already published, or by the issue of original works, the utmost care should be taken to accept only those of the highest merit and of a permanent interest. It is hoped that in this way it may come at length to be regarded as a recommendation to a book if it have a place in one of these libraries. The Committee recommended that this plan be followed up as fast as the receipts from the Book Fund of the Association will allow; and that in the matter of contracting for printing, paper, binding, &c., the Association will gladly avail itself of the practical experience and successful business ability which has been kindly offered for its assistance.

The report, of which the above is an abstract, was accepted, and its suggestions were unanimously adopted.

A special meeting of the Committee was held January 25, 1855, at which only a quorum of the Board was present.

Votes of thanks were passed to Messrs. James Munroe & Co., to Rev. T. B. Fox, and to Messrs. Hickling, Swan, & Brown, for the gift of valuable books to the library of the Association.

The Secretary made a statement of the terms on which Mr. Channing would supply the Association with one thousand copies of Channing's Works, and the Secretary was authorized to contract for the same.

The subject of the preparation of a new Commentary on the New Testament came up for consideration. It was felt, that, in addition to the valuable Biblical aids already furnished, there was a call for a book of a different character from any now accessible ; and that an important service would be rendered to families, Bible-classes, and

Sunday-school teachers, if we could supply them with *one cheap volume*, containing the results of the best scholarship, explanatory of the historical books and epistles of the New Testament. The importance of a condensed but thorough treatment of this subject, in the spirit of faith and reverence, and under the lights of a broad and sound investigation, was felt on all sides ; and the subject was referred to the Publishing Committee, in the hope that some plan for meeting this want may soon be reported.

It was voted that the subject of affixing a title to the Book of Prayers now in press be referred to the President and Secretary, with full power.

February 12, 1855. At the regular meeting of the Committee, this day, all the members of the Board were present.

The Secretary having stated that valuable presents to the library of the Association had been made by Hon. James Savage, Rev. William Mountford, Hon. J. G. Palfrey, and Messrs. Crosby, Nichols, & Co., it was voted that the Secretary communicate the thanks of the Association to these gentlemen.

The time of this meeting of the Committee was mostly taken up in considering two subjects, as important as any that ever came before the Board. These were the establishment of a missionary station in India, and the adoption of Rev. James Tanner as the Missionary of the Association among the Chippewa Indians, in Minnesota Territory. We shall be expected to dwell on both of these subjects at some length.

Ever since the return of Rev. Charles T. Brooks from Calcutta, which place he visited last summer, the Committee have desired to give our Unitarian brethren in India some token of our sympathy. The report of Mr. Brooks, which may be found in the Journal of last October, need not here be quoted. It will be recollected by all who read it, that he found Unitarians in Calcutta, that he visited Rev. William Roberts in Madras, and accompanied that earnest and devoted laborer to the schools, which, amid circumstances of much privation, he continues to sustain. It was not from these alone that there came an earnest entreaty for a missionary and books. A spirit of inquiry had arisen among Mussulmans, who desired to know something of our views of Christianity. Believers in the undivided unity of God, they were repelled from the instructions of Trinitarian missionaries, and felt a great curiosity to learn how we, Unitarians, interpreted the religion of Jesus Christ. The letter they sent to the Association, under their own hand, is a most interesting document; and their earnest call for light was felt to be one to which it was our Christian duty to respond. The Executive Committee placed much reliance upon the judgment of Rev. Mr. Brooks, who, not only in the report above referred to, but in personal interviews, expressed a strong desire that help might be sent to India, as he believed that missionary service could be there rendered with hopes of encouraging success. One short paragraph from Mr. Brooks's report may here be recalled. Writing of Madras, he says : —

" I felt that there was something of the moral sublime in this little handful of poor people thus continuing to hold forth, year after year, the light of the simple Gospel, between the native idolatry, on one hand, and the Trinitarian idolatry and Calvinistic superstition (which, while nominally warring with it, are also working with it), on the other. I look upon them as a little band of martyrs, for poverty and obloquy are their only earthly reward. I was moved solemnly to promise them and myself that I would plead for them with my brethren in America, — which I now do. They seem to me to need, immediately, and deserve, our pecuniary assistance. If the Association would vote them a sum, say of $ 500, and afterwards an annual appropriation, it would be money well spent; it would plant roses in the wilderness, and kindle the star of hope in a dreary sky. It would trim a light for the Gentiles and for them that sit in the shadow of death. And, then, I would submit whether, by and by, our Association might not combine with the British, in sending out a missionary, who, assuming the general oversight of the stations, Calcutta, Madras, and the interior, might perhaps make his head-quarters at the first of these places, and there organize a Society."

One good effect of publishing these statements in the Quarterly Journal was early brought to our notice. They awakened a missionary spirit in many hearts, and several persons conversed with the Secretary on the subject of their undertaking a mission to India. During the last winter he was in communication with them touching this matter; but of them all, Rev. Mr. Dall appeared to have the best qualifications for this work. After repeated interviews, Mr. Dall was asked to draw up a paper setting forth his feelings in regard to this enterprise, which paper the Secretary presented to the Executive Committee. It is as follows : —

"GENTLEMEN OF THE COMMITTEE : —

" After a study of some weeks concerning the practicability of establishing a Unitarian Mission in the East Indies, — with the co-workers we have already there to direct the way, — I come before you to say that I am willing to go and labor there as God shall give me power and opportunity. ' How shall they go except they be sent ? ' is the Apostolic question that brings me to your door for aid. I am not able to go at my own charges; and I pray your answer to the inquiry, what your Board would be able to do, if they shall conclude that it is best to accept such services as I have to offer.

"I well remember the anxiety with which both of the sainted Wares sought the highest welfare of the Unitarian Church, in the establishment of a mission to the East Indies. I was then almost a child; yet from that day, and through a course of theological training at their hands, and fourteen subsequent years of home missionary life at St. Louis, in Baltimore, in Canada, &c., I have never wholly parted with the wish and prayer to go forth bearing the cross of such a mission.

"I believe that a missionary spirit, longing to embrace the world, struggles for expression in the enlarging heart of the Unitarian Church, not less, but much more, than it did twenty-five or thirty years ago. I see the self-sacrificing work of a foreign mission connected more intimately than ever with our religious life as a denomination. Now, more than ever, we must water the desert and solitary places, if we would be freshly watered from on high.

"'Five years is the average term of life granted to American missionaries in the East Indies,' says the revered 'Adoniram Judson, after an observation of more than thirty years upon the ground. Still, 'He that loseth his life for my sake, and the Gospel's, shall find it.' And, 'Whoso hateth not his own life for my sake cannot be my disciple.' Such words of our Lord and Saviour Jesus Christ have rung in my ears from the first day I was able to read them until now. And now *shall I be sent,* in a way to engage *many* hearts around me here to bless and be blessed by *many* there, — going with no wisdom but Christ's love to perishing men, and an utter faith in him as the single and only God-commissioned Saviour of the world? The special plans of labor that I believe myself competent to execute, I shall gladly lay before your respected Board at an early day, — if you see fit to entertain the offer and aid the prayer of your fellow-laborer for Christ and his 'little ones.'

"C. H. A. DALL.

"*Boston, February* 12, 1855."

After the reading of the above letter, Mr. Dall appeared personally before the Committee. A long and free con-

28 *

ference ensued. Much information which he had previously obtained was laid before the Board. It related to the number and wants of those in India who are open to our influence, to the best means of ministering to them, to the probable expense of the proposed mission, and to the spirit and aims in which it should be undertaken.

Upon Mr. Dall's withdrawal from the Rooms, a free consultation was held, and it appeared that but one impression was left upon all minds. That impression was, that the case called for the Christian action of the Committee, and that Mr. Dall's education, experience, and heart all fitted him for usefulness in the sphere to which his affections have been led. The following votes were unanimously passed : —

" *Resolved*, That this Board establish a missionary station in India.

" *Resolved*, That the appointment of a Missionary for this station, and all other necessary arrangements for the execution of the foregoing resolve, be referred to a special committee, consisting of Messrs. Fearing, Briggs, Lothrop, and Miles, with full power to act, and to appropriate any amount of money not exceeding one thousand dollars per annum."

The action of this special committee, and the instructions they gave to their Missionary, may be found detailed in this Journal, under the head of " Mission to India."

After the disposal of this subject, the Secretary stated that he had invited Rev. James Tanner to meet the Committee, and present some plans to them which he desired to lay before the Board. A brief notice of Mr. Tanner's life may be found in this Journal, under the head of " James Tanner." Mr. Tanner had been in Boston several weeks, and had had personal interviews with several members of the Committee. Some time was consumed in giving the Board a brief history of the facts narrated in the article just referred to. When it was understood who and what Mr. Tanner was, he proceeded to speak of the purpose for which he had desired this interview. He had been in the employ of the Baptist Home Missionary Society, and his station had been among the people of his own tribe, — the Chippewas of Minnesota. Some differences of opinion had sprung up between him and that Society in regard to the best mode of converting the Indians to a Christian state. The funds of the Society had been raised solely for preaching the Gospel. But experience proved that much must be done in addition to this. The roving habits of the Indians must be broken up; they must be gathered into fixed communities; they must be attached to the land; the arts of agriculture must be introduced and taught; schools must be formed, and local churches organized. Without all this, converts to Christianity can be subjected to no oversight and training; they wander away on hunting or warlike expeditions, and the foundations of a civilized community are not laid. He had had long experience among the Indians, and he thought he saw the causes of the failure of nearly all missionary attempts. Finding his views unsupported by the Baptist Missionary Society, he had declined an appointment to be their servant. He had come to Boston to obtain aid from his religious friends in this city. But he had found most of the churches closed against him, by a notice from the Missionary Society. In this case he was on the point of returning in despair, when he was introduced to some Unitarians in this city.

We should be glad to give the particulars relating to this point in Mr. Tanner's life. We must content ourselves by a general allusion to them. At the table in his boarding-house a theological question had been started, — whether God suffered and died on the cross. He was shocked at certain opinions he had heard expressed. His assertion that the Great Spirit could not suffer and die, and that it was the Son of God who died on the cross, was met with the charge of Unitarianism. He had before heard of that word, and had been told that it was something " as dreadful as that with which some mothers frighten their children " ; but, now, resolved to learn what it was, he had been to Unitarian meetings, he had conversed with Unitarian ministers, he had procured books from the Unitarian Rooms; and as the result of his inquiries he would say, that on the subject of the Great Spirit, and of his Son Jesus Christ, he held the same views which the Unitarians held, and had always held them ever since he was a converted man, and he did not believe that one of his Indian converts in his tribe was a Trinitarian.

While, then, through a doctrinal sympathy with Unitarians, he could work heartily with them, believing that their prayers, and preaching, and interpretation of the Scriptures, would have the most favorable acceptance among the people of his tribe, the question was, whether the Association could aid him in the work which was near his heart. To answer this question, the Association must know fully his Christian character, and his plans of action.

Mr. Tanner then presented a large number of credentials, consisting of a certificate of his church-membership and Christian character; of recommendatory letters from Baptist clergymen in St. Paul, Minnesota Territory, Chicago, Cleveland, Brooklyn, N.Y., and Boston, and from Rev. Silas Bailey, President of Franklin College, Indiana, in which institution Mr. Tanner has a son, a lad of twelve years of age; of letters, also, addressed to Hon. Wm. L.

Marcy, Secretary of State, speaking in high terms of Mr. Tanner's devotedness and efficiency ; and of two communi‑cations which we must give entire. The first is from the chief and braves of the Chippewa nation, and is addressed to "His Excellency, N. A. Gorman, Governor of Minne‑sota," dated "Crow Wing, Min. Ter., Oct. 23, 1854." It reads as follows : —

"Our Father, — Hearing of the love thou hast for thy Indian children, and of the efforts and desire thou hast for our civiliza‑tion, which was made known to us by our former teacher, Mr. Tanner, for which, our father, we feel grateful, although we but lately heard of it; also hearing of the provisions made by your government at Washington, to assist us to become a civilized people, and to live as the white man does ; —

"We, the undersigned, do therefore by this apply to your In‑dian Department at Washington, through you, our father, for assistance, to get us some farming implements, and also some teachers to teach our children to read, and to learn them to work.

"We have no one to assist us, or to teach us how to get along in work, and as it is very probable, on account of the troubles be‑tween the Sioux and our nation at Pembina, that our former teach‑er, Mr. Tanner, will fail for yet a while to form a settlement with the Chippewas at that point, if he can be had, we would recom‑mend him to your Excellency to be appointed as our assistant or teacher in these things. We would also make known to you our improvement towards farming. We have at present, in all, on and within the premises of Lake Winnepeg, between thirty and forty acres of land under cultivation, with corn, potatoes, and pumpkins. We have been now three years in doing this. We are also in number forty-five families that belong to this place. And as it was Mr. James Tanner who was the first to teach us this kind of work, and as we are all well acquainted with him, and he with us, this is our reason for recommending him to your notice ; and for which assistance, if granted, we shall truly feel very thankful, and promise, if intrusted in right hands, our father shall never have occasion to say that he has assisted us but to no purpose. We remain your unworthy, but hope obedient children.

(Signed,)   "EAGLE, *Chief of Lake Winnepeg*,"
And four Braves.

The other credential is as follows : —

"*Executive Office, St. Paul, Nov.* 6, 1854.

"SIR, — I inclose two letters from the Chippewa chief at Pembina and Lake Winnepeg. It will be seen that I have recommended Mr. Tanner as a proper person to receive ($ 500) five hundred dollars as Missionary Teacher at Pembina.

"The appeal made in these letters draws strongly on my sympathy, and I hope you may think proper to help them. Mr. Tanner is a Baptist Missionary, and a most exemplary man, and well worthy to be intrusted with this duty. He visits Washington and New York to see the Board of Missions and your Department. He is a half-blood, with a pious education, and feels deep solicitude for his relations in that far-off region.

"Respectfully, your obedient servant,
"N. A. GORMAN, *Governor Min. Ter.*
"TO THE COMMISSIONER OF INDIAN AFFAIRS, *Washington.*"

In regard to his plans of action, Mr. Tanner said he had drawn up a brief statement, which he would ask leave to read. He proceeded to read the following paper, which we give as it came from his hand.

"*Boston, Feb. 9th,* 1855.

"1st. It is my desire to introduce amongst my nation the arts of civilization with Christianization ; for in order to save the soul, we must save the body.

"It is found to be one of the first laws of God to man after his fall, that he shall till the soil ; and it was a garden that God chose to place man in after his creation for man's place of happiness ;

and it is God's will to choose for man all that will tend to make him happy: therefore, to show forth the Spirit of God in one thing, we must show it in another. God shows forth his love to man by his works; therefore, to support amongst us Indians the truths of Christianity, we must do it by works, and let those works be of God's own appointment. Then when faith, love, and works go hand in hand, then we go in God's own way; then we have the promise of his approval and assistance, for we then show our faith, our love, by our works. With this wall we surround the Indian's strong fortress of suspicion, and you conquer him. No more he looks on you as a spy, but as a loving and kind brother, true and faithful in what you say, faithful in carrying out what you preach. Then when you preach to him on love to our God and to our fellow-man, and God's love to man, he believes you by and from your works.

"2d. In order to do this, I am striving to get and carry out to them farming implements and other tools for civilizing our people, which tools, after got on the ground, instead of giving them for nothing, I propose to sell to each one as they stand in need only at cost, for furs or Indian curiosities, and then to send those articles to your Treasurer in Boston, to be disposed of at your own discretion, and the money to be used or spent in getting more implements or such things as we shall call for.

" This will tend to keep up a spirit of self-dependence in us, and be a source of encouragement to you, and will also tend to unite our hearts more together. But as for poor widows, or such as are entirely unable to purchase, to them either to give or lend as the case may demand. Therefore, in order to do this upright, you give me a bill of all implements or tools, and I give you my receipt, and at the expiration of six months from the time I get all on the field at Winnepeg, Upper Mississippi, for me to send to you a bill of tools and implements sold, given, or lent, or remaining, with the proceeds of those sold, and so on every six months. But that a certain portion be kept for the purpose of lending to those whose case shall require it, and that a necessary portion be kept exclusively for the use of the mission. It is also my desire, if possible, to get the irons for the erecting of a saw-mill, which mill, if I succeed, shall be public property until the sale of our lands, then the mill to be sold either to the government or Indians, and the money got for the mill to be used for the mission, or opening of a new mission amongst some destitute parts; and I intend that those Indians amongst whom I make a beginning shall make an annual collection for the purpose of sending help, or opening new missions in other places, which will be the means to increase the spirit of love one for another, and perseverance; for the Indian, as well as the white man, finds it to be more blessed to give than to receive.   I am also striving to open a school amongst the Indians, and to have the children taught in the English language, and at the same time to learn them to work.   Therefore it will be necessary to get a school-teacher; but the teacher must be a man that is accustomed to work, and who will be willing to put his hand to any kind of work, and not to confine himself only to school-teaching, for in all of our movements we have to keep before us constantly in view so to act as to wean from the mind of the Indian that spirit of suspicion that he ever looks on the white man with.

" I also intend to keep up at least a monthly correspondence with your several churches, through their ministers, or some other way; also with your Sabbath schools, which will tend to make us all more and more acquainted and interested one for another.

" Dear brethren, I have briefly laid before you my plans, which plans, if carried out, must require faith, love, works, patience, and perseverance; and when I look upon it all, and the many difficulties in our way, both from the side of the Indian, and from the side of the many ill-meaning white men, and the almost impossibility of laying before the white man the true spirit of the Indian; and again, when I look at the position of my own family and of the many oppositions and old systems we must contend with and break up, and then, looking at my own weakness and many failings, it at times appears to me as it appeared to Israel of old, when brought on the shores of the Red Sea with Pharaoh's host at their rear, and I am constrained to cry out, Who is enough for this great work, to bring to birth and to life a whole nation, and that to be done in a day?   I hope you clearly see that what is to be done must be done quickly, or soon nothing but the mere name of the Indian will be left. I therefore, in our distress, cry up to the Great Spirit, and to you, his children, and say to you, Help, help, or we perish!

"From your unworthy brother,

"JAMES TANNER."

The reading of the foregoing paper was followed by a free conversation between Mr. Tanner and members of the Board. A large number of questions were put to him, which elicited prompt and satisfactory replies. From these the Committee understood that the Indians of the Chippewa tribe number about two hundred and fifty thousand, that they occupy a large territory near the head-waters of the Mississippi River, that they have manifested a desire to be instructed in the arts of civilization and the truths of the Christian religion, that settlements may be formed, and schools established, and churches organized, and the foundations be laid of growing and prosperous communities. The well-known fact of the general failure of all attempts to civilize the aborigines of this country was adduced as a discouragement to any further effort; but the cause of these failures, it was contended, might be found in the cupidity of the white man, in the ignorance on the part of most missionaries of the real character of the Indian, in misdirected methods of influence, and especially in neglecting to break up the roving habits of this people, and to attach them to the soil.

As was before remarked, Mr. Tanner had been several weeks in Boston, had become acquainted with members of the Committee, had attended our religious meetings, and had addressed audiences deeply interested in himself and his plans. The impression he had made was confirmed by this examination before the Committee. It was evi-

dent that he was a man of rare native endowments, of good
practical judgment, of a penetrating knowledge of human
nature, of much power in address, of a sincere and devoted
piety, and willing to meet any sacrifices for the improvement of the people he loved.   From all the information in
the possession of the Committee, it was also evident that he
had attained a position of much influence over that people,
while his plans, though discouraged by respectable Missionary Boards, seemed the most practicable and promising
methods of influence which had been devised.   Inquiries
had also been made of the light in which he was regarded
among those with whom he had formerly acted, and of the
real causes which resulted in his separation from them ; and
the answers to these inquiries only strengthened the interest
that was felt in him.

On Mr. Tanner's withdrawal from the room, the question, what was the duty of the Committee in this case, presented itself for consideration.   On the one hand was the
danger of committing the Board to an uncertain and hazard-
ous experiment, and one, perhaps, not contemplated as
likely to fall within the sphere of our action ; while on the
other hand were these questions : Is there nothing providen-
tial in the appearance of such a man before our Board, and
in his earnest entreaty for help ?   To the friends who have
committed trusts to our hands, to our own consciences, and
to the voice of God's providence in this opportunity of usefulness, can we justify a refusal to act ?   Are we not appointed to the places we occupy, that in our best judgment
we may improve every hopeful method of diffusing far and
near the truths of a pure Christianity, and if the benighted
red men of our Western wilds come and ask us for the blessings of that Gospel, shall we turn them away empty ?

An important fact cast a light upon these questions which

aided the Committee to see the course they finally adopted. So strong had been the interest already felt in Mr. Tanner and his plans, that it was quite evident that this mission would receive a distinctive and adequate support. Offers of money and implements had already been made. Others, as it was already certain, would be received. The adoption of this mission would not call for the expenditure of funds placed in our hands before such a field of action was contemplated. By assuming the management of this mission we might give it a stability and effectiveness and chance of success, which, without such oversight, it could not have. Even should it ultimately fail, as the experiment, it must be confessed, was attended by many doubts, we should have the satisfaction of feeling that, without endangering any of the funds committed to our hands, we had tried our best to do a good work.

We have indicated but a few of the points discussed and of the thoughts entertained in the session of the Board of which we are now writing. We must hasten to the votes finally adopted, with entire unanimity, which were these: —

" *Resolved*, That, from the information laid before this Board, it is our opinion that a favorable opportunity is offered for the establishment of a mission for the diffusion of Christianity and civilization among the Chippewa Indians, in the neighborhood of Lake Winnepeg and Pembina, in Minnesota Territory.

" *Resolved*, That a sum not exceeding five hundred dollars a year be appropriated towards the support of Rev. James Tanner, as a Christian missionary among the Chippewas.

" *Resolved*, That a sum not exceeding two hundred and fifty dollars per annum be appropriated towards the support of a school-teacher in Minnesota, to work under the direction of Mr. Tanner.

" *Resolved*, That all arrangements necessary to carry into effect the preceding resolutions be referred to the special committee charged with the oversight of the mission to India."

An account of the arrangements which this Committee finally made with Mr. Tanner will be found under the article " James Tanner " in this Journal.

We have taken up much space in describing this session of the Executive Committee. To commit the Board to the work of Foreign Missions was felt to be a measure full of solemn interest. The duty to engage in this work, as opportunity invites and means allow, can be questioned only by those who doubt whether the Gospel of our Lord Jesus Christ be a blessing to the world, and whether the oft-quoted words have any meaning to us, " Go ye into all the world, and preach the Gospel to every creature." And as we close this extended account, we wish to state distinctly two or three principles which have governed our action, and which should be borne in mind.

1. We have embarked in this enterprise in no mere imitation of other denominations, in no hostility to their work, and with no intention of interfering with any of their plans. We believe that the daily prayer, *Thy kingdom come*, demands works corresponding with the spirit of this petition ; and that some devoted and self-sacrificing exertions to promote the coming of that kingdom are a manifest Christian duty, which has always been felt by many in our body, who will now, we believe, rejoice to see that duty publicly acknowledged and undertaken.

2. Yet while this is true, we have not at the same time been eager to enlist in any Quixotic experiment. The opportunities we propose to improve are not such as we have devised and made. They bear the marks of having been

made for us. They have sought us. The call has come to our Rooms, in tones of all sincerity, as we judge, and earnest and solemn entreaty ; and it is in the exercise of the best judgment we can use, and after cautious inquiry, and earnest and prayerful consideration of our duty, that we have resolved to act.

3. Though the two spheres of activity into which we propose to enter are far remote from us, and are on the opposite sides of the globe, yet they have one thing in common ; they are places where our belief in the undivided unity of God will give us great advantage for Christian effort. They are places, therefore, which it rightfully belongs to us to occupy. We go among those who have always held to the belief in the oneness of God, and who are shocked when they hear that the Godhead consists of Three Persons, one of whom suffered and died. Such can be more easily converted to the Christianity which we profess, and it is towards such that our sympathy and Christian efforts naturally turn.

4. Still, we do not embark in this work merely for denominational extension. We would keep higher aims and ends before our eyes. To those who sit in darkness we would give light, and to thousands oppressed by ignorance, superstition, and sin we would impart the temporal blessings of the Gospel, with the hope that is full of immortality. In the persons of those whose benighted condition we may help, we would see him who said, " Inasmuch as ye have done it unto the least of these, ye have done it unto me," and would be thankful if we may cast seeds of truth and grace into any corner of that field in which many noble missionaries of the cross have long labored.

5. We cannot foresee what success may attend our efforts. They may have no success. Two years may prove

that we can do no good in either of the fields we enter. Failure will reflect no disparagement upon our present motives, and efforts, and prayers. If these are right in the sight of Him who searches the heart, they may then, with increased purity and strength, be led to some more hopeful channel. Thus may we leave all with Him

> " To whose all-pondering mind
> A noble *aim* faithfully kept is as a noble *deed*,
> In whose pure thought all virtue does succeed."

6. We believe we do not misinterpret the feelings of our friends when we express our confidence that they will sustain us in the steps we have taken. Increased activity and usefulness, a more earnest and devoted Christian enterprise, — how many hearts are there among us that have longed for these! How have we needed them as a cure for our hypercriticism and our selfish isolation! What opportunities of advancing the truth as it is in Jesus Christ are open before us, if only we have the courage to enter upon them! Will not every faithful effort we make be more than recompensed in the deeper sense of the preciousness of our faith, in the increased fervor of our devotion, in the manifold fulfilment of the saying of our Lord, that it is more blessed to give than to receive?

MISSION TO INDIA.

THE reader will find in this Journal, under the " Meetings of the Executive Committee," a full account of the steps that led to the establishment of this mission. After a long discussion of this subject before the whole Board, a special committee was appointed to carry out the votes that were then passed. That committee consisted of Hon. Albert Fearing, Rev. G. W. Briggs, the President, and the Secretary.

A meeting of this special committee was held on Wednesday, February 14th; all the members were in attendance, and, by invitation, Mr. Dall was also present. A free conference took place in regard to the best plan of carrying out the purposes of the Association, and much additional information relating to the possibility and' hopes of useful missionary action in India was communicated. Mr. Dall was unanimously appointed the missionary, and he informed the Committee that he should be ready to sail in the course of a few days.

It only remained to secure a passage for him, to draw up his commission, to select two large boxes of books for his disposal in India, and to prepare a letter of instruction containing a full statement of the wishes of the Committee. The commission bore date, February 22d, and on Wednesday, February 28th, Mr. Dall sailed from Boston in the ship Napoleon, Captain Barnes, bound for Calcutta. The following is the letter of instruction he took with him : —

LETTER OF INSTRUCTION TO MR. DALL.

DEAR SIR : — You will find in this letter a brief statement of all the points taken up and considered by the special committee of the Board of the American Unitarian Association, in their interview with you, February 14, together with the results which the Committee reached, and which they regarded as their instruction to guide your course in the mission upon which you now enter. They are here drawn up in writing, that you may take them with you to India, and a copy will be duly filed in the Rooms of the Association.

You will bear in mind the circumstances under which this mission is established. Nearly forty years ago, an able Trinitarian missionary was sent from England to Calcutta. He there became acquainted with that eminent man, a native of India, Rammohun Roy ; who, dissatisfied with all the forms of religion which rare and extensive learning had enabled him to examine, had at length turned his attention to Christianity, and had become a believer in the unity of God, as revealed through Jesus Christ. In the interviews and discussions that followed, the missionary was converted to the Unitarian faith, and subsequently became pastor of a Unitarian church in Calcutta.

In 1823, a correspondence took place between Rammohun Roy and the converted missionary, Rev. Mr. Adam, on the one part, and the late Dr. Ware, senior, Professor of Divinity in Harvard College, on the other part. Its object was to obtain information, for the use of American readers, relating to the prospects of Christianity in India. From this correspondence it appeared that one of the chief obstacles in the way of converting the natives to Christianity was the preaching of the doctrine of the Trinity; and that both Mussulmans and Hindoos " would be more likely to embrace Unitarian than Trinitarian Christianity." It also appeared that schools for native children might be established, and the Holy Scriptures and other books circulated under a good hope of imparting the temporal blessings of the Gospel, and the hope of salvation, to this people. A strong desire was felt in many hearts to send an American Unitarian missionary to India, and this measure was advocated in the journals of that day.

This, however, was not done. The causes of this neglect need not here be dwelt upon. They arose in part from the smallness of our body, from the difficulty of finding a suitable missionary, and from the demand for all the means in our hands for the diffusion of the truth at home. It may be added, that meanwhile we have occasionally heard of the condition of things in India, but more minute and exact information has come to us quite recently, through Rev. Charles T. Brooks, who visited that country last season. He reports that he found Unitarians there who earnestly longed for a preacher of their faith ; he found schools in which the children of the natives were taught, but which were greatly in need of books, and he brought with him letters addressed to our Board, from those already converted to Christianity, and from a number of Mussulmans, both of whom sent us a Macedonian cry, " Come over and help us." These letters you have read in the Quarterly Journal for October, 1854, where also you found the interesting and affecting report made by Rev. Mr. Brooks.

These facts have revived the interest formerly felt in India, and the improved condition of our body seems to impress upon us the duty of entering at once upon missionary labor in that country. In voting, therefore, to establish a missionary station there, and in appointing you to visit that land, you will remember that you are charged with the double duty, first, of ascertaining in what place ór places missionary labor may be most advantageously bestowed, and secondly, of entering upon such labor yourself, wherever Divine Providence may open the most favorable door.

This duty of exploring the needs of different places, and of comparing the opportunities they present for beneficent action, will, of course, claim your first attention. For this purpose you are instructed to proceed first to Calcutta, and to examine thoroughly what field for Christian usefulness from us is there offered. You will obtain information from the source mentioned by Mr. Brooks, (Hodgson Pratt, Esq., Under-Secretary of the Bengal Government,) and will ascertain what number of persons would probably attend upon your preaching, what number of children can be gathered into schools, and whether good results may be anticipated from the circulation of tracts and books. You will not fail, also, to make inquiries in regard to the " Society of Vedantists," referred to by Mr. Brooks, and to learn if there are any hopeful ways of extending Christian influences among them.

You are instructed to proceed from Calcutta to Madras. Here you will seek at once Rev. William Roberts. We wish for full information in regard to his chapel, his schools, his wants, the number and character of the persons that come under his influence, and whether, through any agency of ours, that influence may be extended. We need not remind you of the great interest we feel in the labors of this devoted man, both for his own and his father's sake, and we desire that whatever you may learn in regard to his means and hopes of usefulness you will communicate to our Board.

From Madras you will go to Secunderbad and Salem, from which place Mr. Brooks says there comes "a strong cry for a shepherd." You will obtain for us information relating to those places like that already indicated in regard to others. We wish to know how many persons here may be brought under our Christian influences, and what hopes these places may hold out for useful missionary effort.

Should you hear of other places where Christian efforts from us may promise to bring forth good fruits, you are instructed to visit them, unless good reasons may forbid; in which case, and in all cases above alluded to, we must leave much to your judgment at the time, as it may be affected by considerations of distance, expense, sickly seasons, &c.

This exploration of the religious wants of this country, and this ascertainment of the place or places where Christian exertion may be most advantageously bestowed, we regard, as was said before, as your first duty. You will communicate to us the results of your observations as often as you can, so that we may have a connected Journal of your mission. You will receive further instruction from us. From the nature of the case, we cannot at present determine how long your absence from your native country may be required. No interference on our part will suspend your faithful labors; still, the result of your inquiries may show that we cannot at present undertake any useful labors in India for the extension of Christian truth. We have now a strong impression that we can, and believe that these hopes of usefulness, and the entreaty even to tears that we would send a pure Gospel to those in ignorance and want, demand at least these inquiries from our Christian sympathy and faith. Unless otherwise advised, you will, after making the above-named inquiries, fix yourself in the place where your labors may promise to be attended with the most extensive and hopeful results. And there you are instructed to enter upon the work of a missionary; and whether by preaching, in English or through an interpreter, or by school-teaching, or by writing for the press, or by visiting from house to house, or by translating tracts, or by circulation of books, you are instructed, what we know your heart will prompt you to do, to give yourself to a life of usefulness as a servant of the Lord Jesus Christ. You go out as a *Unitarian* missionary, because we have reason to believe that many will receive the Gospel as we hold it who reject the errors which we believe others have added to the faith once delivered to the saints. But you are not expected to carry mere doctrinal discussions and sectarian strifes to those distant lands. "God so loved the world that he sent his only begotten Son to seek and to save the lost," — this is to be the grand burden of your message ; and we need not remind you, that, as a Unitarian believer in the Lord Jesus Christ, you will enjoy a great advantage in the simplicity of your doctrine, the intelligibleness of your faith, and its accordance with the correct and obvious teachings of Scripture. We wish you, wherever you may meet missionaries of other denominations, to cultivate friendly relations to them, and to try to make them feel that you are laboring, not for a sect, but through a love for the souls of our fellow men, and in obedience to his words who said, "Go ye into all the world and preach the Gospel to every creature." Whatever information you can obtain in regard to the operations, successes, or disappointments of other missionaries will be gladly received.

You will be intrusted with a large package of books, catechetical, practical, devotional, and doctrinal, and these you are instructed to offer for sale wherever they can be sold, and to bestow them gratuitously when you may judge they will be of most use, not forgetting to offer a sufficient supply to those Mussulmans who, in their letter to us, have asked for our publications.

We shall inform the British and Foreign Unitarian Association of your visit to India, and you will be glad, we know, to receive and answer any communications you may receive from them or any of their agents.

Signed,   HENRY A. MILES, *Sec. A. U. A.*

JAMES TANNER.

On a previous page, under the head of "Meetings of the Executive Committee," will be found a statement of the manner in which Mr. Tanner became known to the Association. Supposing that our readers would naturally feel some interest in his previous history, we present to them the following sketch of his life, which we draw up from particulars communicated by Mr. Tanner himself.

Near the beginning of the present century, a white family by the name of Tanner resided on the banks of the Kentucky and Ohio rivers. The father had been a clergyman, was well known and respected, and was rearing a large family of children on what was then the border line between the white and Indian races. In some of the predatory incursions which the Indians made, they seized one of his sons, then seven or eight years of age, who was soon adopted by an Ottoway chieftess, and was taken to the Red River of the North, which empties into Hudson's Bay. This was John Tanner, father of James.

For thirty years John Tanner lived among the Indians,— learned their language, adopted their mode of life, married an Indian woman of the Chippewa tribe, and, under the name of Shaw-shaw-wabe-na-se, — The Falcon, — became renowned for his adventures. In 1830 his life was published in New York, in a large octavo volume of over four hundred pages, entitled, " A Narrative of the Captivity and Adventures of John Tanner, during Thirty Years' Residence among the Indians in the Interior of North America. By Edwin James, M. D."

In 1823, Lord Selkirk, who had come to this country to settle some difficulties between the Hudson's Bay and North-west Fur companies, found John Tanner among the Indians; and, becoming interested in him, inquired into his history, and advised him to return to his friends in Kentucky. Yielding to this advice, he went to Sault St. Mary and to Mackinaw, and thence to Detroit. Lewis Cass was at this time Governor of Michigan, and to him Tanner brought a letter. Governor Cass had heard of the Tanners of Kentucky, and of the captivity many years before of a little boy. He kindly helped John, who was soon in the arms of his brother Edward, after a separation of thirty years.

The season following, John Tanner brought his Indian wife and his children to Kentucky. Among them was James, who was put to school. Their Indian blood made their situation somewhat unhappy, and in the course of a year the father went with the family to Sault St. Mary. Here he became United States Interpreter, under Schoolcraft. Governor Cass, at this time Superintendent of Indian Affairs, often saw the Tanner family at Sault St. Mary, and bestowed many kind attentions upon the little boy James. He paid for his clothing and schooling for two years; and among James's early recollections he distinctly recalls the time when Governor Cass placed his hand on his head and said he " must grow up to be a useful man." Last year, at Washington, James Tanner reminded Mr. Cass of this incident, who remarked that he " felt rewarded for all that he had done for the Chippewa boy." James Tanner went to school, in all, about six or seven years. He was also at one time in a Sunday school. His teacher was Miss Delia Cook, of whom he speaks in terms of great affection, and whose gentle and faithful instructions inspired him with a respect for the truths of Christianity, to which he attributes his subsequent conversion. His father died in 1847, but to the very last retained his fondness for Indian life, preferring the society of Indians to that of the whites.

On coming of age to act for himself, James Tanner went to Lake Superior, and engaged in the Indian trade. Here he was successful, and acquired property. He married Margaret Chapman, a quarter Chippewa Indian. She was a member of the Roman Catholic Church. In 1846, they were both converted, and joined the Methodists. From the day of his conversion he resolved to be a missionary among his people. He gave up his business, went to Sandy Lake, built a log-house for his wife, and commenced the life of a missionary. He labored two years at Lake Winnepeg, and one year at Pembina. In the winter of 1853–4 his mind was troubled on the subject of his baptism, as he had come to believe that immersion was the only true mode for him. Accordingly he and his wife went to St. Paul, in Minnesota, on snow-shoes, a distance of more than five hundred miles. He offered himself for baptism at a Baptist church. After some delay, occasioned by his refusal to subscribe to the articles of a creed offered for his signature, which he maintained the church had no right to require of him if he complied with the Scripture requisition, " If thou believest in the Lord Jesus Christ, thou mayest be baptized," he was immersed, and was advised to go to New York, to be appointed a missionary of the Baptist Home Missionary Society.

Accordingly, he visited New York, and was called before a council of Baptist ministers, preparatory to ordination. Here was still further delay and perplexity. Tanner could not assent to the covenant and creed of the Baptist Church. He could neither bind himself to close communion, nor profess his belief in the doctrine of the Trinity. These objections to his ordination were finally overruled, and he was ordained in May, 1853.

The following summer was spent in travelling in Rhode Island, Connecticut, and different parts of New York, making collections of money and farming tools for the Chippewas. Through the kindness of Governor Gorman, who gave one hundred dollars for Tanner's personal expenses, and one hundred and fifty dollars to transport the farming tools, these had been removed by ox-teams from St. Paul to Crow Wing. At this place they were stored in the United States warehouse, preparatory to their removal to Pembina. A fire broke out and consumed the warehouse and all its contents, — a heavy blow to James Tanner, who lost the fruits of a year's labor, and tools to the value of two thousand dollars.

The last spring and summer was passed at Pembina. The Chippewas were at war with the Sioux, and many a time Tanner' preached " with his Bible in one hand and his rifle in the other." Finding it impossible to establish a salutary and permanent influence over his people without gathering them into settlements, and for this end needing tools, books, and teachers, he wrote to the Baptist Board in New York for assistance. Last October he came on through St. Paul, Chicago, and Cleveland, and went to Washington to consult with the Bureau of Indian Affairs. He bore with him the letters that will be found under the " Meetings of the Executive Committee." He received encouragement in Washington, and came to New York, where he learned that the Board of the Baptist Home Missionary Society had offered to commission him, on the condition that he would confine himself to preaching the Gospel, and for this purpose would return to Minnesota. This offer he felt constrained to decline.

Leaving New York, Mr. Tanner came to Boston to interest his Baptist friends in his wants. Of the reception he met in Boston, and of his introduction to new friends, we have already given a brief account in the "Meetings of the Executive Committee." It only remains to be added, that, after the appointment of Mr. Tanner as Missionary of the Association, donations of tools and money passed through the hands of the Treasurer of the Association, to whom Mr. Tanner is to account for the same. On Sunday evening, February 25th, he addressed a large audience in Bedford Street Church in Boston; and on Friday, March 2d, he started for his home towards the setting sun. He has appointments to fulfil in various places, and bears with him letters commending him to the sympathy and aid of our friends. A large number of books, seeds, and farming implements have been shipped for St. Paul, and a school-teacher, procured by the Association, is on his way with Mr. Tanner, under whose direction he is to act. The scene of their labors will be the upper part of Minnesota Territory, remote from any danger from the incursions of the hostile Sioux, and where communities of the Chippewas can at once be formed. It is Mr. Tanner's purpose to arrive there in sufficient season to commence spring work. Any information we obtain hereafter in regard to the practical results of this experiment will be laid before our readers.

The following notice of the meeting in Bedford Street Church is reprinted from the Christian Register of March 3d.

"The meeting in Bedford Street Church was held last Sunday evening, as was 'advertised. The church was filled at an early hour. Prayer was offered by Rev. Calvin Lincoln, and Dr. Lothrop briefly made known the purpose of the meeting. He alluded to the great interest which belongs to the history of the aborigines of this country, and to the efforts which we ought to make to civilize and Christianize the remnants of the race whose hunting-grounds we now possess. It must be confessed, he remarked, that, compared with the amount of time, labor, and expense directed to this end, but a small harvest of good fruits had been gathered; but he believed it was not because the Indian was incapable of civilization, but because proper methods had not been adopted. Mr. Tanner had presented himself before the Executive Committee of the American Unitarian Association, and had asked our aid. The Committee listened to his plans, inquired into his history, had obtained the most satisfactory assurances of his integrity, ability, Christian devotedness, and commanding influence over his tribe; they found that heretofore he has been connected with our friends of the Baptist denomination, with whom, however, Mr. Tanner has never fully agreed in opinion, as both he and all the Indian converts to Christianity among his people are believers in the undivided unity of God, and in the derived nature of our Lord Jesus Christ. Mr. Tanner comes from a large tribe, the Chippewas, now living near the head-waters of the Mississippi. They number 250,000 souls. They are ready to receive ` the arts of civilization and the institutions of the Gospel. Mr. Tanner wishes to take back with him a school-master, and books, and farming tools, and his whole plan seems so reasonable, practicable, and hopeful, that the Committee of the Association thought they should be doing a good Christian work to place in his hands the means to carry out that plan, and subject it to a fair and full trial. Accordingly they had voted to adopt Mr. Tanner as their missionary, to send out with him a school-teacher, and one had already been engaged for this purpose, and to furnish him with needed books and tools. Mr. Tanner's story is so full of interest, and his plans so full of promise, that friends had already contributed liberally, and over six hundred dollars in implements and money had been raised. The present meeting was called merely to hear the parting words of this missionary, who will leave Boston this week, and he would now introduce him to the audience.

" Mr. Tanner then came forward upon the platform, in front of

30 *

the pulpit, a well-formed man of medium size, with marked Indian
features, though not much more tawny than many of the whites.
His address occupied one hour and forty minutes. He had no
notes, but still followed a connected and· clearly conceived plan.
He began by alluding to the condition of the Indian tribes when
our fathers landed at Plymouth. At that time, the aborigines
had some arts of civilization, and were friendly to the whites.
They offered corn to the starving strangers that had come among
them. As a race, however, they are not more civilized to-day
than they were two hundred years ago. Why not?

"He proceeded then to give a brief history of the treatment the
Indians had received from the Europeans, who drove them from
their hunting-grounds and from the graves of their fathers; and if
missionaries ever came among them, it was with rifles and bayo-
nets, so that missionaries and land-robbery were associated in the
Indian mind. Now they were gathered in large numbers where,
as they have been assured, they shall be undisturbed, and from
which place they are determined they will never be driven out.
And the question is, What shall be their condition there?

"The first object to be kept in view is to form them into fixed
and permanent settlements, to break up their wandering mode of
life, and to teach them agriculture and the arts of civilization. On
this point some differences of opinion had sprung up between himself and the Baptist friends with whom he had formerly_ acted.
They were ready to preach the Gospel. But suppose they make
converts to Christianity, what becomes of them? They are in
one place to-day, and in another to-morrow, and the missionary
soon loses sight of them. We must settle them in communities,
and keep them under our eye, and gather their children into
schools. Hence, beside preachers of the Gospel, we want farming
tools and schoolmasters. He had come to Boston to get aid from
his Baptist friends. While here, he accidentally fell into conversation with persons who told him of the Unitarians, and that he,
Tanner himself, was a Unitarian. He had, he confessed, great
prejudice against those who bore that name; but he determined to
know more about them; he attended their meetings, conversed
with their ministers, read their books, and he found he was one

with them, as were all those who had been converted to Christianity in his tribe.

" Mr. Tanner then proceeded to relate the circumstances under which he presented himself before the Board of the Association. He had determined in his mind, if he should be unsuccessful here, to go back in despair. But when the Association voted to adopt him as its missionary, he thanked God, and took courage. He went to his boarding-house, with the young Chippewa who is with him, and who cannot understand a word of English; and when he had heard what was done, they both kneeled down, and poured out their hearts in thanksgiving and prayer to God. He could now assure his brethren of the Unitarians in Boston, who had befriended him, that they never should regret the tie that had now been formed with the Chippewas, and he proceeded to shadow forth the consequences that might result from this small beginning.

" In this part of his address Mr. Tanner became truly eloquent. He gave proof of sagacious thought on subjects of state policy and national interests. His plans are far-reaching; for by civilizing the 250,000 people now open to our influence, he hopes to extend the blessings of our arts and institutions to other tribes beyond, that all may at some future time become a member of our confederation. Mr. Tanner closed by expressing his heart-felt gratitude for the kindness he had received. He assured his friends that they should often hear of him. Reports of his mission will be received every quarter, and will be published in the Journal of the Association. We understand that it is expected that three native Chippewas will enter the Meadville Theological School this autumn, that they may become missionaries under Mr. Tanner."

EXTRACTS FROM THE JOURNAL OF OUR MISSIONARY.

In making my first Report, I trust I shall be allowed to indulge in a remark, which will show my expectations, and be at the same time the gauge of my own estimate of success or failure.

The body of Unitarians is not large. It numbers less than many other denominations, but in proportion to its numbers its wealth is not exceeded by any other body of Christians.

Such an assertion gives us nothing to flatter our pride. Stewards of God's bounty, our responsibility is in proportion to our ability. In view of the means at our disposal, our own convictions of neglect must humble us. The Unitarians recognize the greatness of human nature, — the worth of immortal souls. From the first we have recognized the great claims of a common humanity, though abused, bruised, and depraved. With such sentiments, what could be expected of the denomination but a missionary spirit? What but such a spirit could make it consistent? I have long felt we were not faithful to our means. Hoping and trusting, however, that we were awaking to our missionary duties, I was induced to become the agent of the Association, intending to appeal to the love we have for the great principles of the denomination and of the truths which we cherish; to the desire to spread religious knowledge and the real benevolence which the denomination feel towards those needing instruction and aid; but above and beyond all, to the sense of duty inspired by the Great Teacher, whose first command to the disciples was, " Go, preach the Gospel to every creature."

In some places I have met with a hearty response. In

others I have not.   Some seem to look upon their gifts as a
personal favor to me, and of course feel not the claims of
my mission.   Under short and impatient refusals I confess
I have despaired for the cause.   But when manner or matter has said, "God speed you," it has been like a gleam
of sunshine, renewing my spirit, and awaking the hope
that the day was not distant when we should be fully alive
to our duties and responsibilities.

But let me give a brief report of the answer I have met
with in the several places I have visited.

I commenced my work as missionary and agent in the
manufacturing village of Waltham.   At the time of my
visit all classes were feeling the pressure on the money-mar-
ket.   Business stood still, and men felt poor; but still they
responded to the several objects I presented, to the amount
of $ 173.93.   The interest manifested by the young men
and women of this large parish was an encouraging *prospect*
for its future.

I went from Waltham to West Roxbury.   Here I found
a small, but by no means a *poor* parish.   I had an opportunity to address the people before I solicited aid.   But I not
only found here the hardness of the times against me, but
among many of the most able there was an entire want of
sympathy with our benevolent projects.   Still, many gave
me a good word, and some of the young men exerted themselves to fill out the subscription to the Book Fund; but
thirty-six dollars was *all* that my sale of books, and subscription to Journals and Book Fund, amounted to in this parish.

In Watertown and West Cambridge I commenced work,
but found they were not ready; and desisted, after working
in them a day or two, to resume at a more favorable time.

At North Andover I found an old and rich parish.   The
manufacturers were feeling deeply the pressure of the times,

but, with all the allowances for hard times, I must say that I was saddened and disappointed at the result. Forty-six dollars and forty-three cents for the yearly subscription to the Association, to the Book Fund, and sale of books, — this was all, in the strong parish of North Andover.

At Fitchburg, alive to every good work, I at once gathered as their yearly subscription $ 100.11.

Next in my visits was Concord. Here the parish has age and wealth. An old and honored layman led off the subscription to the Book Fund with fifty dollars, the pastor gave ten, a young merchant twenty-five, and the remainder of the parish thirty-three dollars. I did not canvass this parish for the Quarterly Journal, but sold books to the amount of twenty dollars. Thus ended my mission at Concord.

I spent a few days at Lexington the same week. This old parish seems to be enjoying a revival. They have by great effort paid off their old debts, and with new zeal are bearing on the ark of the Lord. It was deemed best to leave the thorough canvassing of this parish until some time in the spring.

At Plymouth a few friends voluntarily put into my hands seventy-five dollars for the Book Fund.

I spent three days at Bridgewater, and obtained three subscribers to the Quarterly Journal, in addition to those already taken there.

I worked a week in New Bedford. The result there was the sale of books to the amount of $ 14.63.

Sunday, March 11, I spent at Sterling. Presented the claims of the Association and they at once subscribed forty dollars.

I have also visited East Bridgewater and Quincy; but as my work in these places is not finished, I will defer report until another time.

I have presented the various benevolent objects of our body on the Sabbath to ten different congregations.

I am aware that my report is not very encouraging. If judged by dollars and cents, it is a failure. But in judging of the work in the light of pecuniary aid to the Association, two things are to be borne in mind ; — a depression of every branch of business such as has not been felt for fifteen years before, with increased cost of living such as has rarely been known in the country, and a scarcity of money almost unprecedented among us.

These would be enough to account for the meagre subscription list. But this is not all. We need a missionary constantly in the field to stir up Unitarians to their great work. We need to form the habit of giving regularly throughout the denomination. And shall we not persevere until such a habit be formed?

GEORGE S. BALL.

OBITUARY.

THE GOOD PHYSICIAN.

UNDER this appropriate title, some notice has been taken in the public journals of one who will long be missed from the church where he loved to break the bread of Christian remembrance; from the firesides of the poor, where he ministered with a generous hand; from the public schools, where he had assiduously served for so many years; from a large circle of professional practice, endeared to him by his genial kindliness as well as his enlarged experience; from the cherished home, where his "old-school" heartiness shed around him a perpetual sunshine.

DR. Z. B. ADAMS, whose funeral services at the Federal Street Church, on the twenty-ninth day of January, drew together so large a concourse of professional brethren and sympathizing friends, was graduated at Cambridge College in the class of 1813, in company with Rev. Dr. Brazer, Dr. John Ware, Professor Paine, and others of note in the various learned professions. Nearly forty years ago, he commenced practice in Boston; and gradually, as his faithful devotion to his useful calling became known, gathered around himself a constantly enlarging circle of earnest friends. But he was not merely a professional man. Deeply interested in this city of his adoption, the cause of public education engaged his attention, occupied years of his ever-active life, and found him always foremost to bestow time and labor without either emolument or praise. The Common Schools of Boston are more indebted to him than they will ever know for his constant, wise, and energetic supervision. No teacher found in him anything but a hearty friend, an experienced counsellor, and a ready assistant. Many an hour has he given to the examination of school manuals, and the preparation of committee reports, because there seemed to be no one else on whom the duty should devolve, and because it seemed to him a work of the first moment.

As a guardian of the young, a protector of the widow's interests, it was his delight to befriend those who were friendless, and cheer those who were depressed; giving not only his successful medical help, but (where that was evidently needed though not asked) of his ever-open purse. His patient sympathy prevented any such burden from weighing in the least upon himself, or being borne otherwise than to the perfect acceptance of those who looked up to him as a father. Even where his own means were temporarily embarrassed, he could not dismiss the call of charity without a generous response, though he loved better to give where there was no solicitation, and best of all where the giver was unsuspected; and these constant benefactions never seemed to himself more than the simplest duty, for which he expected no return and shrunk from any acknowledgment.

His professional career was always marked by generous self-devotion, winning cheerfulness, entire honesty, and manly independence. He was conservative in his practice as in his opinions; he never could endure to try experiments on his patients, and it grieved him to the heart if they resorted to any new-fangled specifics. But when their case became severe, his hopeful smile cast its mellow sunshine over the bed of sickness; when they drooped, he uttered words of holy promise; when they were sinking, he put beneath them the arm of Christian trust. Hating above all things any exhibition of the most private feelings of the heart, at such moments he showed himself unaffectedly religious; his eye kindled at the expressions of religious peace, his hand grasped warmly the hand uplifted in filial petition.

And when his own end came on so suddenly, at the age of sixty-two, but before his eye was dimmed or his natural force abated, the strength of his unuttered convictions was a support to all around him. The dark valley had to him no shadow, and the narrow vault no gloom. His favorite Sunday recreation had been singing with his family the most cheerful hymns of Watts and Doddridge to the tunes which his boyhood had made dear, and these became the relief of his last hours. As long as his voice was at his control, it mingled with his daughters in those ever-blessed words, " Sweet fields beyond the swelling flood," or,

" While thee I seek, protecting Power," or, " How blest
the righteous when he dies," or, " My God, I thank thee."
And the last sign of his ebbing life was, as one of these
old psalms of trust had just been breathed over his pillow,
the exclamation, as he lifted his wasted hands, " O I am so
happy, — so happy, — so happy ! "   Surely

> " The chamber where the good man meets his fate
> Is privileged beyond the common walk
> Of virtuous life, quite on the verge of heaven."

NOTICES OF BOOKS.

MESSRS. Phillips, Sampson, & Co., are publishing a standard
library edition of the British Poets. We have seen the following : —

The Poetical Works of JOHN MILTON. *With Notes and a Life of
the Author, by* JOHN MITFORD. 2 vols., with a fine engraving
of Milton.

The Complete Poetical Works of WILLIAM COLLINS, THOMAS
GRAY, *and* OLIVER GOLDSMITH. *With Biographical Sketches
and Notes, by* EPES SARGENT. 1 vol., with engravings of the
Poets.

The Complete Poetical Works of SAMUEL ROGERS. *With a Biographical Sketch and Notes, by* EPES SARGENT. 1 vol., with
engraving.

Poems, Plays, and Essays, by OLIVER GOLDSMITH. *With an Introductory Essay, by* HENRY T. TUCKERMAN. 1 vol., with engraving.

The Poetical Works of THOMAS HOOD. *With a Biographical
Sketch, by* EPES SARGENT. 1 vol., with engraving.

The Poetical Works of HENRY KIRKE WHITE. *With a Memoir,
by* ROBERT SOUTHEY. 1 vol. with engraving.

All the above books are stereotyped in Boston, are bound uniformly, and in a substantial and attractive style. Of Mr. Sargent's fitness to edit those he has prepared for publication we need not here speak, and he appears to have done his work with excellent judgment and taste. On the whole, this seems by far the best library edition of Selections from the British Poets, and speaks well for the enterprise, as we think it will also prove the sagacity, of its publishers.

We may take this opportunity to allude to the new store of Messrs. Phillips, Sampson, & Co., at No. 13 Winter Street, and to assure our distant readers that they may look forward to a visit to one of the largest and most attractive bookstores to be found anywhere, as one of the chief pleasures of their next trip to Boston.

———

Hypatia: or, New Foes with an Old Face. By CHARLES KINGSLEY, JR., Author of " Alton Locke." Third Edition. Boston : Crosby, Nichols, & Co. 1855.

THIS is a picture of life in the fifth century, and chiefly in Alexandria, the seat of the most memorable events of that age. Our readers remember the marked success with which the late William Ware reproduced the times of Aurelian and Zenobia. Hypatia is an attempt in the same direction, and it is made with all the command of style, and power of description, and skill in dialogue, which distinguish the author of Alton Locke. Alexandria, with its splendid architecture, and immense commerce, and contending factions, and noisy rabbles, and hordes of monks, is placed before us, and we live in the midst of the struggles and barbarisms of its palmy days. We are not surprised that this work has proved so great a favorite, that a third edition is called for. We anticipate a still more extended sale. The course of Lectures on the Fathers, delivered during the last winter, has awakened much interest in the age of which Hypatia treats ; and if we wish to have a graphic, living picture of their times, we shall find it here unrolled with rare interest and instruction.

*A Treatise on English Punctuation; designed for Letter-writers,
Authors, Printers, and Correctors of the Press; and for the Use of
Schools and Academies.* By JOHN WILSON. Third Edition,
enlarged.

THIS is a work which should be on the table of every literary
man. Probably no one has studied the art of punctuation more
than the author of this Treatise, and already he is an authority to
which all defer. Few are the books which would be more useful
manuals to young persons of both sexes in finishing their education. Through a defect in their early training, the habits of most
writers are careless and inexact in the division of their sentences ;
and many a public speaker, using a manuscript, would deliver his
discourse far more intelligibly and forcibly, if his manuscript had
been properly pointed. This beautiful volume of 334 pages is a
specimen of the printing which one may command at the office of
its author.

———

The Elements of Intellectual Philosophy. By FRANCIS WAYLAND,
President of Brown University. Third Thousand. Boston :
Phillips, Sampson, & Co.

THIS volume contains the substance of the lectures which have
been delivered to successive classes in Brown University. They
are marked by the well-known characteristics of their author, — a
rare clearness of conception, and unrivalled precision and force of
expression. As they were prepared for oral delivery in the reci-
tation-room, they have a directness of address, a freedom of illustration, and an air of earnestness, not often found in works of this
class. The work is designed not so much for original discussion
as for the immediately practical purpose of giving prominence to
the views which unfold the best helps for mental improvement;
and it will take its place by the side of the " Moral Science," as
one of the best text-books which a teacher can use.

———

Early Piety; or Recollections of Harriet B——. Boston : American Unitarian Association.

THIS is a small but beautifully printed book, designed as a present to members of the older classes in our Sunday Schools. It was written by a pupil in a Bible-class in one of our churches, and describes the character, sickness, and death of a young girl, of whom with peculiar emphasis it might have been said, "Of such is the kingdom of heaven." Its tender and holy lesson is, that religion is a reality, and God and Jesus and heaven are realities, the power of which may now be felt, and felt to give a deeper joy, and a diviner beauty, and an unfading peace. We recommend it to parents and teachers seeking gifts for the young.

The Altar at Home. Prayers for the Family and the Closet. By Clergymen in and near Boston. Boston: American Unitarian Association.

THIS is a new book of devotion, which appears from the press simultaneously with the issue of this number. It has been known that a work of this kind was in preparation, and we hope it may meet the expectations that have been awakened. Perhaps we can give our readers an idea of the plan and spirit of the work in no way so well as by the following extracts from the Preface: —

" It is in no disparagement to good manuals of devotion now in use that another is offered to the public. The following work will perhaps be found to reflect more accurately the religious spirit of the present day. Prepared at a time when controversy is suspended, when there is less tendency to extremes, through a mere reaction against error, when the aspect of the Gospel which has most deeply interested the heart is that which regards it as a divine spiritual force for the conversion and regeneration of man, this book will be found, it is believed, to recognize more fully the truths which are the springs of the spiritual life, and to breathe more fervently some of the deepest longings of the soul. As a reflection of the spirit now inspiring many hearts, it derives special interest from the manner in which it was made.

" The Association, desiring to undertake such works as shall best promote the spiritual growth of our churches, sent a circular to several clergymen, soliciting forms of prayer for use in domestic and private worship. The following morning and evening prayers

31 *

were written by twenty-five ministers, whose services are among those most highly esteemed in this community. This work, therefore, is not the composition of an individual, nor is it the exhortation only of one person to a devout life. Let it be received as the earnest desire of many,—the reader's own minister, it may be, uniting his voice with others,—that our families may be families that call on the name of the Lord. In the remembrance of the mercies that crown our daily lot, in the great needs that press on all human souls, their voices are with us, leading us to the Giver of all good, and to the Rock that is higher than we.

"The manuscripts of these prayers were sent to the editor without designation of any one subject as the leading thought of each. It became his duty to adapt to each an appropriate passage of Scripture, and to arrange them all so as to secure a variety and natural order of subjects. This was done in order to present a wide choice of topics, some one of which may be suited to the worshipper's frame of mind at the time. In this way may be avoided a feeling of insincerity arising from using a prayer merely because it is marked for the day, while it may have no adaptation to our present feelings. From the necessity of the case, however, the fitness of the prayer to the scripture, or of the scripture to the prayer, could not be very close, as the editor did not feel at liberty freely to interpolate the manuscripts. Perhaps sufficient adaptation may be found to make the subject indicated the true key-note of the devotional exercise."

"It will be observed that this book is lettered as the first of *The Devotional Library*. Other books in this library will follow, as fast as the Book Fund of the Association justifies the prosecution of the plan, and other libraries are projected, such as *The Biblical Library*, *The Theological Library*, *The Christian Youth's Library*.

"To thousands of families scattered far and wide, but one in the faith and hopes of our Lord Jesus Christ, this little volume is now offered. May it find a place on our tables, and near our hearts. May it be a mother's gift to her son leaving parental watchfulness to encounter the temptations of the world; may it go with the traveller, reminding him that, if he dwells in the uttermost parts of the earth, God is there, and his hand shall guide him. In our hours of gladness may it furnish a voice to show forth our praise; in our times of sorrow may it invite us to him who is our only sure refuge and helper. In the circle of endeared domestic ties may it set up an altar of worship; and in the chamber of sorrow, and on the bed of sickness and death, may it direct to that peace which the world cannot take away!"

We will only add that the book contains 350 pages, is printed on good paper, is neatly and strongly bound, and it is sold at the low price of sixty cents.

PAMPHLETS. — WE have received the interesting *Historical Discourse* preached by Rev. A. B. Fuller, on the occasion of the re-occupation of the New North Church, after it had undergone extensive repairs. The pastor very properly improved the occasion to review the past; and though he walked in the steps of one who diligently gathered up the facts relating to that church, he has gleaned many curious details, which are presented in a clear and earnest manner. — *The Twenty-Second Annual Report of the Seamen's Aid Society* is a well-written document, presenting the facts pertaining to one of the most energetic and successful charities. Our readers know that this society is managed by ladies; it has annual receipts to the amount of thirteen thousand dollars; and during the past year eighteen hundred and two seamen found a temporary home at the Mariner's House. — *The Incarnation. A Sermon preached at the Ordination of Mr. Calvin S. Locke over the Unitarian Church and Society in West Dedham.* By REV. OLIVER STEARNS. (With the other ordination exercises.) Mr. Stearns points out some of the influences of Christ's birth into our world, as consecrating maternity and childhood, regenerating the individual soul, transforming worship, laws, and social life, and affording a demonstration of supernatural grace. The reader will enjoy the union of sound evangelical thought with a style of great dignity and power. — *An Address delivered in Petersham, July 4, 1854, in Commemoration of the One Hundredth Anniversary of the Incorporation of that Town.* By EDMUND B. WILLSON. To one of the most interesting occasions which our rural municipalities present,

Mr. Willson brought the fruits of diligent research, and presented them in a form of much grace and beauty. The address, with the sentiments and speeches at the dinner, will be read with great interest by many from the northwestern part of Worcester County, as well as by natives of Petersham.

PORTRAIT OF DR. CHANNING. — Mr. J. A. Whipple, the distinguished artist, has presented to the Rooms of the Association a beautiful crystallotype portrait of Rev. Dr. Channing. It is taken from the painting of Gambardella, and it has a softness and tenderness of expression which make it superior to the painting itself. By relatives it is pronounced the best portrait of Dr. Channing, and for the sum of ten dollars any one may ornament a study or parlor with an accurate representation of this eminent divine. We feel grateful to the artist who has added this attraction to our Rooms.

RECORD OF EVENTS AND GENERAL INTELLIGENCE.

ON Wednesday, December 6, 1854, Mr. Calvin S. Locke was ordained pastor of the Unitarian Church and Society in West Dedham. Sermon by Rev. Oliver Stearns of Hingham.

ON Monday, December 11, Mr. Caleb Davis Bradlee was ordained pastor of the Allen Street Society in North Cambridge. The Sermon was preached by Rev. Mr. Huntington of Boston.

ON Wednesday, December 20, Rev. Charles J. Bowen was installed pastor of the new Church and Society in Williamsburg, New York. The Sermon was preached by Rev. Mr. Weiss of New Bedford.

ON Wednesday, January 3, 1855, Rev. William A. Fuller was

installed pastor of the First Congregational Society in Barre, Mass. The Sermon was preached by Rev. Edward E. Hale of Worcester.

———

ON Sunday, January 7, Rev. William R. Alger entered upon his duties as pastor of the Bulfinch Street Church and Society in Boston, having preached his farewell Sermon to the Mount Pleasant Society in Roxbury the Sunday before.

———

ON Sunday evening, January 14, Mr. William G. Scandlin, a graduate from the Meadville Theological School, was ordained in Hollis Street Church as a Minister at Large in Boston. The Sermon was preached by Rev. Dr. Gannett.

———

ON Wednesday, January 31, Rev. Horatio Stebbins, late of Fitchburg, was installed pastor of the First Congregational Society in Portland, Me. Sermon by Rev. George E. Ellis of Charlestown.

———

ON Sunday evening, February 11, Rev. Henry F. Harrington was installed pastor of the Lee Street Church and Society in Cambridgeport. Sermon by Rev. Mr. Huntington of Boston.

———

STATISTICS OF THE METHODIST CHURCH IN THE UNITED STATES. — From the minutes of the Annual Conference of the Methodist Episcopal Church in the United States we gather a few facts of interest. The whole number of persons reported as in connection with the Church is 679,282, — probationers, 104,076. There has been a net increase of 30,372 members during the year. The number of travelling preachers in the several conferences is 5,483. Of these 4,814 are now laboring. There were 42 deaths among the travelling preachers during the year. The number of local preachers is 6,149. The change in the Methodist Church indicated by this great proportion of local preachers, as compared with travelling preachers, will not escape notice. The amount of missionary contributions last year was $299,049. The largest contributions in proportion to the membership were from the New

England Conference, which gave an average of nearly 58 cents a member. In Cincinnati they gave 43 cents, in New York 42 cents. It was stated by Hon. Albert Fearing, in his speech at the Montreal Convention of Unitarians, last October, that the contribution of only twenty-five cents from all the Unitarians of New England would yield the Fifty Thousand Dollar Book Fund of the American Unitarian Association. While this sum is not yet raised among the Unitarians, their comparatively poor neighbors, the active and enterprising Methodists, raise every year more than twice that amount — 58 cents — from their members.

REPUBLICATION OF SOME OF THE WORKS OF ERASMUS. — We see by recent English Reviews that the "Pilgrimages of Walsingham and Canterbury," by Erasmus, have lately been newly translated, and an edition, illustrated by quaint engravings, has been published. The book abounds in curious information relating to pilgrimages generally, supplied in the notes of the editor, whose translation, it is said, most delicately preserves the eloquence and irony of the original. A writer in a London paper remarks: "There could not be a better antidote to the morbid yearning for the revival of mediæval religious practices, than the contemporaneous exposure of what these practices really were, from the impartial pen of Erasmus."

THE BURNETT PRIZES. — The two prizes offered at Aberdeen, one of $9,000 and the other of $3,000, for the best treatises on the "Being and Attributes of God," were awarded on the 20th of January last. Rev. Robert A. Thompson of Lincolnshire, and Rev. John Tulloch of St. Andrews, were the successful competitors. Two hundred and eight treatises were offered for examination. The sealed envelopes were opened in the Town Hall in Aberdeen, in the presence of a large assembly of the principal citizens. The next prizes will be given forty years hence, at which time the sum of money offered will be greatly increased.

REV. WILLIAM JAY says in his Autobiography: "I always found one thing very helpful in the choice and study of my *sub-*

jects for preaching. It was the feeling of a rightness of aim and motive, i. e. a simple regard to usefulness, and a losing sight of advantage, popularity, and applause."

———

PRESENT PROSPECTS OF JERUSALEM. — A writer quoted in the February number of the Gentleman's Magazine, referring to the revived interest felt in the condition of Jerusalem, says: " While other cities of the Turkish Empire are falling to ruin and decay, being depopulated and barbarized, Jerusalem is rapidly springing up into new life. European manners and European wants are bringing in civilization and enterprising industry. Good hotels are found to accommodate most travellers better than the Casa Nuova, so long the only shelter for the Frank pilgrim of whatever nation or religion. There are shops where dealers of all kinds of European goods find a ready sale for their commodities; carpenters, watchmakers, blacksmiths, glaziers, tinmen, dyers, laundresses, shoemakers, &c. exercise their various callings. There are three flourishing European tailors. The daily markets are supplied abundantly with good mutton, and poultry and eggs are cheap. Fruit and vegetables are abundant, and good bread is made by several bakers. New houses spring up on every side. By new houses are meant new fabrics upon old foundations, for as yet the waste places are not reclaimed, and one half the ancient city is a desolation, while other parts are crowded. The mighty tide which during three centuries impelled half the nations of Europe towards the rocky shores of Palestine — then ebbing during the temporary ascendency of Rome — is now rising annually higher." This writer estimates that $ 300 would be ample allowance for all expenses incurred by one year's residence " among Bible scenes."

ENGAGEMENTS.

On Sunday, December 10, 1854, the Secretary preached in
Charlestown, to the Society of which Rev. George E. Ellis is
pastor.   To a very large audience he discoursed on the importance of cordial denominational co-operation, closing with a brief
mention of the plan of a Book Fund.   The reasons which called
for this movement were alluded to, as were the successful results which might confidently be anticipated.   The pastor of the
church followed, in a few earnest remarks, commending a measure
which he had from the first advocated, and the progress of which
he had watched with great interest.. He felt sure that no work
which Unitarian Christians can at present take up was more wisely
adapted to the wants of the times, could meet with more hearty
unanimity, or could be presented with more triumphant success.
He referred to a little incident of which he had a day or two before read.   In one of the crowded steamboats that ply between
two large cities, a man was seen going round carefully collecting
all the tracts, and taking them to his state-room.   On being asked
why he did this, he said it was not because he wanted to read
these publications himself, but because he wanted no one else to
read them.   He believed them injurious, founded on false views
of religion, filled with superstitious errors, and pernicious doctrines, and therefore he would remove them from the eyes of all.
Now, said Mr. Ellis, had this man done one thing more, had he
left, in the place of what he took away, books and tracts inculcating true views of Christian doctrine, and breathing a pure, healthy,
and strengthening spirit, placing them where all might see them,
and read them, and be blessed by them, what a greater service
would he have rendered!   This is what we would do, not only ·
discourage men from communion with error, but encourage them
to commune with the truth, that the truth may sanctify them and
make them free.   Not only in our public conveyances, but in
every place where men read, we would have words of truth and
soberness under their eye; assured that in an age like this, when
everybody reads, and opinions and guiding views of life are so

much gathered from books, we can use no more effectual instrument to enlighten the mind, and to bless the heart. Slips of paper had been previously prepared and distributed in the church, and sums of money were pledged, which, added to subscriptions obtained afterwards, will bring the aggregate contributed in Charlestown to at least five or six hundred dollars.

On Sunday, December 17, 1854, the Secretary preached in Lexington, to the Society over which Rev. Mr. Staples has recently been settled as the pastor. The signs of new life and interest in this ancient parish are of the most encouraging kind. The attendance on the public services of the Sabbath is so large as to fill the church, and an evening meeting during the week has been fruitful of good influences. It is among our sincerest wishes that a connection so full of promise as that between the pastor and the people of this place may long be a mutual blessing to them, and a cause of prosperity to our common interests of Christian truth and righteousness. At the close of the morning sermon, a brief allusion was made to the plans and hopes of the Association, though it was announced that no call would at that time be made for aid, as it was judged best, for many good reasons, to defer any solicitation until this spring. The parish in Lexington has not been in the habit of giving annual assistance to the Association. Its contributions have been few and at long intervals. We are permitted to cherish the hope that hereafter it will regularly and cordially co-operate with our other churches in sustaining plans of Christian enterprise and faith.

On Sunday, January 21, 1855, the Secretary preached to the Society of Rev. Mr. Sears, in Wayland. The Society is not large, but it is composed of those who deeply prize the religious privileges which they enjoy. An auxiliary to the Association is here sustained, on the footing introduced several years ago. It has its annual meeting, and choice of officers, and reports from committees. This is the season of the year when the annual meeting occurs. In the discourse in the morning some of the reasons were stated why our churches may be expected to feel an interest in the plans of the Association, and to accord to them a steady support. The regularity of our Wayland friends deserves a grateful acknowledgment. It is but a small sum that is contributed ; but this bestowed without failure, year after year, in a little while gives an aggregate exceeding the fitful charities of much larger and more wealthy societies. The pleasure and instruction of the day spent in the country parsonage will not soon be forgotten.

On Sunday, February 11, 1855, the Secretary preached to the Rev. Dr. Gannett's Society, in Federal Street, Boston. The greater religious activity our churches show in the direction of humanity and philanthropy, rather than in that of efforts for the diffusion of Christian truth, was taken as the subject of a discourse, which offered a plea for a ministration to other and higher than physical wants. A single closing paragraph, relating to the Association, was all that seemed called for in a place where the history of the Association was well known to all; where its anniversary meetings have always been held, where the pastors have been its steadfast friends, — one there speaking, as only *he* could speak, in behalf of its principles and aims, and the other giving it years of oversight and care as its first Secretary, and afterwards its presiding head. Dr. Gannett followed the sermon with a few remarks, announcing the fact that the contribution to the Book Fund then amounted to more than two thousand dollars, and giving notice that the members of the Society would soon be invited to give their annual contribution to the general purposes of the Association. For twenty-five years, without a single exception, has the Federal Street Society contributed annually sums varying from two to ten hundred dollars. It is an instance of methodical and persevering charity which has no other parallel in our body, though one or two other parishes may present very nearly a similar record. The unusual effort in favor of a Book Fund might have been regarded as a reason for omitting the annual contributions. But such omission was not to be allowed; and the hope was expressed by Dr. Gannett, that, under the brightening auspices of the Association, and in the passing away of the clouds that had darkened the financial world, a generous and large expression of interest would now be offered.

On Sunday, February 18, 1855, the Secretary preached in King's Chapel, Boston. At the invitation of the pastor, Rev.

Dr. E. Peabody, he presented the claims of the Book Fund. It is a fact of much satisfaction that a Society which, though the first Unitarian Society in the United States, has never felt itself closely allied to the Unitarian denomination, yet takes an interest in the circulation of our religious literature. Some account was given of the willing reception which thousands in this country now give to this literature, and of its peculiar fitness to meet some of the greatest moral dangers of our age. It was understood that further details in regard to the plans of the Association would be presented by the pastor at a vestry-meeting; and expressions of interest in these plans lead to the hope of a generous aid from this large and wealthy parish.

On Sunday, February 25, 1855, the Secretary preached in the Hawes Place Church, South Boston, of which Rev. Mr. Dawes is the pastor. Few of our parishes are more regular in the contribution of aid to the Association. The Society is in the possession of a fund, which makes the burden of sustaining public worship very light. The fact constitutes a strong reason for a generous support of plans designed to extend the blessings of religious institutions to others. The duty of hearty co-operation for this end was set forth in the discourse; and the pastor gave notice that he should call the attention of the Society to the same subject in a discourse soon to be preached, in the hope that both appeals might lead to a generous response.

The annual times for collections for the Association occur in the following Societies on the days here named: —

April   1. Rev. Mr. Alger's, Marlborough.
"   8. Rev. Mr. Briggs's and Frothingham's, Salem.
"   15. Rev. Mr. Morison's, Milton.
"   22. Rev. Mr. Ware's, Cambridgeport.
"   29. Rev. Mr. Knapp's, Brookline.
May   6. Rev. Dr. Hill's and Rev. Mr. Hale's, Worcester.
"   13. Rev. Mr. Frost's, Concord.
"   20. Rev. Mr. Whitney's, Brighton.
June 10. Rev. Mr. Bartol's, Lancaster.

ACKNOWLEDGMENTS.

In the months of December, January, and February, the following sums have been received : —

1854.

Dec.	2. From sale of books by George W. Fox,	$ 9.62
"	" " " " " M. W. Willis,	9.00
"	5. 1 Sears's Regeneration,	.37
"	6. 1 Channing's Works,	2.00
"	" 9 Subscribers to Quarterly Journal,	9.00
"	8. Sale of books in Lynn,	15.34
"	12. Subscriber to Quarterly Journal,	1.00
"	" 10 " " " Dublin,	10.00
"	" 1 " " "	1.00
"	13. Sterling, in addition,	1.00
"	19. Fitchburg, through Mr. Ball,	75.00
"	" 1 Subscriber to Quarterly Journal,	1.00
"	" H. W. Miller, 2d, pay towards Life-Membership,	10.00
"	" Sale of books at office,	35.94
"	" Charlestown, N. H.,	10.00
"	" 1 Subscriber to Quarterly Journal,	1.00
"	" Lancaster, N. H.,	9.00
"	" Chicopee,	14.00
"	" Sale of books in Northampton, N. Y.,	6.00
"	" Mrs. Fay of Northampton, for Book Fund,	5.00
"	" Sale of books in Saco, 1 Quarterly Journal,	30.00
"	" 1 Subscriber to Quarterly Journal,	1.00
"	" Sale of books by Dr. Burnap,	25.00
"	18. 1 Subscriber to Quarterly Journal,	1.00
"	22. From Concord, Mass.,	10.00
"	" " Lexington,	10.00
"	" " Subscriber to Quarterly Journal,	1.00
"	23. " Billerica,	23.00
"	25. Books sold at Jamaica Plain,	11.63
"	" Subscribers to Quarterly Journal,	18.75
"	" Books sold in Perry, Me.,	8.00

Dec. 26. West Cambridge, in addition,	. . .	$2.00
" " East Boston, auxiliary,	. . . .	23.20
" 28. From Fall River,	. . . . .	28.00
" " " 1 Subscriber to Quarterly Journal,	.	1.00
" " " Sale of books at office,	. . .	53.69
" " " 2 Subscribers to Quarterly Journal,	.	2.00
" 29. " Books at office,	. . . . .	.60

1855.

Jan. 2. 1 Subscriber to Quarterly Journal,	. .	1.00
" 3. East Boston, in addition,	. . . .	3.00
" 4. 1 Quarterly Journal,	. . . . .	1.00
" " Books sold in Springfield,	. . .	20.00
" " 8. From Ladies of Dr. Hill's Society to make Mrs. R. Newton and Mrs. Levi Lincoln Life-Members,	. . . .	60.00
" " 9. 2 Subscribers to Quarterly Journal,	. .	2.00
" " 7 " " Providence, R. I.,	7.00
" " Plymouth, for the Book Fund,	. . .	74.00
" " Sale of books in Plymouth,	. . .	1.45
" " " " Brookline,	. . . .	30.04
" " Concord, Mass., for Book Fund,	. .	115.00
" " 3 Quarterly Journals,	. . . . .	3.00
" 11. 2 " "	. . . . .	2.00
" " Sale of books at office,	. . . . .	2.00
" " From the Unitarian Society in Deerfield, Mass., to make Rev. Mr. Moors a Life-Member,	.	30.00
" " 1 Subscriber to Quarterly Journal,	. .	1.00
" " Books sold in Hingham,	. . . .	45.00
" 12. " " Bolton,	. . . .	28.44
" " Friends in Dedham,	. . . .	40.00
" " " Danvers,	. . . .	32.00
" " " Haverhill and Lawrence,	. .	25.00
" " Walpole, Quarterly Journal,	. . .	30.00
" 13. Sale of Books for Calais, Me.,	. . .	8.06
" " 10 Quarterly Journals,	. . . .	10.00
" 15. 2 Subscribers to Quarterly Journal,	. .	2.00
" " Miss E. P. Dillingham towards the Book Fund,	5.00

32 *

Jan. 16.	3 Quarterly Journals,			$ 3.00
" 17.	Rev. S. J. May, sale of books,			40.00
" "	1 Quarterly Journal,			1.00
" "	From Books in Chelsea,			10.49
" " "	2 Quarterly Journals,			2.00
" " "	Sale of books at office,			38.48
" " "	Templeton auxiliary,			64.00
" 18. "	Sale of books in Kennebunk,			5.00
" " "	3 Quarterly Journals,			3.00
" 19. "	1 " "			1.00
" " "	Auxiliary in Northfield,			50.00
" " "	1 Quarterly Journal,			1.00
" " "	Auxiliary in Northborough, Mass.,			20.00
" 23. "	1 Subscriber to Quarterly Journal,			1.00
" 24. "	1 " " "			1.00
" " "	1 " " "			1.00
" 25. "	Friends in Salem Book Fund,			150.00
" " "	O. G. Steele, books sold in Buffalo, N. Y.,			27.50
" " "	Books in Bridgewater,			1.56
" " "	1 Subscriber to Quarterly Journal,			1.00
" " "	Books in Concord, Mass.,			14.82
" " "	Concord, Book Fund, in addition,			3.00
" 26. "	A. A. Livermore, sale of books in Cincinnati, Ohio,			75.75
" " "	Sale of books at office,			1.00
" 27. "	1 Subscriber to Quarterly Journal,			1.00
" " "	1 " " "			1.00
" " "	Fitchburg, in addition,			21.95
" " "	Watertown, towards Book Fund,			4.00
" " "	Sale of books at office			79.00
" " "	Books sold in Concord,			1.87
" " "	1 Quarterly Journal,			1.00
" 31. "	Sale of books in Roxbury,			35.00
" " "	" " Shirley,			10.62
" " "	Auxiliary in Leominster,			58.43
Feb. 1. "	1 Subscriber to Quarterly Journal,			1.00

Feb. 2.	From	sale of books, ...	$ 3.50
"	3.	"	1 Subscriber to Quarterly Journal, .	1.00
"	"	"	3 " " " .	3.00
"	"	"	Auxiliary in Saco, Me., . . .	30.00
"	"	"	Sale of books at office, . . .	1.67
"	"	"	Mrs. M. S. Jones, Enfield, . .	2.00
"	7.	"	Sale of books in Portland, . .	9.00
"	8.	"	Subscribers in Framingham, . .	55.50
"	"	"	Books in New Bedford, . . .	12.25
"	9.	"	Rev. Mr. Coolidge's Society, Boston,	331.36
"	"	"	Deerfield, Quarterly Journal, . .	22.00
"	"	"	1 Subscriber to Quarterly Journal, .	1.00
"	10.	"	1 Clarke on Prayer, ...	.30
"	"	"	1 Channing's Works, . . .	1.50
"	"	"	Sale of books in Augusta, Me., .	30.80
"	"	"	Sterling, Quarterly Journal, . .	40.00
"	"	"	1 Subscriber to Quarterly Journal, .	1.00
"	"	"	Sale of books in office, . . .	14.22
"	"	"	3 Subscribers to Quarterly Journal, .	3.00
"	19.	"	Subscribers to Quarterly Journal, Roxbury, ...	28.85
"	23.	"	Rev. Dr. Newell's Society, Cambridge,	81.21

WESTERN DEPARTMENT.

[Under the editorial care of Rev. W. D. HALEY, of Alton, Illinois to whom all communications for its pages are to be addressed.]

The Western Department, for this quarter, will not contain much variety. Anticipated communications have not been received. Very severe storms in the northern part of Illinois have so completely blocked up the roads, that the portions farther south have not received any mails for nearly a month at the time of writing this paragraph. All business and postal arrangements have been at a complete stand, affording our merchants the slight consolation that, if their notes due in the Eastern cities are protested, it can hardly be a commercial disgrace, when it is so utterly impossible to forward the means to meet them.

The poor who depend upon daily employment and daily wages for their bread are the greatest sufferers, or would be but that the Western people have hearts too large to permit suffering to exist when they can relieve it. Thus even the complete stagnation of business has its bright aspect in the manifested conviction that all men are brothers and must share each other's misfortunes. In St. Louis, for example, the stoppage of all communication, and the failure of two prominent firms, have produced a monetary pressure said to be unequalled in the history of that city; but it has borne the shock nobly, and instances of mercantile fraternity and kindly consideration have been exhibited which have not only saved the whole Mississippi valley from a frightful crash, but have evidenced the existence of the Christian leaven in the mercantile world. Brighter and more cheering than all is the fact, that, in the midst of all this severe pressure, the most active and efficient measures have been taken for the relief of every case of deserving poverty in that great city. Foremost, as usual, in this movement has been the Unitarian Church ; which has, through the agency of its most earnest and devoted Minister at Large, Rev. C. G. Ward, and his zealous assistant, Mrs. Plummer, disbursed (or will have before the season closes) in the neighborhood of *two thousand five hundred dollars*. These very devoted friends of the poor have toiled almost literally day and night among the suffering, visiting in obscure alleys and damp cellars, and distributing, in the chapel of the Church of the Messiah, provisions and fuel and clothing, and thus ministering commonly to fifty cases per diem.

PRESBYTERIANISM IN ST. LOUIS.—Rev. Dr. Rice, who has earned what some people would consider an unenviable notoriety for his pugilistic encounters with anything that throws a shadow upon the infallibility of Old School Presbyterianism, has published a book in which he endeavors to unchurch the New School portion of his own sect, virtually pronouncing them heretical, and pathetically warning all good Christians to keep out of the New School churches. To this Rev. Mr. Hanes of the New School, a man of too much liberality of thought to be much beloved by his Old School brother, has emphatically demurred, in a series of lectures delivered on Sunday evenings to his own congregation. The friends of the latter think he has demolished the arguments of Dr. Rice for the divine right of the Old School faction, and convicted him of arrogating to himself a right of censure which even the Old School leaders have expressly denied. At the last accounts this controversy had become most unclerically personal.

Verily there is a power at work upheaving the old strata of thought; and these breakings out of the old Reformatory spirit of liberty — these re-assertions of the right of individuality, which underlie all the agitations of orthodox conservatism — betoken the coming of the rightful supremacy of " pure religion and undefiled " over the merely speculative and dogmatical.

Hillsboro, Ill. — This is one of the most delightfully situated villages in all the West. It is about forty-five miles from Alton on the railroad to Terre Haute, which road will soon furnish a more direct and more speedy communication from the Mississippi with the Eastern States. A Unitarian Society has existed here for several years; it embraces several of the most prominent men in the place, and possesses a neat church unencumbered with any debt. Owing to its inland position, Hillsboro has not grown with the rapidity of the river towns, but its present population of seven hundred will soon be largely increased by the opening of the Alton and Terre Haute Railroad. We are not authorized to " call " a minister for our brethren at Hillsboro, but we give it as our impression that some young man might find a delightful home and a fair congregation to begin with, and after a few years of faithful labor, a good compensation and a large audience. We know of no place in which one would be more likely to find a quiet and most useful pastorate; the climate is very healthy, and free from most of the objections which our Eastern friends allege against the river towns, albeit we know that these prejudices are very mythical. We cannot bear the association of a rusty lock in connection with a church dedicated to our liberal faith in a country where such churches are greatly needed, and we will most gladly correspond with any of our brethren who may think of looking westward for a field of usefulness. Let some man go to the brethren in Hillsboro next autumn with the spirit of a prophet, and doubtless he shall obtain a prophet's reward.

SHURTLEFF COLLEGE. — This institution is located at Alton, Ill., and is under the auspices of the Baptist denomination, with a Faculty and Board of Trustees, composed of gentlemen of great liberality. It is very refreshing, amidst the exclusiveness of the religious bodies in the West, to find occasionally a man of sufficient largeness of heart, and intellect, and culture, to look outside of the domain of his own theoretic predilections, and to "fuse" with other workers in the common sphere of humanity. We have been favored with a generous interchange of thought and of the courtesies of life by Rev. Dr. Wood, the President of Shurtleff College, which have been only the more grateful and refreshing from their contrast to the universal "cold shoulder" with which the gentlemen of the clerical profession have usually seen fit to greet us. With the other gentlemen of the Faculty our acquaintance has been slighter, because they live at a distance. We know, however, that, highly as they value their own opinions, they are men of too much culture to condemn others for theoretic differences. We rejoice in the prosperity of Shurtleff College, in the prospect of its ample endowment, in its able Faculty, and in its increasing number of students. While faithful to its mission of educating the young men of this great valley, and while performing this mission in the generous and catholic spirit which now animates its government, it will be no less respected and beloved by men of other opinions for its connection with the

respectable denomination to which it belongs, nor can we
believe that its usefulness in that denomination will be less
because of the liberality of its government.

PEORIA, ILL. — We are glad to be able to chronicle the
safe arrival of Rev. J. R. McFarland at this beautiful city
and most interesting field of missionary labor.   We predict
for our brother a delightful ministry and most complete
success.   The Society has commenced its existence under
the most favorable auspices, and that its influence is strongly
felt in the community is evident from the following extracts
taken from a highly laudatory notice of the opening services
in one of the secular papers.   By the way, we congratulate
our brother that the Peoria papers have independence
enough to venture so lengthy a notice; we know of some
quarters in which three lines countenancing Unitarianism
are indicative of courage, ten display recklessness, and
twenty betoken heroism.

"*A New Religious Society.* — In the forenoon of Sunday last,
the First Independent Unitarian Church of the city of Peoria was
organized, at the Unitarian Chapel on Main Street.   We have before spoken of the intention made known to us by some of our
most prominent citizens of establishing a church in this city, the
object of which shall be the maintenance of a liberal system of
theology, based upon an implicit belief in the truth and divine origin of the Holy Scriptures, and an earnest desire on the part of the
communicant to lead a holy and an upright life.   The services on
this occasion were of a deeply solemn and impressive character,
consisting of prayer, the reading of the holy word, and the enun-
ciation of the twelve articles of agreement, which are to be the
chart, so to speak, of the new society.   These articles of agreement were most judiciously drawn up, and embodied the simplest
as well as the deepest principles of our most holy religion.   The
sermon preached in memory of the occasion, by the Rev. Mr.

McFarland, awakened in our mind remembrances that we may not readily forget. The reverend gentleman selected for his text the words to be found in the sixth chapter of Galatians and tenth verse: 'As we have therefore opportunity let us do good unto all men, especially unto them who are of the household of faith.'

. . . . . .

"To our mind Mr. McFarland seems to have studied the various adaptations of the Gospel for the relief of human misery with an earnestness and religious patriotism that assist him in his able and eloquent efforts to commend it to his hearers, as a matter of present and everlasting importance, with far more than the ordinary degree of success. He has made it the subject of interesting study, for the telling purpose of proclaiming it with effect 'to them that are lost,' by showing them how it expands the intellect, purifies the affections, exerts a salutary influence on the vicious, comforts the afflicted; how it 'gives to life its highest joys, and takes from death its deepest stings.' Mr. McFarland's cast of mind is truly liberal, that is to say, comprehensive, and to an eminent degree discriminating."

Rev. L. C. Kelsey was ordained in December last in Dixon, Illinois. Mr. Kelsey was of the last Meadville class, and has taken his position in the West with the intention of building up the cause of Liberal Christianity. We speak from past and pleasant personal knowledge, when we say that in mind and heart and spirit we believe him well fitted for the task he has undertaken. Although living in the same State, we regret that this is the only method we have of bidding him welcome into the great harvest-field. By the way, it may not be uninteresting to the friends of the Meadville Divinity School to be reminded that six of the sons of that school of the prophets are now resident and preaching Liberal Christianity in the State of Illinois.

Dixon, Ill. — We clip the following paragraph from a

secular paper, as it affords information respecting an important missionary post in Illinois, which is being developed by an esteemed brother : —

"Dixon is a fine growing place, situated on rising ground, flanked by a rich prairie, with Rock River flowing in front, furnishing unsurpassed facilities for manufacturing, with an abundance of timber along its borders, with the Galena and Chicago Railroad running through it, as also the Illinois Central, the former of which is now in operation, and on the latter the track is laid so that construction trains are now passing over it. Thus the commerce of the northern and southern portions of the State will be brought together here on its way to and from Chicago. The town now contains about 2,500 inhabitants, having doubled in this respect in the past two or three years. It has several extensive mills now in operation and in process of construction, with long ranges of splendid brick stores building in different directions. The surrounding country is uncommonly rich and productive, and the place has every indication of a brilliant future."

KANZAS. — We hope to be able to furnish in the next number of the Quarterly Journal some information of the missionary prospects in this important region. If not prevented by some unforeseen event, we shall hope to be "prospecting" (theologically) early in the month in which this number appears.

QUINCY, ILL., is temporarily supplied by Rev. L. Billings, formerly of Bridgeport, Ct.

MILWAUKEE, WIS., is also supplied by Rev. A. S. Ryder, formerly of Cannelton, Ind.

ROCKFORD, ILL., is supplied by Rev. J. Murray, of the last class of the Meadville Divinity School.

THE WESTERN CONFERENCE AT BUFFALO IN JUNE. — Before the next issue of the Quarterly Journal, the Conference of Western Unitarian Churches will have held its session at Buffalo. The *Western* churches will all be represented; our Western friends do not consider it a great undertaking to travel eight or nine hundred miles to go up to their annual Pentecost. Will our Eastern brethren endeavor to be present also? Come, brethren, with your ripe culture and matured experiences, and commune with the earnest men and women who at the outposts of Liberal Christianity bear the reproach of our common faith. The Conference will probably last several days; statistics of the churches will be presented, and many matters of general interest will be discussed, which will amply compensate for a journey from Boston to Buffalo. Moreover, it should be borne in mind that the Conference this year assembles at its easternmost boundary, and it will be several years before we can expect so good an opportunity for the mingling of the East and West. Remember the second Wednesday in June.

To THE WESTERN CHURCHES. — We take the liberty to remind our brethren of the passage of the following resolutions at the last session of the Western Conference. Rev. R. R. Shippen, of Chicago, was appointed Chairman of the Committee referred to.

" *Resolved,* That a Committee of three be appointed to obtain exact information in regard to the churches connected with this Conference; the number of families and individuals in the congregations; the number of communicants; of teachers and pupils in the Sabbath schools; and upon the basis of this information to prepare a report upon the condition of the churches, and upon the best means to be employed, both by pastors and people, to promote the welfare of our churches, and make them instruments of the highest good.

"*Resolved*, That all the churches connected with the Conference be requested to furnish the Chairman of the Committee with the information desired, on or before the first of May, that ample time may be given for the preparation of the report."

MARIETTA, OHIO. We are glad to be able to clip the following from the *Marietta Intelligencer*, for two reasons; because we rejoice in the frequently repeated announcements of new Unitarian Societies in the West, and because the organization of this Society is a fresh proof of the usefulness of energetic laymen. For years N. Ward, Esq., has been preaching Unitarianism, by his life and by the distribution of books and tracts, and now he begins to see results which reward his faithful perseverance. May his example encourage our laymen to faithfulness. Much, very much of the progress of Liberal Christianity depends upon the zeal with which laymen are animated, in places to which our ministers can rarely have access.

"At a meeting of the friends of Unitarian Christianity, held at the Court-House in Marietta, on Saturday evening, February 3, 1855, in accordance with a call made through the *Marietta Intelligencer*, by Nahum Ward, Esq., for the purpose of ' forming and organizing a Unitarian, liberal, rational, religious society in this place, for the worship of God in Unity, and *not in Trinity*, in accordance with the plain, unmystified letter of the Bible,' Nahum Ward, Esq. addressed those present in regard to the object of the meeting, and of man's duty to God and his fellow-man, and submitted the following as a basis of organization : —

" ' We, the undersigned, citizens of Marietta and vicinity, in the county of Washington, and State of Ohio, disbelieving in the triune nature of God, not on account of any mystery connected with the doctrine, but because it is entirely destitute of proof from nature, reason, experience, or Scripture ; in all those commonly defended views of the principles and results of the Divine government which appear to us to involve a vindictive character ; in the current dogma of the total depravity and helplessness of human nature ; in the Deity of the "Holy Child Jesus" ; in the abritrary election of some to eternal bliss, and condemnation of others to eternal torture ; and in the resurrection of a fleshly body at any future day of judgment ; — but, on the other hand,

" ' Believing in the unity and in the paternal character and merciful government of God ; in man's natural capacity of virtue and liability to sin ; in the supernatural authority of Jesus Christ, as a Teacher sent from God ; in his divine mission as a Redeemer ; in his moral perfection as an example; in the remedial, as well as retributive office and intention of the Divine punishments ; in the soul's immediate ascension, on release from the body, to its account and reward ; and that salvation rests not on superficial observance of rites, or on intellectual assent to creeds, or on any arbitrary decree, but, under the grace of God, on the rightness of the ruling affection, on humble faithfulness of life, and integral goodness of character ; —

" ' Overlooking all minor differences, sinking all alienating controversies, in the generous and conciliatory spirit that becomes us best ; wishing to go forth and live the Christian life, not as a form, but a principle, — with a warmer philanthropy, a holier consecration, a deeper piety, a more united front than we have yet shown ; in the fear and affection of God, in the faith and love of Christ ; —

" ' Do form and organize ourselves, and such persons as may hereafter unite with us, into a church and society, to be known and called the " First Unitarian Society of Marietta." We rejoice and believe in God, as our Father, who is in " Christ reconciling the world unto himself"; in Jesus Christ, the Son of God, as our Redeemer, and who is to us " the way, the truth, and the life " ; in the Holy Spirit, proceeding from the Father, as our Comforter and Guide; and in the Bible, as our only creed and authority in belief.' "

33 *

" The foregoing basis of organization being then signed by a few persons present, Nahum Ward, Esq. was elected Chairman of the meeting, and John C. McCoy, Jr., Secretary.

" A series of By-Laws was then adopted for the government of the affairs of the Society.

" On motion, it was

" *Resolved*, That the first three persons whose names are signed to the paper forming and organizing the ' First Unitarian Society of Marietta ' be elected Trustees, in accordance with the first By-Law of said Society.

" Whereupon Nahum Ward, William S. Ward, and J. C. McCoy, Jr. were elected said Trustees.

" NAHUM WARD, *Chairman.*

" J. C. McCoy, Jr., *Secretary.*"

LETTERS TO EASTERN UNITARIANS.

FROM A WESTERN UNITARIAN.

DEAR BRETHREN : — As the Quarterly Journal finds its way into all your churches, I take the liberty to make it the medium for offering some information concerning the interests of our common faith in this Western world. I do this the more freely, because my happiest associations are with the localities in which you live, and I have always formed in private a desire for information upon the topics which I propose to discuss in these letters. I make no pretensions to literary excellence ; I do not write for critics ; but I do claim to have viewed many things through the medium of common sense, and I shall endeavor both to use that capital faculty in what I have to say, and also to address myself to those who are governed by it in their life and in their reading. I wish, so far as is possible, to da-

guerreotype the experiences of a Western missionary life,
so that the farmers and manufacturers among the pleasant
hills and valleys of New England may know what their
faith and loyalty to truth require at their hands in this
distant country, which is being settled by their sons and
daughters. It would be a difficult task to convey to those
who have always been favored with the regular ministration
of Liberal Christianity in New England an adequate conception of the idea which is entertained of Unitarianism in
places where it has none of the prestige of social respectability which attaches to it in the East. In the West there
are two elements, distinct in their character, and antago-
nistic in their nature, against which Unitarianism has to contend, and which indeed I am sanguine enough to believe it
is our mission to encounter and to demolish, or rather to
harmonize, — removing from the one its unscripturalness
and absence of the humane, and from the other its negativeness and want of faith.

Bald Calvinism, of the description which might be found
in Connecticut forty years ago, is one of these forces. In
the West, Calvinism is not the mild and evangelic pietism,
so courteously liberal and kind as to give a positive con-
tradiction to its written and printed articles of faith, which
it is in New England. Here the most earnest and devoutly
pious Unitarian could never be suspected of leaning towards Orthodoxy. It preaches the Westminster Confession
and the Athanasian Creed (damnatory clause included),
vaunts its belief in infant perdition, exults with a profound
unction over the torments of the elected to God's wrath,
tells you boldly that there is no salvation outside of the
Genevan dogmas, and carries its haughty pretensions into
private life, so that in many instances even the suspicion of
a denial of its arrogant claims is sufficient to produce a loss

of business patronage, and a lack of courtesy in the con-
ventionalities of society.

Then, on the other hand, there is a large body of the most
intelligent men of the country, who, having been taught to
identify Christianity with Calvinism, in their repugnance to
the dogmas of that system have-been borne to the opposite extreme, of wholly denying revealed religion, and are
either actively or passively favorable to infidelity. Indeed,
there are not a few to be found who avow their infidelity,
and imagine that in demolishing the arguments of their Orthodox opponents they are in fact disproving Christianity.
To this latter class, many of whom have strong religious
tendencies, Unitarianism especially commends itself, by
reconciling their intellectual difficulties and pouring a new
light upon the Scriptures. I am convinced, that, because a
state of irreligion is unnatural, no man is contented with it,
and when something positive, and yet rational, is presented
to this class of minds, it will be accepted as far preferable
to the negative element which at present characterizes it.
Indeed, I know that it is so, for I have seen more than one
instance in which the presentation of a reasonable religious
hypothesis has removed the strong antagonism of doubt
which previously stood in the way of any acceptance of religion.

In this classification I have not included a most important
element of the religious condition of the West, but it must
not be overlooked in considering the subject from the stand-
point of denominationalism. I mean the members of Unitarian churches who are scattered all over the country.
There is scarcely a town of any considerable size in all the
West in which one, two,.or half a dozen earnest Unitarian
laymen (or laywomen) may not be found. And the very
circumstance of their isolation from any organized Unita-

rian sympathy creates a positiveness and a zeal for Liberal Christianity which they never dreamed of while they were habitual attendants upon Unitarian services in New England.

Now take these three leading facts, in connection with one or two circumstances which I will mention, and it will become evident, I think, that we have a work to perform which is full of encouragement. Largeness of soul is characteristic of Western people. I do not wish to use any mere boasting, but I give it as a deliberate opinion, that Unitarianism is the natural theology of the West; there is an expansiveness in Western mind to which the liberality of our position is especially commended. In addition to this, the marvellous increase of population is of itself, apart from any theological peculiarity, sufficient to warrant the most earnest and faithful efforts for the spread of our views. I have no hesitation in saying, that if a missionary is sent into any of the rapidly growing towns which are springing up every day on the banks of our rivers and in the midst of our great prairies, if he be a pious, devoted man, with his soul illuminated by constant communion with God, and his pulse throbbing in sympathy with the common experiences of the human heart, and if his pulpit ability is of an average order, he will in ten years, irrespectively of the power of a liberal theology, but simply as a result of residence and Christian intercourse with the people, have gathered a large and devoted congregation about him. That several of those years will be full of toil and self-sacrifice there can be no question, — much, however, of that it is in your power to lighten, — but the result will come, if heart and health can bear the tug and strain; and if not so, depend upon it, no seed thus implanted shall fail of germination. Now add to this the facts which I have mentioned above, and is it not evident that there is something real and momentous at the basis of those often-repeated calls for aid to the West ?

I know very worthy gentlemen, very profound scholars, very eloquent preachers, and very devoted pastors have decided that it is not well to invest any more Unitarian money in Western " brick and mortar." With the most delightful complacency, they will philosophize about the course which *they* would adopt if their lot were cast in this Western vineyard. *They* would never appeal for aid to the East. They would preach out of doors until they gathered a congregation.

Now, with the profoundest esteem for these gentlemen, I assure you I believe they would do nothing of the sort; because they are Christian gentlemen and would not wish to be made a laughing-stock for a low mob such as their proposed course would assemble. Discouraging enough it is to forsake all the pleasant associations of one's home in New England and to minister to the progress of Liberal Christianity, and the religious wants of our common brethren, so far from one's kindred, even when buoyed up with the generous sympathy of the Eastern churches; but there are few of us who could endure it, if local separation is to make us of another nation, and to deprive us of the co-operation of those who are at ease in their established prosperity.

Depend upon it, Christian friends, the power of Love, and the Christian obligation to mutual aid, are not bounded by the Alleghanies, or lost on the prairies, or ingulfed in the lakes. There is a path as direct from heart to heart, over the mountains and across the continent, as when both throb within the limits of the same township. Why should it not be so ? We are your brethren in thought and purpose; many of us have sat in the same school seats, and walked to the house of God in company with you ; — nay, even closer ties bind us ; we are of your blood, and our children are called by your names ; we utter the same prayers, and toil for the same common good that you desire. Out of your churches, and at the entreaty of your pastors, have gone forth young men to prepare for the ministry ; after years of anxious preparation, and in the belief that God and their brethren needed their services where at least the first years of their ministry must be full of self-sacrifice and uncompensated toil, instead of seeking a comfortable support among you, they have turned their faces toward the setting sun, and trusting God, who works by you, they are to be found scattered along the banks of the great rivers, and in the midst of the forests and prairies of the West. Among strangers, buffeted with scorn, and proscribed by bigotry, they are contending for the faith which blesses your lives, and makes God and Christ and the immortal life realities to your souls. Out of this band, — who, if they succeed here, could certainly succeed where our faith is established, and our churches are built, and our parish committees provide for the yearly expenses, — out of this band occasionally some brother, compelled by a pressing emergency, makes sacrifice of his sensitiveness and ventures to ask you for aid ; not for himself, however badly he may need it, but to erect a shelter under which he may, with better advantage, and to larger congregations, preach the word, and thus have a fair opportunity to present the views which both you and he are agreed only need presentation in order to their acceptance.

And now, what if such appeals *are* numerous ; that ought to cause rejoicing at the rapid spread of Liberal Christianity. Some of you have given a great deal, and very often, and God has blessed you for it, if you have given in the right spirit. Look at the prominent churches of the West, are they not working also?　Read the Report of the Conference of Western Unitarian Churches; see how men are preaching in court-houses, and stores, and garrets; see, too, how they gain and maintain a footing in spite of the most severe antagonism.　Do you not think the burden is at least equally borne by those of the West?

I could tell you of a physician, who, without compensation, labors as faithfully and efficiently as any colporteur; who never visits a patient without preaching Unitarian Christianity, and who distributes tracts and books with as much conscientiousness and system as he dispenses medicine for physical ailments.　I could tell you of a friend who travels much on railroads and steamboats, collecting for large firms in New York, and who considers it one of his chief commissions to talk Liberal Christianity wherever he can find opportunity.　But time would fail to tell of all who devote time and money to the dissemination of Unitarianism in the West; but fair specimens of them may be found near Marietta, Ohio, Owensboro, Ky., New Albany, Ind., and Carrolton, Ill.　There are many more than you imagine, who are laboring and giving, not because they live in the West, but because they love Liberty and Love, and do not believe Providence and duty are limited to localities.

But I find I am likely to exceed my limits without reaching the topic which I had directly before me when I commenced this letter.　I will therefore defer until my next the consideration of the " Book Movement," which I am glad to see is being agitated amongst you.　With the most earnest wishes for your prosperity, and for the spread of " pure religion and undefiled,"

Fraternally yours,
Occident.

THE

QUARTERLY JOURNAL.

VOL. II.   BOSTON, JULY 1, 1855.   No. 4.

THIRTIETH ANNIVERSARY OF THE AMERICAN UNITARIAN ASSOCIATION.

THE Thirtieth Anniversary of the American Unitarian Association was celebrated in Boston, on Tuesday, the twenty-ninth day of last May.

According to previous notice, the meeting for business was held at nine o'clock in the forenoon, in Freeman Place Chapel. There was a large attendance, many auxiliaries having accepted the invitation to send delegates to this meeting. From one society in the country there were six delegates present. We thus had the happiness of seeing new faces at this annual gathering, and were animated and encouraged by this proof of interest in our cause.

On taking the chair, the President, REV. DR. LOTHROP, called upon REV. MR. PALFREY, of Belfast, Me., to open the meeting with prayer. The Treasurer's Annual Report was then presented by that officer, CALVIN W. CLARK, ESQ., and it was referred to HON. BENJAMIN SEAVER and HON. HENRY B. ROGERS, to be audited.

The President stated that, as the Secretary would read the Annual Report of the Executive Committee at the public meeting this evening, it might be well that only a brief synopsis of its contents should be presented now. The Secretary accordingly gave a statement of the most material facts contained in that Report, and it was voted that the further consideration of this subject be referred to the evening meeting.

The Association then proceeded to a choice of officers, which resulted in the election of the following persons : —

Executive Committee.

Rev. SAMUEL K. LOTHROP, D. D., *President.*

Hon. STEPHEN FAIRBANKS,
Rev. EDWARD B. HALL, D. D., } *Vice-Presidents.*

Hon. ALBERT FEARING.

Rev. GEORGE W. BRIGGS.

Rev. WILLIAM R. ALGER.

Rev. CALVIN LINCOLN.

GEORGE CALLENDER, ESQ.

CALVIN W. CLARK, ESQ., *Treasurer.*

Rev. HENRY A. MILES, D. D., *Secretary.*

REV. DR. LOTHROP thanked the Association for this renewed expression of their confidence and approbation. He had looked forward to this anniversary as the time when his official connection with the Association would cease. For twenty years had that official connection been enjoyed, as a member of the Executive Committee, for four of which he had been President of the board. But he confessed not only to a willingness, but to a desire, to remain in his present position a little longer. He wished to see the completion of the enterprise to the accomplishment of which they stood pledged, — the collection of the Fund of Fifty Thousand Dollars. He hoped and believed that result would soon be brought about; and, having taken part in the councils of the Association in its days of weakness and struggle, he had found his present relations to it, in its days of prosperity and growth, a source of great satisfaction-

HON. STEPHEN FAIRBANKS remarked that he felt that he might well ask to be excused from serving any longer in the position which, through the favor of the Association, he had enjoyed; but he found his connection with his associates of the Committee too pleasant to permit him to decline. The other officers accepted *sub silentio* the trusts to which they had been reappointed.

HON. BENJAMIN SEAVER and HON. HENRY B. ROGERS were appointed auditors for the ensuing year.

On motion of REV. MR. PALFREY, the subject of the Secretary's salary was referred to the Executive Committee, with full power.

THE SECRETARY expressed the great satisfaction that was felt in the presence of so many members, and delegates from auxiliaries. He believed that if these business meetings could be made also meetings for a free interchange of opinions and feelings in regard to the Association, they would be interesting and profitable, and we might hope for a large gathering of our friends in years to come. For his part, he wished that the presence of delegates from auxiliaries might be something more than a silent attendance, and that we may be favored with the counsels and instructions of our friends. If a topic for consideration was wanted, he would propose one which was of great importance to the best interests of our cause, — the best method of increasing the income of the Association. Through the extension of their operations, the Executive Committee would need a large increase of means, and the question was how these means could be raised.

On motion of Rev. Dr. Hall, it was voted to take up
that part of the Annual Report of the Committee which related to this subject; and accordingly the Secretary read all
that is contained in the Report under the third head. The
subject thus presented was the plan of Districts, and of employing District Agents.

Hon. John Prentiss, of Keene, expressed a decided
opinion in favor of individual appeal to each member of our
parishes. He believed that laymen would give to a greater
amount if only the cause was distinctly stated to them
individually. He detailed the manner in which the Society
with which he was connected had contributed for the Book
Fund. Believing it was a good object, it was presented to
each member of that Society by its pastor, Rev. Mr.
White, to whose earnestness and faithfulness he desired to
bear witness. He had been in hopes that the whole of that
Fund would have been raised at an earlier date than this.
He was sure it might now be raised at once, if our Societies
would present the great duty of charity in the form of a
personal appeal.

The President remarked, that he could not but respond
to what his friend from Keene had said. No Society had
acted more promptly or munificently than the Society in
that town. It had set an example which, if we had all followed, a far larger sum than that proposed would long ago
have been raised. He desired to thank that earnest and
generous parish, and to express his belief that their action
would yet be imitated in many places.

Hon. Stephen Fairbanks remarked upon the manner
in which two thousand dollars for the Book Fund was
raised in the Federal Street Church in Boston, of which he
is a member. It was by a personal appeal. He had himself called upon every individual from whom aid might be

expected. He desired to say distinctly and emphatically, that one thing had surprised and pleased him. It was the cheerfulness with which all had contributed. Laymen are far more ready to give than many suppose. We must present to them a good object, clearly and manifestly so; and this was felt to be a good object. This Book Fund was just what is wanted. Everybody saw it in this light. Importunity was not needed. All had been glad of an opportunity to give. The collection of the sum of two thousand dollars had been a labor of love. One member of the Society, unintentionally passed by, had actually complained of the neglect. He hoped that in all our Societies there would be this personal appeal.

REV. MR. FROST, of Concord, desired to add one word, suggested by his own experience, in favor of presenting this cause to every member of our Societies. In his own town a committee of ladies was appointed, one for every district; and they went from house to house. This had been done annually for several years. The people had thus been educated to a habit of giving. They expected to be called upon at a certain season of the year for this object, and they gave cheerfully, and he was glad to observe they increased their gifts from year to year. He might mention the case of one who had declined, but who confessed, a year from that time, great regret that she had done nothing to help send the Gospel to others, and a determination to give then, and every subsequent year, to this cause. We must not content ourselves by merely speaking upon this subject from the pulpit. That must be followed up by personal and individual appeal.

REV. MR HALEY, of Alton, Illinois, said he was glad to see the friends of true Christianity earnestly moving in the direction in which so much good can be accomplished;—

the circulation of books. Illinois, Indiana, and Missouri, —
those three States alone need, at this moment, and would
profitably use, all the books the Fifty Thousand Dollar Fund
can furnish. He narrated repeated and striking instances,
and in the case of leading and prominent men, where our
books accidentally falling in their way had revolutionized
their minds, and had given a new and holier direction to
their lives.

MR. KENT, of Concord, New Hampshire, expressed his
regret that the Unitarians of that place had as yet not co-
operated with their brethren in other places in carrying on
this work. The reason was probably known to most who
heard him. A calamity had taken from them their house
of worship, and had devolved the heavy expense of providing a new one. When the parish had recovered from the
burden which they had thus been called to bear, he felt sure
that it would promptly and generously do its part in this
good work which the denomination is now carrying on.

HON. ALBERT FEARING said he was afraid that we are all
too timid in asking our fellow-Christians to give. Why
should we not put it to the rich directly and plainly, Will
you assist in sustaining this cause ? What an unspeakable
good will it do to them ! How many are the rich men who
could hardly receive a greater blessing, than to have their
hearts and hands opened to help on the kingdom of holiness
and truth ! He felt mortified when he thought what a
small matter it was for us to accomplish the work proposed,
and yet it is unperformed. He believed that the very children of our Societies might compass it, — surely they
would do it if all would contribute as liberally as those in
some Societies had done, who had raised over one hundred
dollars for other objects. He would repeat the remark
made last autumn at the Montreal Convention, that the con-

tribution of the small sum of twenty-five cents from every man, woman, and child in our denomination would give us the entire Fund, and would ask if we will not all pledge ourselves to that amount at least !

Other interesting remarks were made by Rev. Mr. Casewell, lately of England, Rev. Mr. Palfrey of Belfast, Rev. Mr. Thurston, and Rev. John Bellows; at half past eleven o'clock the Association adjourned, to meet in the Federal Street Church at half past seven o'clock this evening.'

TREASURER'S REPORT.

Receipts and Expenditures.

RECEIPTS.

To Cash balance former account, .	$ 69.03	
" " from Auxiliaries and interest permanent fund, . . .	5,592.33	
To Cash from scattered subscribers to the Quarterly Journal,	541.35	
" " for Book Fund, .	11,619.46	
" " " Book Fund investment,	500.00	
" " " Sales of Books, .	2,888.19	
" " " Chippewa Mission,	534.03	
" " " Meadville Theological School, . . .	40.00	
		$ 21,784.39

EXPENDITURES.

By Cash paid expenses at office, &c., . $ 2,032.04
"   "   " Publishing Books,   10,925.87
"   "   " Chippewa Mission,   759.26
"   "   " Kanzas Mission,   200.00
"   "   " India Mission,   .   790.00
"   "   " Meadville Theological
              School,   .   .   40.00
"   "   " Agents, Sales Books,
              &c.,   .   .   585.23
"   "   " Aid to Feeble Socie-
              ties,   .   .   .   2,207.91
"   "   " Salaries,   .   .   2,250.00
"   "   " Investment Book Fund, 1,250.00
"   "   " Balance to new account, 744.08
                                   ————— $ 21,784.39

Er. Ex.

CALVIN W. CLARK, *Treasurer.*

Boston, May 29, 1855.

Boston, June 4, 1855.

The undersigned has examined the accounts of the Treasurer, and finds them correctly cast and properly vouched.

BENJAMIN SEAVER.

THE church in Federal Street was filled with a much larger audience than has of late assembled on the anniversary of the Association. At half past seven o'clock the chair was taken by the President, REV. DR. LOTHROP, who invited REV. DR. HALL, of Providence, R. I., to open the meeting with prayer. The Secretary then presented the following

REPORT OF THE EXECUTIVE COMMITTEE.

In the history of the Association we have reached a point of peculiar interest. We are assembled to celebrate its thirtieth anniversary. For a period as long as is usually assigned to a generation, has this organization maintained its existence. In its power of ready adaptation to meet the varying wants of the times, and in the gradual but sure enlargement of its means of influence, we may see prophecies of its continued life through other cycles of generations. It will be little in accordance, however, with the noble spirit of reform in which it was instituted, if we strive to perpetuate its name and body after its true life has departed. If it does not serve a higher purpose than that of being a relic of the past, if it does not vindicate its existence by the good it does now, if the spirit of the living God does not animate it, and, through it, carry on the divine purpose of unfolding ever fresh forms of truth and life, then by quietly laying it aside, with other things that have had their day, and by giving our interest and strength to more promising modes of influence, we shall best honor the men who, thirty years ago, were its originators and founders.

The occasion permits us to indulge the feelings of affectionate respect with which we revert to those men. The first meeting called to consider the expediency of forming a Unitarian Association was held in the vestry of, this church thirty years ago the twenty-seventh day of last January. A circular had been previously sent out, stating that " the design of the proposed meeting is, to bring together from distant parts of the country gentlemen who are known to take a deep interest in religion, and are supposed to have similar views and feelings on the subject, in order to confer together on the expediency of appointing an annual meeting for the purpose of union, sympathy, and co-operation in the cause of Christian truth and Christian charity." It was further stated, in another paper drawn up soon afterwards in explanation of the purposes of the proposed Association by its first Executive Committee, and by them sent forth to the churches, that the object to be kept in view was the promotion, " not simply nor chiefly of those views which distinguish the friends of this Association from other disciples of Jesus Christ, but of those great doctrines and principles in which all Christians coincide, which constitute the substance of our religion. We wish to diffuse the knowledge and influence of the uncorrupted Gospel of our Lord and Saviour Jesus Christ. Great good is anticipated from the co-operation of persons entertaining similar views, who are now strangers to each other's religious sentiments. Interest will be awakened, confidence inspired, and efficiency produced, by concentration of labors. The spirit of inquiry will be fostered, and individuals at a distance will know where to apply for information and encouragement."

These were the feelings which led to the call of that first meeting of January 27th, 1825; and as that time drew nigh, a plan of " procedure " was drawn up by the late Henry Ware, Jr., in conference with another friend of the cause. The original paper, which is preserved in the records of the Association, sketches a plan of organization essentially like that which was afterwards adopted. The first item entered on that paper stands recorded in these words: "Take no account of the prejudices, lukewarmness, or opposition of our own body; but ascertain our means and our duty, and commence operations prudently, systematically, and perseveringly." The need of this caution has not, perhaps, yet wholly passed away; still are we too apt "to take account" of the lukewarmness and prejudices " of our own body," and to forget that there is nothing like prudent and persevering action to remove indifference and opposition.

At the meeting, January 27th, the opinions of thirty-one persons were represented, either by personal attendance or by proxy and letter. The names of such of those persons as have since departed from this life may here be repeated. Of the clergy, there were Dr. Channing, Dr. Parker, Dr. Bancroft, Dr. Thayer, Dr. Abbot, Dr. Freeman, Dr. Allyn, Dr. Pierce, Henry Ware, Jr., Professor Norton; and of the laity, there were Judge Story, Judge Howe, Hon. Leverett Saltonstall, Hon. Alden Bradford, Hon. Charles H. Atherton, Stephen Higginson, Esq., and others. The conference was opened by prayer by Rev. Dr. Channing; and the minutes of the Secretary, Rev. James Walker, which are preserved in our records, give us a knowledge of the opinions which the discussion developed.

On the question of the formation of the Association there was not entire unanimity. Some thought that all that could well be done for the promotion of true views of religion could be accomplished by friends of that cause in their individual capacity, while injury to it might accrue by adopting a party name and presenting an object of attack.

The measure, however, was advocated by many speakers, among whom Dr. Channing and Professor Norton may be particularly named ; and the opinions of a large majority preponderated in its favor.

It was not, however, until the Anniversary Week in the month of May following that the object aimed at was fully accomplished. On the 26th of that month, 1825, the Constitution of the American Unitarian Association was adopted, and its first officers were chosen. A few extracts from letters from influential men, in various parts of the country, will show the feelings with which the proposal for an Association, and its establishment, were regarded.

Hon. Judge Howe, of Northampton, under date of January 24th, 1825, writes : " Nothing would afford me greater pleasure than the opportunity which such a meeting would present of becoming acquainted with the views and sentiments of yourselves and other gentlemen on the subject of religion. In saying this, I have of course expressed my opinion in relation to the propriety of establishing an annual meeting for this purpose. I think much good would result from an establishment of this kind, and I cannot but believe it would be a subject of general interest through the Commonwealth. My engagements have been such as to prevent my being able to consult with many gentlemen in this vicinity on the subject ; but so far as my inquiries have extended, there has appeared to be but one opinion in relation to it. . . . . . I have showed your letter [the circular above referred to] to Judge Lyman, and though it will not be in his power to attend the proposed meeting, yet I shall urge him to communicate to you his own views on this subject, though I know they agree substantially with my own."

Under date of January 26th, 1825, Hon. Leverett Saltonstall, of Salem, thus writes: " From the best consideration I have been able to give the subject, I think some such measure is expedient and will tend to promote the cause of Christian truth. All other classes and denominations around us have associated in this way, and, undoubtedly, have found it beneficial. Why should not we do the same ? Would it not give strength and confidence to our friends ? I am inclined to think it would. Far be it from us to become a sectarian, proselyting party, and to resort to any of their arts to increase our numbers. But when our views are so misunderstood and misrepresented, and so many systematically excite a fear of our sentiments, and of opinions which we conscientiously believe to be the truths of the Gospel, why should we not show that we have confidence in them ? And why should we not desire all the aid and comfort we can obtain from mutual sympathy and encouragement, and from cultivating acquaintance with those whose general views on religious subjects are similar to our own."

Under date of July 30th, 1825, and in relation to the office of President of the Association, to which he had been elected, Rev. Dr. Bancroft, of Worcester, thus writes: " Your plan of executing the purposes of the Association of Unitarians meets my fullest approbation, and I duly appreciate the honor done me in my election to the presidency. Though I have attained to an age which warns me of the propriety of retiring from public stations rather than entering into new and responsible situations, yet, if you have not already filled this respectable office with a more suitable character, and your committee still suppose that I can in that capacity be of any use to the society, I will not decline your request."

Hon. Judge Story, then of Salem, under date of August

26th, 1825, writes as follows : " I entirely approve of the plan and objects of the American Unitarian Association, and should not hesitate a moment to become a subscriber to it. I wish it every success, and am confident that it will be found highly useful to genuine, rational, and liberal Christianity. In respect to accepting an office of Vice-President of the society, I have more difficulty, not from any disinclination to being known as an avowed and un-equivocal Unitarian, but from a consciousness that I shall have little opportunity to take an active part in the concerns of the society. With me it is a rule not to hold offices the duties of which my other avocations prevent me from fulfilling; and although I am sometimes induced to act where I cannot perform all the duties, I do so with very great reluctance. My time principally belongs to the public, and I fear the example cannot be good of accepting offices where we can expect to do little. I shall not be less a friend of the institution because I may have no office, nor less a Unitarian because my aid is given only in private. Still, however, if the society feel that I can be of more use to them as a public character than as a private subscriber, I will not shrink from a performance of their wishes, though I should feel better pleased with having my place supplied by a more active and punctual officer."

Only one other extract will be made. The following, written October 2d, 1825, is from a letter from the late Hon. Henry Wheaton, for many years the distinguished Minister from the United States to the Court of Berlin : " My absence from New York has prevented my returning an earlier answer to your letter of the 15th of August, announcing my appointment as a Vice-President of the American Unitarian Association. I beg leave to return my thanks for the honor done. me by the Association, whose objects I most heartily approve. I can only regret that it will not probably be in my power to contribute essentially to promote those objects. I have long thought that a more intimate bond of union between the friends of liberal Christianity throughout the country was very desirable, and am glad to see that it falls within your plan to assemble an annual convention of delegates."

The writers of all these letters, and many of their distinguished associates and faithful fellow-laborers, have passed away from the scenes of earth. Others, who rendered most valuable service in the formation and early stages of the Association, we have still the happiness — long may it be ours — of meeting among its honored friends and supporters. It is good to recur to the words they left on record thirty years ago, to set forth their comprehensive plans and noble purposes. To add another to the list of narrow religious sects was not at all their intention. There is in their plans an air of freedom, inquiry, progress, charity, and generous co-operation with liberal-minded men of all parties, which it will do us good to breathe. Only as we sympathize with the spirit of religious liberty and true progress, wherever found, are we worthy to stand in their places and to take up their work. As compared with the intolerance and denunciation of a third of a century ago, what a change in the prevailing temper of the religious world has been brought about! How little could this change have been anticipated at the time when the foundations of our Association were laid by the men we have named, and how would they have rejoiced to see it! The fact that Unitarianism has made so little outward progress has been often pointed to as an evidence of the failure of the plans of its friends. The reply is, that those friends did not propose to act the part of propagandists of a creed. They aimed to diffuse a generous and liberal spirit. The history of no other denomination in this country records a more manifest and wide-spread diffusion of its prevailing idea. Towards the accomplishment of this result our Association has probably contributed as much as any other one human agency. Every year its Annual Report has given true words of encouragement and hope. And returning from this passing allusion to the founders of the Association, its Executive Committee would now proceed to relate the facts in the history of the last year which may here properly be named.

In order to present in some convenient plan the various topics which may claim consideration, they will be taken up in the following order : —

1. The Association's Book Fund and Books.

2. The Missionary Enterprises recently undertaken.

3. An explanation of a new method adopted by the Committee for the promotion of systematic charity.

4. An allusion to some of the feelings and purposes which our position and prospects should inspire.

1. The Association's Book Fund and Books. Fifteen months ago a pledge was given by the friends of the Association for earnest and persevering efforts to raise the sum of fifty thousand dollars. In several of our societies, that part of the responsibility of this pledge which rested upon them has been promptly and munificently redeemed. The sum of twenty-one thousand dollars has been raised. But a little more than one half of this has been contributed during the past year. The friends of the measure preferred not to press its claims in a season of financial stringency and embarrassment, believing they should win greater favor to it by awaiting the return of

more prosperous times. For this reason action in many of our largest and wealthiest parishes has been delayed. Time, which so often divides opinion as to the importance of new enterprises, and evaporates the ardor which marked their inception, has only strengthened the belief so generally entertained of the value, usefulness, and entire feasibility of this undertaking. Every argument urged in its favor stands even stronger to-day than it stood fifteen months ago. This good at least has come from the gradual progress of the plan, that we have been assured that we are not deceived by unfounded hopes of usefulness in the direction here proposed, and may now add to our appeal arguments drawn from a year's successful experiment.

Some minute details as to the actual working of this experiment the Committee will now proceed to present, believing that the facts will show, not only some diligent use of the means intrusted to their hands, but their confidence that they would be supported in undertaking plans for the accomplishment of which the entire amount at first named for the Book Fund will be required.

By the terms of subscription, that Fund, and any part of it, was to be used *as capital* by the Executive Committee, who, instead of investing it in stocks, and appropriating only the accruing interest, would make it available, as a book-business firm would its capital, in the purchase of editions, and in contracts for printing, paper, and binding. Believing that the sum placed a year ago at their disposal authorized a beginning of the business contemplated, the Committee entered upon the work of which they are now to give some account.

Their first want was that of the assistance of practical knowledge and skill in the business of book-publication. That want was not left unsupplied. A gentleman of long

35 *

and successful experience in that business in this city met sub-committees of our board, gave them the benefit of his time, his careful examination of our interests, his judgment, and advice, and for months has rendered assistance of the greatest value and importance. The Committee cannot withhold the expression of their gratitude for the generous aid which, through his interest in our plans, he has so kindly bestowed. The Committee have contracted for the continued publication of the Quarterly Journal, — the circulation of which has now attained to six thousand copies. They have stereotyped two thousand five hundred pages of our Tracts, so that we can now furnish entire series of the twenty-six volumes, and any numbers of the nine volumes bound up according to subjects. Not to mention several smaller books that have been published, such as " Sin and its Consequences," and " Early Piety," the Committee have got out new editions of Sears on Regeneration, Eliot's Discourses, Grains of Gold, The Gospel Narratives, and an edition of a thousand copies of Channing's Works, in three volumes. In order to supply the most important theological and religious publications of Dr. Channing at a very low price, they have published an edition of five thousand copies of a select volume, which is volume first of a Theological Library. As the second volume of this Library, they have contracted for an original and able work, by Mr. John Wilson, of Boston, entitled, " Unitarian Principles confirmed by Trinitarian Testimonies," which is now passing through the press, and will soon be issued. The third volume of this Library will be Norton's " Statement of Reasons for not believing in the Trinity," with a sketch of the life of the author, to be published in the course of a few months. With two scholars and divines in our denomination, whose names would be the sufficient guaranty for every needed qualification for the work, the Committee have contracted for the preparation of a new commentary on the New Testament, — a work which will be the first volume of the Biblical Library. Of the Devotional Library, the first volume has already been published, entitled " The Altar at Home." Of this book we may add that four editions have appeared within the short space of ten weeks. It will soon be followed by a second volume in that Library, to be entitled " The Rod and the Staff," by Rev. Thomas T. Stone, of Bolton. A third volume in that Library may be published this season, to be entitled " Anastasia, or Immortality," by Rev. Mr. Sears, of Wayland.

In addition to these statements, it might be added that the Committee have other manuscripts under consideration, and propose to reproduce other works of established character and value in the series of libraries that have been projected. Enough perhaps has been said to give an idea of the plan of the Society's operations, and to furnish some indication of the manner in which the Committee have used that portion of the Book-Fund which has been placed at their disposal.

As to the call for such books as the Association furnish, the Committee would express their belief that it is steadily increasing. During the past year there have been sent out from the Association's Rooms over 16,000 volumes, 4,000 being the number sent out the year before. Some of these were gifts to public institutions; some were sent to the eighty-two different persons by whom our books are kept on sale; some, too, were carried to distant places by our missionaries; and many have been sold for cash at the rooms. The sales last year amounted to over $2,800, against $700 in the year before. As the character of our publications and the mode of our influence become more widely known, the Committee see no reason why the business of the Association may not be greatly enlarged, so that in a few years it may amount annually to many thousand dollars, and the Association retain substantially the capital intrusted to its care. Especially may this extension of operations be hoped for, if pains are now taken to establish business connections, and make the publications of the Association known in various and distant parts of our country. To this point it is believed that immediate attention should be directed.

The Committee will here close their remarks on this first head of the Report, as they believe they have presented the material facts in regard to the plans which have now been detailed. If these plans have been formed wisely, and are full of promise for the promotion of higher views of truth, the Committee will not believe that their action will be left to be crippled for want of means. The most important work we have ever undertaken, commending itself at once to the universal common sense, by its being suited to the character of the age, making available the hiding-place of our power, — our able and attractive literature, supplying the existing want of preachers, preaching in a thousand places to which preachers could not go, doing more, probably, at this moment, than all other agencies put together to diffuse the truth, and doing it in a manner which returns the original outlay, to be used over and over and over again, — it now remains to be seen whether this work shall stop or go on. To the contribution of the full sum originally named for the Book Fund, the honor of the denomination is pledged ; and it is not for the Committee to doubt that there will be generous and persevering action till that pledge be redeemed.

2. While the Committee have thus endeavored to use

with some diligence the most promising methods of diffusing a pure and earnest Christianity here at home, they have not been unmindful of the duty of improving opportunities of usefulness in distant places, opened to us by the directing providence of God. In approaching the second topic of this Report, namely, the Missionary Enterprises recently undertaken, it is not necessary to do more than allude to the frequency and urgency with which, on previous anniversaries of this Association, both in reports and addresses, the importance of cherishing a missionary spirit has been affirmed. It was not doubted that the time has come to translate these words into actions. The increasing numbers and enlarged means of our societies forbid that *we* should do nothing to extend the domain of that Gospel which is to be preached to every creature through the zeal and courage of those who believe it to be of God; nor can it be forgotten that we need the transforming and renewing influence which comes as the divine compensation for every sincere and self-sacrificing effort, and which is seen in drawing hearts together that are now apart, each in its own isolation, and in giving them a deeper sense of the preciousness and power of their common faith.

In regard to the choice of fields for missionary action, the Committee felt that they had but one rule to guide them; it was to keep themselves in the attitude of watchful and careful observers, and to be ready to follow any intimations of the leadings of Divine Providence. Nearly eight months since, the return of the Rev. Charles T. Brooks from India, to which place he had gone for the benefit of his health, put the Committee in possession of recent and exact information in regard to the condition and prospects of a pure Christianity in that country, and revived the deep interest which was here felt on this subject, twenty-five years ago.

During the whole of this period of a quarter of a century, we have had the thought present to our minds, that there are brethren of our faith in that distant land who need a word of encouragement from us; and that many, nominally connected with an ancient form of religion which sends its roots back into a dim and mysterious past, would from us, and perhaps from us alone, learn of that Saviour, who, in these later times, has come as a messenger of God's grace. The report which Mr. Brooks made of the results of his personal inquiries, and of the earnest entreaty of residents in India that a missionary might be sent to them, has been published, and need not here be repeated. The Committee could not doubt that this was one field of usefulness to which they were called. And when, a few months later, an offer was made to them of services as a missionary from one who was favorably known by his varied experience, his skill in teaching, the gentleness of his spirit, and the courage and perseverance of a warm and devoted heart, the Committee closed a contract with him, with a gratifying conviction that, whatever the final results of this mission may be, the Association has responded to a call from which it ought not to turn away.

Rev. Mr. Dall sailed for India on the 28th of last February. He took with him a commission as Missionary of the Association to Calcutta, Madras, Salem, and other places, and minute instructions to guide his course, and large packages of books to be sold or bestowed wherever they may be of use in promoting Christian truth. It will, of course, be many months before we hear of the results of his labors. Since his departure, the Committee have had letters from Rev. William Roberts, of Madras, giving a further account of the state of his schools and church, from which we learn that, in the three charity schools established in that place, there are at present one hundred and fifty-five pupils, of whom there are heathen children, ninety; Mahometans, eleven; Roman Catholics, thirty-nine; Trinitarian and Unitarian, fifteen. Services are regularly maintained in his church, and during the past year he has had many converts from the heathen. He writes in feeling terms of his need of books, and of a missionary from our country; and we rejoice that a voice of encouragement and Christian fellowship is on the wide waters that roll between him and us, and will soon greet his ears. It is an interesting fact, that from our new country, and from one of the most recent growths of our Christian civilization, a missionary has gone, bearing a fresh word to those old hives of the world's population, — a restored Gospel, — appearing something more than an imitation of their own triune emanations and metamorphoses, and addressing them in the purity and majesty of the one living and only true God.

On the 12th of last February, the Executive Committee voted to establish a missionary station among the Chippewa Indians, beyond the Minnesota Territory; and at the same time, Rev. James Tanner, a half-blood Indian, and an ordained minister of the Gospel, was appointed Missionary of the Association. After a few weeks' conference with the Committee, Mr. Tanner left Boston on the second day of March, accompanied by Mr. Robert Clark, who has been engaged by the Committee as a school-teacher, to assist Mr. Tanner; and both, with books and farming utensils, have now entered upon the work of attempting to civilize and Christianize the native tribe above named.

Of the previous history of Mr. Tanner, of his former connection with the American Baptist Home Missionary Society, of his introduction to the Executive Committee of the American Unitarian Association, and of the plans he has

formed for the instruction and elevation of his tribe, full
accounts have been published in the Quarterly Journal of
the Association.   During his stay in Boston, many became
personally acquainted with him, and formed an opinion as
to his intelligence, honesty, piety, his love of his race, his
willingness to labor for their good, his probable ability to
improve their condition.   It cannot be forgotten what a sad
history is that of the aboriginal tribes of this country, since
their hunting-grounds were first invaded by the white man.
The entire failure of nearly all attempts to bring these
children of the forest within the pale of our civilization, is
the most signal disappointment in the enterprises of modern
philanthropy.   The most sagacious plans have again and
again been baffled; and before the advancing flood of the
violence and vices of a border life, the Indians have constantly retreated westward, every year perishing by thousands.

Under these circumstances, it was hardly to be expected,
perhaps, that the Committee would engage in so discouraging a work, requiring, for a hopeful prosecution of it, an
amount of missionary experience, an array of numbers, and
an affluence of means which we cannot command.   There
were circumstances, however, which seemed to make it
imperative, in the judgment of the Committee, for them to
assume the oversight of this mission.   These circumstances
arose less from the theological sympathies which Mr. Tanner and his Indian converts are believed to have with our
form of faith, than from a conviction that, if it be possible
for the Indian to be blessed by our civilization, Mr. Tanner appears to be, in many respects, remarkably fitted for
attempting this work.   From the time of the first addresses
he made to audiences in Boston, it was evident that *he*
would collect means nearly sufficient to sustain his mission

for a year, — a result which has since been accomplished,
— and it appeared to be clearly our duty to give the wisest
and best direction in our power to these charities ; nor can
we doubt that, through the Divine favor, we may be able to
carry the hope of salvation to thousands, if we can act
through the instrumentality of one who thoroughly understands the condition and feels the wants of the Indian, and
who, by his sincerity, eloquence, and Christian devotedness,
appears to have obtained a commanding influence over the
people of his tribe. All accounts agree in representing that
large numbers of that people are ready to abandon their
roving habits, to adopt the manners and arts of civilized life,
and to listen, with willing minds, to instructions pertaining
to the Gospel of Jesus Christ, which they will more easily
receive in the form held by us than in that set forth in
Trinitarian creeds.

By the terms of a treaty made at Washington during the
last winter, communities and individuals of the Chippewa
tribe, as fast as they become civilized to a certain extent,
are to be admitted to all the rights and privileges of American citizenship. It is the first time that this experiment has
been tried. A stronger motive than has ever before been
held out will thus operate to induce the Indian to adopt our
mode of life ; and it is believed by those who are familiar
with the subject, that it will be the beginning of a new era
in Indian civilization.

It is not improbable that a call may come to us for other
school-teachers, and other preachers of the Gospel. Two
native Chippewa Indians, it is expected, will enter the
Meadville School in the coming autumn. This may be the
small beginning of a work which may grow larger, and extend longer, than we can now foresee. The Providence
which has directed the steps already taken may have great

designs to accomplish, — trying our faith and courage, tasking all our postponed exertions, and giving us the satisfaction of feeling that to us it is permitted to do something towards paying that debt to the red men of the forest which centuries of wrongs have accumulated.

The two missionary enterprises we have now described have historical sympathies connecting us with the ancient idolatry of the East, and with the primitive monotheism of the West. The Executive Committee have recently established a third missionary work, bearing upon the great question which marks the middle of this nineteenth century, — the strife between freedom and slavery, which seeks its battle-ground in the central Territory of this continent. In alluding to this subject here, the Committee open no sectional agitation, and take sides with no political party. But they would be false to all the convictions of their minds, and do violence to all the instincts of their hearts, if they manifested no interest in the crisis which is fast approaching. Accordingly, they desired to send to that new Territory, where thousands of the sons of New England are now gathering, some one who should be a fit representative of the Gospel of Jesus Christ as we understand it, and who should there lift up its voice in favor of the inalienable rights of man, of freedom protected by law, and secured by institutions of learning and religion. A prudent, conciliating, but earnest and devoted man, they wanted, — willing to cast in his lot amid the hardships of a new settlement, ready to adapt himself to all classes, able in address, and wise to win souls. It was felt that such a missionary was so much needed in Kanzas, that the Committee would be held inexcusable if they did not send one to minister to numerous families of our own household of faith who are removing to that Territory, to lay the foundations of religious societies which may there spring up, to circulate the Scriptures and other religious books, to preach wherever he may gather hearers, and in all ways in his power to pour the lifeblood of freedom, truth, and righteousness into the heart of that new commonwealth. On the 12th of last March, Rev. Ephraim Nute was appointed to this work. The Committee have congratulated themselves that their choice was directed to one who combines as many qualifications as any person to them known. On the 3d of April, Mr. Nute was installed a missionary of the Association by a public service in the church in Chicopee, in which, for several years, he has served as pastor. On the evening of the 13th of April he addressed a meeting in Boston in explanation of the purposes and plans of his mission, and on the 19th of the same month he left this city for his distant scene of labors, taking with him a large number of our books, and followed by the earnest wishes and fervent prayers of many friends.

Thus during the past year three missionary stations have been established, and four missionaries have been appointed, all of whom have either reached or are now on their way to their several posts of duty. As the first attempt at foreign missions ever undertaken by the Association, they will make the past year memorable, not only by the extent to which the work has been begun, but, as we hope, by larger and more vigorous enterprises that may be dated from this point. Already it is apparent that they have given us a position of more respect and influence in the religious world. Earnest efforts to teach the Gospel, as we understand it, in distant and remote parts, with which we have no ties but the ties of Christian sympathy, are proofs which come home to every man's breast that that Gospel is an object of our love. Theologians may say what they will about the defects and

negations of our creed; but when it prompts to self-sacrificing efforts to seek and to save the lost, it gives evidence
which cannot be impugned that it is vital with the spirit of
Christ. The effect of this movement upon ourselves, also,
cannot be overlooked. The spirit of missions enters so
deeply into the heart of Jesus and his Apostles, that, wherever it is cherished, it seems to carry with it something of
the awakening and transforming power of Apostolic days.
It was through the spirit of missions that Romanism in the
sixteenth century was pervaded by an enterprise and energy unknown in her whole previous history, so that she in
part recovered from the blow inflicted by the Reformation.
It was through the spirit of missions that Protestantism
shook off the embrace of a sceptical philosophy, and drew
that more earnest breath of life which has marked the last
half-century. If these historical illustrations bring to view
works whose magnitude we cannot hope to emulate, they
may at least suggest the steps by which some new vigor
may be infused into our branch of the Christian Church.

We have now presented some details relating to the
missionary enterprises of the past year. Meanwhile all
the operations of the Association, established in former
years, have been continued ; such as the regular supply of
the publications of the Association, the employment of col-
porteurs for the distribution of our books, and the care of
feeble Societies which need our fostering aid. It will be
seen, therefore, that if the past year has been marked by a
signal extension of our labors, it has been marked also by
an increase of our expenses.

3. We are thus brought to the third topic of our Report,
which is an explanation of a new method adopted by the
Committee for the promotion of systematic charity.

Under this head, the Committee feel it to be their duty to

call the attention of the Association to a few facts, which shall be stated with all possible clearness and brevity.

To sustain the present operations of the Association, there is needed, setting aside altogether what may be given for the Book-Fund, the annual sum of twelve thousand dollars.

During the last five years the average amount contributed annually for the general purposes of the Association has been seven thousand five hundred dollars.

For years to come, the Executive Committee will be obliged to do one of two things, either to increase the *income* of the Association annually to the extent of four thousand five hundred dollars, or to suspend some of the present operations of the Association. The Committee cannot doubt which of these alternatives will be accepted.

Beside the ten or fifteen thousand dollars to be raised every year for the Book-Fund till that be completed, the twelve thousand dollars to be collected for the general purposes of the Association seems a small sum, considering the number and wealth of our churches. Less wealthy denominations in New England easily collect larger sums, through the habits of systematic charity established among them. Here is our great neglect. A few facts present this subject in its true light.

Setting aside the number of feeble Societies from which no contribution can be expected, we have in our denomination at least one hundred and eighty parishes, from which, every year, some aid might be given. Twelve thousand dollars divided among them is but a fraction over sixty-six dollars each.

But we have included in the one hundred and eighty parishes several that cannot give sixty-six dollars a year. But as an offset we have also included some that give an-

nually two or three times that amount each, and one that
does not let a year pass without its gift of one thousand
dollars to the general purposes of the Association. The
main thing is, to have each Society give something, give
what it can, if it be but five dollars, — to give that *every
year* without fail, as an expression of its sympathy and
good-will.

But it is only a small number of our societies that contribute regularly every year. During the last five years
the average number annually contributing is only fifty-
seven out of the one hundred and eighty, — that is to say,
less than one third. In the denomination at large, there are
about twenty Societies that are sure to make annual returns.
A contribution for the Association is a part of their established charities, not to be omitted, whether an agent of the
Association visits them or not. In the remaining one hundred and sixty Societies a contribution is taken up only now
and then, — once in two, three, or five years, as it may happen ; hardly ever, however, if an agent is not present to
solicit it.

A view of these facts has led the Committee to ask, if
some plan cannot be adopted to remedy this great irregu-
larity ; and as the entire experience of the Association
shows that but few Societies contribute without the solicitation of an agent, is it not possible to increase the number
of agents, so as to have the claims of the Association presented to every parish once every year ? The Committee
are deeply impressed with the conviction, that the support
of the present operations of the Association is dependent
upon the adoption of some plan of this kind. It seems indispensable as an instrument in educating our people to
habits of missionary charity, and is demanded that we may
take the place as an efficient Christian and Christianizing

power which our numbers and wealth require that we should assume.

It is not here necessary to go into the details of the measure which the Committee have adopted. They will be fully set forth in a circular, to be sent to the churches. Our Unitarian Societies are divided into districts. In each district a District Agent is appointed, — a clergyman, who will be asked to present the claims of the Association, some time during the year, to each Society in his district, in the course of his usual exchanges. The Sundays of the Secretary will be employed in some of these districts ; but, as he cannot address every year more than one third of our parishes, this plan is designed that *all* Societies may annually be reached. It is obvious that its efficiency will depend upon the favor, with which it is received, and upon the willingness of ourc lergy to co-operate for the great end we have in view. Should the plan be cordially tried, the Committee believe that its effect will be to increase the number of Societies that annually contribute, and to enlarge the amount of our annual receipts ; while a semiannual meeting of District Agents for mutual conference and encouragement may be expected to diffuse a knowledge of the operations of the Association, and to make friends of those who labor for its good.

4. In regard to the measure now named, as in regard to all measures for increased activity and usefulness, the Committee are convinced that far more depends than we may at first be disposed to allow upon the general feeling cherished throughout the denomination towards this American Unitarian Association. The remark naturally introduces the fourth and last topic of our Report, — the feelings and purposes which our position and prospects should inspire. Towards this particular agency, with the oversight and care

of which your Committee have been intrusted, towards this
American Unitarian Association, it is not for us to decide
how you, its members, shall stand affected.   That must depend upon a great many causes over which we can have
no control.   It is ours to labor, to *deserve* your confidence ;
and not that only, but that affectionate interest, that heartiness of co-operation, without which our work is " toiling up
the hill," and can end only in disappointment.   Perhaps it
is hardly to be expected that a denomination which has such
an intense love of individualism should very cordially
rally around any institution ; perhaps, among a people impatient of all old things, it seems to some that an institution
thirty years old is old enough, and they have become tired
of its very name ; perhaps others, seeing that the Association does not give its entire influence to collateral views and
measures which for the time may have most interest to
them, may naturally under-estimate the value of the results
it is accomplishing ; perhaps, too, there may be those who
·have fallen into a way, they hardly know when or why, of
looking at all the measures the institution proposes in lights
which alienate from it their feelings, and prevent them
from attracting towards it the sympathies of others.   Apart
from the operation of some such causes as these, it is not
easy to see why it need be difficult to raise every year, not
twelve thousand dollars only, but twice that amount, nor
why the completion of the Book-Fund should be postponed.

Your Committee do not allude to these things in a tone
of complaint.   They know not the class or the individuals
on whom they may rightfully cast any blame.   Blame, if
there be blame anywhere, may rest upon all of us alike, —
and may, after all, spring mainly from too much neglect of
our profoundest Christian convictions, and our most pressing religious duties.   We bespeak for these a more united

and earnest attention. Overlooking minor differences, conscientiously practising the liberality we profess, we need to cherish a juster sense of the value of the truths and interests which we hold in common. It is a position of great influence and responsibleness, this of the Liberal Congregationalists, which we inherit from our fathers. With the restoration in this country of a pure Christianity, and the diffusion of tolerant and kindly feelings on the subject of religion, the history of our Association is identified. It is throughout an honorable history. It is the record of efforts made on a small scale indeed, but made, as we believe, in the spirit of Him who has promised to be even with two or three of his disciples who have come together in his name, and followed, as we would gratefully acknowledge, by that blessing, which, after we have planted and watered, can alone give the increase. It is a chapter in the ecclesiastical history of this country which will make mention of names and measures with which we may well count it an honor to be in any way associated, and a chapter not yet closed, but destined to record, if only we are faithful to our trusts, larger and better things. Bring back the union and love and zeal which warmed the early anniversaries of this Association, and what an interest would go from these meetings to our two hundred congregations! To what a position of influence would this Association be raised! The people, seeing that we thought of it, and loved it, and honored it, and were willing to labor for it, would not withhold a prompt and generous support. It would attract the benefactions of the affluent, and be remembered in the legacies of the dying. A general and hearty attachment to it would make its action vital and efficient; while without this, though we have an organization, officers, agents, and all needed apparatus, we have only a body without a soul. In the signs we discern of a growing union, love, and zeal, we see the fairest hope that brightens the path of the future.

When from this general view of our denomination we look to the condition of individual churches, we find facts to encourage us. They furnish tokens on many sides of spiritual growth. In not a few of them, the past year has been marked by an unusual attention to the subject of religion, and by large additions of members. We have before alluded to the issue of four editions of the prayer-book called " The Altar at Home," within the short space of a few weeks. The tone of feeling in our Societies of which this fact is significant, is one for which we have just reason to thank God, and to take courage for more strenuous labors to promote a life of prayer and faith. Our reference to this work reminds us of the signal service which the pastors of our churches may often render to the spiritual growth of their people, by taking some pains to promote the circulation of good books. Neglect of this is sometimes defended on the ground that families in *our* congregations are capable of selecting their own reading; a plea which, if it was justified by an inspection of family libraries, would not bar the friendly office of the pastor in commending works which might not otherwise be heard of, and which might be no unimportant auxiliary to the teachings of the pulpit in promoting truth and holiness.

Book-distributors of other denominations take advantage of our neglect ; and in thousands of our families works of inferior ability to our own, and charged with what we believe to be doctrinal errors, are found in place of those which we should see furnished to every household. There is not a denomination of Christians in New England that bestows so little care in regard to this matter as we give to it. What might be done through the agency of our literature, not only in distant places, but here at home, if only we took pains to secure its wide diffusion! Some few examples are full of encouragement. Said a preacher in one of our rural churches: "I know of five families who have joined our Society as the result of a general circulation among us of Eliot's Doctrinal Lectures." Some three or four clergymen furnished every family in their Societies with a copy of the Altar at Home, at the reduced price. How much might a life of faith and holiness be promoted, if a copy of that book could be placed in every household in our denomination!

In the relation between pastor and people in the Societies of our denomination, as we think we have good reason to judge, there is springing up a more conservative and sacred feeling in place of the spirit of restlessness and change which has heretofore had so much sway. The readiness to yield to the ministry a more adequate support, and the large number of instances which have occurred during the last year of reconstruction or repair of places of public worship, are gratifying indications of the strength of attachment for the institutions of religion. It is deeply to be regretted that these indications do not attract a greater number of young men to the sacred profession. The want which must press heavier and heavier on our churches is the want of a larger supply of ministers of strong powers and devoted hearts. Well is it that attention is turned to the importance of securing a more effectual alliance of religious influence with the processes of academical and collegiate education; and a measure, recently consummated, providing for this result in the neighboring ancient University, cannot be referred to without expressions of interest. The brother who leaves one of our largest Societies to take upon himself the trusts and duties of a new office will be followed by the prayers of many hearts, that strength and grace may be given to him to guide souls " to Christ and the Church." The Theological School at Cambridge is fulfilling the hopes of its friends, in giving to our churches, this year, a large class of promising young men. Should events transpire requiring generous efforts to place this institution on some new basis of enlarged usefulness, these efforts will not be withheld from an object of such vital interest to the prosperity of our churches. Of the School at Meadville we are happy in being able to say that it is still experiencing that measure of success and promise which have marked its career from the beginning.

Turning from this glance at the condition and prospects of our own body; the Committee may be permitted to add one word in regard to other denominations of Christians. With no remarkable expansion in the growth of any sect, there is, as we judge, a healthy vigor in the life of all. We deem it a fact which calls for devout gratitude, that the religious world is, to so great a degree, free from fierce and bitter sectarian controversy; that points of difference are subordinated to the things which make for peace ; and that so many are seeking higher forms of truth, less through disputation, which seldom leads to such results, and more through a higher spiritual life, — the decisive way to know of the doctrine whether it be of God.

Your Committee will close a Report already too greatly extended, by subjoining one word in regard to the spirit which they hope may mark this anniversary. Perhaps, on surveying the reports and addresses on the previous returns of this celebration, it may be perceived that one tone has somewhat largely pervaded them ; and while it is doubtless a good thing to rejoice in what God has done for us, and to cherish faith in the future, and to congratulate ourselves that our affairs never stood so well, and prospects were never more cheering, yet it would be a regret if the enthusiasm thus awakened evaporated in the ebullitions of a vague hope, and none of it was directed to the one great condition of success, which is WORK. In what the Committee have narrated as the brief history of the past year, it must not be forgotten that we have occasion to record as yet but little that is *done*. Plans, not results, are the burden of their story. To translate these plans into results, — this is the call for *work*. Give us that encouragement which holds out new incentives to *work*. Give us that encouragement which comes from the pledge of your co-operation in *work*. In the solemnity of these closing words we call to mind the image of an earnest workman, whom we shall no more see at these our annual greetings, and who, in the walks of business life, as a publisher of our Association, as pastor of one of our churches, as a missionary in California, — everywhere, and in all stations, — was marked by his untiring and devoted work. It is that spirit of faithful and self-consecrated toil in all, ministers and laymen, that we most want, rather than great talents or better opportunities. Give us a spirit to work with the talents and opportunities we have, and years hence, by God's blessing, we may talk. of success, and may fill out our words of congratulation with a fuller meaning than ever yet they have had.

PUBLIC MEETING.

THE church in Federal Street was early filled by a large audience, assembled to celebrate the thirtieth anniversary of the Association.   At half past seven o'clock in the evening the chair was taken by the President, who invited REV. DR. HALL, of Providence, to open the meeting with prayer. The Secretary then read portions of the above Report, occupying about twenty-five minutes.

The President then rose, and observed that this celebration was one of peculiar interest to him.   For twenty years had he been a member of the Executive Committee, and as he had watched over the interests of the Association in its days of weakness and struggle, he now rejoiced in its growing prosperity and strength.   To-day it is thirty years old.   In man's life, thirty years of age is the period of greatest vigor.   The state of infancy and pupilage has been passed, and the best efforts which human life can render may then be put forth.   We read that the Great Master of Christians began to teach " when he was about thirty years of age " ; and let us hope that our Association, having now attained to this age, may by its enlarged usefulness enter upon a new career, teaching a pure and undefiled religion to our growing country and to the world, as it never has been taught before, and doing it in the Master's spirit and with the Master's power.   He was glad to see present this evening one of the founders of the Association, to whom, more than to any other one, in its early days, it was indebted for a watchful care that never overlooked its interests, for wisdom to plan, and for zeal and diligence to execute.   He would call upon Rev. Dr. Gannett to move the acceptance of the Report.

REV. DR. GANNETT came forward, and addressed the meeting, for nearly an hour, in a strain of great earnestness and eloquence. We regret that we have no means of presenting his speech in full. He began by calling up the images of those with whom he was associated, thirty years ago, in organizing this institution, — the sainted Henry Ware, Jr., the courteous and accomplished Bancroft, and others spared yet among the living, whose heads were whitened with age, but whose hearts were as fresh as ever. The Association was founded for a double purpose, — to wield, if he might so express himself, a two-edged sword, not only to oppose and destroy infidelity and worldliness, but also to resist and to restrain false views of Christianity. Devoutly did he hope that this latter purpose might never be overlooked. For thirty years he had studied the Word of God, and meditated upon the great truths of the Gospel of Jesus Christ, and the conviction had been growing stronger and stronger, till now it was as immovable as the everlasting hills, that our Unitarian Christianity is, in its substance and peculiar verities, the message of God's grace to mankind. If any form of Christianity may take to itself the name of Evangelical, it is this. He had no doubt that Fénelon and Lyman Beecher would both share in the joys offered to faithful followers of the Saviour in the kingdom of Heaven; but as little did he doubt that one would see that the Roman Catholic Church is not infallible, and the other that Jesus Christ is not the Supreme God. He exhorted to greater faithfulness in preaching our distinctive Unitarian Christianity. He did not want to see our Unitarian doctrines encumbered with Orthodox phrases, nor Unitarians themselves working in Orthodox methods. He believed that the type of character which our views of the Christian religion naturally tended to produce was as high as the Christian world had ever seen; and therefore he hoped we should work to diffuse them. He accepted the word which the Secretary had used in the latter part of his Report, — WORK. It is a little word, but it means a great deal; and in the hope that we should all comply with that condition of success, since God had promised success to the earnest and faithful worker, he would move the acceptance of the Report.

REV. CHARLES T. BROOKS, of Newport, R. I., then came forward and spoke as follows: —

Mr. President, — I feel as if the word which I have to say to-night about Unitarianism in India came both too early and too late. Too late for me, because a year ago was the time when I wanted to say it; only, while you were then gathering here, I was fifteen thousand miles off, and if I had been here I should not have had strength enough to utter it. Too late for you, because the imperfect expression which I gave of it on paper last autumn has already done its work, and far more than I dared to expect, in deciding you to send to India, not only money, but a man. And yet, at the same time, I feel as if my present speaking, though in these respects " a day after the fair," were almost premature and presumptuous, when I consider how soon the report of an invalid, who spent only three languid weeks in each of the two great Eastern capitals of India, will be revised, favorably or unfavorably, (and, in either case, superseded,) by the statements of the quick-eyed and strong-hearted laborer who by this time is fast approaching that distant and interesting field.

As, however, it has been thought that a few words from an eye and ear-witness might add to the interest of this occasion, and as the printed paper already referred to left some things unsaid that I wished to say, I will occupy the attention of the Association a few moments.

I confess, Sir, to have been hitherto one of those who have been in the habit of regarding the Unitarian body as not specially called, just yet, to engage in foreign missions; not because

" charity begins at home," for ours has been beginning at home a great while, and my religion tells me that

" My neighbor is the suffering man,
Though at the farthest pole " ;

and my philosophy, that there are deeper wounds and wants than those of the body; but I have simply felt, that, in the work of communicating Christianity to humanity, there was as much to be done in the way of *deepening* as of extending its influence, and that home labors and home missions constituted the department to which Liberal Christianity was at present particularly called and peculiarly adapted.

But within a year or two I have felt that, in fulfilling the call — I will not say of Christ, but of the Christian conscience — to " preach the Gospel to every creature," there were several strong reasons for making India our first *foreign* field, at least.

1. There is much ground to think that India is the region in which the simple and sublime doctrine of Unitarianism was first communicated from Heaven to man. If, as some hold, there was the cradle of the human family, then this was certainly so, for there is no evidence in reason or revelation that Adam knew any doctrine contrary to the unity of God. The doctrine of the Divine unity and a pure rational worship is still extant, not yet dethroned, if not throughout decidedly dominant, in the oldest sacred books of the country. In sending Unitarianism to India, then, we aim to restore an old faith to an old homestead.

2. In this work there are many things to give us hope and help. The general progress of education and civilization has opened the eyes of great numbers of Hindoos to the absurdity and abominations of the existing religion, and placed them in that inquiring state which our simple views of Christianity are best fitted to meet. " Are there Unitarians among the Christians? " said a native gentleman to me, with an expression of great interest. Another young native with whom I became acquainted had become converted to Unitarian Christianity by reading the Gospels and Channing, and had in consequence been disinherited by his father; but he had secured the birthday presents which his father

37 *

had laid by for him from year to year, and they had enabled him to buy a farm, which he now conducts in a Christian spirit. He expressed great eagerness for our Unitarian books. Many others I saw who have lost all faith in the Brahmins, and whom none of the distracting creeds of the Christianity presented to them can satisfy. Among these are some who owe their yearning for a better faith to the influence of Rammohun Roy, and, at present, seek in the Unitarianism of the old Hindoo Scriptures the satisfaction of their spiritual wants.

3. I cannot believe that the race and region which produced the noble advocate of Unitarianism just named are to be for ever given over to a false, distracting, and degrading theology. I feel that there must be an influence surviving his earthly labors which will co-operate with us when we enter the field he opened, and that the memory and example of Rammohun Roy are a call to us from the Father to *go over and help* his countrymen.

4. There are other helpers. The mosques and mausoleums that rise everywhere among the pagodas of India remind us that the followers of one who was not wholly a *false prophet* are numerous in this country; that the Koran is there, launching its indignant, scornful, and often sublime satire against the polytheism of the heathen idolater on the one hand, and of a corrupted Christianity on the other. Even the little Mussulman children may be our allies against, not only heathen, but Christian error; as I was forcibly reminded one day, when, visiting in Madras the vast mission-school of the Free Church of Scotland, and witnessing the quiet dissent which one of the Mohammedan boys manifested to the teacher's exposition of the Gospel, I said, "You find the Mohammedans tough subjects?" "Yes," was his quick and earnest reply, — and it had more point than he thought of, — "because they have *so much* of the truth!"

5. I felt deeply, in visiting the schools of the missionaries, the need of our doctrine and protest, for the sake of keeping the truth before them, our Christian brethren, and defending the simplicity of the native mind against the burden of a false creed, and encouraging all parties to *stand fast in the liberty wherewith Christ hath made them free, and not become entangled in the yoke of bondage.*

It was painful to see how the teacher would watch every symptom of a tendency in the young and unsophisticated heart to break through the snarl of a self-contradictory dogma; how he would meet them at every opening, and drive them back into the maze; painful to see the benighted and bewildered mind, that asked for the bread of revelation, answered with such a hard stone as the Trinity. I am not wanting in admiration for those heroic men who labor in the fields where Judson and Scudder wore out their lives; but I must say it is not by means, but in despite of great and grievous misrepresentations of the Gospel, that they have done what they have. And when, in addition to the mighty obstacles to the conversion of the natives of India presented by their own superstition, sensuality, scepticism, by the power of the Brahmin and the dread of losing caste, we consider the stumbling-block thrown in their way by the inconsistencies, immoralities, or indifference of people from (so-called) Christian nations, who resort thither merely in the scramble for riches and honors, caring little for the natives, except as instruments of their own advancement, — and then, finally, by the irrationalities and inconsistencies, so obvious to all thinking heathen, in the very creed offered them as Christian, — the wonder should be, not that so few converts have rewarded the missionary efforts, but so many.

6. Wherever the language and mind of England (Old England or New England) go, — wherever English common sense goes, — there our common-sense Unitarian idea ought to keep them company. Surely it seems high time that in that great English Empire of the East the liberal principles of theology, which *we* feel to be so extensively identified with the best of our inheritance of freedom, should have " a local habitation and a name." Indeed, the preacher who, " being dead, yet speaketh," had been there before us. The most popular clergyman of the English Church in Calcutta told me that Channing was his constant companion, and that he held him as the first of the religious writers of the age; and I saw in his preaching the influence of Channing's thought. And then I would suggest here that our sons go to the far East as well as to the far West; and amidst the moral dangers

of the East as well as of the West they need all the Christian influence we can supply.

7. But, finally, what has more than all else excited my Unitarian sympathy for India is the fact that I have seen with my own eyes, and heard from their own lips, the trials and the necessities, the desolateness and devotedness, of a little handful of worshippers on that distant and darkened shore, who have for half a century sustained an altar inscribed with the name of the God of Abraham and Moses and Jesus, — an " unknown God " to the multitudes around them, and ignorantly worshipped (it may too truly be said) even in the several denominations of churches and converts who there name the name of Christ.

I refer, of course, to the native Unitarian Society in Madras. I feel that if that little church were the forlorn hope of our cause in India, they would deserve that we should stretch forth our hand, and keep it stretched forth, in their behalf; that it would be a good and great thing, for our own sakes, to keep up a constant communication of heart and help with that noble little household of the faith.

I will mention one anecdote, related to me by William Roberts, the young, ingenuous, and intelligent native pastor of that Society, as showing what influence those poor Unitarians have to struggle under, and to what meanness bigotry will bow men down.   Mr. Roberts was, some years since, the servant of a bishop ; but when his master discovered he had Unitarian notions, he silently dismissed him, and when a gentleman to whom he afterward applied for employment agreed to take him if he would get a statement from the bishop of the reason for his dismission, that dignitary declined giving it !   What an example for a master in Israel to set to the heathen of the spirit of the Christian religion !

But, under all the discouragement and depression of the cause, with a church composed mostly of poor servants, for whose worldly interest it would greatly be to yield to the constant influence exerted to draw them from their faith, this young man works on, nor *abates one jot of heart or hope;* he preaches, he catechizes, he keeps three schools in operation, he writes letters to the missionaries protesting against their misrepresertations or their mistranslations of the Scripture to the heathen, — as when, in one instance, they worded the title of the New Testament, " the Gospel of our God Jesus Christ "; he is instant in season and out of season, and has long asked, and I think he might well ask, that we of America and our brethren of England should give him a steady expression of our Unitarian, our Christian, our human sympathy. We have put forth our hand, may we have no occasion to draw it back!

After Mr. Brooks had closed, REV. MR. HILL of Waltham rose, and spoke in substance as follows : —

I do not intend, Mr. President, to offer any remarks upon the book to which you have alluded, but to speak upon a general topic suggested by its publication and reception.

The fact that a book of family prayers meets with so ready a sale, and is so rapidly coming into circulation, is an encouraging sign. It gives us ground to hope that the error which has been prevalent in our day may be passing away, and a better state of the Christian Church be returning. For it cannot be denied that there has been a grievous error in the world and in the Church of these latter days. It has openly been avowed that belief in particular providence, and prayer for specific blessings, were relics of superstition unworthy the present century, and that study and labor were the true methods of prayer.

These false doctrines concerning prayer are founded upon a truth, and are propped up by two valuable traits of our modern intellectual character. They are founded upon the great truth that the will constitutes the centre and essence of the soul, and that therefore every earnest desire must take the form of a purpose ; every heart that is in earnest is as ready to act as to talk. But this is not new. The prophets said, " Cease to *do* evil, learn to *do* well." The teachers of old did not regard this doctrine of labor as inconsistent with the doctrine of prayer. The prophets and apostles, from whom we have the most powerful exhortations to active goodness, have also given us the most earnest entreaties and invitations to prayer. And our Lord himself, who bids us judge men by their fruits, and who tells us that they who cloak their lack of righteousness with long prayers shall receive the greater damnation, tells us also that men ought always to pray, and never to grow weary. He bids us look into our own hearts, to know whether prayer is of value. "Will any of you give a stone to your child asking you for bread? If ye, being evil, know how to give good gifts to your children, much more will your Father who is in heaven give good things to them that ask him."

Nor is there, in reality, the least inconsistence between the doctrine of prayer and that of labor. The foundation of the doctrine of labor is in the consciousness of a will. And when a man is once awakened to an earnest, living consciousness of the freedom of his own will, that mighty sentiment, rising in irresistible strength and sweeping away the green withs and new cords of the Dalilah of indolence and the Philistines of necessitarian logic, bears away also the gates and boundaries in which Pantheism would hedge up our idea of the Divine Power. When a man really feels himself to be a free man, he feels also that his Creator is an Ever-living God, able and free to do whatever he pleases in heaven and upon earth. There is a loftiness and grandeur in this Hebrew representation of God which no generalizations of Plato concerning the unity of the beautiful, the good, and the true, — no speculations of Spinoza concerning substance, — no dreams of Hegel concerning the genesis of being and non-being, — ever reached. The reasonings of philosophers concerning the Divine Being may command our assent, or may arouse us to vehement denial, but they can never bring us to bow in the deep spirit of adoring wonder as we do at the simple announcement of the Hebrew prophets of the wisdom, power, and eternal life of the Almighty God. "In the beginning God created the heaven and the earth; He hath garnished the heavens; He hangeth the earth upon nothing; He formed man in his own image, and breathed into him understanding. Lo! these are the borders of his works. How faint the whisper we have heard of Him, but the thunder of His power who could comprehend!"

When a man is fully awakened to the consciousness of his own freedom, he feels also the certainty of God's freedom, and no miserable sophistry can persuade him that it is impossible for God to act on his universe except as a whole. He replies, " Nay, the Being in whose image I am created is able to do at least all that I can do, since he can do infinitely more. If I can grant the request of my children, he can grant mine ; and I therefore will ask him for whatever I feel the need of."

The truths which lie at the foundation of the modern erroneous views of prayer are not, therefore, truly consistent with the structure built upon them. It is of course possible to build well a bad superstructure upon a good foundation ; but in this case not only is the superstructure bad, but it is badly built.

I have already said, this superstructure is propped and sheltered by certain valuable elements in our modern state of society. I refer to the practical and scientific character of our efforts. The colonization of America and Australia has called out an amount of practical effort, — I mean of individual struggle with physical difficulties, — such as was not before known. The contest with nature in the other continents had been gradual, and in proportion to the state of the race in its successive development.

But when civilized colonists, accustomed to the subjugated condition of nature, were placed upon continents where all was wild, and were thus intrusted anew with the work that God had heretofore given only to savage tribes, this was a new mode of the education of the race which has produced and is producing the mightiest effects. Requiring so much labor, developing so much strength and ability, it has led to a great deal of practical self-reliance ; to a high estimate of the power of man to do for themselves what they have ofttimes asked from God. This feeling spreads to other subjects than those concerning which it was first awakened, and men doubt not of their own ability to work out their own salvation, and to convert and save the nations. So that the practical spirit of our age discourages prayer in a twofold manner ; — first, by leading us to exalt the importance of practical effort above any state of heart, the importance of labor above any petitions or thanksgivings ; secondly, by puffing us up with a conceit of our own ability, by making us forget our dependence upon a higher Power, and filling us with the spirit of Mezentius, which cries, " This right arm is my saviour, these instruments of my own invention are my divinities."

It needs no argument to show that this is not a true and legitimate effect of the practical spirit of the age. It is simply one of the multiform disguises of Satan, who transforms himself sometimes into an angel of light. It is not an effect which will always last. The novelty of invention wears away, the impotence of human strength becomes again apparent, and we see again that all our wisdom and all our strength are nothing in comparison of Him upon whom aloue we can lean, and find our trust never disappointed. Our practical spirit will indeed legitimately lead simply to a more earnest reliance upon the aid of the Holy Spirit. We may have lost for ever all admiration of that sanctity which contents itself with retreating from the world, and spending its days in meditation and prayer ; but we only shall admire the more that saintly heroism which leans boldly upon the arm of God, and goes armed with prayer and faith into the strongholds of vice, and into the abodes of misery and crime, on its Christ-like mission of mercy.

The scientific character of our age is perhaps even more remarkable than the practical. The progress of practical invention is steady and uniform, but that of scientific discovery goes on with accelerating speed, and no man is able to foresee the result. In practical inventions our sphere is somewhat limited, — limited by the nature of the material in which we work, limited by the limited ends for which we work. Science, it is true, does something to enlarge these limits by the discovery of new processes, and even of new substances. But such enlargement of the sphere of practical invention supposes an enlargement of the sphere of science, and that is already boundless. No man can say, of all the myriad problems which science has already proposed, how many are soluble by the power of the human intellect. In every department of human research, men are achieving new success, in reducing the various questions of nature to questions of pure quantity, and thus bringing them under the control of the mathematician's analysis. And the mathematicians of the world are constantly inventing new processes, and discovering new principles, by which they have a more complete control over the new problems submitted to their examination.

The results which are attained by scientific men are now rapidly spread before the public by means of scientific journals, and even of newspapers. Even those who do not understand what is meant by the language in which the announcement is made, perceive that at least a scientific truth is said to have been discovered. And the great activity, and at least apparent success, of the students of physical science stimulate a vast deal of pretension to scientific knowledge. Every pursuit is called a science, and every teacher styles himself a professor. Persons without a thorough scientific knowledge are misled by those pretensions, and the triumph of scientific discovery is thus supposed to be even greater than it is.

Now this has a very decided effect on the tone of the human mind. We cannot avoid it if we would. When we know that the mysterious northern light, and the bright and terrible lightning, move by fixed and known laws, and that the same power which forms them carries our telegraphic messages and moulds metals for us without the aid of heat, — when we know that planets, too small or distant for sight, have been discovered by the aid of calculation, — when we know that these triumphs of the human intellect are but single specimens among thousands that are continually being achieved, we cannot avoid receiving from it a tone of thought. We insensibly begin to feel that all things are under the control of fixed laws, and that, when scientific men attain to a knowledge of those laws, they will be able to understand and foretell all events with the same confidence and certainty with which the chemist foretells the result of a new mixture, or the astronomer predicts the occurrence of an eclipse. And the first effect of this enlargement of our ideas of law and harmony in the universe is frequently a destruction of faith in particular providence, a resolution of all providence into the wisdom of the general laws of the universe. This spurious science, this dilution of science through the medium of newspapers and conversation, destroys, therefore, the spirit of prayer, since it makes the only answer to prayer consist in the natural effect of prayer upon the mind of the petitioner. Say not that I am fighting a man of straw. This view of prayer has been even approved by men carrying the title of Doctors in Divinity, and has been ingeniously and plausibly presented in books that have enjoyed a wide popularity.

Yet what is it but an atheistic, or at best a pantheistic, doctrine? It is not a legitimate fruit of science. It will not be permanent in the world. The age of faith must return, and a deeper acquaintance with science will but strengthen faith.

For what is science? It does not consist, as Comte falsely affirms, in a knowledge of the positive facts of nature, even when that knowledge can be generalized in a brief formula. To call a mere knowledge of facts science, or to say that science is a mere knowledge of facts, is to confound the distinction between knowledge and science, between practice and theory, between natural and artificial schemes of learning. Science looks behind the facts of Nature to the thoughts of the God of Nature. Science has never fully attained her end until she has led the soul into communion with the wisdom of God, and unfolded a part of the Divine plan on which the universe is built. Science, therefore, in going behind the fixed order of the universe to the cause of that order, shows that order to be no inexorable decree of Fate; but the wise and reasonable action of an Infinite Father, who is, to say the least, as able to grant the prayers of his children as we are to grant the prayers of our children.

No mortal man is able to solve all mysteries; and should I attempt to show the manner in which the Father of All, acting by general laws, brings particular events to pass, I should be as presumptuous as those who, upon a little knowledge of science, picked up at fourth or fifth hand, assuming that science is our only safe guide, and that the Gospel, with its doctrines of providence and prayer, is now outgrown, presume to affirm that God cannot act upon a part of his universe at a given time, but must act only upon the whole universe at once, and continue that action through eternity the same. It is enough for me to show that science joins with sound philosophy and with the Christian Scriptures in declaring God to be almighty, all-wise, all-good, able and free to do whatsoever he pleases, in whose image we are made, and whose powers must be, to say the least, as great as ours, because infinitely greater.

Whatever difficulty there may be in understanding the consist-ence of a particular providence, and answer to prayer with a fixed order of nature, there is just the same difficulty in reconciling the freedom of man with that fixed order. If there is any fixed order of events to include human actions, and afford an opportunity for pious men to trace the footsteps of God in history, or for scientific men to establish the existence of laws of trade, laws of political economy, and theories of social science, that fixed order certainly does not interfere with our ability to grant or refuse the requests of our children, and therefore much less can it interfere with God's ability to grant or refuse the requests of his children. Whoever is not deterred, by philosophical doubts of human freedom, from asking a favor of his fellow-man, may be assured of some error in his heart as well as in his head, if he allows such doubts to keep him away from the mercy-seat in Christ Jesus.

God invites us to pray. His invitation comes to us in the course of his providence dealing so gently and kindly with us; it comes in the instincts of paternal love that make us ready to hear our children; it comes through the revelations of science, which is daily showing that we are indeed by creation the children of God; it comes through the influence of the Holy Spirit, prompting us to prayer; it comes through the tender words of Jesus, telling us that men ought always to pray, and not to faint, — that, although God forbear long, he will certainly in the end more than fulfil the hopes of all that put their trust in him.

God invites us to pray, and promises to grant our requests. It is only by prayer, and by the prayer of faith, that we can gain any courage to labor, and to carry on the warfare against sin; but leaning by prayer upon the strength of God in Christ Jesus, we shall find ourselves willing and able to do and to bear all that is appointed for us.

REV. MR. HALE, of Worcester, being called upon by the President, offered a few words in regard to the mission to Kanzas. He would not, at that late hour, take up any more time; but would content himself with an expression of his deep interest in this action of the Association, believing that the Committee had rendered a good service to the freedom, peace, and prosperity of the country.

It was expected that Hon. T. D. Eliot, of New Bedford, would speak upon the mission to the Chippewa Indians; but the lateness of the hour forbade. The President expressed the deep regrets of the Committee. The vote accepting the Annual Report was unanimously passed. The audience united in singing the doxology, " *From all that dwell below the skies*," and then withdrew.

LETTERS TO AN INQUIRER.

III.

MY FRIEND, —

Having in my first letter aimed to show that Christianity is to be viewed, first of all, as an historical fact, not an opinion or dogma, — and in the second letter labored to prove, I hope with some success, that the evidence on which the truth of Christianity stands is the same in kind as other evidence, and in degree superior to most that sustains remote and undisputed facts generally, — I would direct your mind now to the manner in which the question was treated by the early *assailants* of Christianity. The testimony of an opposer or enemy is always considered valuable, as far as it goes. In the present instance it is the more to be valued, as demonstrating two facts, both of which are important: first, that in the beginning there were very few opposers or sceptics of sufficient note and power to send down to us even their names; and next, that not one of them denied or professed to doubt the genuineness of our present Gospels in their day, or attempted to disprove their material facts; they only attempted to explain the facts in some other way than by admitting their supernatural character.

Perhaps the best way of seeing the ground on which Christianity has been opposed, is by dividing its whole era into three periods: the first comprising the four first centuries, particularly the time that preceded the civil enthronement of the religion by Constantine; the second covering the whole interval between that period and the Reformation, an interval of twelve centuries, yet distinguished by no important assaults upon the genuineness of the Gospel records; and the third including the time that has elapsed since the Reformation began.

The first period has this peculiarity, — that, being nearest the time of Christ and the Apostles, it afforded the best opportunity for a thorough investigation, and a formidable, even fatal assault, if any could be fatal. It is matter of congratulation that objectors and opposers appeared as early as they did. It prevents the suspicion of general collusion, proves the existence of that which is assailed, and must have induced a careful inspection of alleged facts, so recent and so extraordinary.

To begin with the Jews, the earliest objectors. That they had an interest in settling the authority or exposing the falsity of the new pretender is self-evident. That they should have admitted the essential facts on which Christianity rests, and, with all their reasoning and captiousness, assumed the integrity of the Old and New Testament, is much to our purpose. It is seen in the earliest controversy of which we have any record, so far as I know; namely, that between Justin Martyr, born of Gentile parents in Palestine about the hundredth year of our era, and Trypho, the learned Jew, supposed by some to be an imaginary character, but, whether imaginary or actual, bringing out the strongest arguments of the Jew against the Christian. Trypho's work is still extant, making three hundred folio pages ; and we may therefore suppose it contains all there was to be said on that side. Enough to know, that in all this mass of controversy there is no denial or impeachment of the existing record of the Gospels, no questioning of the fact that Jesus had lived and wrought, as is said in that record, but the full admission of these facts, without any imputation of fraud on the part of the disciples. Remember that this was within a century of the alleged time of Christ, that it was a controversy with the Jews, all whose prepossessions were against Christianity, and whose knowledge and opportunity, as well as interest and wishes, would make them sure to seek and find any good ground of accusation. If *they* found none, — if these original and prejudiced antagonists attempted not to subvert, nor pretended to doubt, the essential facts of the new religion, and brought nothing in opposition except that its Author did not correspond with their interpretation of the prophecies and their sanguine expectations, — I commend it to your fair mind to say whether the first form of unbelief, in the Christian age, works most to the injury or the aid of Christianity. `

You may object, if you know the fact, that a greater and earlier witness, and an historian of the Jews, says nothing in favor of Christianity, and scarcely notices it, — Josephus. There is a difference of opinion as to the fact whether Josephus does notice the new faith, or is wholly silent in regard to it. If two passages ascribed to him are genuine, the reference is very direct and ample ; for one passage speaks of James as " the brother of Jesus, who is called Christ " ; and the other refers to Christ as " performing wonderful works," attaching to himself many Jews and

Gentiles, condemned by Pilate to the cross, appearing again on the third day, and leaving "a sect of Christians, named from him." The genuineness of this passage has been doubted, though it is found not only in the "Jewish Antiquities" as printed, but also in every manuscript copy extant. The ground of doubt seems to be only the improbability that a Jew would write as if he were a Christian believer, as the form of the passage is thought to intimate. But if he wrote it as an historian simply, recording a matter of fact or a prevailingly received opinion, the objection fails, and the testimony is decided. You are to remember, too, that Josephus was regarded by his own countrymen as a traitor, counselling their submission to the Romans; that he was a flatterer of Vespasian, attempting to show that the very predictions of the Messiah pertained to the Emperor; and that he moved chiefly in the higher grades of society, where Christianity was least in favor. These circumstances will explain his saying little about the new heresy. It is a great deal, though it were all, that he says nothing against it, produces no fact inconsistent with it, but so describes the condition of his own people, and the destruction of their city and temple, as corresponds most wonderfully with Christ's predictions and the Gospel story.

There are other more recent Jewish writings, which call for no notice, as containing nothing opposed to Christianity; all admitting its chief features and facts, and objecting to them only as not agreeing, in the opinion of a Jew, with his own Scriptures and cherished hopes. There has been a learned Rabbi within the last century, David Levi, whose writings attracted great attention, consisting of a "Translation of the Pentateuch" and "Dissertations on the Prophecies." It was to him that Dr. Priestley addressed his "Letters to the Jews," aiming to convince him of the divine authority of Christ; to which the Rabbi opposed chiefly the dissensions among Christians, and says of the miracles of Christ, as if admitting them, " Whether it was by art, deception, or supernatural power, it is not my business to inquire." I have in my possession a series of Letters which the same Levi wrote to Thomas Paine, attacking the famous " Age of Reason," and proving the genuineness of the Old Testament Scriptures. Does not such a fact prove something? Paine, in his amusing conceit as well as ignorance, thought he had verily demolished Christianity. But the Rabbi throws at him a distich, not his own, nor very elegant, but worth quoting, as showing the contempt of a Jew for a man whom some Christians profess to honor.

> " It is not easy, I confess,
>   To baffle such a plate of brass;
>   For in my days, I ne'er did hear
>   So impudent a sophister."

Passing from Jewish to Gentile objectors, there are but three whose names are of note, and whose writings have come down to us from so early a date : Celsus, Porphyry, and the Emperor Julian, appearing severally in the second, third, and fourth centuries. Celsus was an Epicurean philosopher, and an able writer. According to the date that Lardner assigns him, he must have been conversant with many who had personally known the Apostles. This gives value to his testimony as to the prevalence and character of Christianity. His chief work, called " The True Word," is lost. But we have nearly the whole of it in the writings of Origen, who took up the book and answered it point by point. And few opponents, or even advocates, have contributed more to the testimony in support of Christian truth. For the very objections of Celsus, beside involving the material facts, are of a nature that we should consider favorable both to the truth and excellence of the religion, — such as its addressing itself to the poor and ignorant, and Christ's voluntarily subjecting himself to sufferings which he had predicted. Other objections relate to alleged incongruities, textual criticisms, and the power by which the miracles were wrought, which Celsus supposes to have been a "magical art" acquired by Jesus while living in Egypt. Now, if a man standing so near the times of the Apostles could find no better arguments against Christianity, or any other explanation of its origin and success, while he admits all we care for, — the facts themselves and the prevailing views of them at that early day, — you will not pretend that a modern opposer has a very easy task in overthrowing the whole fabric.

Of Porphyry, in the third century, little need be said, as he adds nothing to the objections of Celsus. He strengthens the evidence for the original Gospels, by petty criticisms of the text, which only show that it was the same then as now ; while he finds no better solution of the marvellous works of Christ and the Apostles than the trite one of magical and demoniacal powers.

When three hundred years had passed from the death of its Author on the "accursed tree," the religion which had been despised by the great and powerful, and which some whom you know affect to despise now, had given proof of its inherent power, by its steady, onward march against the most formidable obstacles. Already it had passed through the most fiery trials, which had helped both to purify and diffuse its light. From being the religion of the vulgar, the illiterate, and lowly, it had risen to the seats of learning and power, and had found first a secret and then an open advocate in the palace of the Cæsars. To charge upon it impurities and atrocities is no longer safe, for the calumny has become treason. The sword that slew is drawn to defend; and the very emblem of infamy, the ignominious cross, now blazes in the imperial banner. A transition verily ! proving at least as much as anything we have yet found against the religion. Christianity sat upon the throne in name and power. Yet not all of the royal household embraced it. Julian, a nephew of Constantine the Great, and afterward a successor, set himself against the Gospels; first covertly, professing himself a believer, then openly, throwing off the mask, or really apostatizing. The cruelties inflicted upon many of Julian's family by Constantine, and the strictness of the teachers who were appointed to train him as an ecclesiastic, may have had much to do in creating the secret repugnance and the determined opposition which soon appeared. It may help you to understand, not only Julian, but Gibbon, whom you so admire, to read what he says of one whom he styles a hero, a philosopher, and a patriot-prince, and whom he intends to eulogize thus : " As soon as he had satisfied the obligation of assisting, on solemn festivals, at the assemblies of the Christians, Julian returned, with the impatience of a lover, to burn his free and voluntary incense in the domestic chapels of Jupiter and Mercury."

From such a man, Christianity had nothing to fear in open conflict. He brought out no new weapons, unless the sarcasm which he used most freely may have been comparatively new. He repeated almost literally the poor objections of Celsus and Porphyry. He allows all for the Gospels that we need, speaking of them as universally received and revered, and paying a remarkable tribute to the moral character and life of the Christians, though he calls them by hard names. " It is a shame for the impious

Galileans to relieve, not only their own people, but ours also, and that our poor should be neglected by us, and left helpless and destitute." This candid confession and contrast between Christian and Pagan humanity is more than a balance for the force of all Julian's objections.

You have now before you, my friend, both the strength and the weakness of early scepticism, so far as it can be shown in this brief space. You see the nature and the result of the efforts of learned and acute men to overthrow or cripple Christianity in its infancy. Think what you will of their arguments, you must not forget their admissions, or rather the unavoidable evidence furnished by their very assaults. They all bear testimony, free or forced, to the essential truth, that the books of the New Testament were then universally known, and that no one, not even the sceptical and hostile, ventured to call in question the leading facts on which Christianity rests.

The next period referred to — that which covers the whole long interval between those early sceptics and the time of the Protestant Reformation — affords no name so prominent as to call for special notice. This silence, or indifference, may have been owing to the ecclesiastical dominion, then completely established, and, with the penalties it commanded and used, restraining all expression of scepticism and heresy. And when at last this restraint was removed, the iron rule broken, and the fiery ordeal and the slavish fear ceased, it was natural that all opinions, all doubt and denial, should be emboldened again to declare themselves. The Reformation had done a good work, if it had done no more than remove Christianity from the basis of mere authority and subjection, and place it on that of conviction and affection. And a hardly less valuable service was rendered by the freedom given to all opponents, and the fair, open field for the great conflict.

And here, in the third period, appears a long array, if not a formidable army, of disputants and assailants.   Beginning with Lord Herbert, and his famous work against Christianity and the miracles, — the work which he was encouraged to publish by a miracle vouchsafed to himself, as he professed to believe, (mark the consistency of unbelievers!) — we have Tindal, Shaftesbury, Bolingbroke, Collins, Toland, Morgan, Chubb; and then the higher rank, as they are deemed by many, — Hume, Gibbon, Voltaire, Rousseau, and Paine.   Most of these, and all the best of them, differing widely in many other features, virtually agree in this, which is sufficient; namely, that the evidence on which they build their objections to Christianity is almost wholly of the *à priori* kind.   They reason from intuitions, more than from facts.   They attempt not to disprove the facts, but only to question their probability, or deny their possibility, judging by their own intuitive sense.   They assert the sufficiency of nature and reason for all that is or can be wanted; and thence infer the incredibility of anything above nature and reason, or even auxiliary.

And this, my friend, this, which is at present the prevailing form of scepticism and infidelity, I suppose to be your own.   You belong, in tendency at least, to that class of doubters and deniers who say that there has been no supernatural revelation, because their intuitions tell them that it is unnecessary, therefore improbable, therefore impossible.   Now, if this form of argument convinces and satisfies you, there is little use in discussion.   The reasoning that precludes reasoning is final.   I only ask you to see to what it amounts, and to what it tends.   The first age of scepticism admitted the facts of Christianity, but ascribed them to magic or some earthly cause.   The last age, and the present, deny the facts, but only on the ground of their antecedent improbability and their intrinsic impossibility.

Are you satisfied with either of these modes of reasoning? I do not believe it. Search your own heart; not the understanding only, the cold intellect, the confident conceit, but the humble, craving heart. Weigh well the confession which Hume is said to have made, in the end: "I am affrighted and confounded with that forlorn solitude in which I am placed by my philosophy. Where am I, or what? From what causes do I derive my existence, and to what condition shall I return?"

Sincerely your friend,

H.

ELLEN ASHTON. — A SKETCH.

A few evenings since, I attended a meeting of Sabbath-school teachers, and listened to the various opinions which were expressed. Some spoke of encouragement in their labors, while others again, in terms of despondency, doubted if any good were resulting from their efforts. To such I would say, Go on, labor assiduously, look not for immediate results; the future, the eternal future, alone can measure the end of your work. The seed now sown in despondency may be fruitful of good, speaking comfort to the afflicted heart in the house of sorrow, and giving strength to resist in the midst of temptation.

> "The world will come, with care and crime,
> And tempt too many a soul astray;
> Yet the seed sown in early time
> Will not be wholly cast away."

Perhaps, in this connection, the following little sketch will not be wholly devoid of interest.

It was a lovely Sabbath morning in early spring; the busy city, which at that same hour on other days was so bustling and so crowded, was now hushed and calm ; the mart was deserted, the warehouse closed, and a holy quiet lingered upon every object; we seemed to feel a " present Deity," as all slept in " the stillness of that Sabbath morn."

I love such a scene ; to me it is sacred in its deep repose. I love to feel, that in my own heart, and in that of the thousands around me, the spirit of worldliness may, for a season, be repressed ; that purer and holier feelings may find an entrance into that temple too often defiled by the love of gain, the unsanctified throbs of ambition, or the degrading pursuit of pleasure. It speaks of that purer, deeper nature of man, of that spirit which allies him with the Divine, and it assures me that there is an under-current, which, though the mad waves of passion, of ambition, and of avarice may foam about, still may arise in its power, and, in some calmer moment, impel the soul's frail bark to a harbor of safety.

On such a morning, and occupied with such reflections, I directed my steps to the scene of my favorite duties, the Sabbath-school room, and as I asked myself the question, How shall I meet my class this morning? in what way can I most effectually arrest their attention? how bring to their minds the most important truths? I determined to speak to them of some of the prominent and distinctive features of our own belief. For my own experience as a teacher has fully convinced me that this is a part of Sabbath-school instruction which is too often neglected, with those whose minds are sufficiently mature to receive it, and that to this neglect may be traced those apparent defections from our faith which are really the result of an inability to give a reason for the " hope that is in them."

As I entered the room, group after group was gathering there. The benevolent expression on the features of those around me who were engaged in this work of love lent animation to my own feelings, while the happy, innocent faces of the children furnished the strongest appeal to the hearts of their teachers. On joining my own little circle, a new face greeted me. It was that of a mild and pensive girl of about seventeen, who begged to join the school.

There was a frank confidingness in her manner which irresistibly attracted me towards her. School commenced, and after the prayer, the hymn, and the introductory remarks were over, I told my class, that, were I addressing children, I should studiously avoid bringing before them points of a doctrinal nature, but should confine my instructions exclusively to those plain views of duty which all may feel and understand; and to them, to us all indeed, these should ever be the grand objects of interest and attention, compared with which modes of belief sink into insignificance;—and yet, while we would always deem them of minor value, the very fact that God has made a revelation to us, and endowed us with minds capable of comprehending it, places us under imperative obligations to recall, reflect, and seriously inquire, " What is Truth ? " As all action, all practical effort, must be founded upon some doctrine, or a belief in some principle, a correct form of faith is of great moment to us. These questions once satisfactorily answered to our own minds, that spirit of charity which " hopeth all things " should be our guide in all our intercourse with those who differ from us;— honestly, we doubt not, though through a different intellectual medium, the rays, more or less refracted, have reached them from the same great Source. If the result in both cases be to illumine the devious pathway of life, and clearly point out the course of duty, why should we murmur at those shades of difference, assured as we must be that *his* light is the purest who brings the most devoted tribute of love and obedience to the Father's shrine ?

The little circle around me listened with much apparent interest, and when the lesson of the morning was over the stranger, whom I shall call Ellen Ashton, lingered for a few moments after others had left the room. She begged me often to converse with them upon those subjects, " for," said she, " I long to know more of them. For three or four years I have been unable to attend a Sabbath school ; I am a stranger in this city, having been here but a few weeks, and there are few here who take any interest in my happiness, or even know me. I feel that the Sabbath school will be my haven of rest, — that it will make me happier and better."

What an appeal was this to the heart ! how long did I meditate upon it, and how earnestly did I desire to be made an instrument of good to this gentle and solitary girl ! I soon learned the further particulars of her history. She was the daughter of respectable parents, who, by a long train of adverse circumstances, had been deprived of the slender property which they had hoped would secure them comfort in the decline of life ; but poverty came, and sickness too. Ellen was the eldest of four children. She determined to be active in the exertion of all her powers for those who were at once so helpless and so beloved. For the first time in her life she left her early home, and came to the city of L——, to engage in one of the manufacturing establishments in that place. She was alone, far from her home and childhood's friends, and she was exposed to great and peculiar temptations ; but a high and holy trust sustained her. She was acting in obedience to the great principles of that Gospel which teaches us to honor our parents and sustain them in the hour of need, — which inculcates the great truth that duty is immutable, — that it is the same in the eye of Heaven, whether pursued in the more elevated or humble walks of life, — that one act of duty is more acceptable before the throne of God than the loudest professions or the most costly sacrifices.

Such were the principles which actuated her life. For several years she was constant in her attendance at the Sabbath school. She had succeeded in placing her parents in a situation of comfort, and bringing forward in the same course of industry her younger sisters ; while she had not failed to improve every opportunity for advancing her own education.

We toil, we struggle, we suffer, but amidst all our petty interests the great current of time is passing rapidly on, bringing its changes to all ; the wheel of fortune, in its swift revolutions, sports with our plans and prospects for the future, while the web of real life has lights and shades which so deeply contrast with each other as to throw into obscurity the wildest dreams of romance. So was it in the history of Ellen Ashton. The solitary, humble stranger, the devoted daughter, the self-sacrificing sister, is now the happy and honored wife of one whose name stands high among the educated and gifted of the land. I have seen her in her own family circle, carrying out, in her new sphere of duty, the same principles which formerly governed her in her humble walks of industrious effort. She tells me that she often recurs, with gratitude and pleasure, to the first morning she took her seat in the Sabbath school ; "for," said she, "it was then that the two paths of life stretched before me ; I stood at the dividing line. It was then that I needed a pure, simple, effective faith, which

39 *

would enlighten my mind and guide my life. I found that which met my wants and satisfied my highest aspirations. Under the blessing of God, it was that which enabled me to resist the peculiar temptations by which I was surrounded, and which sustained me amid a thousand depressing circumstances."

Who can estimate the amount of influence for good which she may exert as a wife and mother, a daughter and a friend ? Truly, when a powerful influence is brought to bear upon one mind, we may hope that, like the ripple upon the water caused by the smallest pebble, it may widen and widen in its sphere, till eternity alone can measure its extent.

> " O, sweet it is the growth to trace
> Of worth, of intellect, of grace,
> In bosoms where our labors first
> Bid the young seed of spring-time burst,
> And lead it on, from hour to hour,
> To ripen into perfect flower ! "

SUNDAY-SCHOOL SUCCESS.

[From an excellent Address on this subject, by Rev. A. R. Pope, we are permitted to make the following extracts.]

IT has always seemed to me to be unworthy of this scheme of human amelioration by the application to the young of religious principle by personal communication, to be looking constantly for present results. If they offer themselves to notice, very well ; let us thank God for the blessing. But to seek them we must look back, when all the hopes of ultimate success lie before us. Besides, it seems to involve a wavering of the faith, which we do not easily reconcile with the highest purposes. That the irreligious neither desire nor believe in the attainment of great advantage by the religious training of the young, is nothing strange; that men possessed of great plans of outward activity, personal ambition, and temporal aggrandizement, do not give us a hearty hand of encouragement, is not more strange; the wave that baptizes into the name of Christ the heads of social enterprise must be previously swelled, ere it can reach them, by the ready accession of the influence of large masses of persistent laborers for goodness. But that a teacher, so impressed with the desire to take each little one in his arms and to bring him to Christ, so actuated by a zeal that estimates personal sacrifice and discomfort as small in comparison with earnest hopes of usefulness, as to enter upon the performance, — that such an one should only be suited with the encouragement which belongs to the harvest, and not to the seed-time, somewhat surprises me. It is a pity for any one to undertake this work without being furnished with a full faith in its reality and practical success, — without having counted the cost, the hours of preparation which ought to be given to it, the hours of pleasant and profitable reading and conversation with which it must interfere, the inconvenience of faithful attendance at all seasons, in all weather; for the result in such a case is not concealed in a distant future. Such an one will either very soon part with his zeal and give up his class, or come to a new conviction, which is the only earnest of success. Every superintendent, to say the least, knows what I mean.

But when I come to speak to a different kind of Sunday-school teachers, to such as enlist for the struggle against indifference, irreligion, and spiritual ignorance in youth, to pursue the work till God shall be done with them in this world, I know that they do not look for outward testimony concerning the good there may be in this kind of labor; and to them certificates of success only seem to touch individual cases of toil. All the teachings of analogy, and all the conclusions derivable from what we know of the natural connection of cause and effect, offer to them better evidence, which the faithful can fully appreciate. They are thus taught that, if earnest hearts bind themselves to carry forward the work of their Divine Master, and not only *suffer* little children to come unto him, but take them in their arms to the Saviour's feet, such action brings its own necessary result; — the sowing cannot all be lost when the seed is truth, and human hearts are the soil, and human love is the husbandman! And just in proportion as this soil is left uncultivated, or is likely to be sown with tares by injudicious culture or evil influences, let me say again, will the work be greater for him who can save the child of neglect or abuse, and bring him through Christ to God.

Does any one, knowing this, ask whether the Sunday school has been of any signal advantage? It is no matter to me if a single case of benefit cannot be produced. The Indian chief's answer to the captious inquirers whether the missionaries of Christ had benefited his tribe, is the best reply: "Does the Great Spirit cause his sun to shine upon his red children? And does the dew drop upon the red man's fields? And will the good seed fail to grow when the sun is warm and the soil is moist?" Add to this natural logic, which should shame the weakness of our Christian belief, the material fact, that children bring with them into the world not only the necessity to be trained, but the precise elements of character suitable to culture and progress, and an inquiry whether an effort, even though very feeble, in the right direction, has done any good, is almost an insult to the understanding. Nor is it at all surprising that we cannot look upon a boy and discover where the lines which his Sunday-school teacher traced lie in his character. If he have grown into full goodness, then some good influence has mightily worked upon his heart; if he be not altogether base and unworthy when exposed to a thousand temptations, some persuasive love has evoked an answering chord of moral hope in his soul. When, where, by whom, only He knows who so knows our outward frame that He can tell what nutriment has sustained the animal strength, or brought it to a full maturity of powers.

We can more readily dispense with the view of outward results by being more precise than is usual in considering the true object and office of the Sunday school. If it is to teach history or geography, or to give to the child any attainment which he can readily display, that is something which not to be able to see argues its absence. Or if it is chiefly to teach the commandments, and the catechism, and the articles of belief, there is something which a pastor by a quarterly examination can exactly measure. But if its idea embrace, besides all this, not only or principally the making of a boy honest and a girl decorous, but the adding to the life the motive of honesty and decorum, — that is, the familiarizing the life with the elements of a true spiritual experience, — it is obvious that we are hoping for results which, in the nature of the case, will not be likely very decidedly to manifest themselves, except in marked cases, until the child begins to act in a wider sphere. And yet every one who entertains a full idea of the Sunday school will see that its pupils, if it be possible, are to be so trained that they may by and by think, speak, act, and feel as religious beings, — as if they recognized their spiritual relation to God, as well as their physical relation to this world of time and sense.

Of course teaching, as an auxiliary, is one of the means by which the fuller office is to be answered; and the highest teaching may encourage such new ideas of life as to kindle up holy motives and earnest purposes. But my point is, that mere information concerning the life of Abraham, Isaac, and Jacob, and the *recitation* of these important religious facts, will not amount to much, even though it come under the general term of Biblical knowledge, — a very fine kind of knowledge too, and one not half enough sought after and secured; but it will not amount in the life to anything until it can be worked into real experience by a quickened, converted, spiritual life. Our best manuals, which I do not mean to speak slightingly of, the value of which these words do not intentionally underrate, are only good tools with which the living heart may work upon another heart; and poor manuals will answer no purpose except as crutches for the very halt.

I need not add, except for completeness, that these thoughts suggest at once what kind of preparation every teacher requires for absolute success. Living souls can be acted upon only by living souls. The warm hearts of childhood can be reached and wrought into newness only by the warmth of a corresponding enthusiasm, quickened by religious fervor. Every one knows what kind of training a music-teacher requires to teach music, or the writing-master to instruct in his art; and to make a child proficient in the greater harmony of a soul at one with God, or in the nicer art of living according to God's will, the sweetness of a pure desire must mingle in his teacher with the consciousness of an immortal nature, and of the experience which belongs to it. An irreligious teacher must not expect to impart a religious influence to his pupils. Is not this plain enough?

I can conceive of no higher office than that which embraces such an advantage to others; and its success cannot be questionable. It may not, indeed, have caused all the boys and girls to occupy the uppermost seats in God's kingdom of love; but no more has the day-school which they have attended made them all wise, or completed for them a proficiency in art and science. I am willing to accept any testimony a faithful teacher may be able to bring; but I can get along without it, and still have faith in the Sunday school. Its influence may be compared to the electric current, which traverses continuously and quietly along the wires over our heads, and never intimates its presence except as it ceases to pass on its circuit; and when it stops for an instant a thousand men are alarmed, and rush forward to avert the destruction which impends.

I have greater faith in the Sunday school when its friends come together to lament its inefficiency, and to strive for new methods, than when they meet to congratulate each other upon its success. In the former case, they always tell me that they have a greater idea before them than has been attained. That is always hopeful. In the latter case, they seem to have come to a stand-point in religious life, which is salutary neither for themselves nor for those whom they can influence. To be sure, this lamentation may become morbid, and lead to a worse inaction than the opposite way of exaltation. But have we not had a great many exaggerated statements of the success of the Sunday school? And does it not often happen that, when a faithful laborer at fifty years of age can come among us bringing his sheaves with him, *the product both of his early and his late sowing*, we may so puff up the ambition, or so stimulate the hope of young teachers, that in a year's time they pass into despondency, and relinquish their work in dismay? I have had many teachers say this to me. If we can avoid both extremes, it is better, of course. But while there seems to me to be encouragement enough in the very office to be wrought, I think it not unwholesome, but hopeful, when the difficulties, the dangers, ay, the partial failures, are all brought to view. I say again, I have the greatest faith in an institution that has set before it such a goal that earnest efforts, directed by great zeal, have not one half reached it. It will be better yet if it still keep in view an end little less than absolute perfection.

OLD PATHS AND NEW PATHS.

MANY years ago, as the writer was passing through the classic grounds of Harvard in company with the younger Henry Ware, he was led to notice here and there a deviation from the regular, established walks, which were laid out with a design to keep all pedestrians within the beaten track. The design, to some extent, had failed, as in cases of this nature it often does. Here was a shorter path, which those most interested had made for themselves; cutting off the corners, in utter disregard of all authorities, either present or past. There was a devious, winding course, where careless or wayward feet had wandered; as if they were resolved to assert their independence, and to go where they pleased over grounds appropriated to their use. The remark was made, that " there seemed to be some difference of opinion in regard to the questions, what walks were needed, and what ways were best." And the reply was given : " Yes, men will strike out new paths for themselves. They cannot always be made to follow the old. They will not always be content to move in paths which others have prepared for them, and in which others have walked before them or may still prefer to walk." And the answer was true, and full of important suggestions.

There never was a time, perhaps, when men were more inclined than they are at present to make for themselves new paths in relation to everything that pertains to their religious belief and their principles of duty. There are multitudes, all through the land, who seem in their hearts to be determined, and who in many cases are ready to express the determination, that they will not follow in the track of others; and who must have new ways of their own, or else they will have none at all. But there are many, also, of an opposite class, who are equally determined that they will never abandon the old paths in which they and their fathers have been accustomed to walk, let the disadvantages and the inconveniences be as great as they may.

Hence, upon the one hand, we see many who are diverging from the old ways, at all points and in all directions ; and, upon the other hand, we see many who are plodding along in them, notwithstanding there are shorter and better and pleasanter routes which they might take if they chose ; while there are yet others who, having forsaken the old paths and entered upon the new, and becoming alarmed at what they perceive or imagine to be the tendency of their course, are continually crying out to those who may be behind or before, " Go back ! Go back ! There is a lion in the way ! " Perhaps neither class is wholly in the right, and neither class is at all times in the wrong, so far as may relate to the course which they actually pursue. There may be sufficient reasons for choosing sometimes one path and sometimes another, according to the circumstances of each particular case; and there are always sufficient reasons to justify one who finds himself pursuing a course which is leading him astray in changing it for another which is safer and more direct. But the proper inquiry for every one to make is not, Which is the old way, and which is the new? but, Which, on the whole, is the best? And if the old should be best, let him follow that; or if the new should be preferable, then let him follow that.

To speak without a figure, and to assert only what is familiar to all, and what all will admit, there are very many at the present time, who, becoming dissatisfied with the traditionary faith and forms in which they were educated, and which have come down to them through many successive generations, have felt constrained to adopt others which they deem more consonant with Scripture and reason. There is a still larger number of those who seem resolved, at all hazards, to adhere to the ancient formularies; and who appear to regard any material deviation from them, and the adoption of any different creed, as the direct road to perdition. And there are yet others, who, forgetting that the best things are those which are most liable to be abused, and that the greatest blessings are not unfrequently attended with corresponding dangers, and seeing to what an extent many are disposed to carry their principles of moral and religious freedom, and what consequences have sometimes followed, become filled with apprehensions in regard to the result, resolve to forego all the advantages which liberty offers, and voluntarily submit themselves again to the yoke of bondage, — just as the Israelites of old, when they had effected their escape through many remarkable deliverances, became discouraged by the perils which surrounded them in the wilderness, repented of their choice, and " in their hearts turned back again into Egypt." So, upon all sides, from those who have remained behind and from those who have advanced too far, and whom we meet in their returning course, we hear the constant cry : " There is danger ahead ! You will make shipwreck of your faith ! " And then they quote Scripture, and say : —

" Thus saith the Lord, Stand ye in the ways and see ; and ask for the OLD PATHS, where is the good way, and walk therein, and ye shall find rest for your souls."

The Scripture is good, and the paths which are recommended in it are safe, and will, if we follow them, undoubtedly lead us right. But it is by no means improbable that they will be found to be entirely different paths from those which most persons have intended, when they have taken it upon them to offer this advice. It is well to give heed to the words of the Prophet ; for in the present case the " old paths " are best. It may not be well to follow where such guides would lead us ; for it is certainly possible that they may not have found the right paths themselves. These three objections may be urged against taking the paths which others have marked out for us ; and they may be supported with very satisfactory reasons : —

1. They are not *old enough.*
2. They are not *good enough.*
3. If we return to them, *they will fail to give us rest.*

What has commonly been the meaning of those who have had the most to say in regard to the importance of walking in the old ways ? The correct answer to this inquiry will, of course, depend upon the denomination or party to which they may have chanced to belong. If the

individual was a member of the Church of Rome, then his
meaning was, " Come back, and seek out the good old way
of the Romanists, from which all Protestant sects have departed." If he was a member of the Church of England,
then the meaning was, "Come back, and seek the old path
of Episcopacy, from which all dissenters have strayed
away." If he was a Presbyterian, then he meant the old
path of Presbyterianism ; and so on, through all the various
forms of church organization. If he was a disciple of Saint
Athanasius, he doubtless intended the way which is indicated by the Athanasian creed. If he was a Calvinist, he
intended the rugged way of stern old Calvinism ; and so on,
through all the multitudinous systems of religious belief.

Now, the question very naturally arises, How old is
the oldest of all these different ways to which this brief
reference has been made ? Some are much older than
others, but it may be said with safety that there is not one
of them which equals the age of the Gospel. It was not
until many hundred years after the crucifixion of Jesus that
the Metropolitan Bishop of Rome pretended to occupy the
chair of Saint Peter, and to rule as the Vicegerent of
Christ upon earth. And it was not until a much later period
that the various Protestant sects took their rise. Athanasius was not born till about the year 300 of the Christian
era, and neither wrote nor saw the creed which bears his
name. Calvin flourished only about three centuries ago ;
and many of the sects and opinions now prevalent are of a
much more recent date. Indeed, as if it were designed to
turn the whole matter into a burlesque, there are sects
which have arisen since the commencement of the present
century, that begin to complain of innovations, and to talk
of their old ways. *The Gospel is older than all of them ;*
and therefore, if we would seek the oldest, we must go back

beyond Calvinism, beyond the Episcopacy of England, beyond Romanism, and follow Him alone who declared, "*I am the Way, and the Truth, and the Life : no man cometh unto the Father but by me.*"

Again : these ways of more recent origin are objectionable, because they are not good enough.

In the first place, they deprive men of their Christian freedom. Those who walk in them are under authority ; not that of Christ, not that of conscience and the law of God, but that of fallible beings like themselves. They are subject to the control of spiritual overseers, who will not allow them to choose a path for themselves, nor to turn aside, nor to turn back. They are compelled to wear shackles, which often prove galling and oppressive ; and which, if they were able, they would gladly cast off. In plainer words, liberty of conscience, and the rights of private judgment, are either expressly denied them, or else are permitted under such narrow restrictions that no great advantage is gained.

In the second place, it is a fault in nearly all of these different religious systems, that they make such representations of the nature and character of God, and of the condition and destiny of man, as tend to baffle our reason, to shock our sensibilities, to confound all our ideas in relation to moral distinctions, and to paralyze human efforts, by declaring them to be utterly unavailing, and thus taking away every motive to exertion and all responsibility for moral action. If God has foreordained whatsoever comes to pass ; if from all eternity he has fixed the condition and destiny of man by an unalterable decree ; if he has made him by nature incapable of thinking a good thought or of performing a good deed ; and if there is even one of Adam's race whom he has determined to punish endlessly for

40 *

being just such as he has created, and for doing what it
was impossible for him to avoid, — then not only are the
preceding statements true, but God becomes to us indeed
the " hard master," who would gather where he has not
scattered, and who would reap where he has not sown.
We need and desire a better way than that.

In the third place, it is an objection to many of these
systems, that they place mere speculative belief and the
mere observance of forms higher in the scale of Christian
graces than the practice of every virtue and the greatest fidelity in the fulfilment of moral obligations.   The
former alone appear to be regarded as among the things
which are strictly essential, while the latter, though they
may be deemed profitable, and in many respects important, are evidently allowed to hold a subordinate place.
With reference to this matter, the proverb may be applied, that " actions speak plainer than words."   A person is admitted into the church, or debarred from its privileges, according as he is able to receive, or is compelled
to reject, its creed; and not on account of his declared
purposes or the fitness or unfitness of his moral character.

But perhaps the greatest evil of all, and one which seems
indeed to be inclusive of all, is, that they tend to lead men
away from the simplicity of the Gospel.   Religion, in its
essentials, is a very simple thing.   It is only to fear God,
and to work righteousness.   This the Scriptures themselves
declare to be " the whole duty of man "; and this, an Apostle assures us, is sufficient to render any man acceptable to
God.   But how many are there, among all the differing
sects of Christendom, who would be contented with this?
How many who have not added to what the Gospel declares essential many other conditions of their own ?

We " have not so learned Christ." It is not thus that he has taught us concerning the Father. It is not such a representation which we find in the Scriptures concerning those who are " his offspring." Christ has shown us " a more excellent way."

One thing more. These different ways of man's construction are all objectionable, because they can never fulfil what they have promised us, — they can never give us rest.

Rest from what? from the commotions which are agitating and convulsing the world, in the present great conflict of opinions? Can we anywhere, in the many numberless paths which men have marked out and prepared for our use, find rest from these? Why, there is not one of all the multitude of sects into which Christendom is divided that is not at this very moment riven to its centre from these same causes. In spite of the claims of infallibility, in spite of the exercise of human authority, in spite of confessions and creeds, in spite of anathemas and excommunications, and restrictions of every.kind, and penalties of every degree, differences of opinion exist, and cannot by any means be prevented ; and exciting controversies from time to time break out, which cannot be quieted until they subside of themselves. And it is a matter of common notoriety, that those very sects which have exerted themselves the most to maintain a uniform standard of belief, and to avoid differences and debates upon important questions of theology, have suffered most from them, and have been most distracted by them. If any exception is to be made, it is only in those countries and in those cases where men have ceased to interest themselves at all in such matters, and mental activity has terminated in spiritual stagnation and death.

There is but just one way in which a living church can

ever have rest in relation to things of this nature, and that is, to abstain from every attempt at coercion, to abandon all pretensions to an uniformity of dogma, and to fulfil the law of love, by allowing every one to become fully persuaded in his own mind, and by endeavoring, amid all diversities, to maintain " the unity of the spirit in the bond of peace." He that would find rest must go to Christ in the full enjoyment of that liberty of thought and utterance " wherewith Christ hath made us free." Then and thus he will find rest to his soul.

These are among the objections which, as Liberal Christians, believing in the truths of revelation and in the principles of the Gospel, we are compelled to make, when men would persuade us to leave the way which our judgment and conscience assure us is right, in order to follow theirs. We do not judge others. We do not wish to compel them to walk in our ways, if our ways should differ from that of the Bible ; but we desire that both they and we may return to Christ, the true and living Way, and walk together in peace. We are not seeking after new paths ; we have no inclination to follow the untried, but our desire is to discover and to reopen the old, which has long been unused ; and which even now is encumbered and obstructed by the rubbish of ages. We are doing the very thing which the Prophet recommended. We are standing in the midst of the ways, and seeking and asking " for the OLD PATHS, where is the GOOD WAY," in order that we may " walk therein," and in this we hope to " find rest." We are glad when others are disposed to aid us, and to walk with us ; but shall not abandon our efforts, though left to search and toil and travel alone.

MUTUAL FAITHFULNESS.

In St. Paul's epistles to the various churches under his charge, we find that, instead of confining himself to the inculcation of strictly theological truths, he earnestly enjoins upon all the Christian converts the necessity of sincere and disinterested dealing with each other in the affairs of daily life; for, says he, " we are members one of another," as well as " members in Christ."

From the frequency with which he reiterates this charge, we are led to infer that there was a peculiar deficiency in this respect among the people to whom he was writing; which the Apostle regards as a relic of their heathen condition, a sign that they had not yet " put off the old man." But, alas! we of this late day need the admonition quite as much as the Ephesians or Romans could have done, although we can point to no former state of Paganism as an excuse for our short-comings. In no respect has the world made so small advances, in proportion to its opportunities, as in the simple recognition of our mutual rights and claims. Yet no man can advance many steps in the career of self-seeking, ere he becomes aware that, whatever his advantages may be for the attainment of his end, there is no completeness in himself alone. He is constantly compelled to seek the aid of others in carrying out his plans, and frequently required to pause in the race to see that justice is done to some one whose rights he has been wholly disregarding, otherwise he can neither reach the goal he is seeking, nor reap any advantage from the steps already taken.

The merchant should take the common membership into the account when he arranges his plans for amassing wealth, so that the same process by which his own fortune is acquired may prove the source of many others, which will be little streams flowing side by side, deepening and strengthening the current of his own prosperity. But, alas! we too óften find him paying no heed to these considerations, until, when taking some step which conscience does not sanction, he destroys his own prospects, and finds, to his dismay, that hundreds perhaps are involved in his ruin.

The mechanic does not remember how strong a claim the public has upon his fidelity when he seeks to make his contract for buildings or machinery more profitable to himself by careless labor or unsuitable materials, until he is painfully reminded of it by some calamity which endangers the safety and even .life of great numbers of his fellow-creatures, who, but for his unfaithfulness, might still be in the enjoyment of life and health.

The employer forgets the tie of brotherhood, when he fails to provide for the highest welfare of those under his care; when he regards them as *mere laborers*, and not as *men* with powers and wants similar to his own, substituting for the office of guardian and friend that of the selfish, exacting taskmaster.

The person to whom large pecuniary trusts are confided would shrink with horror from the thought of dishonesty, in the common acceptation of the term; and yet, when temptation assails him in the form of speculation, or some other speedy method of gaining wealth by the *temporary* use of more means than he can command, he sometimes forgets that the treasure around him has other owners, whose defrauded rights will one day call loudly for settlement. In an evil hour he yields to the tempter; detection is inevitable, and he feels compelled to take one fatal step after another in order to cause some delay of the dreaded moment; until, at last, despair overcomes his manhood, and, that he may escape an arraignment before an earthly tribunal, he dares to rush unbidden into the presence of his Maker, vainly hoping that by a change of worlds he shall find a change of laws.

The vender of intoxicating liquors thinks only of the gain he may derive from his nefarious traffic, and goes on unscrupulously trifling with the peace and safety of his fellow-men, urging them more and more rapidly down to the depths of degradation and misery.

At length some member of his own family falls into the snare which he had so industriously spread for others. Then the wretched parent is compelled to pause in his dread career, and, as the iron enters his own soul, he is led to turn his eye in upon some of the other homes whose light he has helped to quench, and upon the hearts which his cruelty has crushed.

Then there is another class of poisoners, more insidious, but not less dangerous. These are the writers and circulators of those pernicious fictions, whose false and corrupting views of life are as sure to poison the hearts and minds of those who learn to relish them, as noxious drugs to destroy the body. How sad is it that persons who are sufficiently gifted intellectually to assist in forming the public taste should ever forget that the common membership entitles all men to the truth, and pictures based upon truth and virtue, which always must be pure. Every reader has a right to claim the best an author has to give; and if he can contribute nothing good to the common stock, it were far better that he should withhold his pen than to " scatter firebrands, arrows, and death."

The clergyman who rises in the pulpit and sees around him hungry souls waiting to be fed with the Bread of Life which Jesus brought, should not attempt to satisfy these wants (as the manner of some is, in these days) with the crude vagaries of his own mind, scarcely yet formed into thoughts; by telling his hearers, under the guise of a deep sympathy with the woes of humanity, that the respect which they have been taught to feel for the Scriptures is an antiquated superstition, and that he is by no means sure that these records are true. The evidence of the Saviour's holy mission, he thinks, is insufficient; and the law of man's own intuitions is of far higher and more enduring authority than anything contained in Holy Writ. Such a man goes through with the appointed exercise, and leaves the church without once exhibiting credentials entitling him to enter a Christian pulpit while rejecting the Christ, but not without making injurious impressions upon some of his hearers, and wounding the consciences of many more.

So closely are we bound to each other in every walk of life, and so essential is this tie of brotherhood, that, if it be broken, the keystone is removed from the arch, and the foundations of human welfare are laid in ruins.

Our Divine Master has shown us how fidelity to our neighbor can exalt the bliss of heaven; and he has also declared that a fearful discipline of sorrow and remorse will await us if we refuse to admit his claims. The Saviour tells us, too, that he regards each imprisoned, destitute, suffering man as his representative; and that he shall measure our love of him by the manner in which we discharge our obligations to each other.

MISSIONARY EXPERIENCES.

I HAVE thought these would interest the readers of this Journal more than any other contribution within my power. Having travelled a vast deal in all parts of this and other countries, I have had, of course, my share of adventures ; and these are what one person is never tired of telling, nor others of hearing or reading. But to my story.

On one occasion I had been spending a Sunday at Cleveland, Ohio, occupying a Universalist pulpit morning, afternoon, and evening, and talking between whiles pretty steadily. The next day a little party was made up for me to visit a pretty village not far from Oberlin College, where a Sunday school had paved the way for theological discussion, and a number of intelligent, influential people had got upon our platform without knowing it, — without hearing any Unitarian preacher save conscience, or reading any Unitarian tract except the Bible.

We started — I remember it as if it were yesterday — immediately after dinner, with a pair of horses, over a plank road, and for seven miles all went well ; but then, alas ! we merged into mud of unmitigated blackness, and 't was necessary to walk as well as we could, creeping sometimes along fences, sometimes plunging bravely into a dismal swamp. As the guest of honor, they were inclined to keep me in the carriage ; but I could not bear to be housed up like a sick girl, and when there was walking to be done I was in for my share of it ; — and I had had some acquaintance before with Western roads, and should like to see the man who could take the lead of me in a fair field.

But, what with creeping on the wheels and creeping by them, the October day slipped away, and night came heavily on ; and though the appointed hour had arrived and past, still we were not *there*, neither was any " there " to be seen, — nothing but this swampy highway, and deserted fields, and funeral-looking woods. However, it was no use to groan. I had not sought the opportunity, it had found me ; and there was plainly enough a providence about it all.

Finally, when horses and men were equally uséd up, and a cold rain had set in, lights burst upon our clerical drowsiness. We could thank God, with the Apostle, for the taverns, and make a rush for the place of meeting, where the Apostle's text on patience had been practised, if not preached, by an excellent audience, " considering." We were too much exhausted to extemporize ; even the very earnest intelligences gathered in this chapel could not make up for weariness of the flesh. So, determining that the forty adult brethren, a member of Congress, a doctor, an editor, &c., &c., should see the spirit of the faith to which God's spirit had so freely led, we contented ourselves with giving a discourse on Christian holiness ; knowing very well that those who had come to question would go away to speak well of us, those who wanted to find some handle of reproach would soften their asperity a little, and those who had only fastened upon the boughs of our tree would find there was choice fruit farther on.

My purpose was answered. I could see the general acquiescence with what was said. A considerable number attended me to my lodgings to express their sympathy and desire to hear more. It seemed a very little thing to come all the way from Boston to do, and yet it was plainly dropping good seed into rich soil. They entreated me to stay over the next Sunday, offering to bear my expenses and procure me a crowded church ; but I was already too late for the Mississippi, and another week's delay might be fatal, — indeed, very nearly proved fatal as it was. So the next noon we parted, mutually interested in one another; they to do the good work of spiritualizing, unsectarianizing Christianity around and within their homes, I to toil and suffer as an apostle to the Gentiles, for aught I knew to the Kickasaws and Chickapoos.

But I never saw an opening which pleased me more, and I have seen many. None of the usual acrimony attended this introduction of the "sect everywhere spoken against"; no heaving asunder of society, no breaking up of church connections. The new brethren could not be talked down, nor prayed out, nor worried into bitterness of soul. Having worked their way to Christian liberty, they were not to be frightened out of it. Having slowly taken hold of advanced views, no pulpit-thunder could drive them back. Having been led by God's hand to this high table-land, they seemed to look down serenely on the fogs and mists floating below. For the lack of missionary spirit among us, they may not be built up into a separate congregation in that quiet, rural community; the same interest in their peculiar opinions may not always continue. The probability is, that, in the constant dispersion of the more active and hopeful of Young America, one of these brethren may be a pillar of the faith at Kanzas, another a corner-stone at California, another a firm buttress of the new church in China; but, anywhere and every way, building up "the kingdom."

The second "experience" was more remarkable. I was hurrying home, quite homesick. The constant ice on the Ohio had tried my patience to the utmost, and brought me to my Virginia landing on Friday night instead of

Thursday morn. It would require two days to reach the nearest Unitarian church, and make my Sunday profitable to anybody. I rushed up, the moment we touched the shore, and inquired out an old "Christian" friend, — a kind-hearted, right-spirited brother, by the name of Blackmarr. He was a little unwell and quite discouraged, but glad to see me. "Now," said I, "do you want me to stay?" "O, certainly!" said he. "But," said I, "it is impossible without we have preaching." "Ah!" said he, "that's another thing; there are no Unitarians here except ourselves." Then his wife, his better half, spoke: "I 'll promise you an audience, Mr. ——, and a place; so go back to your hotel, and sleep in peace. And, now I think of it, we have arrived at the fifth week of an exceedingly interesting debate, and you can help us in it." So I went back content to the dingiest of hotels, and thanked God that there was always work enough to do for those who were willing to do it.

The heavens smiled upon me that Sunday. The best hall of the city was half filled morning and evening with the right sort of people; but the great affair was the afternoon. A free Sunday school had been gathered, irrespective of doctrine, at the southern part of the settlement. In the course of instruction the teachers split upon the doctrine of the Trinity; so, after teaching their pupils what they knew, they continued their own meeting, to see if they could not know a little more.

I found them, as the discussion went on, in a very chaotic state; floundering, I should say, in deeper mud than any prairie roads. The parties alternated, for ten minutes each, in very Christian and courteous style. But, while there was on the Trinitarian side some educated, professional talent, our side was maintained in singular ignorance of the science of hermeneutics, and, as I thought, of all our strong points. I kept still and bit my lips, while one party proved, and the other disproved, that Christ was in the burning bush which spake to Moses, — was here in some obscure prophecy, and there in some two-sided phrase. Meanwhile, I watched the more ingenious Trinitarians, and saw their exultation, and heard them " count their chickens," and noted thankfully that the sun was going down, and that the time of reckoning had come. As a stranger, I claimed ten minutes of the floor. Not six people knew on which side I was. My friend Blackmarr had the chair. Everything was propitious. My first shot must be at their spread sails. I took their triumphant proof-texts in order, beginning with the " Let us make man in our image " of Genesis, and ending with the " I am Alpha and Omega " of the Apocalypse. I had not written one of these passages down ; they seemed scarred upon my skin anew, as I saw them telling like well-aimed " broadsides " upon the awed audience. In ten minutes I had given our explanation of them all ; and, dropping in a few of our strongest Scriptures at the close, sat down just as the hammer fell, not having wasted a second, omitted a passage which had been strongly proved against us, nor entangled myself in any of the cloudy defences which our friends had been casting up of dreamy dust.

A Dr. Somebody rose on the other side, stated that the discussion had taken a new phase, that he felt hardly prepared then to go on with it, and wished to ask me a question or two, (in which I surprised him by giving the chapter and verse for the passages which he was fumbling after, as well as by the quickness of my replies,) and closed with a desire that I would speak a second time. This was all I wanted, and worth the whole two hours to me. . The ground

41 *

was perfectly clear of rubbish; it was now time to build. I was never to have such opportunity again. Praying most earnestly for help, and giving the whole audience time to request me to close the discussion, I began with laying down the Divine Unity as the great revelation to mankind by Moses; and, closing with that chapter in the " Revelatlon " where Christ is standing before the throne, receiving the book from God upon the throne, and those passages in Paul where Jesus is seated at the right hand of the Father, I implored them not to take these greatest truths on trust, but to know for themselves, by prayer, study, and comparison of Scripture with Scripture, in whom they believed and to whom they prayed.

Then the assembly dispersed, as it was twilight; and the next day my face was turned towards Boston, where, shortly after, I received a well-signed petition for help in sustaining Unitarian services, and had the pleasure of contributing something myself for erecting a temple to Liberal Christianity, which our Secretary ought to go out and recover from its temporary misfortune.

I do not recall this as anything of an achievement. Clerical readers will not think the task of breaking down pasteboard walls of any account. I only rehearse it as an invitation to others to seek such occasions and make the most of them, and not confine themselves to the old milltrack, nor to the drowsy corners, where, like myself, they may have strangely enough dropped down.

THE RELIGIOUS ELEMENT IN MODERN FICTION.

A GREAT stride has been taken lately in the religious tendency of novels. When we compare those of the last half-century with those which now issue from the press, it seems almost as if one could trace each upward step.

Miss Edgeworth stands between the old and new. Hers are not religious novels, but highly moral. One enjoys them, and learns good lessons from them; but there is nothing which excites or inspires to nobler aims. Her heroes and heroines are outwardly perfect, and, measured by the world's standard, superior beings; but the reader would not imitate them; he feels himself capable of far more, not perhaps than what they attain, but than what they appear to feel. We should never call them noble; not even the greatest among them. The dear old lady has, however, gray-headed champions, whose gratitude for many an hour of pleasure will prompt them to stand forth valiantly in her defence, if we were so forgetful of the enjoyment she has afforded us as to find fault with her. But she is perfect in her sphere.

Such books, however, as those which are now most popular amongst us bear a different stamp. It proves a new era in religious progress that such can be written, and, still better, that there is such a demand for them. We find them in houses where a few years ago a book was almost an unheard-of luxury; and they are enjoyed and appreciated, too, by those whom one would hardly suspect of such a taste. How great an influence they must exert!

Dickens, we think, is our oldest friend in the department of authorship to which we refer. How deeply we enjoy the variety he gives us in every story, the warm heart he shows us, and the innumerable friends and acquaintances he pictures to us, a little overdrawn oftentimes, but all the more easily recognized.

Kingsley is by far the most suggestive writer in this same department. How much food for thought he gives us in those soliloquies in Hypatia! How the pictures he draws stand out in the brightest of colors!

The "Heir of Redclyffe" is the book, more than all others, that finds the invisible gateway to the heart, and creeps closer to us than we care to acknowledge. It stands as a type of what novels should be, with its high moral tone, its closeness to nature, and its living pictures of life and character. The interest never flags throughout the whole, and the most superficial reader cannot escape its lessons; for a thread of the highest religious principle runs through the whole fabric, and brightens every part as it meets the eye, — the true religion which is not forced upon the world, but lies hidden, perfecting the character till trial and affliction call for its services, and then it starts up, like a faithful soldier, ready armed, to fight in its master's cause, or like a gentle, loving wife, faithful and watchful, and always ready to soothe and comfort, and to soften every blow.

This is the kind of religion wanted for every book which finds its way to so many homes as a popular novel. Something that is practical, something that can be taken directly from the story, to be laid up among the treasures of the heart for a time of need. Not an indefinite, vague idea that good women always come to their reward (i. e. a husband), and that undeserving ones either find bad husbands or none at all, — the greatest punishment that can be inflicted. It is not always so in real life. We know many a dear old maid who here on earth lives a great deal more in the kingdom of heaven than hundreds of married women; and sometimes evil deeds never find their punishment in this world, except the punishment of an uneasy conscience, while great sacrifices are often never known, and only bear fruit upon the character.   Give us a book where even good people have trials and struggles and sufferings, and are not finally richly rewarded, but where those trials develop and mature the soul, and thus bring their own compensation with them.   This seems to be the way God works in the world, and shows his great love for his children.

Such a book is "Experience of Life."   We care less for the story than for the instruction we gather from Aunt Sarah.   This is one of those rare books where neither of the two principal characters was married or was beautiful; yet we find them just as interesting as any young rosebud of a heroine.   It is a book that will have its marked passages, to be read a page or two at random, and never closed without an addition to the heart's riches.

Miss Sewall goes a step deeper than most writers in her moral teachings.   Her heroines not only plan and do good, but learn to give up those plans cheerfully, and see them executed by others when circumstances demand the sacrifice.   That is a lesson hardly learned, even in every-day life; for only deeds come before the world, but the sacrifice of intentions, and the struggle it costs, the world does not see, and sometimes not one's dearest friends.   Such teachings, therefore, are welcome strangers, — no, dear old friends, whom we are very glad to meet out of their accustomed retirement.

It has been said that Miss Yonge was evidently an admirer of Miss Sewall.   Perhaps so.   But we do not find the proof, and indeed, much as we admire all of Miss Sewall's writings, we are rather jealous of the imputation; for, if she drew her inspiration from her, the pupil has, in many respects, far surpassed the teacher. The moral and religious tone in both are of the same high stamp; but in the painting of characters, while those of the one are dim and undefined, most of the other live and breathe.

Among so many books as there are now, one hardly knows what to choose. It is worse to read too many than too few, and where every day a new one tempts, it is almost as difficult to resist the numbers as to find time for all.

The public voice — not through the press, but by word of mouth — is an excellent adviser. What is recommended continually we may be pretty sure to find, in some measure, worth reading. Among the thousands who read "Uncle Tom's Cabin," because so many praised it, was there one who did not add his voice to the multitude, and say to the next benighted friend he met, "Read it"?

We have spoken, of course, of the better class of novels. They have enemies, as every positive for good must have its negative for evil; but we know little about them, except the general color of their covers as they lie in the shop-window. We will not do human nature the injustice to suppose, that, while books of the better class are so easily obtained, the majority prefer the mental food which inflames their worst passions, and leaves them disgusted with the duties which every one must meet in life. Every good book that can interest one reader does something, however little it may be, to crush one of the opposite class. It enlarges, though imperceptibly, the love of the good and the beautiful, and leaves less room in the heart for a corrupt taste.

UNITARIANISM.

For fifty years this has been an object of dread to thousands in New England. Pious parents have looked upon it
as the greatest moral peril which their children would encounter. Sunday after Sunday from innumerable churches,
and night after night from countless family altars, has gone
up the prayer that this evil might be abated. In how many
religious circles have its principles, tendencies, and prospects been anxiously discussed, and counsel been given and
taken as to the best method in which this distemper is to be
treated, and the most hopeful remedies to be used! What
sums of money have been contributed to support champions
of the truth, to establish lectures and meetings where error
might be resisted, to erect churches as dikes to stay the
incoming flood! How many newspapers and reviews have
set themselves with all due formality to cast the horoscope
of this dire phenomenon, at one time announcing with profound lamentation its growing ascendency, at another joyfully predicting its sure decline!

Out of New England the case is worse still; though, to
tell the truth, we have always suspected that the horror of
Unitarianism, elsewhere expressed, was somewhat exaggerated and feigned, as a foil to New-England boasting. If
in the South or the West a son of the Puritans says a word
in favor of his native land, the fact of this awful defection is
sure to be adduced. What a noble system of public instruction! "Yes, but see the godless infidelity it has led
to." Mark her enterprise and industry! "And that is all;
mere morals, the form of godliness without the power
thereof." See her beautiful villages, with spires pointing
to heaven. "And half of her churches denying the Lord

that bought them." She furnishes nearly all the writers
and books of the country. "And what streams of poison-
ous heresy are filtered through these channels." What
sums of money she gives every year for philanthropic purposes ! "Though they were ten times as large, they would
be no equivalent for her dreadful, God-defying Unitarianism."

What is this Unitarianism which is so much abhorred at
home and abroad ? Much, doubtless, goes under that name
with which we have no sympathy whatever. It is no strange
thing for a name to be assumed as a cover for opinions
which would meet with little favor under their own proper
title. So it was in the beginning. The sceptical, the radical, the revolutionary, flocked to hear the first Christian
teacher. " The kingdom of heaven suffered violence, and
the violent took it by force." Time soon proved who embraced it because it was the wisdom of God and the power
of God to salvation, and who pressed into it as a cover for
their own wild opinions and selfish ends.

Time is doing the same thing with us. A winnowing
process has been going on for nearly two generations. The
result will by and by be seen by all, if it be not now most
obvious. The world around will understand who they are
who hold Unitarian Christianity as a supernatural revelation
from the Father of lights, and who as a product of their
own philosophy ; who they are who accept Jesus Christ as
a divine messenger from heaven, and who as simply a wise
and good man ; who they are who believe the Bible to be
the inspired word of God, and who regard it as only a mere
human production ; who they are who look to the cross of
Christ as one of God's chosen means for man's redemption,
and who see there only a martyr's constancy and trust ;
who they are who maintain the necessity of conversion to a

spiritual life, and who believe that the good morals of a fair and upright walk are sufficient.

When these points have come to be clearly understood, what will Unitarianism be seen to be? It will be seen to be the faith of the Universal Church, the doctrines of the Apostles' Creed, the religion held by Christians of all names who are aside from sectarian influences, the substance accepted by all sects without the additions made thereto by each. Perhaps we can give no better definition of Unitarian Christianity than to say, that it is the Christianity common to believers of every name, when divested of the peculiarities of all parties and sects.

If it seem incredible that so simple and divine a system as this should be the terrible bugbear against which thousands have labored, exhorted, and prayed, let it be remembered that these persons have been frightened by their own misconceptions. To some image dressed up by their fancies and fears, to which they impute certain gross errors of belief, and a doubting, denying, rationalizing, and self-righteous spirit, they apply the name " Unitarian," and then they call upon God to destroy it and upon man to hate it. We do not join in such prayers, first, because we do not like to encourage men to hate anything, and secondly, because we do not feel like invoking so freely the name of God against the conjurations of one's own brain. As to their image of Unitarianism, we should not probably like it any better than they do. As we have said, much goes under this cognomen which we utterly reject. But the name does not bring up to our minds any thoughts of these outside misconceptions. With us the name stands for all the central truths and the common substance of the religion of Jesus Christ. It embraces all that is sound and vital in any church, and in any party, and in any believer, in Christendom. It brings us to

that common fountain of truth at which Fénelon and Cheve-
rus, Doddridge and Watts, Penn, Wesley, Channing, all
drank of the waters of life and were satisfied.

This view of Unitarianism as the faith of the Universal
Church, when separated from the peculiarities of sects, involves two facts as two distinct stages through which it
must pass.

First, the fact of universal antagonism. Every denomination will be against Unitarianism, because Unitarianism
is against the peculiarities of all denominations. And it is
to its peculiarities that each sect will at first be most strongly
attached, its lifeblood will most circulate in that part of its
system, its nerves will there be most sensitive, till a longer
and deeper experience has driven it back to the grandeur
and greatness of those central truths which are the common inheritance of believers. This stage will come by and
by. And then we shall have,

Secondly, the fact of universal fraternization. For it cannot be doubted that Unitarianism presents more points of
sympathy to all denominations than any other one denomination whatever. Just as fast as the idiosyncrasies and as-
perities of all denominations are worn away, just so fast
will they come to that tone of mind and cast of spirit which
we denote by the word Unitarian. And though doubtless
we have many misconceptions to correct, and errors to lay
aside, and sins to repent of, yet we believe that Unitarianism, Christian, Evangelical Unitarianism, is the high and
broad table-land on which all Christians will stand when
they come to have " one Lord, one faith, one baptism, one
God and Father of all, who is above all, and through all,
and in us all."

MEETINGS OF THE EXECUTIVE COMMITTEE.

March 12, 1855. All the members of the Board were present, with the exception of Rev. Mr. Lincoln.

The subject which occupied the chief attention of the Committee at this meeting was the establishment of a mission in Kanzas. The vast importance of sending out an earnest and active man to that new Territory had, months ago, presented itself in a strong light, and a correspondence had been opened, through the Secretary, with several persons with reference to undertaking this work. The Secretary stated that he had obtained information which led him to suppose that Rev. Mr. Nute of Chicopee would accept an appointment as our missionary in that field. There was much feeling on this subject in the towns on the Connecticut River, and several of Mr. Nute's parishioners were soon to remove to Kanzas. They were solicitous that he should accompany them. Mr. Nute was well known to every member of the Board. It was felt that no arrangement could be more satisfactory and full of hope. The subject was finally referred to the Committee on Missions, with full power, and with a recommendation to engage Rev. Mr. Nute as a missionary.

The Secretary stated that a beautiful crystallotype portrait of the late William Ellery Channing, D. D. had been presented to the Association by the artist, Mr. J. A. Whipple of Boston. A vote was passed directing the Secretary to return the thanks of the Association to Mr. Whipple for this highly acceptable gift, and to have it framed and placed in our rooms.

Copies of " The Altar at Home," just published, were placed upon the table, and it was voted that the price of

of annual contributions in aid of its objects, the Unitarian Societies in this country be divided into Districts.

"2. *Resolved*, That those Districts for the present be as follows : —

District No. 1. Includes all the Unitarian Societies in Boston.

District No. 2. Includes the Societies in Cambridge, Cambridgeport, East Cambridge, West Cambridge, Brighton, Brookline, Charlestown, Medford, Somerville.

District No. 3. Includes the Societies in Concord, Carlisle, Lowell, Billerica, Westford, Chelmsford, Tyngsborough, Lincoln, Lexington, Bedford, Woburn, Andover, Lawrence.

District No. 4. Includes the Societies in Watertown, Waltham, Weston, Wayland, Sudbury, Natick, Needham, Sherborn, Newton, Stow, Marlborough, Framingham.

District No. 5. Includes the Societies in Roxbury, West Roxbury, Dorchester, Milton, Quincy, Hingham, Cohasset, Scituate, South Scituate.

District No. 6. Includes the Societies in Dedham, Canton, Medfield, Walpole, Easton, Mansfield, Dover, Mendon, Uxbridge, Upton.

District No. 7. Includes the Societies in Taunton, Norton, Bridgewater, East Bridgewater, West Bridgewater, Fall River, Providence, Newport, New Bedford, Fairhaven, Nantucket.

District No. 8. Includes the Societies in Plymouth, Kingston, Duxbury, Pembroke, Brewster, Sandwich, Barnstable.

District No. 9. Includes the Societies in Worcester, Northborough, Westborough, Grafton, Sterling, Lancaster, Clinton, Leominster, Fitchburg, Leicester.

District No. 10. Includes the Societies in Groton, Pepperell, Shirley, Ashby, Harvard, Lunenburg, Townsend, Littleton.

District No. 11. Includes the Societies in Salem, Marblehead, Beverly, Lynn, Danvers, Gloucester, Newburyport, Chelsea.

District No. 12. Includes the Societies in Templeton, Petersham, Barre, Hubbardston, Greenfield, Deerfield, Fitzwilliam, Montague, Athol, Brattleborough, Windsor, Northfield, New Salem.

District No. 13. Includes the Societies in Springfield, Northampton, Chicopee, Brookfield, Ware, Holyoke, Hartford, Bridgeport.

District No. 14. Includes the Societies in Concord, N. H., Peterborough, Dublin, Charlestown, Walpole, Keene, Manchester, Nashua, Wilton.

District No. 15. Includes the Societies in Portland, Portsmouth, Dover, Exeter, Bath, Brunswick, Hallowell, Augusta, Saco, Kennebunk, Standish.

District No. 16. Includes the Societies in Bangor, Belfast, Thomaston, Perry, Eastport, Calais.

District No. 17. Includes the Societies in New York city, Staten Island, Brooklyn, Williamsburg, Jersey City.

District No. 18. Includes the Societies in Albany, Troy,
. Trenton, Vernon, Union Springs, Syracuse, Rochester, Buffalo.

District No. 19. Includes the Societies in Chicago, Detroit, Cleveland, Milwaukee, Cincinnati, Meadville, Austinburg, Rockford, Geneva, Marietta, Wheeling.

District No. 20. Includes the Societies in St. Louis, Louisville, Alton, Quincy, Peoria, Dixon.

" 3. *Resolved*, That there be annually appointed by the Executive Committee an Agent for each of the above Districts, — a clergyman who shall be expected to preach once every year to all Societies in his District on the plans and wants of the Association, if his services for this purpose may be accepted, and if, in his judgment, it may be expedient to bestow them ; it being understood that he will do this in the course of his usual exchanges, and that he will take up a collection in aid of the Association ; and the General Secretary of the Association shall act as Agent in one or more of these Districts, as may be determined by the Committee.

" 4. *Resolved*, That it will be expected of the District Agents that they will make a written report to the Secretary by the first of May in each year : and for the purpose of keeping them informed of the measures and needs of the Association, as well as for the sake of mutual conference and encouragement, there shall be two meetings every year of the District Agents with the Executive Committee, at such time and place as the latter may appoint.

" 5. *Resolved*, That as there are other Unitarian Societies in this country beside those embraced in the foregoing Districts, but which, from their position, cannot conveniently be arranged in any District, — such as the Societies in Burlington, Vt., Lancaster, N. H., Montreal, Philadelphia, Baltimore, Washington, Charleston, Savannah, New Orleans, and San Francisco, — we hereby invite them to co-operate fraternally with us in an annual contribution in behalf of the Association."

After the adoption of the above Resolutions, it was voted that the appointment of District Agents be made by the new Executive Committee at its first meeting after the approaching Anniversary.

Copies of the Select Volume from the writings of Dr. Channing were laid upon the table, and it was voted that the price be sixty cents retail, with twenty-five per cent off at wholesale.

The Secretary then read his Annual Report, which, after some amendments, was adopted as the Annual Report of the Executive Committee, to be presented at the Annual Meeting.

EXTRACTS FROM LETTERS.

FROM Rev. James Tanner we have had several letters. The first he wrote after his leaving Boston was from New York city, in which he says : —

"I met here a large delegation of Chippewa chiefs and war-chiefs, on their way home from Washington to the head-waters of the Mississippi. O what a meeting that was! They have made the desired treaty with the United States government, and my countrymen are saved! Stand by me, and we shall yet have that whole nation. The Indian Agent highly approves of my plans, and hopes that your Association will go on in the course begun."

A few days later he writes : —

"There is much talk on my account. Some say, We separate from Mr. Tanner on account of his Unitarianism. Others say, No, we will stand by him. Two reverend gentlemen asked me to-day if I had changed my views. I said, No. They said the Unitarian paper described me as differing from the Baptists. I replied, Brothers, you know I always differed from you. I differed at the time you ordained me. Where I stood then I stand now. I believe in the existence of one God, not in two or three. I believe in the Son of God, but do not believe that the Son of God is God himself. I leave here to-morrow for home. Pray for me. I am a poor creature knocked about here and there. Remember me to my many friends with you."

Some time later we had another letter from Cincinnati, in

which he speaks in grateful terms of the kindnesses he had experienced there, and in all places through which he had passed. Word has also reached us of his arrival in St. Louis and St. Paul, in both of which places he awakened much interest. We hope to be able in our next Journal to present full accounts of his labors in his mission.

Just as we go to press we receive a brief letter from Rev. Mr. Nute, which, though it gives but little information, reveals the spirit with which he improves every opportunity of influence. We accordingly print it entire.

                              " Lawrence, Kanzas,
                          Monday Morning, May 28, 1855.
    " REV. DR. MILES : —
" My dear Friend, — The mail which leaves this place but once a week is just closing, and I have time to write only a few lines.

" I reached here a week ago last evening, by the first trip made by a steamboat up the Kanzas. I stopped only to the next morning, when I went on to reconnoitre as far as Fort Riley, to decide upon the best place for me to locate. The boat got aground several times, so that we were five days getting up to within six miles of Topeka, which is but twenty-five miles west from here by the California road. I was detained on the boat by the sickness of a passenger who had committed himself into my care to stand by him to the last, attend to his burial, take charge of his effects, and communicate the intelligence of his death to his family if he should be taken away. He died on Friday morn, in cheerful trust, a rational Christian of the Unitarian stamp, though reared a Methodist. One of his last and most earnest charges to me was for his children, that they should be educated free from all sectarian bias, to draw their religion directly as possible from the very words of Jesus. His heart overflowed with gratitude for the new light which had broken upon his mind. This was indeed a true-hearted Christian man. His disease was the cholera, and very distressing until within a few hours of his death. I stood over him most of the time for twenty hours, and feel thankful that strength was granted me so to do. This was the fourth case of cholera on our boats, two of which have terminated in death. The others are now re-covering, — one of them stopping now in the next cabin to that where I abide for a day or two.

"Many opportunities offered themselves to me on the way to exercise the offices of my mission, so favorable, that I believe one of the most fruitful fields for permanent usefulness would be that of travel on the great rivers of the West.

"I preached on three boats, and made the acquaintance of many whom I have met and am daily expecting to meet in the Territory. In Griggsville, Ill., I preached twice to congregations of a hundred persons, the second time by request, to state the Unitarian belief,— a rare opportunity, as *notice was given in all the three churches in town that I was to speak in the evening, and that I was a missionary of the American Unitarian Association.*

"Quite a number came forward at the close, and expressed their interest and assent. Some of these reminded me of my services in that place five years ago. It will not be long before there may be a prosperous society of our fellowship in Griggsville.

"Last evening I preached under circumstances novel and pecu-liarly impressive. All the rooms suitable for public service were occupied, which was but one. In the morning I attended, but not to my edification ; heard an old-fashioned, gloomy funeral sermon, calculated to depress the minds of the people, and therefore most inappropriate to the condition and state of feeling in which most of them are placed. The teacher's topic was the probability of sick-ness and death, the certainty that many of us would be sick and die in the course of a few months ; his conclusion was, that we should frequently think of our winding-sheets and coffins and the worms that would soon be eating us in the grave, and should flee from the wrath to come. I have found no one who liked it, and most condemn it in strong terms, among whom are ministers and church-members of several denominations.

"Several expressed to me a desire to hear a discourse that should present some of the cheerful aspects of our religion adapted to our condition. I made an appointment to meet those so disposed on the top of a hill, a little more than half a mile from the village, at the hour of sunset. More than a hundred (about 150) responded to the invitation, though the notices were given out after four o'clock. One of the most beautiful scenes that I have ever beheld was spread before me and fixed for ever in my mind. From the top of the eminence which I had chosen, an extensive view is presented of the town, the winding rivers, the Kanzas to the north and west, and the Wakarcusa to the south, and a panorama of indescribable beauty for more than twenty miles in every direction, and twice that distance in several points; — thousands of acres of the most fertile, undulating prairie, dotted with the tents of the emigrants gleaming in the light of the setting sun, with hundreds of cattle grazing in groups here and there, — the long white wagons drawn by strings of mules and oxen, sometimes to the number of twenty, the prairie-ship of the Santa Fé and California emigrant, slowly crawling over the great sea of grass, unmarked except by the dark brown track on which they are moving ; — to the north and west, and beyond the Kanzas, boundless tracts of forest. But I must leave all this for what more particularly belongs to the occasion. Standing on the topmost height, I look down toward the village, (I should say the city,) from which are moving the people who are to compose my first congregation in Kanzas, men and women and a few children scattered all the way along the road, some just climbing the hill. I think of the hill-sides of Palestine, of the Great Teacher, and hear him say, as he did when waiting for the people who were coming out from Samaria, ' Lift up your eyes and look · on the fields, for they are white already to the harvest.'

"Soon I am surrounded by a number about the size of that which tarried in Jerusalem for the outpouring of the Spirit by the command and promise of their ascended Lord.

"We sing a hymn about the Good Shepherd who leads his flock by the fair pastures and pleasant waters. I read the opening of the Sermon on the Mount and the 17th of Acts, and take for my text, *The Unknown God, him I declare unto you*, &c.

"Here I must stop for the mail. The rest next week, or sooner if I have an opportunity by private hand.

"Yours as ever,

"E. NUTE."

NOTICES OF BOOKS.

Lingard's History of England. A new Edition, in thirteen volumes. Boston: Phillips, Sampson, & Co. 1855.

THE publishers have rendered an important service towards promoting a taste for historical investigation by giving to the public this excellent library edition of a valuable standard work. The merits of Lingard are so well known that they need not here be repeated. No one can have a correct knowledge of the course of English history who shuts his eye from the view taken by this learned, and generally impartial, Catholic historian; and although this is not the book to be read by those whose time confines them to one historian alone, the mental discipline arising from a comparison of this writer with others will be one of the most valuable exercises to which the mind can be subjected. We remember that, more years ago than we care about numbering, we were advised by a wise instructor to take the three histories of Goldsmith, Hume, and Lingard, and read the paragraphs in each which relate to the same events or men, carefully observing the difference in representation, and forming our own opinion as to the probable truth. It is undoubtedly the best possible way of reading history. It breaks up that indolent habit of quietly accepting all statements as true into which we so easily slide as we follow the polished sentences of any one writer. A thorough comparison and independent judgment, carried on through one period of history, will give an insight into the secret springs of character, and help form a habit of historical criticism which will be of the greatest importance in all one's subsequent reading. The work which this eminent Boston house has published is printed on good paper, is neatly bound, each volume has an engraving, and the whole is supplied with a copious index. We may add, that the publication has been superintended by an editor whose learning and taste have amply qualified him for this undertaking.

Westward Ho ! The Voyages and Adventures of Sir Amyas Leigh, Knight, in the Reign of her Most Glorious Majesty, Queen Elizabeth. Rendered into Modern English by CHARLES KINGSLEY, Author of Hypatia, Alton Locke, &c. Boston : Ticknor and Fields. 1855.

EVERY work from the pen of the author of Alton Locke bears the unmistakable mark of genius. In this volume he reproduces the good old days of Queen Bess, with notices of some of the remarkable men of her court, Raleigh and others, and of the great events of her reign, such as the destruction of the Spanish Armada. The story turns upon the love of maritime discovery and military adventure which so strongly distinguished that age. The tale we think is too long, and the chapters are of very unequal interest; but it sets forth in a faithful and spirited manner one phase of that reign of which we have another in Sir Walter Scott's Kenilworth ; and it is high praise to say that a reader fresh in his admiration of the latter work will not lose a relish for the former.

———

1. *The Daily Life : or Precepts and Prescriptions for Christian Living.* By REV. JOHN CUMMING, D. D. Boston : John P. Jewett & Co. 1855.
2. *Sabbath Morning Readings on the Old Testament.* By REV. JOHN CUMMING, D. D. *Book of Leviticus.* Boston : John P. Jewett & Co. 1855.
3. *Sabbath Evening Readings on the New Testament.* By the REV. JOHN CUMMING, D. D. *St. Luke.* Boston : John P. Jewett & Co. 1855.

MOST of our readers know what a large library of books the industrious minister of Crown Court, Covent Garden, London, has published. Though their theology is not at all to our liking, we are obliged to confess that for the most part they relate to practical duties common to all Christians, that they are written in an easy, rapid style, and now and then present pleasing and forcible illustrations.

Essays. By Theophilus Parsons. Third Edition. Boston: Crosby, Nichols, & Co. 1855.

The subjects of these Essays are, Life, Providence, Correspondence, The Human Form, Religion, The New Jerusalem. They are written in the tranquil and dreamy style so common with the followers of Swedenborg, and partake largely of the cheerful spirit by which his disciples are distinguished. We were not a little surprised at some of his representations of Unitarianism. According to Professor Parsons, the only thing Unitarians agree in is the rejection of a personal God, which doctrine was believed before it was revealed in the Trinity only by the faith that an incarnate God would appear on earth.

The Philosophy of Sectarianism: or a Classified View of the Christian Sects in the United States, with Notices of their Progress and Tendencies. By Rev. Alexander Blaikie, Pastor of the First Presbyterian Church in Boston. Boston: Phillips, Sampson, & Co. 1855.

The title of this book is deceptive. The work is a plea for Presbyterianism, which is represented as standing in the middle, safe, and apostolic ground between Prelacy on the one hand and Congregationalism on the other. From the author's point of view he criticises all denominations but his own in respect to church government, worship, the administration of the sacrament, discipline, revivals, missions, domestic training, Sabbath schools, influence on civil polity, &c., summing up the results in certain "deductions" at the close, a few of which are these: "that Presbyterianism is the Scriptural form of church government"; "that it is most conducive to the civil and religious happiness of man"; "that the government of the United States, if overthrown, must be subverted by Prelacy or Congregationalism," &c. The book is written with a good deal of spirit and wit, and though Unitarians are brought in for their full share of censure, we have read it with pleasure. The author deals his blows with a pretty liberal hand upon the faults, follies, rivalries, ambitions, and apish imitations of all sects, and it is instructive to see these held up in caricature, though it be somewhat extravagant.

———

The Daily Monitor; being a Portion of Scripture, an Anecdote, and a Verse of a Hymn for every Day in the Year. By REV. JOHN ALLEN. With an Introduction by REV. E. N. KIRK. Boston: John P. Jewett & Co. 1855.

THIS is a little pocket monitor to aid in holy living. Some of the anecdotes, we think, might have been chosen in better taste, and from one or two statements of doctrine we might dissent. But as a whole we deem this a useful collection, and do not doubt that a daily reference to it will help promote a life of holiness and true piety.

———

The Mayflower, and Miscellaneous Writings. By HARRIET BEECHER STOWE. Boston: Phillips, Sampson, & Co. 1855.

THIS collection of Mrs. Stowe's tales and essays, published many of them before she had achieved her great distinction as the writer of *Uncle Tom's Cabin*, will prove that she had been an industrious and remarkable authoress prior to the appearance of that famous book, which was no sudden blooming out without previous stages of growth and promise. From the fact that we have seen many beautiful stories from her pen which are not included in this volume, we have no doubt that another collection of the size of this might be made. They are all marked by her rare cheerfulness, vivacity, good sense, close observation, dramatic power of description, and her believing and devout spirit. Many readers will thank the publishers for this beautiful and interesting volume, which is adorned with a steel engraving of the writer, somewhat idealized, and yet so near to the original as to be recognized at once as a likeness.

A Boy's Adventures in the Wilds of Australia; or Herbert's Note-Book. By WILLIAM HOWITT. With Illustrations. Boston: Ticknor and Fields. 1855.

THIS book dates from Melbourne, and purports to have been written amid the scenes it describes. Lovers of wild adventure in new and strange scenes will here find it to their heart's content. Over all the hardships of a new settlement, the perils of an unknown land, the difficulties that taxed ingenuity, the encounter with original characters, the occurrence of unexpected events, the view of the wild scenery and interesting natural history of Australia, William Howitt has spread the charm of his clear, easy, and attractive style, and to thousands of young readers this book will prove a great favorite.

Ironthorpe: the Pioneer Preacher. By PAUL CREYTON. Boston: Phillips, Sampson, & Co. 1855.

ANOTHER description of life in the wilds, amid the adventures of first settlers. But the scene of this book is nearer home. It describes the struggles, privations, disappointments, and successes of a family journeying westward forty years ago, when the Genesee Valley was an untrodden wilderness, and Western New York was the land of promise. The commanding influence of a frontier preacher, named Ironthorpe, is set forth in a striking light, in which we see how great was his influence, and the influence of the religious sentiment, upon the moral condition and temporal prosperity of the colony. We commend the work as highly interesting and instructive.

Woman in the Nineteenth Century; and Kindred Papers. By MARGARET FULLER OSSOLI. Edited by her Brother, ARTHUR B. FULLER. Boston: John P. Jewett & Co. 1855.

A GRACEFUL and affectionate tribute to the memory of a beloved sister has Mr. Fuller here rendered, in superintending the republication of her most remarkable production, and in the warm testimony he bears to the heartiness and Christian power of her

life as it unfolded itself at home.   We do not agree with some of
her views.   A great subject when first discussed is never seen in
its proper light and just proportions.   To Margaret Fuller will always belong the honor of being among the first to commence a
needed reform in the general estimation of the position and rights
of woman, and of treating this subject with unmistakable evidences of learning and genius.   To her treatise on the subject,
which has given a title to the book, Mr. Fuller has very properly
added some of his sister's best articles in the New York *Tribune*,
with extracts from her letters to kindred and friends.   These, with
an engraved likeness of the writer, constitute an interesting memorial of this gifted woman.

———

*Christianity, its Essence and Evidence; or an Analysis of the New
Testament into Historical Facts, Doctrines, Opinions, and Phra-
seology.*   By GEORGE W. BURNAP, D.D.   Boston : Crosby,
Nichols, & Co.   1855.   pp. 410.

A SERIES of twenty-five sermons presents a classification of the
contents of the New Testament.   Nine discourses are devoted to
a statement and proof of the *Facts* of the New Testament, such as
the reality of persons, times, and places therein mentioned, the
resurrection, claims, and sinlessness of Christ, the personal consciousness which was the basis of his action, and the perfect mo-
rality which was the substance of his instruction.   Six discourses
relate to the *Doctrines* of the New Testament, among which are
stated the personality and paternity of God, efficacy of prayer, forgiveness of sins, immortality, and retribution.   Five discourses
treat of the *Opinions* of the New Testament, by which are meant
"the impressions and habits of thought which were current at the
time of Christ upon subjects collateral to religion, which he did
not deem it expedient to criticise."   These opinions are the interpretation of the Old Testament, a personal Devil, and the return of
Christ to the earth.   The remaining six discourses relate to the
Phraseology of the New Testament, so much of which was the
conventional diction of that age, not invented or introduced by
Christ, but adopted by him with the intention of filling it out with

a higher and nobler signification. Of this the phrases, kingdom of God, Christ a king, Jesus the Son of God, priesthood of Christ, the sacrificial language of the Epistles, and regeneration, claim a discourse for each.

From this statement of the purpose and contents of this volume the reader will see how happily chosen is its title, and how admirably arranged are its topics. The author exhibits in this work the power of logical argument, the clearness of style, the wide range of reading, and the marks of original investigation and observation, which in many preceding books have made a wide circle of readers his debtors. We think we should have preferred the recasting of this matter in some other form than that of sermons, and the addition of several topics the omission of which leaves chasms in the discussion. It must be confessed, however, that the former objection is greatly relieved by the singular directness with which the writer approaches his subjects, and by abstinence from the usual homiletic exhortation. Of course such a wide range of discourses must include those of varied importance. That on *Prayer* seems to us to present only the least significant aspect of that subject. The sermon on the *Consciousness of Christ* is striking and profound. It develops an argument for the truth of Christianity with a clearness and power which present it with all the freshness of an original view. Our whole reading public have been laid under fresh obligation to this industrious and scholarly pen.

———

A Translation of the Gospels, with Notes. By ANDREWS NORTON. Vol. I. *The Text.* Vol. II. *Notes.* — Also one volume, in uniform style, on the *Internal Evidences of the Genuineness of the Gospels, with Particular Reference to Strauss's "Life of Jesus."* By ANDREWS NORTON. Boston: Little, Brown, & Co. 1855. pp. 443, 565, 309.

WE have at length the great work of Professor Norton, the fruit of his lifelong study, in these three splendid volumes, which would have satisfied the nice eye of their author, while they reflect the highest credit upon their publishers. Volume first is a new translation of the Gospels. It uses to a great extent the phraseology of the common version, but by an occasional change in the words or structure of the sentence, it clears up obscurities and corrects misconceptions. The text is printed in paragraphs like other books, with marginal indications of verses; and many will find fresh interest in these narratives of the Evangelists, as they read them in the clear, simple, and carefully chosen language of this translation. In family reading of the Scriptures, this volume, we hope, may come into general use, for it will be found to be singularly fitted to arrest attention and to awaken thought.

Whole libraries of learning and long years of study are condensed in the second volume, which will have more interest to clerical and critical readers. A perusal of it has carried our minds back to the time when we enjoyed the instructions of Professor Norton in sacred criticism; and while we recognize the explanations of many passages which then sunk deep into our memory, as stated in his slow and silvery tones, we have also been struck with the fact that he has since modified some of his expositions, and given evidence of continued research and completer mastery of his subject to the very last. This is not the place to enter into any criticism of his interpretation of particular passages, even if we were competent for that task. One merit will strike the eye of every observer. There is no exhibition of learning and profusion of commentary on unimportant texts. The strength of the book is given to the development of certain correct principles of interpretation, and to the unfolding of the true sense of leading words and phrases; and we believe it is the opinion of those who are competent to pronounce a wise decision, that few Biblical scholars have shown more power in this department of labor than Mr. Norton. To his many pupils, scattered throughout the land, and to thousands of other earnest seekers after truth, this book will be a priceless treasure.

The third volume contains matter which is more new and fresh to us, and we have read it with the deepest interest. It is the complement of that honored monument of his scholarship, — The Genuineness of the Gospels, — the former developing the internal, as the latter the historical or external evidences of Christianity.

The chapter "On what Essentially Constitutes the Value of Christianity and of the Gospels" shows how clearly the early class of Unitarians saw the truth that Christ is a manifestation of the Father, and how high-toned and evangelical were their statements on this point. The argument drawn from the consistency of the narrative in the Gospels with facts which must have existed, though unrecorded and unexplained, is stated so clearly and convincingly, that it seems like a fresh confirmation of the truth.

But we are enticed into remarks beyond our proper length. It is with a feeling of greater personal wealth, and of sincere thankfulness to Him who has raised up this teacher, that we place these volumes on our shelves. Their appearance during the Anniversary Week gave increased interest to that pleasant season. We only regret that some one of our Biblical scholars had not been called upon to express our common pleasure and gratitude. To our lay readers who may desire to make a valuable addition to the library of their pastor, we may say, you can select nothing more useful or welcome than the six octavo volumes of Professor Norton, which will be sold at the Association's Rooms at the reduced price of eight dollars and a half.

The History of Massachusetts. By JOHN STETSON BARRY. Boston: Phillips, Sampson, & Co. 1855. 1 vol. 8vo.

MR. BARRY has lately been known as one of the most diligent and painstaking students of our early annals. The fruit of many years of investigation is presented in this noble volume, whose eighteen chapters bring the story down to the beginning of the last century. To complete the annals of our Commonwealth according to the plan here begun will require at least three or four other volumes. Though Mr. Barry's path has often been traversed by diligent observers before him, yet he gleans many curious and interesting facts which were never before historically stated. He has investigated points with a rare minuteness of research, and has presented a narrative distinguished for its clear and agreeable style. The book is a rich contribution to our historical literature, and we shall look with interest for the appearance of the subsequent volumes.

Diary in Turkish and Greek Waters. By the Right Honorable the EARL OF CARLISLE. Edited by C. C. FELTON, Greek Professor in Harvard University. Boston: Hickling, Swan, and Brown. 1855.

IN 1853 the Earl of Carlisle, formerly known as Lord Morpeth, and now Lord Lieutenant of Ireland, visited Dresden, Vienna, Constantinople, Troy, Smyrna, Rhodes, Athens, Alexandria, Malta, Corinth, Venice, returning home by way of Milan and Switzerland. He kept a diary, in which are recorded the remarks of a sensible, well-informed, hearty, and genial observer. Professor Felton, who, near the same time, passed over much of the same ground, furnishes a Preface and numerous instructive and entertaining notes. Altogether, it is the most interesting book we have taken up for many a month. The exact information it gives of many of the localities which are now the seat of the great European war makes its publication most timely; while, independent of this temporary interest, its classical allusions and criticisms will give it a permanent value. The work contains twenty-five illustrations, taken from Smith's History of Greece. No more agreeable and instructive pages can be found.

A School of Life. By ANNA MARY HOWITT. Boston: Ticknor and Fields. 1855.

THIS is another illustration of the good judgment and good taste which guide the selection of books published by this firm. We commend the interesting story, the many beautiful lessons, the sweet and devout spirit, of a book to which the eye will at once be attracted by its uncommonly neat and delicate appearance. It sketches the career of a young artist who early consecrated himself to the pursuit of the beautiful, and unfolds the varied lessons he received in the school of life. We are glad that the papers read in their original form by a brother in the wilds of Australia are now published, for the entertainment and instruction of a wide circle of readers.

Tricolored Sketches in Paris, during the Years 1851, -2, -3. New
York : Harper and Brothers. 1855.

THESE Sketches formed a series of letters to a New York paper,
and present a pretty fair view of the course of events during the
most memorable era in the modern history of the French capital.
Mingled with anecdotes of public characters and events are frequent notices of details in Parisian life, the whole constituting a
very readable and pleasing book.

Louis Fourteenth, and the Writers of his Age. By REV. J. F.
ASTIÉ. Translated by REV. E. N. KIRK. Boston : J. P.
Jewett & Co. 1855.

MR. ASTIÉ delivered nine lectures in French to select audiences
in New York, reviewing the age of Louis the Fourteenth, and the
writers, such as Pascal, Corneille, Fénelon, La Fontaine, Boileau,
Racine, Molière, who made that age one of the most memorable
in history. Such a *résumé* must necessarily be very general and
superficial. Mr. Kirk's Introduction shows an ability to treat this
subject with more power than the lecturer.

RECORD OF EVENTS AND GENERAL INTEL-
LIGENCE.

ON Tuesday, April 3, Rev. Ephraim Nute was installed as a
Missionary of the American Unitarian Association to Kanzas.
The services were held in the Unitarian church in Chicopee,
where Mr. Nute has for years ministered. The sermon was
preached by Rev. Mr. Huntington of Boston.

, ON Wednesday, April 18, Rev. Thomas Weston was installed
pastor of the Unitarian Church in New Salem, Mass. Sermon
by Rev. Mr. Briggs of Salem.

ON Wednesday, April 18, the Unitarian church in Eastport, Me., which had been remodelled, and made one of the most attractive churches in the State, was dedicated to the uses of public worship. Sermon by the pastor, Rev. Henry F. Edes.

———

ON Wednesday, April 18, the new and beautiful stone church erected for the use of the Unitarian Society in Rockford, Ill., was solemnly consecrated to the worship of one God, the Father. Sermon by Rev. R. R. Shippen of Chicago. In the evening of the same day, Mr. John Murray, late of the Meadville Theological School, was ordained pastor of the Society worshipping in this church. Sermon by Rev. Mr. Conant of Geneva.

———

ON Thursday, April 19, Rev. Mr. Nute, Missionary of the American Unitarian Association, left Boston for Kanzas Territory, the scene of his future labors.

———

ON Sunday, April 29, Rev. O. B. Frothingham preached his farewell sermon to the North Church and Society in Salem, Mass., preparatory to his assuming the care of the new Society in Jersey City, N. J.

———

ON Saturday evening, May 19, the Unitarian church in Lee Street, Cambridgeport, was entirely destroyed by fire. Immediate measures have been taken to secure the erection of another house of worship in its place.

———

THE usual anniversary meetings were held in Boston during the last week in May. As far as we have been able to judge, they appear to have been marked by a spirit of harmony, love, a tender and deep interest in the cause of Christian truth and of man's salvation. As full reports have been given in the papers, it seems needless to present here any details. We may only remark generally that the meetings of interest to us as Unitarians were well attended, and must be productive of good results. The *Morning Prayer Meetings* were crowded. There was no want of speaking, and for the most part the speaking was good. In the hushed silence, and eager attention, and spiritual response to every devout utterance, it seemed apparent that there was a Presence there greater than man's, — a Spirit that takes the things of God and shows them unto man. — The *Collation* was more largely attended than in former years; and though the speaking had not the interest of other days, the occasion was delightful for its kindly greetings and cheerful and animating hopes. — The *Anniversary of the American Unitarian Association* was well attended, though the absence of some on whose presence we had confidently counted was painfully marked. Too much time, we fear, was taken up in reading extracts from the Report, and in premeditated speeches. Should we see another annual meeting, we hope that the reading may not occupy more than ten minutes, and that the speeches, limited to that amount of time, may be of a more spontaneous kind. Our readers will find a report of the proceedings of the celebration on another page of this Journal, and the excellent addresses of Messrs. Brooks and Hill. — Two valuable addresses were given to the *Ministerial Conference*, one by Rev. Dr. Peabody of Boston, the other by Rev. Samuel J. May of Boston. — The *Sunday-School Society* held a meeting in the Bedford Street Church, at which an important paper was read by Rev. F. D. Huntington, on *Order, Instruction, and Christianization* in our Sunday schools. Rev. Stephen G. Bulfinch has been appointed Secretary of this Society, and he made a short, but interesting and highly practical address. Great hopes of increased usefulness and vigor are cherished from the services of a Secretary who has so many eminent qualifications for that office. — The sermon before the *Convention of Congregational Ministers* was delivered by Rev. Dr. Lothrop. The text was the words, " As in Adam all die, so in Christ shall all be made alive." The object, subject, and power of the Gospel were treated in a style of much manliness and power, far exceeding even the high expectations of the preacher's friends, and extorting the warm commendations of those who do not belong to his school of Christian thought. Rev. Dr. Sweetser of Worcester is the first preacher for next year; the second preacher, just elected, is Rev. President Stearns of Amherst College. — A most spirited meeting of the *Children's*

Mission Society gave great delight to a large audience, and a fresh impulse to that favorite charity. — Mr. Clapp's sermon at the administration of the *Lord's Supper* was a tender and solemn utterance from a deep religious experience, and the service of commemoration was conducted reverently and impressively by Dr. Farley, of Brooklyn, N. Y.

ENGAGEMENTS.

ON Sunday, April 8, the Secretary preached in the afternoon to the Rev. Mr. Holland's Society in East Cambridge, setting forth the plans and needs of the Association. The pastor had previously commended the subject to his congregation, and the attendance was good for an afternoon service. A contribution was taken up. There has been an Auxiliary established here for some time. The late O. H. P. Green, Esq., whose recent death is much lamented, has hitherto had the care of it.

On Sunday, April 22, he preached to the Unitarian Society in Mansfield, Rev. Daniel W. Stevens pastor. This is a small rural congregation, and but a shadow of the large parish known fifty and a hundred years ago in this ancient town, when one minister gathered nearly the entire population for public worship. Of late its fortunes have revived. The church has been repaired, and it may invite its share of the new population which hopes of business may bring to the place. The Society was addressed in the afternoon upon the subject of the Association. Copies of "The Altar at Home" were afterwards sold there, and subscriptions received for the Quarterly Journal.

On Sunday, April 29, he preached in Brookline, to the Society of which Rev. Frederic N. Knapp is pastor. The present interests of the Association were presented in the forenoon's discourse, and a contribution was taken up in aid of its objects. The occasion was made more interesting by the appearance of the pastor at church, who, after an absence of many months, confined to his house through lameness, was now able, for the second time this spring, to attend the services of public worship, and to take part in them. The Brookline Society remembered the annual day for its contribution, and we hope it will not hereafter let it pass by unnoticed.

On Sunday, May 13, he preached to the Society in South Scituate, Rev. Mr. Stetson the pastor. This is one of the few places left in Massachusetts where the centre of the town has but one place of public worship. Unity may sometimes promote indifference, and competition and rivalry may be needed to awaken life and interest. The Society here has not been in the habit of contributing to the Association. A sermon on the subject of the services we should render for the diffusion of Christian truth was followed by a few words from the pastor, commending the claims of the Association to his people. A contribution was taken up, which we hope will be repeated every year.

On Sunday, May 20, he preached to Rev. Mr. Whitney's Society in Brighton. This is the Sunday for the annual contribution in this parish for the Association; and few Societies are more regular and systematic in their charities than this. A rainy day did not prevent a good attendance, and an encouraging attention was given to an exposition of the reasons which call for more earnest activity towards the promotion of our views of the Gospel. The amount of the contribution will be found stated in its proper place. It followed immediately after a subscription for an organ for the vestry. We are glad to notice the continued prosperity of this united and earnest parish.

During the two years of the publication of the Quarterly Journal, the Secretary has given in each number some statement of his engagements during the succeeding quarter. As the plan of District Agents, as described in-this number, both in the Annual Report and under the head of Meetings of the Executive Committee, is now to be tried, there will be no further call for any mention of the Secretary's engagements, which will accordingly be hereafter omitted.

ACKNOWLEDGMENTS.

In the months of March, April, and May there have been received the following sums : —

March 1.	From the Society in Groton,		$40.00
" 2.	" subscriber to Quarterly Journal,		1.00
" 6.	" Second Unitarian Society in Portland,		40.00
" "	" sale of books in Union Springs, N. Y.,		54.34
" "	" " " in West Roxbury,		1.56
" 9.	" subscriber to Quarterly Journal,		1.00
" "	" sale of books at office,		1.00
" "	" ladies in Church Green, Boston,		53.50
" 10.	" friends in Chicopee, Book Fund,		52.00
" 13.	" West Church, Boston, for Mr. Tanner's mission,		110.13
" "	" West Church Sunday School, for do.,		32.21
" "	" sale of books at office,		.60
" "	" " " in Quincy,		50.00
" "	" " " S. J. May,		25.00
" 15.	" " " Blooming Grove, N. Y.,		30.00
" "	" subscriber to Quarterly Journal,		1.00
" 16.	" Auxiliary Society in Taunton,		73.00
" "	" subscribers to Quarterly Journal,		5.00
" 19.	" " " " "		1.00
" 21.	" books sold at the West,		40.00
" "	" subscriber to Quarterly Journal,		1.00
" 22.	" sale of books at office,		1.20
" "	" subscriber to Quarterly Journal,		1.00
" 23.	" Clement Willis, Esq., Life-Member,		30.00
" 24.	" subscribers to Quarterly Journal,		3.00
" 26.	" sale of books from office,		30.00
" 28.	" subscriber to Quarterly Journal,		1.00
" "	" a friend, for Mr. Tanner's mission,		10.00
" "	" sale of books,		.60
" 29.	" " "		.80
" 30.	" Auxiliary, Peterborough, N. H.,		32.12
" "	" sale of books at office,		121.12
" "	" " "		50.00
" "	" subscriber to Quarterly Journal,		1.00
" 31.	" sale of books at office,		3.30
April 2.	" " "		1.20
" "	" Miss Penhallows, of Lowell,		5.50
" 6.	" sale of books in Lawrence,		25.22
" "	" subscribers to Quarterly Journal,		2.00
" "	" Auxiliary in Wayland,		20.00

April	7.	From Hon. John C. Gray, donation,	.	$25.00
"	"	" John Dorr, Esq., donation,	. .	20.00
"	"	" Mr. Cotton, donation, . . .	.	5.00
"	9.	" sale of books by T. D. Howard,	.	5.00
"	10.	" " " by T. J. Mumford,	.	20.00
"	"	" a friend, for Meadville student, .	.	40.00
"	"	" sale of books at office, . .	.	49.66
"	11.	" " " at Mobile, . .	.	15.00
"	"	" Auxiliary, Dover, N. H., . .	.	39.00
"	13.	" Quarterly Journal, . . .	.	6.00
"	16.	" Auxiliary, East Cambridge, .	.	45.00
"	"	" Quarterly Journal, Rev. J. A. Kendall,	.	1.00
"	17.	" Female Auxiliary, Marblehead, .	.	25.00
"	20.	" Quarterly Journals in Boston,	.	89.00
"	"	" sale of books at office, . .	.	77.55
"	21.	" " " "	. .	19.11
"	"	" Quarterly Journals, . .	.	5.00
"	"	" sale of books, . . .	.	36.80
"	23.	" " " . . .	.	2.50
"	24.	" " " . .	.	3.00
"	"	" " " by Rev. A. Harding,	.	30.00
"	28.	" " " at office, . .	.	17.80
"	"	" " " "	.	31.55
"	29.	" Auxiliary, Brookline, Mass., .	.	50.00
"	30.	" sale of books, Walpole, N. H., .	.	6.00
May	1.	" " " Brookfield,	. .	3.00
"	"	" " " Baltimore, .	.	5.00
"	2.	" " " "	. .	28.47
"	3.	" " " at office, . .	.	7.75
"	"	" " " Thomaston, Me.,	.	5.00
"	"	" Quarterly Journal, . . .	.	1.00
"	4.	" sale of books, Brattleborough, Vt.,	.	2.00
"	"	" " " Lancaster, N. II.,	.	3.00
"	"	" " " at office, . .	.	19.80
"	"	" " " "	. .	4.55
"	"	" Quarterly Journals, . .	.	82.00
"	"	" Miss G. Hallett, Life-Member, .	.	30.00
"	"	" donations, . . .	.	30.00
"	"	" sale of books at office, . .	.	29.27
"	5.	" Auxiliary in New Brunswick, N. J.,	.	20.00
"	"	" sale of books at office, . .	.	.43
"	"	" " " in Hartford, Ct.,	.	8.00
"	7.	" East Boston, for Book Fund, .	.	117.00
"	"	" sale of books, Brewster, .	.	30.47
"	8.	" " " Waterville, Me., .	.	.40
"	"	" " " Geneva, Ill., .	.	25.00
"	9.	" Quarterly Journals, . .	.	3.00

44*

May	10.	From	Altars at Home in Cambridge Port,	$ 33.75
"	"	"	sale of books in Medfield, . . .	3.97
"	"	"	Hon. Joseph Andrews, Life-Member, .	30.00
"	"	"	Sale of books, ...	37.43
"	"	"	Quarterly Journals in Sandwich, . .	10.00
"	11.	"	sale of books, Deerfield, . . .	31.27
"	"	"	" " Meadville, . .	16.65
"	"	"	donation, E. P. S., ...	5.00
"	12.	"	sale of books in Blooming Grove, N. Y.,	20.00
"	14.	"	friends in S. Scituate, for Book Fund,	46.00
"	"	"	sale of books in Shirley, . . .	9.71
"	"	"	a friend, for Book Fund, . . .	10.00
"	16.	"	" " " . . .	20.00
"	"	"	Quarterly Journals, ...	3.00
"	"	"	sale of books at office, . . .	41.98
"	18.	"	Auxiliary in Northfield, Mass., . .	50.00
"	"	"	sale of books in Burlington, Iowa, .	35.45
"	22.	"	ladies in Uxbridge, ...	25.00
"	23.	"	friends in Montreal, for Book Fund,	300.00
"	"	"	sale of books in Montreal, . . .	40.00
"	"	"	Dr. Hall's Society, Providence, .	187.00
"	24.	"	Auxiliary in Mr. Pike's Society, Dorchester, ...	27.00
"	"	"	do. in Mr. Thayer's Society, Beverly,	50.00
"	"	"	sale of books at office, . . .	26.69
"	25.	"	Dr. Putnam's Society, Roxbury, .	100.00
"	26.	"	Quarterly Journals, S. Scituate, .	13.00
"	"	"	sale of books, ...	6.50
"	"	"	Miss M. Newman, ...	4.00
"	"	"	Rev. Dr. Abbot, for Book Fund, .	20.00
"	"	"	sale of books at office, . . .	1.20
"	28.	"	Auxiliary, Hawes Place, S. Boston, .	100.00
"	"	"	sale of books in Lunenburg, . .	2.24
"	"	"	Auxiliary in Brighton, . . .	116.00
"	"	"	" in Newport, R. I., .	39.00
"	29.	"	sale of books in Stow, . . .	35.70
"	"	"	Auxiliary in Belfast, Me., . .	50.00
"	"	"	friends in Worcester, for Book Fund,	708.00
"	"	"	Worcester, for Tanner mission, .	78.00
"	"	"	Auxiliary in Concord, Mass., .	116.25
"	"	"	Dr. Newell's Society, in addition, .	10.00
"	"	"	a lady, donation, . . .	20.00
"	"	"	a lady, for the Book Fund. . .	20.00

WESTERN DEPARTMENT.

[Under the editorial care of Rev. W. D. HALEY, of Alton, Illinois, to whom all communications for its pages are to be addressed.]

WE regret that our pages cannot offer a greater variety of Western matter. In the next number we hope to resume the History of Western Unitarian Churches with a sketch of the Chicago Church, which has been promised by the present pastor.

MISSIONARY EXPERIENCES IN THE WEST.

No. I.

SCENE. — *A Counting-room in a Western Village.* CLERICUS *has ridden forty miles, at the imminent peril of his life, to preach to the people. He is introduced to* B., *a minister of another faith, and the following conversation ensues.*

B. Do you preach here again, Sir ?

C. Not immediately. In the course of a few weeks I hope to visit your village again, to preach on two or three evenings.

B. I am sorry to hear it; I cannot wish you success, for you rob the Gospel of its glory.

C. I hope not.

B. Yes, you do. You deny the Godhead of the Son, and reject his vicarious atonement.

C. I suppose I do what you mean, if you used a correct phraseology. I deny the Deity of the Son, and reject the human dogma of a vicarious atonement.

B. Yes, Sir; and in doing that you take away all the beauty of the Gospel, and lead deluded souls into perdition. I shall feel it to be my duty to keep everybody from hearing you. I would not listen to the utterance of such sentiments, or read a book avowing them.

C. Now, look here, stranger; I believe you tell the truth, and are just as ignorant as you profess to be. You call yourself a Democrat, and a Republican, and a Protestant, don't you? And yet YOU, an ordinary man, venture to assert the most extravagant claim ever put forth by the Pope of Rome. *You* pretend to tell the people of this village what they may hear for themselves! Do you allow them to read the Bible without a license? Have not the men and women of this village as good powers of discrimination as you are blessed with? Are you afraid that in two or three sermons I shall destroy all truth? It seems to me you cannot have much confidence in your own system, if it is so easily upset.

B. Don't you throw away the Bible, and count the blood of the Covenant an unholy thing?

C. God forbid! I do neither. Allow me to ask, if you have ever read a Unitarian book or heard a Unitarian sermon?

B. No, Sir! I don't depend upon human learning; the Bible is my text-book, and I would be very unwilling to listen to disguised infidelity. You deny the Godhead of the Son, and worship you know not what, not doing homage to the Triune Deity.

C. If you mean that for Scripture, stranger, I am sorry to be obliged to remind you that it is home-made Gospel.

I hope it is not the kind you usually dispense. Now, if you will find in the Scriptures, which I have here in my pocket, the words " vicarious atonement," " Triune God," " Three-in-one," " God-man," and the like phrases which you have been using pretty freely during this conversation, I will agree to preach no more, recant my errors, and join your church.

B. Well, anyhow, you have nothing but a human sacrifice.

C. Supposing that to be true, you are in the same predicament.

B. No, Sir. I dare you to prove it. I have an Almighty Saviour; as Watts says,

> " Till God in human flesh I see,
>   My thoughts no comfort find;
> The holy, just, and sacred Three
> Are terrors to my mind."

C. Well, well, don't get angry; that is poetry, not Scripture. Nor don't exhort, because we are not holding a camp-meeting. Now as to your challenge, let me ask you one question. You say, do you not, that in the person of our Saviour ——

B. Our Saviour !

C. Well, well, my Saviour, then, — you say, in the language of the Methodist Discipline, which I have here in the same pocket with the Bible, but beneath it, " that the Son, who is the Word of the Father, the Very and Eternal God, took man's nature in the womb of the blessed Virgin, so that two whole and perfect natures, that is to say, the Godhead and the Manhood, were joined together in one person, *never to be divided*, whereof is one Christ, very God and very man, who truly suffered, was crucified, dead, and buried, to reconcile his Father to us, and to be a sacrifice, not only for original guilt, but also for the actual sins of men."

B. I believe all that.

C. Now, then, I want to know whether both of the na-tures united in the person of Jesus died on the cross, or if it was only the Godhead, or whether it was the Manhood? If the Godhead " truly suffered, was crucified, dead, and buried, to reconcile his Father to us," that would seem to involve the monstrous idea that Deity died to appease his own anger, and left the universe without God while Jesus was in the tomb. If it was not the Godhead, but only the Manhood, that suffered, please tell me wherein that differs from a human sacrifice?

B. (*somewhat hastily*). I am sorry I have not time to discuss this matter now.

C. So am I, *very* sorry; for you commenced an unpro-voked attack upon a stranger, who desired only the privi-lege of free speech in your community, and I should like to canvass this matter now upon its own merits. I am no lover of controversy, and can respect good men of all shades of opinion; I know many good, pious men in your own denomination, men who are too full of " pure religion and undefiled" to harbor bigotry and uncharitableness. — (Before you go I must give you a few words of counsel.) You are comparatively an old man, and will soon be where the scales of sectarian exclusiveness will fall from all eyes; and I trust, if loyal to my conceptions of truth and duty, I shall reach the same Presence : but depend upon it, the providence and mercy of God even now out-reach the limits of our poor partisan distinctions, and count our love and faith more precious than our spec-ulation. Contact and antagonism of thought there must needs be, because circumstances and minds are various; but there need not be bitterness and enmity. What is it that we are all striving for but the truth? and that is seldom found amid heated animosities; but it comes into the soul when the affections are serene, and the spirit devout, and the trust and love reliant and strong. Let us live in peace, and if we cannot have an unity of theory, we may at least have an unity of the spirit. — (But, bless me ! the man is gone !) Well, friends, live in love ; be strong, be independent, be as devout as you please, but think for yourselves ; — only be sure you do *think*, and do not embrace negativeness as your faith, but " search the Scriptures."

OUR DUTY.

THE following extract from a letter in the " Christian Reformer," dated at Geneva, contains truth which the readers of the Quarterly may profitably adopt and apply to the circumstances of the movement for a Book Fund under the control of the American Unitarian Association.

" My dear Sir, — I strongly feel, on the eve of my departure from the continent, that there is a great stir and agitation coming over the religious mind of Europe, which cannot but issue to the service of truth, if we are only, each of us in our respective positions, faithful to our convictions, simple-minded, and large-hearted. We want bravery and confidence ; we want the encouragement of sympathy and co-operation ; we should multiply our relations as much as possible, abroad and at home, with all such societies as will receive us as brethren, and will work with us in the simple love of truth and the fervent spirit of humanity. I believe there are thousands who would hold out the hand of welcome to us, if they only knew more of us than our obnoxious name. We are frozen to death by reserve and insulation. A grand warfare is going on, under different names, between the religion of Love and the religion of Fear, — the religion that is in harmony and the religion that is in war with the noblest inspirations of our common humanity. I have long made my choice and taken my part; and, with such feeble weapons as God has intrusted to me, I will fight on against Jesuitry and uncharitableness, till I am bidden to retire from the field. On the final issue of the contest I have no doubt, dark and discouraging as may seem for the moment its present aspects; but when the triumph comes, as in God's own hour it must, it will be shameful to feel that we have lost all claim to participation in it, through our own inaction and pusillanimity. I could write much more, but must prepare for my early departure to-morrow morning. Yours faithfully,

"J. J. T."

PEORIA.

WE take the liberty to publish the following extracts from a friendly communication received from the Rev. J. R. McFarland. The letter was written some time ago, and the Society has since been rapidly growing. Peoria is the geographical, educational, and literary centre of the enlightened and prosperous State of Illinois. We know of no point in all the West which at this moment presents more imperative and pressing demands upon the active liberality of our Eastern friends than does Peoria. Its beautiful location and palpable business advantages are rapidly attracting a very large population, and the spoken Word and money expended there during the next three years will be an investment that will by and by return a handsome interest into the common channels of our denominational welfare. The brethren at Peoria need a church edifice, and we most earnestly hope that the zeal they have manifested, and the well-known talents, self-sacrifice, and devoutness of their pastor, will prove arguments sufficient to obtain them the very little "material aid" they seek.

"The initiative step in this enterprise of a Liberal Church in Peoria was taken by Mr. Eliot, who first mentioned the subject to me about a year ago, and through whose mediation a correspondence was commenced between a gentleman of this city and myself, which resulted in an engagement, on my part, to come out and break ground, on the faith of his opinion that material existed out of which a Society might in time be organized. Circumstances of a domestic character delayed my departure till after the winter had set in. . . . . However, having almost passed the ordeal of winter, and perceiving a steady progress, notwithstanding many inevitable and disheartening circumstances growing out of the unfavorable season, I look forward to the opening of the spring campaign with even more of anticipation than I could have indulged had I postponed my coming to a later period. As it is, the trenches are dug, the batteries planted, the plan of attack all settled, and everything is in readiness for the assault, when the spring opens; — and with better prospect of success, I hope, than the Allies seem to have before Sebastopol. . . . . .

"One word in reference to antecedents. A number of years ago, Rev. Mr. Huntoon, now of Marblehead, had a flourishing Society here; and I have no doubt that, if he had seen his way clear to remain, he would have had the largest and most influential church in the city. If he knew, as perhaps he does, with how much respect and affection his name is cherished here, it might help to assuage the sad memories that are associated in his mind with the place.

"In the dismemberment of the Society that ensued on Mr. Huntoon's departure, some of his former parishioners joined a movement; to establish a Swedenborgian Church, of which they subsequently became members. This apostasy from Unitarianism, which would never have occurred had Mr. Huntoon's place been earlier supplied, has lost to his successors some very valuable material. In the long interval that elapsed between Mr. Huntoon's and my own settlement here, the want of settled religious connections drove others into the pale of Episcopacy and Methodism. Some of these may probably come back to us.

"Within a few years, Mr. Learned and Mr. Whitney have each occupied the field for a short time. These several efforts that have been successively relinquished, so far from preparing the way for a more permanent undertaking, have created a prestige that is unfavorable to its success.

"To return now to this more recent movement. Out of a population of fifteen thousand, after deducting the Unitarians in connection with other churches, I found about fifteen persons who were disposed to second my endeavors. I preached my first sermon in the Court-House, to an audience of about twenty-five persons. On the next Sabbath, we met in a rear room, second story, over a dry-goods store. One of our number had, in the course of the week, procured about three dozen arm-chairs. A paper-box, which once contained ladies' shoes, being trimmed slantwise and placed upon a table, served very well to rest my manuscript upon. A music-dealer gave us the loan of a small melodeon for a consideration; we made lawful seizure of a lot of old hymn-books — Greenwood's collection — that we found consigned to the dust and obscurity of a vacant pew, in a hall now occupied by a Presbyterian Society; and, altogether, we felt that our second Sunday showed a decided advance in point of comfort, with some additions in point of numbers. The picture of a locomotive from the Boston Locomotive Works, that hung directly above the pulpit, was taken down, as indicating more *force* than we at that time possessed. I will send it to you if you desire it, to hang up in your new church, a fit emblem of the power of Boston opinions, as the reality is of Boston enterprise.

"The third Sunday we had to borrow some chairs, our congregation numbering about forty persons.

"The fourth Sunday we held service in our little chapel, which will hold about one hundred persons, and which we have fitted up (in the second story of a store) in a style of comfort and taste of which the sooner you have some experience the better I will be pleased. All who have seen it pronounce it to be the most comfortable and attractive place of worship in town. A tin shingle, with " Unitarian Chapel" painted on it, points out its locality. We have a German music-teacher to play our melodeon for us, and we go through Mr. Eliot's service 'according to book.' Indeed, our music is an attraction.

"Our entrance into our new place of worship was thought a proper occasion for perfecting our organization. Accordingly, I presented a series of twelve 'Articles of Agreement,' defining our position, and providing, among other things, for the election of a standing committee of three, a treasurer, clerk, &c. These articles were signed by those present who felt disposed to cast in their lot with us, and we have had occasional accessions since. . . . . .

"In order to bring our people together, I early established weekly social meetings from house to house, — an experiment which has entirely succeeded. As soon as the spring opens, and the children can get to the chapel from various quarters, with an even chance of not being swamped in the mud, I shall open a Sunday school.

"This place offers many advantages for a missionary work. It has a large and rapidly growing trade, and its population is likewise increasing. It will probably, in the next ten years, have reached a population of thirty thousand, and if manufacturing operations should be extensively carried on, fifty thousand would not be too high a figure.

"Of the extreme beauty of its location I need not remind you, who have been here. I have yet to see the place in its glory. It occupies, with reference to the State at large, as you know, a central position, at a point on the Illinois River where it expands into a lake a mile in width, distant from St. Louis about two hundred miles, and from Chicago one hundred and fifty, communicating with both places by railroad. There are no less than six railroads in prospect and in course of construction, which will add to the general prosperity. There is energy, life, emulation, in all departments of the social system. The meeting of the Educational Convention, or Teachers' Institute, recently, has given a good impulse to the cause of education in this city; and a late movement, originating with the teachers in the public and other schools, will doubtless elevate the standard and increase the effectiveness of their instructions. The Presbyterians have shown a commendable zeal in raising among our citizens the amount necessary to secure the location of the Synodical College at this place. This gives significance to our own movement, and renders it all the more important that Liberal Christianity should effect a lodgment here, in order to counteract the 'genius and spirit' of Orthodoxism.

"There has been found sufficient literary taste among us to sustain two sets of lectures weekly. Several weeks ago Josiah Quincy, Jr., all the way from Boston, entertained us in his peculiar vein.

"In morals we are not far behind other Western towns. . . . . . Intemperance is the prevailing vice. We have a large proportion of German population already, and if we have a proportionate increase in the next five years, posterity will have it to say of the new College, as some one said of a certain German university, that 'it is located at a seat of celebrated beer.' But I have already extended this letter to an unreasonable length. If it should meet the eye of my respected friend, Dr. Miles, I hope he will receive it as the interest on the debt I have been so long promising to pay.

"Yours in the faith,

"J. R. McFARLAND."

"P. S. — Since the above was written, our enterprise has shown gratifying progress. First, our usual attendance has increased from thirty or forty to an average of from eighty to a hundred. During part of the day our little chapel is packed close, and we think we have reached that first stage of progress known to Western Societies, having increased up to the limit of our accommodations. We are sadly in want of a church. Where we are, we have no room to grow. We have had some important accessions in the way of immigration from the Eastern States. Our Sunday school was organized a couple of months since, under very hopeful auspices. A larger hall for worship and a little persecution is all we want now to give us another lift.

"J. R. McF."